CULINARY PSYCHOLOGY

CULINARY PSYCHOLOGY

Food Choices and the Mind–Body Connection

Stelios Kiosses, Beth Frates, and Neil Rippington

CULINARY PSYCHOLOGY

KARNAC
firing the mind

First published in 2026 by
Karnac Books Limited
62 Bucknell Road
Bicester
Oxfordshire OX26 2DS

British Library Cataloguing in Publication Data

A C.I.P. for this book is available from the British Library

ISBN: 978-1-80013-232-0 (paperback)
ISBN: 978-1-80013-233-7 (e-book)
ISBN: 978-1-80013-234-4 (PDF)

Typeset by vPrompt eServices Pvt Ltd, India

www.firingthemind.com

MIX
Paper | Supporting responsible forestry
FSC® C007915
www.fsc.org

Karnac Books is committed to a sustainable future for our business, our readers, and our planet. This book is made from Forest Stewardship Council® certified paper.

Contents

About the authors and contributors

Beth Frates, MD is a trained psychiatrist (a medical doctor specializing in physical medicine and rehabilitation) and a health and wellness coach, with expertise in lifestyle medicine. She has received several teaching accolades from Harvard Extension School and Harvard Medical School, where she is an associate professor, part time. Dr. Frates is one of the first fellows of the American College of Lifestyle Medicine and a pioneer in lifestyle medicine. In 2008, Dr. Frates created the first Lifestyle Medicine Interest Group at Harvard Medical School. In 2014, she developed and taught a college lifestyle medicine curriculum at Harvard Extension School, and it is still one of the most well-received courses offered at the school. In 2017, Dr. Frates was selected to be one of four item writers for the American Board of Lifestyle Medicine's inaugural exam for certification in this specialty. She was voted president of the American College of Lifestyle Medicine in August 2020. Dr. Frates served as president until November 2024, and now serves two years as an immediate past president. Dedicated to mentoring, she won the Women in Medicine I Stand With Her annual mentoring award for women mentoring women in 2024.

Dr. Frates coauthored *The Lifestyle Medicine Handbook: An Introduction to the Power of Healthy Habits*, which was ranked in the top 20 by BookAuthority for medical books released in 2018. To accompany the syllabus and handbook, she also cocreated Lifestyle Medicine 101, a full college curriculum with twelve weeks of PowerPoints and a teacher's manual, which is free and accessible through the ACLM website. In addition, Dr. Frates coauthored *The Teen Lifestyle Medicine Handbook* (2020) which, when paired with the Teen Curriculum consisting of a teacher's manual and twelve PowerPoint decks, can be used to teach and empower middle school and high school students to adopt and sustain healthy habits. In 2023, Dr. Frates coauthored *The Lifestyle Medicine Pocket Guide* and coedited *Empowering Behavior Change in Patients.* Most recently, in June 2024, she coedited the book *Essentials of Clinical Nutrition in Healthcare.*

Dr. Frates has created and implemented a twelve-step wellness program, PAVING the Path to Wellness™ for patients and providers. Most recently, she coauthored the book *PAVING the Path to Wellness Workbook: A Guide to Thriving with a Healthy Body, Peaceful Mind, and Joyful Heart.* In addition, Dr. Frates has her own lifestyle medicine consulting/coaching practice where she sees patients one to one and in groups.

Stelios Kiosses is a psychotherapist, course director, and tutor at the University of Oxford, and a pioneering voice in the emerging field of culinary psychology. An Oxford graduate with specialized training in psychodynamic therapy and clinical supervision, he brings more than three decades of clinical experience to his work, focusing on the intersections between food, emotional resilience, and psychological well-being.

His academic career has included roles as visiting lecturer at Goldsmiths, University of London, and honorary senior lecturer in the Department of Psychiatry at the University of Birmingham, where he taught on the MSc in psychiatry (family and mental health). He developed and cotaught the innovative culinary psychology course at Harvard University Extension School, and is currently a featured guest speaker at Harvard Medical School, contributing to its Executive Education program in Nutrition and Wellness.

Beyond academia, Stelios is widely recognized for his media work as presenter of Channel 4's *The Hoarder Next Door*, narrated by BAFTA- and Oscar-winning actress Olivia Colman. He is also the author of

The Power of Talking: Stories from the Therapy Room, a book that explores the transformative potential of psychotherapy. In his public role, he has previously served as patron of The Prince's [now The King's] Foundation School of Traditional Arts, one of the core charities founded by H.M. King Charles III.

Through his clinical practice, teaching, writing, and public engagement, Stelios continues to champion the therapeutic possibilities of food and psychology, inspiring a deeper understanding of how what we eat is inseparably connected to how we think, feel, and live.

Neil Rippington trained as a chef at the Bournemouth and Poole College, before going on to work in Michelin-starred restaurants in France, London, and the New Forest, and other roles in the culinary industry in the U.S.A., Canada, and the Caribbean. In 1999, Neil returned to work in education, and in 2003, he joined Colchester Institute as head of the Centre for Hospitality and Food Studies. In 2010, Neil took up the position as dean of the College of Food at University College Birmingham, where he worked for more than ten years.

Neil's writing career started in 2007 with the publication of *Professional Chef*, produced as a resource for students following the newly developed City & Guilds diplomas in professional cookery (now in its second edition and translated into many languages). He has since written and cowritten several other practical books for students, has developed many educational programs, and teaches subjects across the culinary arts and gastronomy. His research led to the development of degree programs offered at the Edge Hotel School, University of Essex, and he codeveloped a program in culinary psychology at Harvard University, U.S.A.

Neil is a senior fellow of Advance HE. He is also an examiner for City & Guilds of London Institute, an academician of the Royal Academy of Culinary Arts, and chair of its Education Committee. Neil sits on various other committees and steering groups, is a subject expert for hospitality and catering for the Office of Qualifications and Examinations Regulation (Ofqual), and has acted as an external university advisor/examiner in the U.K. and internationally.

In recognition of his work, Neil has received many accolades, including Disciple of Escoffier, honorary member of City & Guilds, and is lead judge for the development of skills at the Salon Culinaire, U.K. Neil is currently the program director for the college community program for the Royal Academy of Culinary Arts, U.K., and the international director for global education with the International Institute of Hotel Management, India.

Professor Charles Spence is a world-famous experimental psychologist with a specialization in neuroscience-inspired multisensory design. He has worked with many of the world's largest companies across the globe since establishing the Crossmodal Research Laboratory (CRL) at the Department of Experimental Psychology, Oxford University in 1997. Prof. Spence has published more than 1,200 academic articles and edited or authored sixteen books, including, in 2014, the Prose prize-winning "The perfect meal," and the international bestseller *Gastrophysics: The New Science of Eating* (2017, Penguin Viking)—winner of the 2019 Le Grand Prix de la Culture Gastronomique from Académie Internationale de la Gastronomie. His latest book *Sensehacking* was published in 2021.

Much of Prof. Spence's work focuses on the design of enhanced multisensory food and drink experiences, through collaborations with world-leading chefs, baristas, mixologists, chocolatiers, perfumiers, and the food and beverage and flavor and fragrance industries. Prof. Spence has worked extensively on the question of how technology will transform our dining/drinking experiences in the future, and has been profiled in *The New Yorker* (http://newyorker.com/magazine/2015/11/02/accounting-for-taste).

Kimberley Wilson is a chartered psychologist with a master's degree in nutrition and the author of influential books linking diet to mental health. In her private practice in London, she integrates nutrition with psychological therapy, advocating a holistic approach to mental health. Her experience includes working in Europe's largest women's prison and serving as a governor for the Tavistock & Portman NHS Mental Health Trust. Kimberley actively engages the public through various media platforms, including podcasts, television, and articles for *BBC Science Focus* and *Psychologies* magazines, to promote a comprehensive understanding of mental health that unites the mind and body.

Foreword

They say food is love, and for me that has always been true. From my family kitchen in Crete to the MasterChef kitchen, I've seen how food gathers people, keeps memories alive, offers comfort, and brings joy. What surprised me when I read this book was how naturally psychology, lifestyle medicine, and food can sit together.

Culinary Psychology is warm, clear, and easy to read. It speaks to something I've always felt but never quite had the words for: the way cooking can soothe us, and how eating connects us with care, memory, and meaning.

Stelios and his coauthors Beth and Neil have managed something quite rare in this book. They've combined knowledge from psychotherapy, lifestyle medicine, and the kitchen in a way that feels grounded but also full of heart. The book offers insight and reflection, but always in a gentle and human way.

As someone who has always cooked from the heart, I felt a real connection to the stories and lessons in these pages. Whether you're a therapist, a cook, or simply someone who has turned to food in times of happiness or struggle, you'll find something here that speaks to you.

It's a joy and privilege to open this book and welcome you to the table—to the ideas, the conversations, and a new way of looking at nourishment.

Irini Tzortzoglou
MasterChef UK winner 2019
Author, chef, sommelier, and retreat host

Preface

It is both an honor and a privilege to write the Preface for *Culinary Psychology: Food Choices and the Mind–Body Connection,* edited by Stelios Kiosses, Professor Beth Frates, and Chef Neil Rippington. This groundbreaking work delves deeply into the complexities of human psychology through the unique lens of culinary experiences. This book holds a special place in my heart, not only because of its subject matter, but also because I have been involved in the development of this concept from its very inception.

The idea of culinary psychology—the intersection of food, culture, and psychological behavior—was one that Stelios and I discussed in the early stages of its development. What began as a simple conversation about the emotional connections we form with food has grown into this remarkable exploration of how our culinary experiences influence our thoughts, feelings, and behaviors.

Stelios Kiosses is truly of a unique mindset. He has the remarkable ability to think outside the box, constantly challenging conventional ideas. What makes him exceptional is not just his ability to think differently—he takes those innovative thoughts and transforms them into something actionable and tangible. Culinary psychology is the perfect reflection of that, offering fresh perspectives on the human psyche in ways that many have never considered.

It was with great enthusiasm that this concept evolved further with the involvement of his wonderful colleagues, Professor Beth Frates and Chef Neil Rippington, at Harvard Extension School. Together, they have played a crucial role in bringing this vision to life. Professor Frates' expertise in lifestyle medicine and Chef Rippington's culinary mastery have added a depth and richness to this work that is truly remarkable.

On a personal note, this book was born out of my own experiences. After receiving the all clear from my battle with cancer, it got me thinking more deeply about the connection between health, medicine, and food. Stelios and I began discussing how medicine and cooking should work far more closely together for the well-being of humans. These conversations became the foundation of *Culinary Psychology*, and it has been a deeply meaningful journey for me to watch this idea evolve into the book you hold in your hands.

Culinary Psychology addresses a critical aspect of human behavior that often goes unnoticed: how the food we prepare, consume, and share reflects deeper psychological patterns. In a world where food culture plays such a central role in our lives, this book offers an enlightening perspective on how our relationship with food is intertwined with our emotions, memories, and even our identities.

This book is undoubtedly a must-read for all inquisitive minds in the hospitality industry, particularly chefs, who play such an essential role in shaping our culinary experiences. It should also have a wider appeal to the medical community, which I hope will work in conjunction with the culinary world to resolve some of the pressing health issues we face globally. By fostering a stronger relationship between food and medicine, I believe we can achieve a healthier, more holistic approach to well-being.

Stelios, Beth, and Neil bring not only their academic expertise but also a genuine passion for this topic, making this book both intellectually engaging and personally meaningful. Their unique perspectives—shaped by years of research and practice—give readers a rare opportunity to explore the human mind in a way that is both profound and relatable.

What makes *Culinary Psychology* particularly special is its ability to make complex psychological theories accessible to a wide audience.

Whether you are a student of psychology, a professional in the culinary arts, or simply someone who has always been curious about the deeper meanings behind our culinary habits, this book offers invaluable insights.

As you read through these pages, you'll discover not just a wealth of knowledge, but also a new way of thinking about something as universal and everyday as food. I wholeheartedly recommend this book to anyone ready to embark on this journey of culinary psychology. Stelios Kiosses, Beth Frates, and Neil Rippington have given us a gift in *Culinary Psychology*, and I am confident that it will inspire and enlighten readers for years to come.

Chef Andreas Antona
Author
Founding Trustee, The Cancer Platform
Founder and Chairman, Bocuse d'Or Academy, UK
Honorary Doctor, University of Birmingham

Introduction to culinary psychology

Stelios Kiosses, Beth Frates, and Neil Rippington

Defining culinary psychology

Stelios Kiosses

Food as a subject is difficult to describe. It is not even clear what it is. It belongs simultaneously to the worlds of economics, ecology, and culture. It involves vegetables, chemists, wholesalers, livestock, refrigerators, cooks, fertilizer, fish, grocers, and more. How much does food shape human nature? Are our culinary practices a fundamental force in defining what it means to be human? Culinary psychology seeks to answer these questions through the understanding and interpretation of food (metaphysics), and experiential (epistemology) as well as sensory perceptions (aesthetics).

The metaphysics of food

Metaphysics in the context of culinary psychology involves questioning the nature and essence of food: What is the role of food in human culture and individual identity? How do we define the meaning and significance of food beyond its material properties? Metaphysics examines food's role beyond physical sustenance and considers how it connects with our consciousness, emotions, and cultural identity. This approach views food not just as a dietary necessity, but as an integral part of human experience and existential understanding.

When considering the metaphysics of food, we must ask ourselves: What is food? Not simply as an object, but as a concept. We can think of food as the following:

- Nutrition, or what is required for sustaining life. Food in this model has objective properties that are not open to interpretation, like carbohydrates, fats, protein, vitamins, and minerals.
- Food as desire, or what fulfills cravings and hunger. A "food craving" is a desire to eat a specific food generated by something other than hunger, such as a memory, psychological motivation, or pregnancy.
- Food as spirituality. Food is central to religious traditions throughout the world. Religions typically prescribe which foods should be eaten and which should be avoided; they assign significance to food production, preparation, and consumption; and they connect dietary regimentation with moral conduct and spiritual salvation.
- Food as culture. In this model, food has symbolic meaning and significance.

As we conclude our exploration of the metaphysical aspects of food, it's pertinent to recognize the broader implications of our dietary choices. Kimberley Wilson sheds light on an often-overlooked aspect, noting, "We often fail to consider how our diet affects our brain. However, the brain is an organ just like any other and needs specific nutrients to function optimally" (Wilson, 2020).

The epistemology of food

Epistemology, or theory of knowledge, is the branch of philosophy that studies the nature, methods, limitations, and validity of knowledge and belief. It asks questions such as: "What is knowledge?" and "How do we know something?" In culinary psychology, the questions are, "How do we know what we like or dislike about food?" and "What experiences shape our culinary preferences and aversions?" Exploring food through experiential learning—such as cooking, tasting, and dining—helps us understand how personal and collective experiences influence our knowledge and beliefs about food.

Different conceptions of food are connected to our different beliefs about it. Obviously, what one thinks food is depends upon how one perceives and judges it. For instance, some cultures view insects such as crickets as food, whereas others consider crickets the things that chirp at night.

The aesthetics of food

Aesthetics is a branch of philosophy that deals with the nature of beauty and taste as well as the philosophy of art. It examines subjective and sensoriemotional values, sometimes called judgments of sentiment and taste. Aesthetics in culinary psychology is not just about the beauty of food presentation but also involves how our senses interact to create a holistic sensory experience. How do these perceptions contribute to our enjoyment and appreciation of food? By examining the aesthetics of food, we delve into the sensory experiences that make dining pleasurable and memorable, influencing our emotional and psychological responses.

The universal meaning of the phrase, "The eye eats before the mouth," is that human beings prefer to eat what is attractively presented. Food has two aesthetic components: First, as the object of aesthetic experience that has a taste and appeals to the senses (e.g., tasty, satisfying, or disgusting). The second is food as art. We describe food in terms of its visual presentation and sensual composition. We attribute aesthetic properties, such as "elegant," "hearty," or "simple." Food in this model is primarily the subject of aesthetic judgment.

A deeper cultural and biological meaning of food aesthetics is that people tend to prepare for eating with their senses. Digestion begins in the mouth; however, the production of saliva is stimulated as we visualize appetizing food, smell food, or remember a meal. Thus, eating is sensory and directly involves our sight, taste, smell, and brain.

The possibility of aesthetic appreciation—whether of food or wine—requires both metaphysics (thinking) and epistemics (beliefs). It's metaphysical because the object must have properties in virtue of which we judge it beautiful or ugly. It's epistemic because we require standards by which we can say that an aesthetic judgment is correct, good, or justified. All of this begs the question, "How do we choose the food we eat?" The question is complicated, especially when you consider the abundance of food choices available.

How we choose foods

There are interesting parallels between the evolution of crayon colors and the variety of food choices we have today. Back in 1903, Crayola offered just eight basic crayon colors: black, brown, yellow, red, orange, indigo, violet, and green. By 1949, the palette expanded significantly to forty-eight colors, with a wider range of blues, yellows, and purples. Fast forward to 2010, and Crayola's collection had grown to 120 colors, including vibrant shades like "neon carrot" and "razzle dazzle rose." A similar expansion has occurred in the world of food: today, we are confronted with an overwhelming array of options. However, this abundance of choice doesn't necessarily lead to better decisions—it can sometimes result in decision paralysis. This paradox underscores a critical aspect of our modern relationship with food: having more options doesn't always equate to making better or healthier choices for our bodies and minds.

In today's supermarkets, the variety is staggering, with anywhere from 15,000 to 60,000 products on the shelves, and this number increases even more when shopping online. This overwhelming selection has contributed to widespread confusion about what to eat, and trust in formerly reliable sources of information has eroded. According to the International Food Information Council's (IFIC) 2024 survey, trust in food information from government agencies has significantly decreased among millennials, high-income households, men, and married individuals. For example, millennials' trust dropped from 56% in 2022 to 42% in 2024. Despite this, 51% of Americans express interest in using artificial intelligence (AI) to help them make safe and nutritious food choices, with younger generations, higher-income households, men, and Hispanic Americans showing the most interest.

Sometimes, the pursuit of healthy eating can become an excessive obsession known as orthorexia nervosa. This condition involves persistent, preoccupying thoughts about consuming only "healthy" foods, adhering strictly to what an individual or group perceives as the "right" diet. Orthorexia is harmful because it transforms healthy eating into a source of anxiety and fear concerning health, food quality, and eating habits (Bratman, 1997; Koven & Abry, 2015).

To identify signs of orthorexia, consider the following checklist, adapted from clinical frameworks (ibid. both):

- Do you spend more than three hours per day thinking about healthy food?
- Are you preplanning tomorrow's meals today?
- Does the virtue of eating healthily outweigh the pleasure you derive from your meals?
- Has the quality of your life diminished as the strictness of your diet has increased?
- Have you become stricter with yourself regarding your diet?
- Does your self-esteem improve from eating healthily, and do you judge others who do not follow your dietary standards?
- Do you avoid foods you once enjoyed to maintain a strict diet?
- Does your diet restrict your ability to eat out, thus isolating you from social interactions?
- Do you feel guilty or experience self-loathing when you deviate from your diet?
- When adhering to your diet, do you feel a sense of total control?

Orthorexia is recognized as an eating disorder, similar to anorexia nervosa or bulimia, but it is treatable (Bratman, 1997). Effective treatment involves the patient learning to relinquish rigid dietary rules, and understanding, with the support of a healthcare team, that flexibility in diet is both safe and beneficial (Koven & Abry, 2015).

While some individuals choose foods based purely on health benefits, others aim to mimic the dietary patterns of our ancestors, believing this approach aligns with human evolution. However, there is substantial confusion and debate regarding the historical accuracy of ancestral diets, which we will explore further.

The evolution of diet

Even though the paleo diet has become popularized as our ancestors' diet, it's difficult to determine what, exactly, our ancestors ate because doing so requires a transdisciplinary approach encompassing prehistory (archaeology), anthropology (bioarchaeology), chemistry, biochemistry, geology, and evolutionary medicine (Alt, Al-Ahmad, & Woelber, 2022). The source material for learning our ancestors' diet is plant, animal, and human remains from archaeological excavations and extrapolation based on archaeobotany and archaeozoology, which study the environmental, economic, and nutritional history, the human impact on the environment, and the economic importance of domestic animals and cultivated plants. From there, by reconstructing the environment, noting the technical achievements, and the traces in the landscape, the diet in various periods can be determined.

It's also worth noting the prehistoric diet was determined by the seasons, the availability of resources, climatic conditions, and the biotope the humans lived in. In other words, humans ate different things in different parts of the world. Regardless though, for survival, stockpiling food was paramount, and "gathering" played more of a role than "hunting," despite what many people believe. According to Alt and colleagues (ibid.), food available to our ancestors consisted primarily of plants (80%) such as leafy greens, sweet grasses, nuts, seeds, tubers, berries, roots, fruits, and pulses, as well as animal proteins from wild animals and fish (20%). Consuming a broad range of different plant foods remained true for all groups of Neanderthals and *Homo sapiens*, based on plant microremains extracted from dental calculus, according to Alt et al. However, it's also important to note that *Homo sapiens* adapted to their ecosystem. The Inuit subsisted mainly on animal proteins, but people in the Andes lived primarily on a plant-based diet.

The hunter-gatherer diet and lifestyle prevented "civilization diseases" or chronic noncommunicable diseases such as diabetes and hypertension. Infectious diseases, on the other hand, were probably the most common cause of death for hunter-gatherers, Alt et al. reported.

After the end of the last Ice Age, the human diet transformed. Around 12,000 BC, the first permanent settlements were established in the Levant, and our ancestors transitioned from hunting and gathering to crop cultivation and animal husbandry. They started to experiment based on wild forms of grasses and legumes such as natural lentils, from which emmer wheat, einkorn wheat, and other varieties were developed. Goats and sheep were the species first domesticated, and land began to be cleared for use as pastures.

Over the centuries, this started to take firmer hold, with more varieties of grains and other cultivated plants such as carrots, radishes, lettuce plants, and herbs taking root. Urban centers started to spring up and that, too, changed diet and lifestyle. The general variety of plants declined in favor of a few varieties that could be stockpiled. During the Neolithic period, cereal porridge and flatbreads were replaced by breads and pastries. Legumes such as lentils and peas were primarily used as dry goods, except during the harvest season; flax and poppy seeds provided fat-rich food and were suitable alternatives to animal-based food, according to Alt and colleagues. Wild plants such as hazelnuts, acorns, beech nuts, apples, pears, elderberries, sloes, wild rose hips, raspberries, and wayfaring tree fruits were used to supplement cultivated crops—especially when those crops failed. At this time, infectious diseases became more frequent, as did degenerative diseases such as osteoarthritis, as certain joints were strained more than others.

Cattle, sheep, goats, and pigs were already domesticated, but animal husbandry techniques varied from one region to the next. This close contact with animals led to numerous infectious diseases that were transmitted from animals to humans and between humans via bacteria, viruses, or parasites. Some of those diseases included tuberculosis, hepatitis B, smallpox, measles, malaria, and typhus.

At the end of the Neolithic period and over the course of the Early Bronze Age, early elites began to emerge, and their status was reflected in the consumption of high-value proteins. The upper classes had access to all kinds of luxuries, whereas poor, rural populations often contended with an unbalanced low-protein diet based on cereals and vegetables. This led to malnutrition and scurvy for some.

In the Middle Ages, the population was made up of serfs and free peasants, a lower and higher nobility, and an urban bourgeoisie, which consisted mainly of tradesmen and merchants. They all had access to different foods and thus were affected by different diseases—some infectious, some not, such as diabetes.

This way of life continued until the Industrial Revolution. The agricultural sector continued to be productive, and there was an increased supply of staple foods such as the potato. Also, high crop yields, new food processing techniques such as canning, and innovations in food preservation permanently changed food production. New preservation technologies added to stockpiling capabilities, and cheap and durable food heralded the beginning of a new age of food consumption. This is also where metabolic disorders and intolerances arose with more frequency, as did cardiovascular diseases like atherosclerosis, heart attacks, and strokes, Alt et al. found.

Social developments once again changed dietary habits, and in the second half of the twentieth century, ready-made meals (TV dinners) came onto the scene, as did fast food, convenience food, and the exposure to foreign foods. And these days, most foods sold in supermarkets are dispensable. There are biological consequences to eating these types of foods in the form of diabetes, heart disease, certain cancers, and a poor gut microbiome, which scientists are still learning about.

More and more, research shows that gut microbiota play an essential role in mood regulation because they catabolize amino acids, whose products can influence the balance of neurotransmitter production, which is critical for proper brain functioning (González Olmo, Butler, & Barrientos, 2021). For instance, bacteria species of the genera *Lactobacillus* and *Bifidobacterium* metabolize glutamate, a free amino acid and excitatory neurotransmitter in the brain, to produce γ-aminobutyric acid (GABA), a major inhibitory neurotransmitter. Another amino acid, tryptophan, can enter the circulation system from the gastrointestinal tract, cross the blood–brain barrier, and initiate serotonin synthesis in the brain. Tryptophan depletion has been demonstrated to affect learning and memory in both healthy and diseased individuals. This again shows the connection between healthy eating, the gut microbiome, and mental health.

Something that upsets the balance of the gut microbiota is sugar, which the modern diet contains high amounts of. Sugar is associated with impaired cognitive performance in older individuals with type 2 diabetes (ibid.). Furthermore, when comparing the gut microbiota of individuals diagnosed with major depressive disorder to those of healthy individuals, there is a reported decrease in species richness and diversity in those with depression; specifically, there are differing amounts of the bacteria *Bacteroidetes, Firmicutes, Proteobacteria*, and *Actinobacteria phyla* in patients with depression, González Olmo et al. (2021) reported. Again, research shows that a healthy gut filled with diversity usually leads to not only a healthy body but also a healthy mind.

The foods we eat can be shaped by our biology—as the gut microbiota change, so, too do the foods people crave—but there are other factors that influence our food choices as well.

The other factors influencing food choices

There are also cultural factors, or how traditions and heritage shape our diet. This could be in the form of holidays, such as eating turkey during Thanksgiving, or more regularly ("We eat pancakes for breakfast on Sundays").

There are social influences, or the role of society and peer groups in our food choices. Social media continue to play a large role. The IFIC survey found exposure to food and nutrition content on social media is up significantly from 42% in 2023 to 54% in 2024. Most people trust the content they see, though fewer trust the content a lot (21% in 2023 to 15% in 2024). There's more food content on social media and also more conversations about food. A current trend, especially among younger people, is an emphasis on eating more plant-based food, as more and more research shows the benefits of eating that way. IFIC data reports that 54% of Americans have tried a specific eating style in the past year, up from 38% in 2019. Of those who are following a vegan, vegetarian, or plant-based diet, 55% report doing so in order to be healthier, and 33% said they are doing it to improve animal welfare. More than a quarter (26%) said they eat that way to help the environment. (The IFIC allows people to select more than one answer.) The impact on the environment is particularly crucial for Gen Z, as they are the most climate-focused generation to date. Some Gen Zs choose to be vegan so they are in alignment with their values about supporting sustainability.

Family dynamics, including upbringing and cultural customs, significantly shape our food preferences from an early age. For instance, children raised in Mediterranean households might develop a preference for olive oil and seafood, staples in their family's diet. Cultural traditions, such as festive foods during holidays, can also create lasting associations and preferences that influence dietary choices throughout life.

Individual preferences are crucial in shaping dietary habits. These preferences are not only influenced by cultural exposure but also by personal tastes and physiological differences. Genetic variations, for instance, can affect how individuals perceive tastes; some people may find certain vegetables bitter due to their genetic makeup, influencing their aversion to or preference for these foods.

Economic status directly impacts food choices, as it affects access to various types of food. Individuals in higher economic brackets may have access to a broader range of fresh, organic, or specialty foods, whereas those from lower economic backgrounds might rely more on processed and less expensive options due to budget constraints. This disparity can significantly affect dietary habits and overall health.

Psychological factors also heavily influence eating behaviors. Emotional states, cognitive biases, and mental health conditions can all alter dietary patterns. For instance, some people may turn to comfort foods that are high in sugar and fat during times of stress or depression to alleviate their feelings temporarily. Cognitive factors like the "halo effect" can lead people to overestimate the health benefits of foods labeled as organic or gluten-free.

Additionally, mental health disorders such as orthorexia highlight the complex interplay between psychological well-being and eating behaviors. Orthorexia involves an obsession with healthy eating driven by a compulsion to consume only foods deemed pure or beneficial. This disorder illustrates how psychological drivers can transform healthy habits into harmful behaviors, underscoring the need for a balanced approach to nutrition that considers both physical health and psychological well-being.

Each of these factors—cultural, genetic, economic, and psychological—plays a significant role in shaping our food choices, influencing everything from what we enjoy eating to how we think about food and health.

What does this all mean for you? Understanding culinary psychology extends far beyond academic theory—it can be actively woven into the fabric of everyday life, especially through the practice of mindful eating. Embracing mindful eating can profoundly enhance both emotional and mental well-being. Jon Kabat-Zinn, the pioneer of the Mindfulness-Based Stress Reduction program at the University of Massachusetts Medical School, defines "mindfulness" as "paying attention in a particular way, on purpose, in the present moment, and nonjudgmentally" (Kabat-Zinn, 1991). Mindful eating, therefore, involves engaging with your food attentively and intentionally, moment by moment, without judgment. This practice fosters a deep appreciation of the present, enhancing the overall eating experience by encouraging a full presence at the meal.

Psychologist Joseph Nelson, in his article for *Diabetes Spectrum*, elaborates on mindful eating techniques (Nelson, 2017). According to Nelson, mindful eating is about immersing oneself fully in the eating experience, from the initial thoughts about food to the last bite. Before you eat, take a moment to assess your feelings. Are you reaching for food out of stress, boredom, anger, or sadness? Is it an emotional need you're trying to satisfy, or are you genuinely hungry? If the hunger isn't physical, what alternative actions could fulfill your emotional needs?

During meals, focus solely on the food. Eliminate distractions such as cell phones or computers. Contemplate the origin of your food—the effort and resources involved in its production. Consider the journey of the sun, water, and soil that nourished what you're eating. Reflect on the distances traversed for it to reach your plate.

As you eat, savor each bite, tuning in to how your body responds. Are you still hungry, or are you beginning to feel full? Let your body's signals guide your decisions about whether to continue eating.

Mindful eating doesn't just enhance your appreciation of meals; it empowers you to make autonomous food choices, relying less on external advice and more on your innate understanding of your body's needs. While nutrition apps, dietitians, and nutritionists provide valuable information, true well-being is found in aligning this knowledge with your body's natural cues. By practicing mindful eating, you may discover a path to greater happiness and health, which is the ultimate goal of culinary psychology.

In conclusion, culinary psychology transcends mere theoretical exploration and deeply influences our daily lives, particularly through practices like mindful eating. This approach empowers individuals not only to enjoy their meals more fully but also to engage with their food choices in a way that promotes better mental and emotional health.

Mindful eating encourages us to be present in the moment, paying close attention to the experience of eating, the flavors, textures, and sensations, and the effects food has on our bodies and minds. It helps us become more aware of hunger and fullness cues, reducing the likelihood of overeating and helping address issues like emotional eating.

Studies in behavioral medicine have shown that mindful eating can help reduce stress and improve dietary habits, leading to better overall health outcomes. This aligns with the principles of culinary psychology, which seeks to understand the deeper connections between our food choices, our sensory experiences, and our psychological well-being.

As we continue to explore the multifaceted relationships between food and psychology, it becomes increasingly clear that our approach to eating can have profound impacts on our lives. By choosing to eat mindfully, we not only enhance our enjoyment of food but also contribute to a healthier, more aware state of being. This holistic approach is not just about nourishing the body but also enriching the soul and mind, fostering a deeper appreciation for the nourishment we consume and its origin.

Culinary psychology, therefore, is not merely about what we eat or how we eat, but about enriching our lives through thoughtful, intentional engagement with food. Each meal becomes an opportunity to practice mindfulness, enhance our well-being, and reconnect with the essential pleasures of eating.

Introduction to lifestyle medicine

Beth Frates

Lifestyle medicine is the medical specialty that uses evidence-based lifestyle therapeutic approaches, such as a plant-predominant eating pattern, routine physical activity, restorative sleep, stress management, positive social connections, and avoidance of risky substances, to prevent, treat, and often put into remission chronic diseases like hypertension, diabetes, high cholesterol, metabolic syndrome, and obesity (ACLM, 2024a).

The foundations of lifestyle medicine come from Ancient Greece. Hippocrates (460–370 BC) stated, "If we could give every individual the right amount of nourishment and exercise, not too little and not too much, we would have found the safest way to health" (Hippocrates, n.d.). Over the years, research studies have demonstrated that there is a great deal of truth to this statement.

Foundational research studies

A 1999 review of the trends in infectious disease mortality showed that in the twentieth century, there was a pretty steady decline in deaths due to infectious diseases, from 797 deaths per 100,000 in 1900 to 36 deaths per 100,000 in 1980, with two exceptions: in 1918–1920, there was a spike in deaths due to the influenza pandemic, and there was a slight increase in deaths from the 1980s to mid-1990s to 63 deaths per 100,000 in 1995, probably due to the HIV epidemic (Armstrong, Conn, & Pinner, 1999). In the last three decades, the list of leading causes of death shifted from infectious diseases like pneumonia, tuberculosis, diarrhea, and enteritis in 1990 to lifestyle-related diseases such as heart disease, cancer, and stroke in 1997 (Centers for Disease Control and Prevention (CDC), 1999). In 2016–2017, according to the CDC, the ten leading causes of death in the United States, age-adjusted, listed in order of severity, were heart disease, cancer, unintentional injuries, chronic lower respiratory disease, stroke, Alzheimer's disease, diabetes, influenza and pneumonia, kidney disease, and suicide (Murphy et al., 2018). In 2020, due to the Covid-19 pandemic, infectious disease again made it into the top three leading causes of death. Of note, heart disease and cancer remained the top two leading causes of death (Murphy et al., 2021), except for a few months, from December 2020 to March 2021, when Covid-19 briefly became the leading cause of death (Ortaliza, Amin, & Cox, 2022). However, considering that people with preexisting chronic disease conditions were significantly more likely to die from Covid-19, lifestyle-related diseases could still be considered the main contributor to the high death rate.

While medicine and science have done a good job battling the causes of infectious diseases, it has become increasingly apparent that the focus should be on lifestyle factors. Our lifestyles are killing us. A landmark study published in the *Journal of the American Medical Association* (*JAMA*) in 2004 looked into actual causes of death, meaning factors that are the root cause of the diseases that are the leading causes of death. The factors listed were tobacco use, lack of proper nutrition and physical activity, and alcohol consumption, the top three leading factors (Mokdad et al., 2004). This article was eye-opening for physicians, scientists, and epidemiologists alike, and it caught much attention then.

Since lifestyle-related diseases and conditions are the predominant causes of impairment and death, there is an increased need to address lifestyle patterns and practices. Lifestyle medicine has gained traction in the past few decades, partly due to researchers sharing their findings in major medical journals and partly due to the burden of chronic disease plaguing the nation and much of the world.

Some of the first research on lifestyle modifications as an intervention for chronic diseases was in cardiovascular health. In their prospective, randomized, controlled trial, Dean Ornish and colleagues determined that lifestyle changes after only one year of implementation may be able to bring about the regression of even severe coronary atherosclerosis without the use of lipid-lowering drugs (Ornish et al., 1990). A follow-up study of patients five years after the original research found continued atherosclerotic regression in patients who sustained lifestyle changes and half the rate of cardiac events in the lifestyle intervention group compared to the control group (Ornish et al., 1998). Results from a study published in 2008 demonstrated that intensive lifestyle intervention in patients with coronary artery disease could have a significant impact. The research showed that after only twelve weeks of intervention, 74% of patients became angina-free, and 9% moved into the mild angina category (Frattaroli et al., 2008). In a 2010 study, CVD patients enrolled in an intensive cardiac rehabilitation program showed statistically significant improvement in their body mass index (BMI), triglycerides, low-density lipoprotein cholesterol, total cholesterol, hemoglobin A1c, systolic blood pressure, diastolic blood pressure, depression, hostility, exercise, and functional capacity after just twelve weeks of the program, with further improvements after one year. Those changes were associated with numerous subjective and objective improvements in health outcomes, and the program had a very high retention rate, with 78% of participants still involved in the program after one year (Silberman et al., 2010).

Lifestyle medicine interventions have also shown promising results in preventing, managing, and putting into remission type 2 diabetes (Kelly, Karlsen, & Steinke, 2020). A seminal study from 2002 compared the effectiveness of metformin (a common and effective medication to lower blood glucose), a lifestyle intervention, and a control group in patients who had high blood glucose levels but were not diagnosed with diabetes (similar to prediabetes today). The lifestyle intervention and the metformin group reduced the incidence of diabetes in these high-risk individuals better than the control group, and the lifestyle intervention proved to be more effective than the metformin (Knowler et al., 2002). Further studies showed that lifestyle interventions have the ability to not only prevent the development of type 2 diabetes but also the ability to put it into remission, though the long-term effects of the interventions require further study (Pot et al., 2020).

Most lifestyle interventions shared several elements: a whole food, plant-based diet, smoking cessation, moderate exercise, stress reduction, yoga/meditation practice, and psychosocial support to initiate and sustain these changes.

Several organizations are dedicated to furthering research, promotion, and wider adoption of lifestyle medicine practices in mainstream medical practice. The American College of Lifestyle Medicine (ACLM)—www.lifestylemedicine.org, American Board of Lifestyle Medicine (ABLM)—www.ablm.org, and International Board of Lifestyle Medicine (IBLM)—www.iblm.com, all offer further education and certification in this specialty. The American College of Lifestyle Medicine was inducted into the American Medical Association House of Delegates in the spring of 2024.

Lifestyle medicine focuses on six pillars, as shown in Figure 1.1 on the next page: Nutrition, Exercise, Sleep, Stress Management, Social Connection, and Substance Use (ACLM, 2025).

Nutrition basics

Nutrition has a significant influence on many aspects of health. Food is an essential part of our lives, and nutrition and diet get lots of attention in research and the popular press. It is the topic of this book. This introduction provides some of the basics of nutrition recommendations and evidence-based guidelines for healthy eating patterns. The various chapters in this book will review physical activity, stress, sleep, social connection, and risky substances as they relate to our eating patterns. Lifestyle matters. Our behaviors impact our health. These six pillars are interconnected. One influences the other. Learning the basics of each

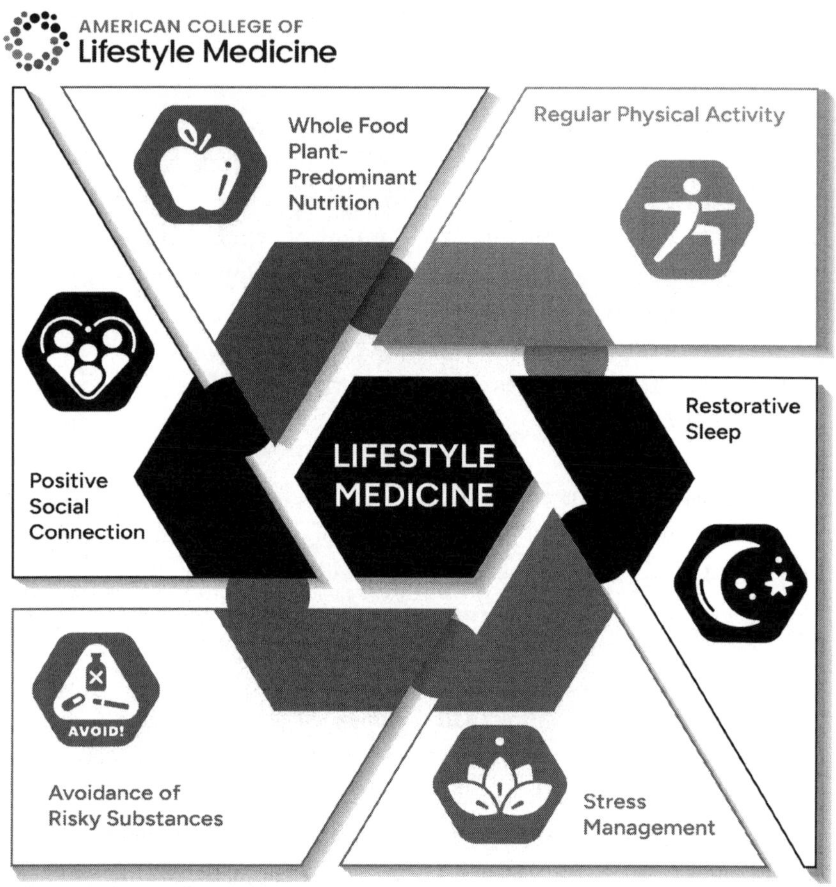

Figure 1.1. ACLM—Six pillars of lifestyle medicine (American College of Lifestyle Medicine. Reprinted with kind permission.)

pillar and how that pillar interacts with nutrition will help people adopt and sustain healthy eating for a lifetime.

A hyper-focus on food and eating is a double-edged sword. While it is good that there is growing awareness of and interest in what constitutes healthy eating patterns, the flip side is the proliferation of multiple fad-diet trends, which can range from overcomplicated and non-efficient to dangerous. It is no wonder that people are confused and discouraged with the idea that they can achieve long-lasting healthy eating patterns. Unclear, non-uniform nutrient labeling and often false advertising create confusion around food.

A question that many people have is, "What diet is best?" Drs. Katz and Miller tried to answer this question in 2014 by identifying all the popular diets at the time (Katz & Meller, 2014). These days, one may add Atkins or Keto to the mix, too. It is important to realize that Keto can also be vegan. Considering all the different diets, Dr. Katz and Dr. Miller identified the health benefits of each diet:

- Low carbohydrate—Emphasis on restriction of refined starches and added sugars
- Low-fat/vegetarian/vegan—Emphasis on plant foods direct from nature, avoidance of harmful fats
- Low-glycemic—Restriction of starches, added sugars, high fiber intake
- Mediterranean—Foods direct from nature, mostly plants, with emphasis on healthful oils, notably monounsaturated
- Mixed/balanced—Minimization of highly processed, energy-dense foods, emphasis on wholesome foods in moderate quantities
- Paleolithic—Minimization of processed foods, emphasis on natural plant foods and lean meats.

In their summary, the compatible, healthy elements found in all the different diets include "limited refined starches, added sugars, processed foods; limited intake of certain fats: emphasis on whole plant foods, with or without lean meats, fish, poultry, and seafood" (ibid.). They conclude that the simple description of a healthy diet can be stated as "Food, not too much, mostly plants" (ibid.).

Current recommendations have moved toward easy graphic representation, allowing flexibility and accommodating personal eating preferences. This approach allows for flexibility for different eating patterns.

One of the more well-known recommendations is the Harvard Healthy Eating Plate (Harvard T.H. Chan School of Public Health, 2023), which concentrates more on the proportions of different food groups rather than specifying what particular ingredients will be used to meet the recommendation. The plate advocates for half of our daily food intake to be vegetables and fruits, a quarter to consist of whole grains, and a quarter to include healthy proteins. The Healthy Eating Plate is similar to the government's USDA My Plate (USDA, 2020) but has some important differences.

For protein, the Healthy Eating Plate recommendations state to choose beans, nuts, fish, or poultry, to limit red meat, and to eliminate processed red meat, while My Plate doesn't have restrictions on red meat and processed meats. It seems that protein is the next great obsession. There was an obsession with fat, which will be discussed in detail later. There was an obsession with carbs, and most recently, there is an obsession with protein. Human beings do need protein, and it is part of all healthy eating patterns. There are many different types of proteins from which to choose. For heart health, plant sources like legumes (including peas, beans, and soybeans), nuts, seeds, and grains like quinoa are excellent options. For people who choose to consume animal products, fish is a healthy option, but people need to be careful about mercury and microplastics. Other animal options are skinless poultry and lean red meats. General recommendations for protein intake range from 0.8 to 1.2 or more grams of protein for every kilogram of body weight per day. People with chronic conditions, the elderly, and athletes looking to gain muscle mass may require more protein. There is a wide range of acceptable protein for consumption. The Dietary Guidelines for Americans list a range of 10–35% of calories that come from protein each day, depending on age and activity level (USDA & USDHHS, 2020). Commonly quoted protein recommendations are 46 grams a day for women and 56 grams a day for men (Harvard Medical School, 2024). Statistics show that in the U.S.A., mean protein intake is 16% of calories for men and 15.7% of calories for women (CDC, 2024b). This is within the recommended level. It is important to realize that people lose muscle mass after the age of thirty, and they need to do strength training and eat protein to maintain their muscle mass. So, protein is critical for health and a recommended part of every healthy eating pattern. What comes with the protein you consume is an important question. With animal protein comes saturated fat, heme iron, vitamin B12, and other nutrients, including zinc, copper, and vitamin A. In animal protein, there is no fiber and no phytonutrients like quercitin, beta-glucan, ellagic acid, or anthocyanidins, as is found in plant protein. B12 is not naturally found in plants. Thus, those people who are consuming only plant protein need to supplement with B12. There is a question about complete proteins. Are plant proteins complete proteins? Do they have all the essential amino acids? Quinoa does, and so do amaranth, buckwheat, spirulina, chia seeds, hemp seeds, nutritional yeast, tofu, edamame, and tempeh (WebMD, 2024).

As it turns out, if you eat a variety of plant proteins you can indeed get all the essential amino acids you need. Are plant proteins bioavailable? Research has demonstrated that "Plant protein in their original food matrix (legumes, grains, nuts) are generally less digestible (about 80%) than animal protein (meat, egg, milk; about 93%)" (Gaudichon & Calvez, 2021).

My Plate allows for any kind of grain, with only the suggestion to make half the grains whole grains, while the Healthy Eating Plate recommends that all grains be whole grains and cautions about eating refined grains. Many people are fiber deficient. They are not consuming the recommended levels of fiber: 25 grams per day (WHO, 2023).

Many of the health benefits of eating plants (fruits, vegetables, and whole grains) are derived from the process of fiber fermentation by friendly microbiota bacteria, which releases short-chain fatty acids (SCFA) (acetate, propionate, butyrate) that play key roles in regulating the host's metabolism, immune system, and cell proliferation (Rastelli, Cani, & Knauf, 2019). These short-chain fatty acids travel through L cells, which line the gastrointestinal tract and secrete peptide hormones, including PYY and GLP 1 (Spreckley & Murphy, 2015). A diet high in fiber and prebiotic-rich foods has been shown to help increase the number and diversity of friendly bacteria in the microbiota (Cronin et al., 2021; Holscher, 2017). The current recommendations for dietary fiber intake are 28 grams for adult women and 38 grams for adult men (Dahl & Stewart, 2015). A fiber-rich diet has also been shown to lower the incidence of type 2 diabetes, heart disease, stroke, colon cancer, and inflammation (Alahmari, 2024; Reynolds et al., 2019).

Outside of the plate itself, the difference is that My Plate recommends servings of dairy and puts milk in a glass for the image. In contrast, the Healthy Eating Plate recommends water as the drink of choice. Hydration is key for health. The recommendation of eight 8-ounce (about 250 ml) glasses of water daily is a general guideline for hydration. There is water in fruits and vegetables, too. In addition, the requirement for water and hydration varies on climate and activity level.

The Healthy Eating Plate suggests consuming some healthy oils, including olive oil, canola oil, and other plant oils (Harvard T.H. Chan School of Public Health, 2012). It is important to note that industrialized, highly processed seed oils are known to be unhealthy choices mostly because of components that get into the oils during processing (Gharby, 2022). The less processed oils are preferred. The American Heart Association maintains that omega-6 fatty acids have heart-health benefits, with the caveat that people should pay attention to overconsumption (omega-6 to omega-3 ratio) and avoid consuming omega-6-containing oils that are exposed to high heat cooking methods and high processing levels that may change their composition (Harris et al., 2009). Most nutrition experts recommend consuming more omega-3s than omega-6s. There are omega-6s in many highly processed foods, and eating highly processed foods is a major health concern. Of note, avocado oil is good for cooking at high heat as it has a high smoke point. Canola oil recommended in the Healthy Eating Plate is the cold-pressed, minimally processed version of the oil that has been shown to have positive effects on lowering total cholesterol and low-density lipoprotein (LDL) cholesterol, as well as improving insulin sensitivity (Lin et al., 2013).

All oils are composed of a variety of fats. The breakdown of canola oil and olive oil are similar in their components. Both contain mostly monounsaturated fats, with polyunsaturated fats as the next most prominent component, and both have a small amount of saturated fat (Caporuscio, 2019). They also have a much lower percentage of saturated fats than palm oil, coconut oil, butter, and lard. Although some emerging research is revisiting the influence of saturated fats on cardiovascular disease development, current recommendations are still to limit saturated fats to less than 10% of total calorie intake, with the American Heart Association recommending keeping saturated fat intake to less than 6% of total calorie intake for people who need to lower their cholesterol (American Heart Association, 2024). Replacing calories from saturated fats in favor of those from unsaturated fats may benefit heart and cardiovascular health (Harvard T.H. Chan School of Public Health, 2023; Maki, Dicklin, & Kirkpatrick, 2021). One of the major concerns with saturated fat is that it increases cholesterol levels (Maki, Dicklin, & Kirkpatrick, 2021).

The *Full Plate Diet* book offers solid nutrition guidance (Seale, Sherard, & Fleming, 2010) and suggests ways to eat nutritiously and feel satiated without falling into the trap of overindulgence in highly processed and unhealthy foods by filling up with fiber and water. Five high-nutrient vegetables suggested by this diet are:

- Five nutrient-dense vegetables:
  - Avocado—monounsaturated fats, folate, vitamins E, K, and B, and potassium
  - Broccoli—vitamin C, beta carotene, assists in making thyroxin, enhancing absorption of iron
  - Spinach—most nutrients per calorie, lutein, and iron
  - Sweet potatoes—potassium, iron, manganese, copper, quercitin, chlorogenic acid
  - Carrots—beta carotene, calcium pectate (soluble fiber that helps remove LDL)
- Five nutrient-dense fruits:
  - Raspberry/Blackberry—antioxidant, anti-inflammatory, vitamin C, folate, anthocyanin pigments
  - Pears—vitamin A, vitamin C
  - Apples—quercetin, fiber
  - Oranges—hesperidin, flavinoids, limonoids, over 170 phytonutrients)
  - Bananas—potassium, vitamin B6, stimulates the production of serotonin.

ACLM has created its version of healthy plate recommendations, shown in Figure 1.2 on the next page (ACLM, 2024b; Hauser et al., 2022).

Several studies in the past two decades strongly support the benefit of predominantly plant-based diets. A meta-analysis of cohort studies following 469,551 participants found that a higher intake of fruits and vegetables is associated with a reduced risk of death from CVD, an average reduction in risk of 4% for each additional serving per day of fruit and vegetables (Wang et al., 2014). The Nurses Study found that in comparison to the people in the lowest category of fruit and vegetable intake (less than 1.5 servings a day), those who averaged eight or more servings a day were 30% less likely to have had a heart attack or stroke (Hung et al., 2004). Research by He and colleagues completing meta-analyses found that individuals who ate

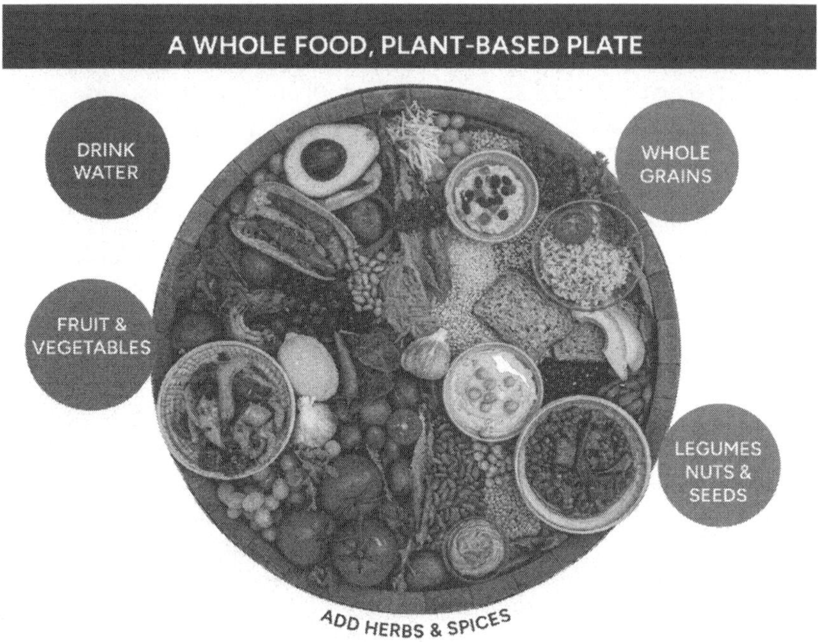

Figure 1.2. ACLM healthy plate (American College of Lifestyle Medicine. Reprinted with kind permission.)

more than five servings of fruits and vegetables per day had roughly a 20% lower risk of coronary heart disease (He et al., 2007) and stroke (He, Nowson, & MacGregor, 2006) compared to individuals who ate less than three servings per day.

Recent research indicates that many of the benefits of healthy nutrition come from a varied whole food, plant-predominant nutrition plan that helps maintain a diverse microbiome. Studies show the benefits and importance of diverse microbiota for multiple endocrine processes in the body (Rastelli, Cani, & Knauf, 2019) and overall physical (de Vos et al., 2022) and mental health (Clapp et al., 2017).

Lifestyle medicine focuses on what to eat: whole foods like vegetables, fruits, whole grains, nuts, seeds, and legumes. It is clear to most people what not to eat: ultra-processed foods. There is more and more data accumulating about the dangers of ultra-processed foods for our health (Mendoza et al., 2024).

The Nova Food Classification scale helps people to better understand the spectrum of processed foods (ECU Physicians, 2018). This classification divides foods into four groups:

- Group 1—Unprocessed and Natural Foods—includes foods that are obtained directly from plants or animals and are not processed or only minimally processed (washing, cutting, grinding, drying, fermentation, pasteurization, cooking, freezing, etc.).
- Group 2—Processed Culinary Ingredients—products extracted from natural foods or nature by the processes of pressing, grinding, crushing, pulverizing, and refining used for cooking or seasoning food.
- Group 3—Processed Foods—industrially manufactured foods by adding salt, sugar, oil, or other group 2 ingredients to natural food to preserve it or make it more palatable.
- Group 4—Ultra-processed Foods—industrial formulations mostly made from substances extracted from foods (fats, sugars, starches, etc.) derived from food constituents (hydrogenated fats and modified starches, or synthesized in laboratories). Group 1 foods make up a small proportion or are absent from ultra-processed foods.

The people promoting these ultra-processed foods are the people who make them. Most healthcare professionals agree that eliminating ultra-processed foods from the diet is essential for health.

Nutrition is a major pillar in lifestyle medicine. This introduction will serve as a foundation of knowledge to be used throughout the book. Each chapter will build on this knowledge. There will be individual chapters on physical activity, stress resilience, sleep, social connection, and avoidance of risky substances, focusing on how they impact eating patterns.

Introduction from a practical culinary perspective

Neil Rippington

We all have a connection with food and drink. We cannot survive without food, as it provides us with energy, the foundation for growth, the development of strength and therefore a natural form of protection.

We also have an appreciation for food and, for many of us, it provides one of life's great pleasures. However, for some, their association with food, for a variety of reasons, is not always positive. For others, certain foods are restricted, sometimes for religious or cultural reasons, health purposes, or due to ethical considerations or simply personal choice. It is this connection, or relationship, that forms the basis for this book and the subject of culinary psychology.

It is, in some ways, ironic that we need food to survive, to drive healthy bodily functions, and to help promote a level of performance to help us to make our way through life and enjoy what it may offer us. As food—including drink, as it has a nutritional value—can also lead to a huge number of health-related issues, including serious illness, disease, and premature death. Food affects us all and drives an activity that we share daily in all corners of the world, namely, eating and drinking.

As creatures of habit (and influence), we become familiar with certain foods, yet many of us gain satisfaction and interest from the exploration of new foods, innovative foods, and dishes that are unknown to us. This sometimes places us in unfamiliar and even challenging situations. Culinary tourism is a huge industry, and our anticipation of others' food cultures and cuisines is often high on the list of priorities when we travel to foreign countries. The culinary tourism market was valued at approximately USD $824.5 billion in 2023 and is projected to reach USD $3361 billion by 2032, with a compound annual growth rate (CAGR) of 16.9% (Grand View Research, 2025). This growth is driven by increasing consumer spending on travel, the desire to try locally sourced food, and a growing number of food travelers exploring new cultures through cuisine (ibid.).

However, why is it that foods and drinks can taste and feel so special in certain environments, yet not the same when recreated in others? Many of us will have experienced a dish from a faraway land or a tropical cocktail on a beach that, when replicated at home on a cold and rainy winter's day, just doesn't have the same appeal or enjoyment. Environmental factors have a huge impact on our enjoyment and recall of positive food and drink associations and memories.

This book has much to explore and challenges us to consider our own relationship with food and drink, and that of others around us: our children, relatives, partners, friends, and people we interact with throughout our lives. Culinary psychology investigates the influences that form decision-making, including how we consider the world around us. Through the media, we are more aware of the issues that affect ecosystems: For example, how the use of fossil fuels has affected the ozone layer, and the consequences of climate change.

Our food supplies travel around the world constantly, filling the supermarket shelves and offering us fresh foods that were picked in fields from farms thousands of miles away just twenty-four hours earlier. The price of this convenience bears more cost than the final financial transaction at the till. Food miles are high on the sustainable agenda, and the use of local, seasonal foods often features as a story-telling selling point on many menus, particularly welcomed by sustainability and ethically minded consumers, as well as many who are keen to support local producers.

From a food production perspective, we consider how intensive farming and industrial fishing practices impact wildlife and the protection of wildlife conservation. For example, meat and dairy farming uses almost a third of the habitable land on Earth, making up 62% of the world's mammals by weight. Humans make up 34%, with wild mammals accounting for just 4% (Ritchie, 2022). This is a startling statistic, and it demonstrates how delicate wildlife ecosystems are in terms of damaging them any further and interrupting the balance of nature.

What we eat makes a difference. Over thousands of years, not only has the human species used a third of habitable land and turned it into farms, but it has also simultaneously overfished a third of global fish stocks. Our food habits and the ecosystems that support them can make a positive difference. Science, technology, and innovation are looking to develop ways in which we can feed the world's growing population by producing more food using less land, leaving space for nature to thrive. Mindful food choices are not only about our own health and well-being but also reflections of our values and ethics, particularly concerning the impact on other species and the health of the planet itself.

In terms of gastronomy and the act of eating and drinking, we investigate how the impact of our surroundings, perceptions, and memories interacts with our enjoyment of consumption. Why should the difference in the number of items on a plate make any difference to our anticipated enjoyment of a dish? Why, often, does an odd number of items appeal more than an even number? It seems obvious that the presentation of food makes a significant difference to our anticipated enjoyment of consuming the food presented, but evidence suggests it goes further than that. The positioning of foods and the way foods, and drinks, are presented have an impact on our perception of quality, enjoyment, and value for money.

The presentation of food has become an art form in certain echelons of the hospitality industry, with leading chefs from around the world creating highly technical, delicious, and aesthetically pleasing dishes. Their creativity and innovations are amazing and deserve the respect and recognition due to an artist and highly skilled professional. The tools and equipment used to supplement the dining experience have also evolved, and the innovation of design in crockery certainly adds a new dimension, helping to augment dishes. However, development in cutlery has not been so innovative, aside from a few exceptions. In the Western world, for example, we have not really progressed from the standard cold stainless steel implements we refer to as a knife and fork. Considering the developments and innovations elsewhere, this seems a little strange. Is this really the best way to transfer food from augmenting crockery to our mouths?

Moving on to the food itself, aroma, taste, flavor, temperature, texture, and mouthfeel are just a few of the sensations we experience as we eat, and each of these nouns can be broken down into countless further descriptors to provide examples of the complexities involved when we consume food and drink. As we go through life, we develop our personal likes and dislikes, but this is not always a permanent state. Our tastes change throughout our lives, sometimes switching on to new foods and flavors, but also, occasionally, we switch off from foods that we have liked in the past. What is it that forms and affects our views, and is it possible to train ourselves to be more open to foods and a wider range of tastes and flavors?

Alongside texture, flavor is one of the most important components in the enjoyment of food and drink. Without flavor, the experience of eating is bland to the point where it can become a task rather than a pleasure. The development of flavor in preparation and cooking, and the ingestion of flavor once in the mouth, is complex. There are thousands of aroma compounds and volatiles that form the flavors we appreciate.

We investigate the importance of our nose in olfaction and breathing, alongside the taste buds on the tongue, to complement the process of eating and drinking. From the initial taste sensations of the infamous "taste map" of the tongue, namely sweet, sour, salty, and bitter, to the more recent savory taste of "umami," research continues with further tastes identified. Since the discovery of the major taste sensations, researchers are suggesting we have far more than the initial four or five, including tastes such as fatty, astringent, pungent, metallic, starchy, and the list goes on.

Physical surroundings and the ergonomics of the environment in which we consume food and drink have a significant impact on our enjoyment of the dining/consumption experience. Large corporations through to independent outlets carefully consider how their physical spaces entice consumers to make their experiences positive, with the aim and intention of consumers returning and sharing their experience with colleagues, friends, and family, and often more widely through social media.

The physical nature of a dining outlet includes design, color schemes, furnishings, and fittings through to the comforts of the dining setting, the seating, and the materials used. The atmospherics add another dimension. For example, how welcoming are your host and venue? How is the lighting, the temperature, the bustle of other customers? Is music being played? What is the genre? Is it too loud? Is there an aroma in the air? Do you like it? Does the opening interaction meet your preconceptions? Are you excited in anticipation of what is to follow? All these additional factors have a role to play in the enjoyment of dining away from the home, and most of the questions above can be applied to operators at every level. The interaction with people also plays a role in the experience of eating. In a restaurant, how important is food service in comparison to food quality? There is a phrase often used in the hospitality industry surmising that "Great service makes the food taste better." This is explored in the chapter "The restaurant journey."

It is natural to develop expectations, acquired from perceptions and/or previous experiences. Even simple associations, such as color, can develop a perception. Why is it that red has sweeter associations than black or green? Which fruit is sweeter, a blueberry or a strawberry? The answer can be found later in the book.

We also make perceptions before we sample goods. Items labeled as low-fat, low-salt, low-alcohol, etc. can produce a negative connotation for many, providing a sense of inferiority or that something is missing in the product. It suggests, perhaps, that there will be health benefits, but at the cost of taste and quality. Will the texture, flavor, or mouthfeel feel the same in the "low" or "zero" product as in the original? Another dimension occurs with low- and zero-sugar products.

How is the sweetness generated, and what are the health implications associated with the ingestion of artificial sweeteners such as aspartame and acesulfame potassium? Is it possible to taste the difference? Many food manufacturers are working tirelessly to produce the "no/zero" and "low" products to the point where the consumer will find it almost impossible to differentiate. Some manufacturers and their developers are getting very close, whereas others have a considerable way to go.

As the final part of this introduction, it is imperative to recognize chefs and their development and contributions over history. Chefs have risen from the depths of dark kitchens, hidden from the stardom of celebrity status that many of today's leading chefs enjoy. Their contributions to the world of culinary arts and the impact they have made over thousands of years have been critical to the development of an art that also supports life and the pleasures of the table. The great gourmand, philosopher, and gastronome Jean Antheme Brillat-Savarin (1755–1826) is quoted in Brillat-Savarin (1825c): "The discovery of a new dish does more for the happiness of the human race than the discovery of a star." This demonstrates the value and appreciation that great food and cooking can have on our lives. Brillat-Savarin also made famous the aphorism, "Tell me what you eat, and I'll tell you who you are." He believed that food defines a nation, and when we examine the health of the world today, and correlate the diets of various nations, there is certainly an alignment.

It is a sad reflection of civilization today that so many people on Earth do not have access to enough food to enjoy a healthy and balanced diet, yet for others in the world, food consumption and poor dietary habits have led to an epidemic of obesity and a range of other food-linked illnesses and conditions. This suggests that we need to eat better and make access to food more equitable. The science and technology are in place to do so.

We can learn much from the past as well as the present and the future. We live in a fast-paced world where some of the traditions of family life have become difficult to uphold. The simple act of sitting together around the table, discussing the day, socializing, and sharing food is much less common than it was just a few decades ago. There is another well-used saying that "a family that eats together, stays together."

However, the final quote is one from one of the world's most contemporary and groundbreaking chefs. Heston Blumenthal explores history, nostalgia, memories, and many other facets in his cooking, one of which is to have good fun, a great time, and create new memories while enjoying fantastic food and drink. "The pleasure we get from food depends, far more than we could possibly imagine, on our subjectivity—on our memories, associations and emotions" (Blumenthal, in Spence, 2017a, p. xii).

We have made major advancements in technology, particularly in the development of AI. This will affect food and drink as it does practically all industries and the way we live our lives. However, the human touch and warmth that is brought via the interaction of people enjoying food and drink in a meal together is one that we have relished since our time began, and long may it continue. It is the foundation of our being.

CHAPTER 1

Neurogastronomy: The study of how the brain processes sensory information relating to flavor

Stelios Kiosses

There is a connection between how the brain creates the perception of flavor and how this matters to human culture. Gordon Shepherd coined the term "neurogastronomy" to describe the interdisciplinary approach that links neuroscience with the culinary arts, psychology, and other fields, emphasizing the brain's role in creating the perception of flavor and its relevance to human culture (Shepherd, 2012).

It's important to clarify that taste and flavor are not the same. Flavor is a complicated mix of sensory data. Taste is just one of the senses that contribute to flavor, but it's an important one because it's a nutrient detector and a toxin avoider. Taste helps you evaluate food and drinks so you can determine what's safe to eat. It also prepares your body to digest food. Humans can recognize several types of tastes. We have receptors for five kinds of tastes: sweet, sour, salty, bitter, and savory. From an evolutionary perspective, taste was a sense that aided us in testing the food we were consuming and was, therefore, a matter of survival.

The various tastes

Starting with sweet, research suggests that we evolved to like sweetness because it helps us recognize energy-dense foods. Sweet foods are often high in carbohydrates, like glucose, which provide our bodies with fuel. It's far easier for many to consume a cookie than a carrot, but you can trick your taste buds. Here's a fun fact: Eating globe artichokes can make other foods taste sweeter. Artichokes contain an acid called cynarin, which causes whatever meets your tongue next to taste a little sweeter than it otherwise would. So mixing artichokes with bitter greens can make healthy salads go down better.

The opposite of sweet is sour. Often spoiled or rotten foods taste sour. It's thought we evolved to taste sourness to identify these types of harmful foods and thus avoid them. However, sourness is still a vital taste. Another fun fact: Sourness makes you salivate. Even just thinking about sourness—like reading this sentence—will make you salivate. Salivation helps with digestion and dilutes the chemicals in your mouth, thus reducing the acidity of sour foods. Being able to detect sourness enables you to judge the ripeness of the food you consume, like fruit. Eating unripe foods can upset your stomach and can lead to inflammation if consumed in large quantities. The less sour, the more ripe, and the more ripe, the better—to a point anyway. Overly ripe becomes rotten.

The next taste is salty. Sodium is essential for electrolyte and fluid balance, and it's believed we can taste saltiness because the body is determining whether it's getting enough sodium. Fun fact: Salt increases the ionic strength of aqueous solutions, making it easier for odorant molecules to separate themselves from food. This is why unsalted soup has no flavor and why adding salt amplifies its odor, which is an important part of flavor.

Bitterness is an interesting taste because it's due to many different molecules. These molecules are usually found in plants like arugula, which you want to eat, but also, many plants with bitter compounds are toxic and you don't want to eat them. Our ancestors evolved to taste bitterness so they could recognize and avoid poison. Fun fact: A study published in the journal *Psychological Science* by Eskine, Kacinik, and Prinz (2011) reported that when college students tasted Swedish bitters—a herbal tonic that tastes very bitter—they were more disapproving of immoral behaviors, ranging from cheating politicians to incest, than participants who tasted a sweet berry punch. This points to how taste is more than one of the five senses and instead has implications for brain functioning, including perception and how we judge ourselves and others. What if life feels terrible not because it is but rather because the food you're eating makes it seem so?

The last accepted taste is savory, which is caused by amino acids. It's commonly brought on by aspartic acid or glutamic acid. The savory taste is also called " umami" or "meaty." Some scientists think tasting savoriness helps increase our appetite and control protein digestion.

Researchers are looking for other sensory cells specialized for sensations besides the five established basic tastes of sweet, sour, salty, bitter, and savory. There are thought to be a few more, such as fatty and alkaline. Newer research suggests there are probably receptors specifically for fat, making fatty the sixth basic taste. However, there could also be other tastes, such as alkaline (brine) and the opposite of sour, metallic and water-like.

We've covered the five basic tastes and the evolutionary basis of them. Our mouths detect the chemicals for salt, sour, sweet, and bitter, but it's our brains that tell us the difference between a doughnut and a lemon. Our brains also signal that sugar is pleasurable and bitter is nasty.

Humans are born with a universal liking for sweet and an aversion to bitter taste, but large individual differences exist in the liking of all the basic taste qualities. These individual differences partly explain differences in short-term intakes of foods varying in taste profiles. Taste also plays an important role in food choice, and a better understanding of the links between the taste of foods, individual taste preferences, food choices, and intakes will aid in the understanding of why some people might select and consume unhealthy foods. But to better unravel this link, we must return our attention to the brain.

Taste and the brain

Charles Zuker, a neuroscientist at Columbia University whose laboratory has transformed our understanding of taste, found that electrically tickling the bitter neurons in the brains of mice caused their mouths to purse and their bodies to shudder as though they were tasting bitter, but when they were given a real bitter liquid and the "sweet" brain region was stimulated, they behaved as though they enjoyed the bitter taste (Peng et al., 2015). This again shows the brain is more deeply connected to taste than people might realize.

We've considered taste in depth but do you know where taste receptors are located? What comes to mind when you think of where they are? Did you imagine the tongue? You might be surprised to know that the proteins that are responsible for our ability to taste salty, sweet, and bitter foods aren't just present on the tongue. People have taste receptors in the pancreas, liver, and testicles (Li, 2013). The function of taste receptors and signaling proteins outside of the taste system is still unclear; however, in some areas, the taste receptors seem to be part of the chemical sensing of sugars or amino acids. The full function of these extra-orally located taste receptors is still unknown, but there's some research as to why taste receptors are found in the testes at least: fertility.

Mosinger et al. (2013) found the taste proteins for sweet and umami not only exist in the testes but also play an important role in mouse fertility—the genetic absence of both taste receptors TAS1R3 and the gustducin α-subunit GNAT3 led to male-specific sterility. Does that apply to humans though? The research team generated a mouse model that expressed a humanized form of TAS1R3 susceptible to inhibition by a class of drugs used to treat high blood cholesterol (clofibrate). They found sperm formation in animals without functional TAS1R3 and GNAT3 was compromised, with malformed and immotile sperm. They suggest these cholesterol drugs could be interfering with human fertility. Focusing on these taste receptors in the testes could make way for new infertility treatments or even lead to male birth control.

That's the testes, but we also have taste receptors in our gut that influence our perception of food. The taste receptors in our gut tell the brain whether we should keep eating ice cream or a cheeseburger and when to stop. It is believed that disturbances in the signaling pathways of these taste receptors play a role in the development of a variety of diet-induced illnesses, from irritable bowel syndrome to diabetes (Depoortere, 2014).

There are also taste receptors in the lungs. These indicate when we inhale something noxious. When that happens, a signal is sent to the brain to make us cough and expel what shouldn't be in the lungs. Lastly, we have taste receptors in the nose. The idea that we taste in our mouths but smell in our noses is not strictly true. Smell has a "dual sense" consisting of orthonasal and retronasal smell. It is impossible to separate retronasal smell from taste because they happen at the same time, in the same place, and come from the same origin, namely, the food you are eating. You're smelling what's outside your body (food) but also what's inside the oral cavity. Sensing the flavor of the food in your mouth is not only done by sniffing but by breathing out, sending little puffs of smell from the food and drink out the back of the mouth and backward up through the nasal passages as food is chewed and swallowed. That is why it's called retronasal smell (retro = backward) in contrast with orthonasal smell (ortho = forward), which is what the common sniffing-smell is called.

Smell is so important that loss of smell (anosmia) can affect a person's well-being. A comparison study examined becoming blind vs. anosmic. It was observed that those who were blinded suffered much more severely at first, but after a year of life with their disability they fared better than the anosmics, who continued to deteriorate over time (Toller, 1999). Anosmics reported feelings of personal isolation, lack of interest in eating, and emotional blunting. It seems that we still have some way to go before the problems associated with anosmia are adequately recognized by the general population and, more importantly, within the medical profession. It's also shown that by regulating the olfactory system, we can control the brain's response to food.

Celine Riera, PhD, is an assistant professor in the Center for Neural Science and Medicine at Cedars-Sinai. Her team's research focuses on mapping the brain circuits to understand pathways that affect obesity. In a recent study, Riera uncovered a connection between olfactory neurons, which control smell, and metabolism, the body's process of converting food into energy (Riera et al., 2017).

Their research found that mice stay leaner when their olfactory neurons, their "smell receptors," were turned off—even when they ate the same diet as mice whose neurons were normal. The mice without a sense of smell burned more calories, stayed more active, breathed more oxygen, and had a higher metabolism. Why? Because olfaction can influence the hypothalamus, an area of the brain that controls hunger.

To return to neurogastronomy, mice who can't smell appear to perceive food differently.

The neurons inside our nose send information to the brain and govern how much food we need, whether to look for food, and how to process the food we eat. The animal research of Riera et al. and others may give us the opportunity to better understand the causes of obesity in humans. One of the causes of obesity—and the reason it is so difficult to lose weight or keep it off—is that hunger and appetite are not something people can control. Hunger happens in the nervous system, at the neuron level, and it is extremely important to understand this aspect of the disease. If we can manipulate hunger response through smell, we could potentially regulate the way the body processes food.

Knowledge of the importance of smell to the perception of flavor and the formation of cognitive and emotional responses to foods and beverages could help to improve health and prevent chronic conditions such as obesity and diabetes. These findings can increase our awareness about the critical relationship between eating habits and senses and could deepen our knowledge of the role that "reward-factor" smell has in various body-shape groups. The reward factor also ties into food liking.

Food liking

Studies show that food liking is one of the most important drivers of food consumption. Tuorila and Pangborn (1988) obtained questionnaire information about women's intended and reported ingestion of four foods and one category of food: milk, cheese, ice cream, chocolate, and high-fat foods. They found that food liking was a stronger predictor of consumption than health beliefs about the food or consumption of the food.

That said, food liking is very subjective, and it is cultural. Different cultures perceive and prioritize tastes differently and have their own culinary traditions. For instance, what some cultures view as a delicacy, other cultures view with disgust. Some cultures use more spice in their food, and that can be too much for the palate of others. Historical, geographical, and social factors influence these taste preferences (and ultimately food liking). It's not only anecdotal evidence that suggests taste is cultural—there are studies that show this too. For instance, Prescott and Bell (1994) looked at Japanese and Australian taste preferences and found there are significant differences in taste discrimination and preference due to cultural backgrounds.

In an earlier study by Prescott et al. (1992), a group of Japanese and Australian participants were asked to rate their liking for seven tastes: sucrose (sweet), salt, citric acid, caffeine, and three umami tastes (MSG, IMP, GMP). The response patterns were similar in both groups for all the tastes, but there were some differences with higher concentrations of citric acid, GMP, and MSG, and also at the lowest concentration of MSG. There were no differences in the hedonic ratings for sucrose, salt, or caffeine. In other words, some food taste preferences are universal.

Some people might say, "It's the artificial flavors that create food liking. Natural flavors don't have the same effect." However, natural and artificial flavors are not that different. Natural flavors are made by extracting chemicals from natural ingredients (plant or animal), whereas artificial flavors are made by creating the same chemicals synthetically. Both natural and artificial flavorings are added to foods for flavor purposes rather than for nutritional purposes, and so neither contributes to any significant health benefits. More specifically, there's no evidence that artificial flavoring itself is harmful to your health, but the food it is included in may not be healthful. In other words, if you're avoiding artificially flavored potato chips in exchange for naturally flavored potato crisps, you're not necessarily doing yourself any health favors.

If there's no difference between natural flavors and artificial flavors, why do companies use natural flavors? Simple: marketing. Research has shown that when "natural" appears on food packaging, people tend to form positive opinions about the product, including how healthy it is (Skubisz, 2016).

If it's not artificial flavors that cause people to overeat, what does? The answer is complicated and in part has to do with emotional regulation, which you can read about in my other chapter. Some people use food to manage their emotions because it feels too scary or difficult to face their feelings.

It's also easy to overeat unhealthy foods, as they are highly liked. Eating an entire box of cookies is more tempting and common than chowing down on Brussels sprouts. But overeating has negative consequences beyond physical ones. Overeating causes people to feel distress, misery, anxiety, or depression. Overeating can also lead to a person feeling out of control and perceiving themselves in a negative light.

Some people think overeating is simply a matter of willpower. Willpower can play a part, as in the case of an obesogenic environment, but overeating is much more complicated than that. For some people, overeating is a learned coping strategy that started in childhood. But there are also mechanisms in the brain and body that affect food liking, taste, flavor, and perception. That's what neurogastronomy teaches us—that food, eating, taste, and weight gain are more complicated than they otherwise seem.

But what also contributes to overeating is an "obesogenic environment," which refers to an environment that promotes gaining weight and one that is not conducive to weight loss within the home or the workplace (Swinburn, Egger, & Raza, 1999).

Creating (or not creating) obesogenic environments

Obesogenic environments are the collective, physical, economic, policy, social, and cultural factors that promote obesity. For example, they may have a high concentration of fast-food outlets and encourage driving over walking.

An obesogenic home environment is one in which the ease, visibility, and access to foods promotes eating unhealthy foods. This is why dieting advice usually includes not keeping candies and chips in the cupboard, as temptation is a deadly force. When unhealthy foods are around, it's easy to grab them in moments of tiredness or hunger. It is possible to create a non-obesogenic environment at home, and this has broader implications for society as a whole, because the healthier people are, the better it is for everyone in terms of how people behave, the strain (or not) on healthcare systems, and more.

In the home, to create a non-obesogenic environment, people can keep healthy snacks visible and easily accessible while storing unhealthy options out of sight. This could mean leaving fruit bowls on the kitchen counter, keeping precut vegetables in the fridge, or buying easily snackable items such as baby carrots or snap peas.

At work, encouraging the availability of healthy food options in the cafeteria and vending machines would help. Ferretti, Mariani, and Sarti (2021) found there is a feedback loop between unhealthy habits (i.e., the consumption of soft drinks) and health outcomes (i.e., the prevalence of obesity). In other words, as the consumption of soft drinks rises, so too does the rate of obesity. Knowing this means that with a little planning, work environments can be healthier environments. In addition to replacing soft drinks with healthier options, workplaces could offer salads, whole grains, and lean proteins as standard lunch options.

A non-obesogenic school environment would involve something similar, and there are case studies that show just how effective small changes can be. For instance, Cornell University researchers conducted a "smarter lunchroom makeover" at cafeterias in western New York (Hanks, Just, & Wansink, 2013). Changes were simple and included a "healthy convenience line" with only submarine sandwiches and healthier sides. Salad was served in see-through, to-go containers, and fresh fruit was displayed in nice bowls or tiered stands. The cafeteria workers prompted students to try healthier options by saying, " Would you like to try …?" and "No veggie? How about …?" They made selecting fruits and vegetables seem normative.

After the makeover, students were 13.4% more likely to take a fruit and 23% more likely to take a vegetable. Selection doesn't ensure consumption, but having said that, the researchers found actual fruit consumption increased by 18% and vegetable consumption increased by 25%. The changes took only three hours to implement and cost less than $50. Related, school gardens also support an increase in healthy food consumption. Holloway et al. (2023) found school gardens do more than increase fruit and vegetable consumption (and thus dietary fiber and vitamins); they also improve body mass index and improve kids' well-being, including by participating in school more.

These changes don't only have to be at school or work. Community initiatives can also make a difference. Supporting local farmers' markets and community gardens can influence health-related behaviors and increase market sales for local farmers. In 2018, the California Department of Social Services (CDSS), CalFresh Healthy Living Program, the Public Health Institute's Center for Wellness and Nutrition (CWN), and the California State Nutrition Action Council created the

Farmers Market Initiative (FMI). The goal was to increase the usage of the Supplemental Nutrition Assistance Program (SNAP), known as CalFresh Food in California, to support participants in stretching their food dollars to purchase more local fruits and vegetables at a farmers' market through the Market Match program. The Market Match program matches customers' CalFresh food benefits dollar-for-dollar.

After this program was implemented, monthly CalFresh redemptions jumped by $401.64 (36.34% increase), and monthly Market Match redemptions increased by $285.82 (42.62% increase) in 2020 and 2021 (Public Health Institute). In addition, average monthly CalFresh transactions increased from sixty-seven in 2020 to around eighty-four in 2021, representing a 24.36% increase.

It's clear that government policies can make a difference in terms of whether people make healthier food choices, as we witnessed with the SNAP program in California. But governments can also support this sort of behavior through food marketing. Folkvord & Hermans (2020) found food marketing is highly effective in stimulating and reinforcing food consumption, in particular for healthy foods. It's well established that showing ads for junk food increases junk food consumption, but so too does showing ads for healthy food increase healthy food consumption. How can governments create non-obesogenic environments? They can ban junk food advertising aimed at children, advertise healthy foods, subsidize healthy food initiatives, and support local farmers.

Again, food is complicated. It's not just food. As neurogastronomy shows us, the field of food science includes all the disciplines relevant to eating such as the culinary arts, molecular biology, neuroscience, psychology, human evolution, and child development, especially brain mechanisms involved in learning and memory, emotions, motivation, and reward. But with a few simple measures, people everywhere can be healthier and happier to boot.

CHAPTER 2

The psychology of sex and food: Do food aphrodisiacs really work?

Stelios Kiosses

Food is not simply fuel—it affects how we think and behave, including sexually. Foods said to excite sexual passion are called aphrodisiacs. The term comes from the Greek goddess of sexual love and beauty, Aphrodite. Her name is derived from the Greek word for foam, *aphros*, which ties in to her origin story: Hesiod claimed Aphrodite was born from the white foam produced by the severed genitals of Uranus after Kronos threw them into the sea.

Anything pertaining to Aphrodite is an aphrodisiac, especially an item believed to make sex more attainable or pleasurable. There are many items that are considered aphrodisiacs but some have that label only because of the direct tie to Aphrodite. For instance, oysters are a symbol of Aphrodite's fertility. She sprang forth from the sea on a shell and promptly gave birth to Eros. Pomegranates are another example, because Aphrodite is credited with planting the first pomegranate. And then there are strawberries. Aphrodite is said to have created strawberries when she wept heart-shaped tears for her lover Adonis upon his death. These are all myths, but they have endured, much like other ancient aphrodisiacs.

The types of aphrodisiacs

Food is a common aphrodisiac, but it's not the only one. There are six types: scents, foods, animal parts, plants and botanical preparations, drugs, and pharmaceuticals. Aphrodisiacs may be classified into two classes: psychophysiological (visual, tactile, olfactory, aural) and internal (stemming from food, alcoholic drinks, drugs, the mythical "love potions," and pharmaceuticals).

The most prominent types of psychophysiological aphrodisiacs are scents and perfumes, which are linked to pheromones, a Greek word meaning "to transfer excitement." Places pheromones are produced are glands at the base of the hair follicles, especially in the armpits and in the genital region. They produce chemicals, and the odor might affect whether a person is considered attractive. There's a debate as to whether perfume is an attempt to mimic "human pheromones" or if it's used to create an atmosphere of positive associations. Instead of floral scents or musk though, you might be more successful with food scents: Research has suggested that certain scents can influence sexual arousal due to their psychological impact and potential physiological effects. The intriguing case of pumpkin pie and licorice stems from studies examining the impact of various scents on blood flow and arousal levels in different genders. For instance, a study conducted by the Smell and Taste Treatment and Research Foundation in Chicago found that the scent of pumpkin pie mixed with lavender increased penile blood flow by 40% among male subjects, while licorice combined with cucumber had a notable effect on women. These findings highlight the role of olfactory stimuli in sexual arousal, suggesting that certain food scents can evoke responses that go beyond mere preference, tapping into deeper physiological and emotional cues (Hirsch & Gruss, 1999).

Turning our attention to internal aphrodisiacs, the most prominent, and readily available, type of internal aphrodisiac is food. While oysters are associated with Aphrodite's fertility, they are also low in fat and high in minerals. That makes oysters a healthy food, especially as phosphorus, iodine, and zinc have beneficial effects on the body. Zinc in particular is said to increase both sperm and testosterone production as well as the secretion of vaginal lubricant. However, research has failed to connect mollusks with actually enhancing sexual drive.

Another such food is onions. Onions are mentioned in many classic Hindu texts on the art of making love, and they were an aphrodisiac in Ancient Greece. They also make an appearance in the famous *The Perfumed Garden*, a fifteenth-century Arabian erotic manual written by Umar ibn Muḥammad Nafzāwī. Onions are mentioned multiple times, but one notable excerpt reads as follows:

> He who peels onions, puts them into a saucepan, with condiments and aromatic substances, and fries the mixture with oil and yolk of eggs, will acquire a surpassing and invaluable vigor for the coitus if he will partake of this dish for several days.

Later, he wrote of a beverage that would not give a man much rest at night because he's so interested in having sex. And if a man drinks the beverage for several days, he will constantly have his member rigid and upright without intermission. The beverage takes one part of the juice pressed out of pounded onions, mixes it with two parts of purified honey, and then warms it over a fire until the onion juice has evaporated.

There's no scientific evidence to back up his claims, but Nafzāwī touted onions nonetheless.

A different food, but one that is a very popular folk aphrodisiac in Poland and the Czech Republic, is celery. The reason why this could be the case is that celery contains androsterone, a naturally occurring steroid that acts as a pheromone in humans (and boars). Some people say eating celery can increase androsterone levels. Also, the vegetable contains androstenone and androstenol, which are male hormones that may stimulate sexual arousal in women.

Truffles were well known to the Romans as a powerful aphrodisiac. However, with the fall of the Roman Empire, the magic properties of truffles fell into oblivion and were rediscovered only in the late eighteenth century. Similar to celery, truffles contain a compound that is like androstenol, which makes it fall into the category of an aphrodisiac.

Saffron is a spice used all over the world, from India to Egypt and Greece. It is said that the herb builds stamina and promotes serenity. Unlike some of the other foods mentioned, saffron has been clinically shown to improve sexual dysfunction such as erectile dysfunction, as well as enhance sexual arousal, sexual satisfaction, and genital lubrication

(Ranjbar & Ashrafizaveh, 2019). Another study (Kashani et al., 2013) found that in women with low sexual desire due to antidepressant medication, taking 30 milligrams of saffron daily over four weeks reduced sex-related pain and increased sexual desire and lubrication compared to a placebo.

While saffron has scientific backing, aphrodisiacs that are based on myth more than science are animal parts. Organotherapy was popular during Roman times as a way of trying to treat sexual problems. This form of sexual therapy is based on the belief that the consumption of a healthy animal organ might cure illnesses in the corresponding human organ—a case of similarity in action. Thus, the Romans ate all kinds of animal genitalia, including penises, wombs, and testes. Note: The treatments were not effective.

Organotherapy practice has detrimental consequences in that some animals are in danger of extinction due to their alleged aphrodisiac properties. One example is pangolins, which are desired in parts of Asia and Africa for their meat, while their scales are ground up for traditional medicines to cure everything from skin rashes to high blood pressure. Their fresh blood is touted as an aphrodisiac. But ironically, consuming pangolin scales is no different than chewing your own nails, as they are both made of keratin. Yet the retail price of pangolin scales has shot up exponentially over recent decades, and in China, these scales can now fetch up to $750 per kilogram. It's a huge problem as demonstrated by a *New York Times* article (May, 2019). The newspaper reported nine tons of pangolin scales were seized in Hong Kong, and that amounted to an estimated 14,000 animals that were hunted and killed.

Another example is the tiger. Tiger parts, such as skulls, bones, whiskers, sinew, and blood, have long been used by Asian people, especially the Chinese, in medicines and potions used to treat rheumatism, rat bites, and various diseases; in the restoration of energy; and as aphrodisiacs. In East Asia, tiger parts—including bones, fat, liver, and even the penis—are considered powerful aphrodisiacs, though no scientific evidence supports these claims. The allure of sexual potency blurs the line between medicine and gastronomy in Chinese traditional medicine. For instance, the Beijing restaurant Guo Li Zhuang has offered dishes made from the penises and testicles of various animals for more than a decade, catering to those seeking virile rejuvenation.

Further illustrating the intersection of belief and tradition, since the sixth century, rhinoceros horn has been consumed in China purportedly to enhance blood circulation during sex. However, scientifically, a rhino's horn is not a true horn but a growth of densely compressed dermal fibers made of keratin—the same material found in human hair and nails. Consuming rhino horn is, effectively, no different from eating one's own fingernails.

Recently, the fungus *Cordyceps sinensis*, which infects the body of certain Tibetan caterpillars, has become popular and costly. This "Himalayan Viagra" can fetch up to three times the price of gold. For context, button mushrooms go for about $4 a pound, shiitakes cost about twice that, and black truffles can run to $800 a pound. *Cordyceps sinensis* sells for $50,000 a pound and fetches such a high price because of its rarity and difficulty of acquisition. Collecting *Cordyceps sinensis* requires excavating soil, and of course finding the caterpillars infected with the fungus. The process has become so intense that biomes of the Himalayan region, such as the Jigme Dorji National Park in Bhutan, are threatened by predatory extinction. A report published by a Bhutanese organization in 2012 said, "[I]f left unregulated and unmonitored, the impacts from the collection of this highly priced fungi while helping improve livelihoods will leave some of the last pristine alpine ecosystems on this planet transformed for the worse" (Wangchuk, Norbu, & Sherub, 2012).

With the exception of the aphrodisiacs that have scientific backing, the most active ingredient in any aphrodisiac is probably sexual innuendo. According to a review of the scientific literature published in 2015 (West & Krychman), none of these rare and exotic-sounding foods (or other substances such as rhino horn, chaste berry, horny goat weed, saw palmetto, or wild yam) have been proven to do much to enhance sexual drive. Food aphrodisiacs such as honey, oysters, and chocolate won't hurt you, as long as you don't gorge on them. For example, studies have shown that cocoa can increase blood flow (West et al., 2014), but when its direct relationship with sexual desire was studied, there was no evidence found to support its use as an aphrodisiac. In fact, no evidence has been found proving that any one food heightens sexual desire. However, don't underestimate the power of sensual suggestion.

Food, sex, and money

Food and sex are biological rewards sought by both animals and humans. These are called primary rewards. Eating, having sex, and making money are rewarding pursuits that drive human behavior. Not all reward-seeking behaviors are biological in need. There are also secondary rewards based on societal importance such as wealth and prestige. A key brain region associated with all reward types is the basal ganglia: a cluster of gray matter nuclei located at the base of the forebrain, originally known for its implication in motor and regulatory function. The reward system is one of the most important systems in the brain. It drives behavior toward pleasurable stimuli such as food, sex, money, etc. And it drives people away from painful stimuli (conflict, homework, etc.) that require more energy or effort. The basal ganglia is where we feel emotions and process those emotions to start or stop action.

Rewards typically serve as reinforcers. That is, they make us repeat behaviors that we perceive (unconsciously) as good for our survival even when they're not. Pleasure is a better reward or stimulus than pain for motivating behavior. Understanding the involvement of brain structures in processing different reward types can help us understand human decision-making mechanisms, from someone's choice of a chocolate bar instead of a healthy breakfast to being attracted to potential mates.

Arsalidou, Vijay, and Sharaev (2020) used quantitative meta-analyses to assess whole-brain and basal ganglia-specific contributions to money, erotic, and food reward processing. Pulling from 190 functional MRI studies, they found concordance in overlapping and distinct cortical and sub-cortical brain regions as a function of reward type. Food reward processing favored the right brain hemisphere; erotic rewards favored the right lateral globus pallidus and left caudate body. Money rewards engaged the basal ganglia bilaterally, including its most anterior part: nucleus accumbens. In other words, the same parts of the brain light up with food, sex, and money, albeit in slightly different regions.

Food and sex share more than the basal ganglia. They also share the orbitofrontal cortex, which is the part of the brain that fires during taste perception and orgasms. It's known that chocolate, particularly dark chocolate, releases dopamine, which is also released during many different euphoric states, including an orgasm. Given the connection between food and sex, it's no surprise that on social media a new iteration of the food–sex link has cropped up with the "foodporn" hashtag, which is often paired with "#foodgasm." At the time of this writing, the foodporn hashtag turns up more than 310 million Instagram posts. The related #foodgasm displays more than 70 million Instagram posts.

These erotic food images can change how much people are eating. Versace et al. (2019) found, when measuring brain responses, that individuals with larger late positive potentials in response to food-related cues are more susceptible to cue-induced eating and, in the presence of a palatable food option, eat more than twice as much as individuals with the opposite brain reactivity profile. More recently, Khosla, Murty, and Kanwisher (2022) found the visual frontal cortex (VFC) lights up when we see food images. The VFC also reacts differently depending on the food—some study participants responded more to processed foods than unprocessed foods. In other words, the brain in some people "wakes up" when seeing a moist, gooey chocolate chip cookie more than an image of kale. What's interesting is the VFC receives, integrates, and processes visual information of faces, bodies, places, and words as well, so the same part of the brain that registers " I like that person" also says "I like that food." Food is a more recently discovered category in the VFC processes and could represent the special significance of food in human culture, meaning food has long been powerful and important for more than just fuel.

Returning to the imagery of food and sex, food companies frequently employ sexually suggestive advertising to appeal to consumers. A notable example is a Burger King ad from 2009, where a woman is depicted with parted lips, facing a burger that is elongated, resembling more of a hot dog than a traditional round burger. The accompanying tagline, "It'll blow your mind away," explicitly draws on sexual innuendo. Similarly, in the U.K., Marks & Spencer is known for its "food porn" advertising campaigns (2019), which emphasize the sensual pleasure derived from its food products. These adverts, renowned for their sultry narration and close-up shots that accentuate the textures and sounds of food, are designed to appeal to the sensory experiences of the viewer. Such strategies underscore a global trend where food marketing leverages sexual imagery to enhance consumer appeal, though the cultural context may influence the specific execution and reception of these advertisements.

It's not only food companies that create sexually suggestive food images—a *Newsweek* cover from 2012 shows a woman's face from her nose to her chin, red lips parted, and two pieces of asparagus dangling close to her mouth. The headline is "101 Best Places to Eat in The World." Not only does sex sell but so does "sexy-looking" food.

Presentation, whether it's overtly sexual or not, affects perception, including taste. Wansink, Payne, and North (2007) gave adult diners a complementary glass of wine that was relabeled to induce either favorable ("new from California") or unfavorable ("new from North Dakota") taste expectations. Those who believed they had been drinking California wine ate 12% more of their meal than those who instead believed they drank North Dakota wine. In combination with a sensory-based lab study, the results show environmental cues can affect the food intake of companion foods. What this points to is the power of the brain. Returning to the topic of food and aphrodisiacs, can food, or even the simple act of eating, put you in the mood for love? The answer is yes. Any provocative effect we get from aphrodisiacs, most researchers believe, is all in our heads. An aphrodisiac is an unconscious survival-oriented behavior characterized by a motivation toward goals that relate directly or indirectly to survival, mating, and reproduction. But that doesn't mean that sex has nothing to do with food. "One cannot think well, love well, sleep well," wrote Virginia Woolf, "if one has not dined well." Food is the foundation upon which so much rests. Without good food, brain functioning changes, and so does behavior, including sexual behavior.

Much of our sexuality is psychological in nature, so perhaps the aphrodisiac foods did what they were supposed to by creating a placebo effect. Foods and the act of eating can suggest sex to the mind, which in turn can help stimulate desire in the body. What we do know is that for people who exercise, have a healthy diet, and enjoy lower stress levels, all these elements work together, and those people have better sex lives.

A study involving nearly 600 women by Giugliano et al. (2010) observed that those with type 2 diabetes who adhered more closely to the Mediterranean diet experienced a lower prevalence of female sexual dysfunction. The Mediterranean diet, characterized by high consumption of fruits, vegetables, nuts, whole grains, and fish, and low intake of red and processed meats and refined grains, has also shown benefits for men. In a literature review, Esposito et al. (2010) found that type 2 diabetic men with the highest adherence to the Mediterranean diet had the lowest prevalence of erectile dysfunction (ED) and were more likely to be sexually active. Furthermore, clinical trials have demonstrated that the Mediterranean diet is more effective than a control diet in improving erectile dysfunction and enhancing sexual function in individuals with obesity or metabolic syndrome.

Many people are looking for a jumpstart to their sex lives and think an aphrodisiac will help them. A food like saffron can help, but ultimately the psychology of food and sex shows that the mind is powerful and the placebo effect is real. Beyond that, the "unsexy" advice like eat well, get good sleep, and lower your stress levels is what will most positively affect your sex life.

CHAPTER 3

The link between diet, crime, and mental health

Stelios Kiosses

Sometimes thought of as disparate issues, diet, crime, and mental health are linked and have profound societal implications. This nexus affects public health policies, educational programs, and rehabilitation methods. By exploring how nutritional factors influence psychological well-being and behavioral outcomes, we can address some of the root causes of crime and mental health issues in society. These insights enable policymakers to craft targeted interventions that promote public safety and wellness, potentially reducing healthcare costs and enhancing community well-being.

While diet, mental health, and crime have been the subject of much research in recent years, there is also a long history to consider. From the Ancient Greek philosophy advocating moderation in all things, including diet, for balanced health and temperament, to the nineteenth-century observations by physicians like Dr. John Harvey Kellogg on the impact of diet on mental clarity and morality, the connection between food and behavior stretches back centuries. However, it was not until the late twentieth century that we began to see a more systematic scientific exploration of how specific dietary components can affect mental health and, by extension, influence antisocial or criminal behavior. This modern perspective is enriched by advances in neurobiology, psychology, and nutrition science, driving a renewed interest in how our meals shape our minds and actions. That's not to say the issue is cut-and-dried, because it's not. The link between diet, mental health, and crime is complex and multifaceted, but more and more, studies are showing a strong connection between what we eat and how we think as well as behave.

It's already well established that poor nutrition affects how a person feels physically. A diet high in processed foods and sugar does not result in feeling healthy and well. Studies have shown this, but there's also plenty of anecdotal evidence to support it. And how a person feels physically feeds into how they feel mentally.

A study by Sánchez-Villegas et al. (2011b) found that a diet high in trans fats was associated with an increased risk of depression. Trans fats are unsaturated fatty acids that can occur naturally or through an industrial process that adds hydrogen to vegetable oil. This causes the oil to become solid at room temperature. Industrially produced trans fats can be found in margarine, vegetable shortening, fried foods, and commercially baked goods. They can also be hidden in frozen pizza and refrigerated dough.

Sánchez-Villegas and colleagues found that people who consumed the most trans fats had a 48% increased risk of depression compared to those who consumed the least. Trans fats clog arteries, but they also affect the brain and increase the risk of depression. On the flip side, there's also research showing that a healthy diet is associated with a lower risk of depression. Parletta et al. (2017) gave 95 study participants either three months of biweekly cooking classes featuring a Mediterranean diet and six months of fish oil supplements or three months of biweekly fun and stimulating social groups along with three additional months of fish oil supplements. All participants received a mood boost, but in the diet group, their depression scores fell by 45% compared to 26.8% in the social group. The reduction in depression was also related to a specific type of food intake, including eating diverse vegetables, consuming nuts, and adhering to a Mediterranean diet overall. A key component of the Parletta study was the addition of omega-3s. Omega-3 fatty acids, which are found in high concentrations in fish, seafood, algae, and flax seeds, positively impact mood and reduce symptoms of depression and anxiety. There is now some evidence that omega-3 fatty acid supplements may be helpful in the treatment of depression, although a definitive statement to that effect cannot be made yet, as per Grosso et al. (2014).

Similarly, B vitamins, which are found in foods such as whole grains, nuts, and leafy greens, play a critical role in brain function and reduce the risk of depression and other mood disorders.

Nutrition affects how you feel, increasing the risk of anxiety and depression depending on what your diet is like, but food also affects how you *behave*.

Influence of nutrition and aggression

A study by Schoenthaler (1983) followed 3,000 juvenile inmates for two years. Subjects were not allowed junk foods, and the facility prepared snacks and treats that did not contain as much sucrose or food additives. They provided snacks such as popcorn and unsweetened orange juice rather than candy bars and soft drinks. In the male population (n = 2,005), antisocial behaviors declined by 21% compared to the previous twelve months. In addition, disruptions/horseplay fell by 42%, and assaults/fights dropped by 25%. There were slight reductions in suicide attempts, verbal threats, and disobedience as well.

Gesch et al. (2002) found antisocial behavior in prisons, including violence, is reduced by vitamins, minerals, and essential fatty acids. Similarly, Zaalberg et al. (2010) found the same to be true in the Netherlands. These studies provide a factual basis for discussions on dietary interventions in juvenile settings. I've thus constructed a hypothetical case study of John, a sixteen-year-old, who had a history of aggressive behavior and frequent incidents of violence at the juvenile detention center where he was placed due to minor offenses. John's diet consisted primarily of high-sugar and high-fat foods, which are common in such facilities. A pilot program was introduced at the center, which focused on improving the nutritional quality of meals. The new diet eliminated trans fats and reduced sugar and salt intake, replacing them with whole grains, fresh fruits and vegetables, and sources of omega-3 fatty acids like fish and flax seeds.

Over the course of six months, John and his peers who participated in the program showed significant improvements in their behavior.

John's incidents of misconduct decreased by 40%, and his overall mood and cooperation with staff and peers improved. Staff also reported fewer disciplinary actions needed during the period.

Analyzing the outcome, the dietary changes were linked to better overall physical health, which in turn improved cognitive functions and emotional regulation. Omega-3 fatty acids, known for their role in brain health, likely played a critical role in tempering aggression and enhancing mood stability, which is backed by research. Golomb and colleagues (2012) published a paper that linked trans fats and aggression. In a study of nearly 1,000 people, the study team found that dietary trans fatty acids were linked with behavioral irritability and aggression. It appears that trans fats interfere with the brain's ability to produce and use omega-3 fatty acids—a nutrient shown to lower aggression, as Benton (2007) found in his research.

Going back to our case study, John demonstrates the potential of dietary interventions as a simple yet effective strategy to improve behavioral outcomes in juvenile detention settings. His results also suggest that such changes could be a valuable component of rehabilitation programs aimed at reducing recidivism and aiding the psychological development of detained youths. It's perhaps for these reasons that prison vegetable gardens, where inmates plant and harvest fresh produce to feed the larger prison population, are gaining popularity in correctional facilities from New York to Oregon (Harrison Green, 2016).

The link between diet and behavior extends beyond any single country's borders, and international research supports the notion that nutritional interventions can positively influence mental health and reduce criminal behavior. Here are a few notable examples.

Brazil: Recent research conducted in Recife, northeastern Brazil, investigated the association between diet quality indices and metabolic parameters among adolescents. The study by Marília Tokiko Oliveira Tomiya and colleagues (2017) highlights the important role of diet quality in influencing not only physical health outcomes but also in having implications for mental health and behavior among young people. This study underscores the broader impacts of dietary intake on health and potentially on behavioral outcomes in educational settings.

United Kingdom: The Food and Mood Centre's ongoing research continues to provide evidence on how diet impacts mental health. One of its studies, the SMILES trial (Jacka et al., 2017), specifically showed that dietary improvements can significantly reduce symptoms of depression.

Japan: The traditional Japanese diet, characterized by a high intake of fish and vegetables, and a minimal amount of processed foods, has been associated with a range of health benefits, including improved mental health outcomes. A study by Nanri et al. (2010) highlights this relationship, finding that "… dietary patterns which are closely aligned with traditional Japanese eating habits are inversely associated with depressive symptoms among Japanese adults." This suggests that the nutritional components of the traditional Japanese diet may play a role in mitigating factors that contribute to depression.

Can nutrition affect brain function and thus lead to poor decision making? Yes. But there are also social and environmental factors that contribute to the link between diet, crime, and mental health.

Social and environmental factors leading to crime

Poverty and food insecurity are major risk factors for poor nutrition, which in turn can contribute to mental health problems and criminal behavior. Food insecurity is defined by Gundersen and Ziliak (2015) as a household-level economic and social condition of limited or uncertain access to adequate food.

These economics professors examined the relationship between food insecurity and health outcomes. They analyzed data from the National Health and Nutrition Examination Survey (NHANES) and the Current Population Survey (CPS). They reviewed previous research on the negative impact of food insecurity on health outcomes, including poor nutrition, increased risk of chronic diseases, and mental health problems. They also discussed the economic and social factors that contribute to food insecurity, such as poverty, unemployment, and low wages.

Nutrition programs such as the Supplemental Nutrition Assistance Program (SNAP), also known as Food Stamps, seek to reduce food insecurity and improve health outcomes. Do they work? According to

Gundersen and Ziliak, yes. These programs are effective in reducing food insecurity and improving nutrition outcomes, but more research is needed to determine their long-term impact on health outcomes.

Overall, Gundersen and Ziliak's study highlights the negative impact of food insecurity on health outcomes and underscores the importance of addressing the economic and social factors that contribute to food insecurity. This is also the case because the food insecurity and poor mental health cycle can perpetuate. Whitaker, Phillips, and Orzol (2006) conducted a cross-sectional survey of 2,870 mothers of three-year-old children, evaluating food security and mental health. After adjusting for sociodemographic factors plus maternal physical health, alcohol use, drug use, prenatal smoking, and prenatal physical domestic violence, the researchers found a link between food insecurity and mental health in the mothers. The more food insecure, the higher the percentage (30%) of depression and anxiety. The same was true in the children: 36.7% experienced depression and anxiety.

The study findings have implications far beyond childhood, as the results demonstrate being food insecure affects development and can lead to increased impulsivity and antisocial behaviors, which are linked to criminal activity. A larger and more recent study from Frongillo et al. (2017) examined the effects of food insecurity on subjective well-being. In a sample encompassing 149 countries, they found food insecurity explained poor physical health and lower subjective well-being beyond other measures of living conditions and was larger than with other explanatory variables such as social support. Food insecurity is a worldwide problem and has implications far beyond physical consequences. Socio-economic factors contribute to a cycle where poor nutrition and mental health problems reinforce each other in community settings. This relates to crime because neighborhoods characterized by high poverty rates often experience higher levels of crime and violence, which can further exacerbate stress and mental health issues among residents.

According to Murali & Oyebode (2004) in *Advances in Psychiatric Treatment*, social deprivation and economic inequality prolong exposure to diet-related stressors, which contributes to mental health disparities and the perpetuation of a cycle where poor mental health and crime feed back into each other. In other words, you cannot solve one without addressing the other, and there must be integrated policy approaches that consider the links between socio-economic status, nutrition, mental health, and crime. Will improving access to healthy foods completely reduce crime? No, but it can help. A study from Clemson University (Caughron, 2016) showed that for every 1% rise in food insecurity, violent crime rates increased by 12%. This suggests that the opposite would also be true—lower food insecurity would lead to a decrease in violent crime rates.

Effective policy interventions that address food insecurity might include improving access to healthy foods in impoverished areas, education on nutrition, and mental health support services. These sound simple, but they are not at all easy. For instance, increasing access to healthy foods means acknowledging that public policy and economic practices have created areas with low access to healthy foods. A word often used to describe such an area in the U.S. is "food desert," which, according to the USDA (Dutko, Ver Ploeg, & Farrigan, 2012), is characterized by large proportions of households with low incomes, inadequate access to transportation, and a limited number of stores offering healthy groceries at affordable prices. However, as farmer and activist Karen Washington states (Brones, 2018), "food desert" is an outsider term used by people who do not actually live in these areas. She says,

> Number one, people will tell you that they do have food. Number two, people in the 'hood have never used that term … When we're talking about these places, there is so much life and vibrancy and potential. Using that word runs the risk of preventing us from seeing all of those things. (Para. 7)

Similarly, in the U.K., areas with limited access to affordable and nutritious food are often discussed in terms of "food poverty" or "food swamps." The term "food swamp" has been used to describe areas where unhealthy, processed foods are more readily available than healthy options, exacerbating nutritional inequality. A study by The Food Foundation (2020) highlights that such terminology may also obscure the underlying social and economic issues that contribute to these conditions, urging policymakers to focus on holistic solutions that address both availability and affordability of nutritious food.

A better term to describe areas with low access to certain foods is "food apartheids." As activist Dara Cooper puts it (Cooper, 2017), food apartheids refer to the

> systematic destruction of Black self-determination to control one's food, hyper-saturation of destructive foods and predatory marketing, and blatantly discriminatory corporate controlled food system that results in [communities of color] suffering from some of the highest rates of heart disease and diabetes of all time.

She specifically calls out the impact of policies on black communities, but food apartheid affects other people of color as well as individuals in poverty regardless of their race. This highlights that solutions to better nutrition, better mental health, and lower crime rates must address economic injustices and the pervasive effects of discrimination that cross racial lines. A grocery store cannot simply be dropped into a community expecting to resolve these issues. Both Michelle Obama and the USDA learned this the hard way. As reported by Nolan Brown in *Reason* magazine (2016), since 2011, the federal government has spent almost $500 million to improve food store access in neighborhoods lacking large, well-stocked grocery stores. States and local governments have also launched programs to attract supermarkets or improve existing stores in underserved areas. However, the problem is that healthy foods don't necessarily sell in certain neighborhoods, and it's not merely proximity to healthy foods that matters as much as household and neighborhood resources, education, and taste preferences. Moreover, price is a crucial factor determining whether or not people purchase certain foods. The USDA found that SNAP beneficiaries were more sensitive to price than to food store access. Participants with very difficult access purchased smaller amounts of perishable foods than shoppers with easy access. However, the prices of different food groups were more important determinants of purchase decisions than access was. When price and demographic factors were accounted for, the effects of food access were negligible. Furthermore, although opening a new supermarket might improve residents' perceptions of food accessibility, it does not necessarily lead to increased consumption of fruits and vegetables. This suggests that addressing food insecurity effectively requires a multifaceted approach that considers a wide array of factors, including economic status, cultural preferences, and educational outreach.

To truly improve nutrition, which has implications for mental health and criminal behavior, communities experiencing food apartheid need more than grocery stores. They need food sovereignty, or the right to have a say in how their food is grown, the right to fresh, affordable, and culturally appropriate food, and ultimately a redistribution of power and ownership. A place to start food sovereignty and reeducation is in schools. Healthy school meal programs have shown positive effects on student behavior and academic performance. Schools with enhanced nutritional meals report fewer disciplinary problems and improve academically and psychosocially. Kleinman et al. (2002) gathered information about a universal free school breakfast program (USBP). Prior to the program, 33% of all study children were classified as being at nutritional risk. Children who were at nutritional risk had significantly poorer attendance, punctuality, and grades at school, more behavior problems, and were less likely to eat breakfast than children who were not at nutritional risk. Six months after the start of the program, students who decreased their nutritional risk showed significantly greater improvements in attendance and school breakfast participation, decreases in hunger, and improvements in math grades and behavior than children who did not decrease their nutritional risk. It's clear that school meals can improve numerous factors, and with that in mind, the best way to ensure these school meals are nutritious is to make sure they include a high ratio of vegetables, fruits, and whole grains while limiting processed foods and sugars.

Related, subsidies can make healthier food options more affordable and accessible because as previously noted, price is a huge deterrent for people with low incomes when choosing foods to purchase. Employing subsidies would potentially improve diet quality because it would incentivize the purchase of healthier food options. This can also tie in to food sovereignty, as government subsidies could support urban agriculture projects that make healthy foods more accessible in underserved areas.

Healthy foods must also be seen as attractive and unhealthy foods as less desirable, because there is a clear link between advertising and consumer behavior, particularly in children and adolescents.

The American Psychological Association (APA) reports that children spend more time (44.5 hours per week) in front of computer, television, and game screens than any other activity in their lives except sleeping. They also reported strong associations between increases in advertising for non-nutritious foods and rates of childhood obesity. Most children under the age of six cannot distinguish between programming and advertising, and children under age eight do not understand the persuasive intent of advertising.

"Advertising directed at children this young is by its very nature exploitative," the APA states ...

> Children have a remarkable ability to recall content from the ads to which they have been exposed. Product preference has been shown to occur with as little as a single commercial exposure and to strengthen with repeated exposures. Product preferences affect children's product purchase requests and these requests influence parents' purchasing decisions.

In other words, advertising has its desired effect—children want the foods that are shown to them on TV. A policy suggestion is to employ strict regulations on the advertising of high-sugar and high-fat foods, especially during children's TV programming and on online platforms frequented by minors. This is only one part of the puzzle, however. Parents must also be educated, and integrative community programs that address both mental health and nutrition can lead to sustainable improvements in public health. Supporting the development of community centers that offer mental health services alongside nutrition education and cooking classes to improve diet and mental health simultaneously can improve outcomes for individuals and the communities they live in.

Diet, crime, and mental health are inextricably tied together, and to truly have thriving individuals and communities, special care and attention must be given to how these issues are connected.

CHAPTER 4

The relationship between religion and food

Stelios Kiosses

Research has shown that religion and spirituality (R/S) has a positive association with health. About 80% of the studies looking at the relationship between R/S and health examined mental health, showing a positive association with well-being, self-esteem, and optimism; lower scores of depressive and suicidal symptoms; and lower stress levels. Numerous studies have also reported a positive association between R/S and physical health, including an association with lower all-cause mortality and lower rates of diet-related diseases such as hypertension, cardiovascular diseases, and cancer. Gillum and Williams (2009) found that after adjusting for age, race, Hispanic ethnicity, nativity, education, and marital status, women who never attended religious services were more than six times as likely to report having four or more risk factors for breast cancer than regular churchgoers. The researchers found the combination of frequent attendance at religious services, very high importance of religion in daily life, and self-identification as a Protestant evangelical were particularly protective.

It's clear that religion and spirituality (R/S) can improve physical and emotional well-being, but what role does food play within these domains? In our culture and religious affiliations, the language we use to describe food often mirrors our unique dietary beliefs, which are deeply intertwined with our spiritual practices. The connection between food and religion/spirituality is multifaceted, reflecting dietary laws, fasting rituals, and the symbolic use of food in ceremonies across various faiths. These practices, rooted in cultural and spiritual traditions, not only serve to purify and express devotion but also strengthen community bonds, highlighting the profound significance of food beyond mere sustenance.

In religion, food is one of the most important parts of religious ceremonies. The role of food in religious culture is an important part of showing respect among their communities, and many of these conventions obey their religious commandments, hence food is prepared in different ways. The meaning attached to food is also an exploration of culture through food. Religious commitments to food are influenced by several different factors, ranging from personal spirituality and experiences to social patterns of belonging as well as ethical, political, and doctrinal convictions related to food and eating. Around the world, people follow different religions. Food is an important part of religious observance for many different religions. Religions which have particular food restrictions or celebrations involving food include:

- Christianity
- Islam
- Hinduism
- Judaism
- Sikhism
- Buddhism
- Seventh-day Adventism
- Rastafarianism
- And numerous spiritual groups as well.

The roles of religion in food choice include communicating with God (e.g., saying thanks and blessing the food); demonstrating faith through following religious rites concerning diets; and developing discipline through fasting.

The religious symbolism behind foods and dietary practices

As mentioned, numerous religions have tenets around foods and dietary practices. Starting in no particular order, observant Jews only eat kosher food, meaning it meets their dietary laws. These dietary laws include no pork or shellfish; animals must be killed in a kosher way. Other kosher rules are that meat and dairy cannot be consumed in the same meal or prepared with the same utensils.

Altogether, the dietary laws are known as *kashrut*. Stone (2023) writes that kashrut carries spiritual and ethical significance within Judaism because, "By adhering to these dietary laws, individuals are reminded of their responsibility to maintain a sanctified life, exercise self-control, and exhibit gratitude for the sustenance provided with a *bracha* over the food. Kashrut serves as a constant reminder of the Jewish people's commitment to their faith and their connection to a larger historical and religious narrative." That narrative continues in each generation in part due to holidays.

There are a number of Jewish holidays that have particular associated food customs. For instance, on Rosh Hashanah (Jewish New Year), sweet foods are eaten to symbolize a sweet new year. Two popular examples are apples dipped in honey and honey cake. Also, the traditional plaited challah is replaced by a round challah to symbolize the cycle of the year. Ten days later is Yom Kippur (Day of Atonement), which is a fasting day. Then there's Pesach (Passover), during which observant Jews do not eat leavened food, or food containing yeast. In its place, some Jews eat unleavened bread called *matzah*. Matzah also plays a special role in the Passover *seder*, a ritual meal that tells the Exodus story. During the *seder*, certain foods are placed on a *seder* plate to symbolize elements of the Jews' escape from Egypt.

In Islam, Muslims do not eat pork or any pork product. Meat that Muslims do eat has to be killed in a particular way, making it halal. Halal food is not just a set of dietary restrictions; it symbolizes a way of life and reflects Muslims' values and devotion to their faith. Anki (2023) wrote that halal food choices are intertwined with cultural identity, as they reflect the culinary traditions and flavors of different Muslim-majority regions. The preferences also often align with health-conscious choices because halal practices prioritize the well-being of animals and emphasize clean and hygienic food preparation.

In terms of special practices that have certain associated food rituals, there are the following:

Ramadan: A month of fasting from dawn to sunset
Eid
Eid-ul-Fitr: A day celebrating the end of Ramadan
Eid ul-Adha: A day that celebrates the end of the Hajj (pilgrimage to Mecca).

Eid can be celebrated with special foods shared with friends and family, such as Eid sweets.

The kosher and halal food markets are substantial, and foods that meet religious dietary standards must be certified. This demand affects food production, processing, and packaging industries globally and leads to a wider availability of these products in mainstream markets. Other religions have specific practices related to food but do not require certified dietary standards.

In Hinduism, some Hindus are vegetarian, whereas others will eat meat. It depends on the branch of Hinduism and where they come from. For some Hindus, their vegetarian diet is rooted in the principle of *ahimsa* or non-harming. The principle applies not only to people, except in the case of self-defense, but also to food choices. *Ahimsa* connects to a broader ethical framework that respects all living beings and asks, "How can I cause the least amount of harm in my food choices?" The answer is to become vegetarian or vegan. In this way, dietary choices can reflect and reinforce spiritual as well as moral beliefs.

For the Hindus who do eat meat, many will not eat beef, as the cow is considered to be a sacred animal. Among the festivals linked to special foods, Diwali (Diipavali) is the most celebrated. The timing of this festival changes because it is tied to the new moon in the month of Karttik, which falls between mid-October and mid-November. Symbolically, the day before Diwali represents a time of darkness, suggesting that light cannot overcome and that evil will continue to dominate society. However, when Diwali arrives, it symbolizes the triumph of light over darkness, good over evil, and the power of knowledge. To celebrate these victories, special sweets are eaten during Diwali to signify and savor the "sweetness of triumph" and the joy of enlightenment that the festival brings.

Sikhs also celebrate Diwali, though their religious observances and dietary restrictions differ from those of other faiths. While Sikhs have few restrictions on what they can eat, they are prohibited from consuming meat that has been ritually slaughtered, unlike Jewish and Muslim dietary laws, which require ritual slaughter. Sikhs believe that sacrificing animals in the name of God is unnecessary and ritualistic, reflecting a deeper philosophical stance that emphasizes respect for all life. According to Sikh principles, true spirituality involves compassion and equality, which extends to not killing animals in a ritualistic manner that places spiritual significance on their death. They argue that such practices may foster a misguided belief that the physical act of sacrifice can lead to spiritual merit, whereas Sikhism teaches that spiritual progress depends on one's actions and devotion to God without the need for such rituals. The congregation eats together after the act of worship in the gurdwara. The langar (sharing a meal in the community kitchen) is an important part of Sikh religious life, and after a religious service, no Sikh will leave without partaking of langar, according to Harvard University's pluralism project (n.d.). "For Sikhs, eating together in this way is expressive of the equality and oneness of all humankind," the project reports. That's because people of all sorts sit together on the floor. No one is better or worse than another, and unlike in the caste system, where there are rules around food and who can eat with whom, the Sikhs reject the idea that anyone is superior or inferior and demonstrate this through the practice of langar. "At the same time, it strengthens the Sikh sense of community. Visitors and guests are readily and warmly included in the great hospitality of the Sikh tradition," the pluralism project says.

Sikhs (but also other R/S groups) demonstrate "commensality," which refers to the positive social interactions that are associated with people eating together. Eating together is a hugely important social activity, with evidence of communal feasting going back at least 12,000 years in the archeological record. A cross-sectional study reported that eating main meals with family members every day was associated with a lower rate of obesity as well as eating balanced meals and having enough sleep. A higher frequency of watching TV during meals was associated with lower vegetable and fruit intake as well as higher fat intake. Research on eating alone suggests it is viewed as a strong experience of loneliness and social isolation.

In Buddhism, one of the key tenets is compassion, and that can translate into dietary choices, with some Buddhists choosing to be vegetarian or vegan. However, it's a personal choice, as many Buddhists are not vegetarian. Some very observant Buddhists will also adopt a vegetarian diet that is free of strong-smelling plants such as garlic, onion, chives, leeks, and shallots, as these vegetables are thought to increase sexual desire when eaten cooked and anger when eaten raw.

In terms of holidays, Wesak is a festival celebrating the birth, enlightenment, and death of Siddhartha, who some people believe to be Buddha. Foods such as eight-treasure rice can be eaten on Wesak. Preserving traditional foods is crucial for maintaining cultural heritage. This effort not only keeps culinary traditions alive but also promotes cultural tourism, where people travel to experience authentic local cuisines. Food festivals and culinary tourism have become popular ways to celebrate and preserve food heritage while promoting cultural exchange.

Christians don't have any restrictions on what foods they eat, but there are a number of occasions where special food may be eaten. This includes Christmas, a day celebrating the birth of Jesus; Easter, celebrating Jesus' resurrection from the dead, three days after he was killed; and Shrove Tuesday or the Tuesday prior to Lent, which is a forty-day period leading up to Easter when Christians remember the time Jesus fasted in the desert. Some Christians give up certain foods during this period to honor Jesus. Shrove Tuesday was traditionally the last chance to use up the foods Christians would not be eating during Lent, such as eggs and fats. This leads me to my next point: fasting.

Religious fasting and its impact on health

Most religions have dietary norms or instructions. These dietary precepts fall into two general categories: 1) a temporal abstinence from all or certain foods (fasting), and 2) stable and distinctive dietary habits that differ from the general population. Religions around the world engage in fasting or restriction of foods as part of their practices. Some such restrictions are daily, monthly, or around holidays.

In Christianity, fasting is mentioned several times in the Bible. Religious fasting is part of everyday life for a number of Christian communities, and as previously mentioned, some take part in partial fasts that deny them certain food types during Lent.

Members of the Church of Jesus Christ of Latter-Day Saints (Mormons) take part in a total fast of food and drink, usually on the first Sunday of each month. During this fasting period, members will abstain from food for twenty-four hours.

Fasting for spiritual reasons is a very important part of Hinduism. Different fasts are observed by each member of the faith and it is a personal choice they take part in. Often Hindus will choose to fast on the day of the week that corresponds with their favorite deity. For example, those who worship Shiva will fast on a Monday, whereas members who follow Vishnu will fast on a Thursday.

For Muslims, fasting is one of the most crucial aspects of their faith, as it's considered the fourth of the "Five Pillars of Islam." These are five basic acts that must be followed that create the foundation of Muslim life. The most notable period of fasting is known as Ramadan—the Holy Month. During Ramadan, followers of the faith should not eat or drink from dawn until sunset.

Religious fasting for Jews involves not eating any food or consuming any drink, even water. The most important and well-known day of fasting for those of the Jewish faith is Yom Kippur, also known as the Day of Atonement. The twenty-five-hour ritual involves abstaining from food and drink before sunset on Yom Kippur eve until after sunset on Yom Kippur itself. In preparation, some Jews take part in a large and festive feast the day before Yom Kippur.

Although each religion takes a different approach to fasting, they all have one thing in common: prayer. Prayer and spiritual strength are the primary reasons why people of all faiths take part in fasting. Because they aren't engaged in meal preparation or dining, they have more time to devote to their spiritual practices. And while religious fasts are observed primarily for spiritual purposes, they also have the potential to greatly affect a person's physical health. Studies indicate that fasting significantly improves several markers of overall health, particularly those related to cardiovascular and metabolic disease.

The Seventh-day Adventists, a widely studied religious group with a distinctive diet and lifestyle, are perhaps the best example. Some Adventists are vegan, excluding all animal products from their diets. Others follow vegetarian diets that include eggs, low-fat dairy, and fish. Still others choose to eat certain meats and additional animal products. The Seventh-day Adventist diet also discourages using products that the Bible considers "unclean," like alcohol, tobacco, and drugs. Some Adventists take this a step further and avoid refined foods, sweeteners, and caffeine. This diet and lifestyle guideline makes Seventh-day Adventists an attractive population to study, and they have been: More than 300 reports have been published in the scientific literature describing the Seventh-day Adventist diet and its health effects.

In general, overall mortality, coronary heart disease, and cancer rates are substantially lower among Adventists, which may be because of their diet or other lifestyle factors. For instance, Fraser et al. (1992) found that exercise makes a difference in terms of coronary risk factors for Adventists. Subsequent studies have revealed that vegetarian Adventists have lower rates of hypertension, diabetes, heart diseases, some cancers, and have greater longevity than nonvegetarian Adventists.

A central rationale in the scientific inquiry of religious diets is that the biological and metabolic mechanisms of diet and health-disease associations in religious people are the same as those in nonreligious ones; thus, much of what is learned in this area of research should be applicable to the general population. Whether it's a "holy" religious precept, "solemn" public health recommendation, or "simple" common sense advice from our parents or neighbors, consuming a healthy diet, regardless of the reason, results in better health for anyone. "Healthy" in this instance means plenty of fruits and vegetables and minimal refined sugars.

On the opposite end of fasting is too much food, which brings us to food waste.

Food waste

Food waste is a problem worldwide. Globally, wasted food amounts to one-third of all food that is grown. The U.S. Department of Agriculture (USDA) estimates that in the U.S., food waste is 30–40% of the food supply. This range is based on estimates from USDA's Economic Research Service of 31% food loss at the retail and consumer levels, which corresponded to approximately 133 billion pounds in weight and $161 billion worth of food in 2010. Of the food thrown away, 33% is fresh food; 27% is leftovers; 15% is packaged and long-life goods; 9% is drinks; 9% is frozen foods; and 7% is takeaways. Playing into throwing away so much food are the dates on food products—sell by, use by, and best before. Almost none of those dates indicate the safety of food, and generally speaking, they're not regulated in the way many people believe, according to a report from the Natural Resources Defense Council (NRDC) and Harvard Law School's Food Law and Policy Clinic (Gunders, 2013).

The current system of expiration dates misleads consumers to believe they must discard food in order to protect their own safety—nine out of ten Americans needlessly throw away food based on these labels. However, the dates are only suggestions by the manufacturer for when the food is at its peak quality, not when it is unsafe to eat. "Sell by" dates are a tool for stock control and suggest when the grocery store should no longer sell products in order to ensure the products still have shelf life after consumers purchase them. "Best before" and "use by" dates are intended for consumers, but they are often just a manufacturer's estimate of a date after which food will no longer be at peak quality; not an accurate date of spoiling or an indication that food is unsafe.

And then there's what happens before food even reaches consumers: an estimated 20% to 40% of fruit and vegetables are rejected even before they reach the shops because they do not match the supermarkets' excessively strict cosmetic standards.

Given that 70% of American food pantries are based in or sponsored by a house of worship, and that 83% of religious congregations in the U.S. host some sort of program to assist needy people in their communities, it's clear that religious organizations could play an enormous role in highlighting the food waste crisis. The relationship between religion and food waste is particularly interesting because religious consumers have been shown to be more altruistic and caring. The influence of religious values and food waste is reflected in religious texts and teachings, which have much to say about food. For example, Judaism has the Talmudic concept of *bal tashchit*, which can be interpreted as "thou shalt not waste." In the Quran, it says: "O Children of Adam! Wear your beautiful apparel at every time and place of prayer: eat and drink: But waste not by excess, for Allah loveth not the wasters" (al-A'raf, 7/31). There is a New Testament passage stating, "When they had all had enough to eat, Jesus said to his disciples, 'Gather the pieces that are left over. Let nothing be wasted'" (John 6:12[NIV]). Many Hindus hold a pantheistic view of God as being in and through everything, including food. Thus, wasting food is, in essence, treating God poorly. In Zen and at many Buddhist retreats, they follow the practice of eating meals "orioki style," which means taking "just enough" food. Orioki synchronizes body and mind by bringing mindfulness to how people eat.

Taking just the right amount of food is essential to practicing the middle way of Buddhism. In the *Vimalakirti Nirdesa* sutra, it is said that "When a person is enlightened in their eating, all things are enlightened as well." This emphasizes the principle of moderation and mindfulness in Buddhism and reflects the core concept of the "middle way" to avoid extremes in all aspects of life. This sutra also highlights the idea that enlightened eating transcends physical nourishment, fostering deeper awareness and interconnectedness with the world. In practice, this happens during meals, because Buddhists are encouraged to eat meals slowly and with full awareness, fostering a deep appreciation for the food and the effort that went into preparing it. This practice is a form of meditation and helps people cultivate mindfulness and gratitude.

There is a Greek parallel with the Temple of Delphi in Ancient Greece regarding the middle way. The maxim μηδέν ἄγαν (nothing in excess) was inscribed alongside γνῶθι σεαυτόν (know thyself), emphasizing the importance of moderation and self-awareness. The maxims are associated with the Oracle of Delphi and are attributed to the Seven Sages of Greece. All of this leads to another concept: ecotheology.

The theology of eating

Ecotheology is a form of constructive theology that focuses on the interrelationships of religion and nature, particularly in light of environmental concerns. Ecotheology generally starts from the premise that a relationship exists between human religious/spiritual worldviews and the degradation of nature. It explores the interaction between ecological values, such as sustainability, and the human domination of nature. It's environmental ethics, consensus for sustainability of the biosphere, and human civilization. The movement has produced numerous religious-environmental projects around the world. Ecotheological approaches include an ethics panel, Earth law, Green Economy tax penalties for depletion and pollution, corporate social responsibility, ecodesign, simple living, and more. On the consumer side, people with strong religious beliefs are more likely to buy fat-free, sugar-free, or gluten-free foods than natural or organic foods, according to research

(Minton, Johnson, & Liu, 2019), which could influence the marketing of those specialty food products. Diet-minded food products do have a particular appeal for religious consumers, likely because they generally prioritize the moral principle of purity, and purity is associated with self-control and behaviors such as restrictive diets.

On a broader level, the International Institute for Islamic Thought, in cooperation with the Eugen-Biser Foundation (Germany), held a symposium titled "Islam, Christianity and the Environment" at the baptismal site of Jesus Christ in Jordan. The symposium was another event in the series of dialogues driven by the global Muslim-Christian interfaith initiative, A Common Word (acommonword.com). It brought together a small group of Muslim and Christian scholars to discuss how each religion views the environment. This exchange helped both sides achieve a better understanding of each other's perspectives and also led to a strengthening of the response from all faiths to the current environmental crisis. Speaking of the environmental crisis, climatic variability can, and does, affect a community's customary food beliefs and behaviors. What was readily available before may not grow as well given the change in climate.

Here's an example: The supply of chardonnay, pinot noir, and pinot meunier, among other wine-making grapes, is at risk, according to new data from a Silicon Valley climate-AI startup, as reported by NPR (Maani, 2024). "By 2050, we're looking at about 85% of the lands that we grow good wine grapes on, actually no longer producing suitable wine grapes," said Jasmine Spiess, the company's head of wine and events in the article. That's because grapes are susceptible to even the most subtle changes in weather. "Wine is kind of the canary in the coal mine for climate change impacts on agriculture because so much of the character of wine is tied to the local climate," said Benjamin Cook, a climate scientist at NASA's Goddard Institute for Space Studies in the *NPR* piece.

It's not only grapes that are connected to the local climate—it's all food. Regions known for growing certain crops may no longer be able to grow them. Foods used in religious ceremonies may be harder and harder to come by. It's unclear how society will adapt, but religions and spiritual groups can play a key role in the adaptation by encouraging new behaviors and taking a leadership role, as we've seen some do already.

CHAPTER 5

Unconscious influences on dietary intake: Why we eat more than we think

Stelios Kiosses

Food is not just food. It's an expression of emotion and is frequently used as a metaphor for consolation, reward, or celebration. We make soup for someone who is sick. We buy something sweet as a treat for a hard day. We bake cakes for birthdays and anniversaries. Food is served to friends, lovers, children, acquaintances, and even strangers. Food is never just food; it's something relational and expressive, these days even more so.

How we relate to what we eat has undergone a substantial shift in the past couple of decades. Eating is an intensely personal act. What we eat communicates to others our beliefs, cultural and social backgrounds, and experiences. According to the 2022 Food Manufacturing Trends Report by the National Food Association, "Today consumers in general want food items that are fresh, creative, and made just for them. That is where the customization trend comes in—and it's hotter than ever in the fast-growing casual segment." There are three main categories of personalization: emotional, preference, and health. Emotional personalization is when products are packaged and customized with names and messages. For instance, putting a name on a soda bottle. Preference is when flavors and textures are tailored to an individual's taste: a spice mix just for them. Health personalization is when products are optimized for specific health benefits or nutritional requirements. This could be a nutrition box for athletes or new mothers.

While adults are the ones driving the personalization trend, it turns out our relationship with food starts much earlier. How we perceive food as adults is rooted in our childhood experiences. Research suggests that children with positive food experiences are more likely to have healthy relationships with food as adults. Cooke et al. (2004) found in a cross-sectional survey of 564 mothers of preschool children that introducing fruits and vegetables during weaning was associated with a higher frequency of fruit and vegetable consumption when they were two to six years old. In other words, the early feeding period is a critical time to be exposed to and learn about a wide variety of foods that will facilitate food acceptance.

There's another connection between food and early childhood, and it has to do with attachment: specifically, how a child attaches to their primary caregivers. We "attach" to our primary caregivers, and depending on how they respond to our needs, we learn how to respond in turn. Attachment patterns are developed within the first year of life and likely solidified by age four. Attachment manifests into two categories: secure and insecure.

Secure attachment occurs when caregivers are regularly relied on for comfort and attention. The baby's physical and emotional needs are met consistently. Insecure attachment is the opposite: either the caregiver sometimes provides comfort, attention, and meets the baby's needs, or they rarely do so. Insecure attachment is characterized as anxious, avoidant, or disorganized depending on how the baby responds to their caregiver.

Those with insecure attachment may develop disordered eating behaviors because the relationship with caregivers sets the tone for the relationship with ourselves, which includes our relationship with food. Furthermore, food may become a coping strategy to fill or avoid a deeper, often primitive emotional void, that of an insecure attachment to caregivers. When food is consumed in this way, it's called emotional eating, because food is being used as a way to process feelings rather than satisfying hunger. This was the case with a patient I'll call Emma, a thirty-two-year-old graphic designer struggling with emotional eating.

Whenever she was sad, she turned to food. It was an easily accessible and constant companion for her when no one else was around. She could count on food the way she couldn't count on her mother.

Emma is not alone in this. A study by Hardman, Christiansen, and Wilkinson (2016) published in *Appetite* found children with an anxious attachment style are more likely to develop emotional eating habits because anxious attachment is characterized by a need for reassurance and fear of abandonment, which can lead to stress and anxiety. Emotional eating is often used as a coping strategy to soothe those uncomfortable feelings.

The researchers also found that if a mother is anxious, her anxiety might influence her parenting behaviors, including how she feeds her child. She might overfeed her child as a way of expressing love and care in an effort to create a sense of security. These patterns are important to understand because they can contribute to long-term eating behaviors and dietary habits as an adult, including becoming an emotional eater.

Emotional eating can be prompted by negative feelings such as stress, loneliness, anxiety, or boredom, as we see with Emma, but emotional eating can also be linked to positive feelings. Some people overeat when they're happy. This could occur in everyday life—for instance, they're newly in love and indulging—or when they're celebrating a holiday or birthday.

Types of food people emotionally eat

Certain trends exist in the foods people want to eat to process their emotions. Generally speaking, happy people want to eat foods like pizza, while sad people prefer ice cream and cookies. Bored people crave salty, crunchy things, like chips. There are also differences along gender lines. One study found that cisgender men prefer hot, homemade meals like steaks and casseroles when they seek comfort. Cisgender women prefer chocolate and ice cream. However, it's also the case that people learn emotional eating patterns: A child who is given cookies to stop crying, for instance, may learn to link cookies with comfort. A child given candy after a big achievement may grow up using candy as a reward for a job well done. It's not only candy—it's any food that was used as a reward in childhood, such as a popsicle, a doughnut, etc.

As adults, we may "reward ourselves" with certain foods after a stressful event, or only feel we "deserve" certain foods if we have worked hard enough and earned a "treat." This was the case with Emma. Her mother gave her a cookie whenever she did something well, and so as an adult she rewarded herself in the same way. However, this behavior ballooned to such a degree that she *had* to have a cookie every time she did something well. She didn't feel satisfied with her behavior without one.

Some parents use food as a reward for eating something else. For instance, "If you eat peas, then you can have ice cream." Here, the child isn't learning to like peas; they're learning to put up with eating peas in order to eat something they *do* like: ice cream. In turn, foods that are used as rewards often become extremely liked and desired more. They are often "treat foods" that may be restricted and as such become "prized." This can be unhealthy, because research suggests such foods tend to be overeaten when freely available. In other words, if ice cream is used as a treat and then freely available, it can turn into a binge food.

Also, the foods that are most often used as rewards tend to be unhealthy. They are usually sugary treats and salty snacks that are generally considered highly palatable and immediately gratifying. This makes them effective in eliciting a positive emotional response quickly. Foods high in sugar and fat trigger the release of dopamine, a neurotransmitter associated with feelings of pleasure and satisfaction. This biochemical response can reinforce behaviors—children learn to associate these pleasurable foods with positive outcomes or emotional comfort.

However, the frequent use of these foods as rewards can lead to several adverse effects such as a nutritional imbalance and the shaping of long-term preferences for these foods. Doing so can also establish unhealthy coping mechanisms, as we've already examined with emotional eating. In the case of "reward" foods, children do not learn healthy ways to cope with stress or achievement. Instead, they turn to food for emotional relief or as a reward, which can contribute to emotional eating habits later in life.

It's important for parents to consider these factors because frequent use of unhealthy foods as rewards can inadvertently promote an unhealthy relationship with food. Encouraging alternative rewards such as activities, small toys, or privileges can be more beneficial in promoting a healthy lifestyle and emotional coping mechanisms.

Some well-meaning parents try to guard against emotional eating by restricting their child's food intake, such as by having a very strict meal and snack structure. However, that might have a boomerang effect and encourage the child to rebel and eat when they aren't hungry. A study by Fisher and Birch (2002) found that when parents restricted their daughters' access to foods at age five, they ate even when they weren't hungry at seven years old.

Eating problem vs. eating disorder

Many people occasionally overeat. It's a common trope to see someone on TV bingeing on ice cream after a breakup, or unbuttoning their pants after a holiday celebration such as Thanksgiving. When overeating is occasional rather than frequent, does no physical harm, and does not impair the individual's quality of life, there is no issue. If, however, the person views their occasional binge eating as a "problem," it is a problem, because every person is allowed to define what works for them and what does not.

Overeating can be segmented into four types: impulsive, compulsive, emotional, and binge eating. Impulsive means not premeditated and occurs on the spur of the moment. It's eating cookies because someone set out a tray of them at work. Compulsive eating is when the person feels they have no choice but to keep eating, even if they're already full. It's buying a bag of chips and finishing the whole bag because they can't eat just a handful. For Emma, it was eating cookie after cookie despite feeling full and wanting to stop. For others, compulsive eating shows up when they consume fast food.

Fast food is more than food that is ready quickly—it's also food that is eaten quickly. Research shows it's the overall atmosphere when you eat out that affects how quickly you consume food. Fast food restaurants are designed with speed eating in mind—and studies show the quicker you eat, the more calories you consume! Many people already categorize fast food as unhealthy; they know what happens when this type of food is consumed on a physical level, but there's a mental and emotional component as well. People who eat a lot of fast food are 51% more likely to be depressed than those who steer clear of it, according to Sánchez-Villegas et al. (2011a). In addition to depression, excessive fast-food consumption is linked to anxiety symptoms. The refined carbohydrates in many fast-food items can cause your blood sugar to fluctuate. Extremely low blood sugar can cause panic attacks, insomnia, and other anxiety symptoms.

The other types of overeating are emotional eating, which we've considered and witnessed with Emma, and then there's binge eating. Binge eating and emotional eating aren't necessarily two separate and distinct processes. Instead, they are one process that occurs on a continuum. The end of the continuum is binge eating disorder (BED).

An eating disorder is different than an eating problem because it's more frequent, causes physical harm, and impairs the person's quality of life either physically (e.g., they ruin their teeth due to frequent vomiting) or mentally (e.g., they are so consumed with thoughts about food and their body that they are unable to be present).

There are four types of eating disorders:

- Bulimia nervosa
- Anorexia nervosa
- Binge eating disorder
- An atypical eating disorder, which is one that closely resembles the other eating disorders but does not meet the precise diagnostic criteria.

It's not uncommon for a person to have a mix of eating disorders, meaning they could restrict food but then binge because something primal takes over, and become so disgusted with themselves or scared of gaining weight that they vomit. Eating disorders can also fluctuate in a person's life if left unchecked. Meaning, in their younger days, a person may have been anorexic but then as they got older, they started bingeing.

For bulimia, three core features are typically present. First, the person experiences frequent binges, meaning recurrent episodes of eating during which genuinely large amounts of food are consumed. Second, they engage in one or more extreme methods of weight control. These include self-induced vomiting, misuse of laxatives, and overexercising. Third, these behaviors are accompanied by persistent concerns about weight, shape, and body image. People with bulimia nervosa "over-evaluate" the importance of their shape, weight, or both; that is, they judge themselves by their ability to control their shape or weight. If they are "thin," which is something they define for themselves, or weigh a certain amount, they feel good about themselves as a person. If they are "fat," again, by their own definition, they think of themselves as "bad," "wrong," "unattractive," "unlovable," etc. In other words, they attach much significance to their shape and size, letting it outweigh their other qualities and characteristics.

The characteristics of anorexia are the following:

1. The person should be significantly underweight, and this should be the result of his or her own efforts.
2. Similar to bulimia, the person over-focuses on their shape and size and makes meaning from doing so (i.e., thin means they're "good").

It should be noted that not all anorexics are underweight. Atypical anorexia nervosa is seen in people with all the symptoms of anorexia nervosa but who have normal body weight. An editorial by Golden and Mehler (2020) reported that this group of patients is under-recognized and under-treated, adding they can be just as sick medically and psychologically as anorexia nervosa patients who are underweight.

The most common eating disorder in the U.S. is binge eating disorder (BED): It affects 3.5% of women and 2% of men. The *Diagnostic and Statistical Manual of Mental Disorders* (DSM-5) states BED includes frequent overeating—at least once a week for three months—combined with lack of control, marked feelings of distress, and an association with three or more of the following:

- Eating much more rapidly than normal
- Eating until feeling uncomfortably full
- Eating large amounts of food when not physically hungry
- Eating alone because the person feels embarrassed about how much they're eating
- Feeling disgusted, ashamed, depressed, or guilty after a binge.

Binge eating falls into two categories: objective and subjective. Subjective binges/overeating are small quantities of food that the individual *perceives* as excessive. Objective overeating/binging is when truly large amounts of food are consumed and that causes psychological and/or physical distress.

The difference between emotional hunger and physical hunger

Emotional hunger comes on suddenly, and often there's a craving for a specific food. In the case of Emma, she craved cookies when rewarding herself and ice cream whenever she felt sad. Eating to fullness isn't satisfying, and there's often a "food hangover," or feelings of guilt, shame, and disgust after a binge. Physical hunger comes on gradually, the person is open to eating any sort of food, when they feel full they stop eating, and there are no negative emotions after the fact.

What spurs emotional eating? Anything from work stress and financial worries to health issues and relationship struggles may be the root of emotional eating. There's also a physiological response. Sometimes what happens is people reach for sugary snacks when they are tired and want to raise their energy levels.

There are two types of tiredness: calm tiredness and tense tiredness. Tiredness is natural in life, especially if you are not getting enough sleep. But if you have anxiety, you may end up feeling more exhausted than is normally expected, which is termed tense tiredness. Anxiety itself is physically and emotionally exhausting. It may also lead to issues like insomnia, which contributes to even further tiredness. Anxiety can also lead to adrenal fatigue, which creates feelings of intense tiredness even when you're otherwise perfectly rested. Sleep hygiene can help with getting more sleep, but if there's anxiety, it doesn't matter how well you practice sleep hygiene—the anxiety needs to be addressed. For some people, there are also physical issues—their poor sleep is the result of an undiagnosed sleep disorder, which can also exacerbate anxiety and create tense tiredness.

On the opposite end of anxiety is depression, and tiredness is one of the most common symptoms. If you are depressed, you'll likely lack energy and feel tired physically, emotionally, and cognitively. Depression can also make sleep less restful and restorative, which then fuels depression. Research by Tempesta et al. (2020) in the *Journal of Sleep Research* found lack of sleep imposes a negative emotional bias on people and has important implications for daily life, as well as in clinical settings. Their study of forty-two subjects looked at "pleasant and neutral images" after five nights of normal sleep and five nights of restricted sleep. The results showed that the participants were more likely to have negative responses to these images after the periods of disturbed sleep than after normal sleep.

How does this relate to overeating or binge eating? As mentioned earlier, tiredness is a trigger. Sometimes eating a certain food will trigger a binge, such as in the case of compulsive eating, but loneliness, a craving, and feeling bored also contribute to overeating. Where do people overeat? In their kitchen, living room, cars, and at work. Why do people turn to food? Because, usually, it's easily accessible, and eating has the ability to change your physical state in an instant. Eating helps soothe anxiety. By filling yourself up with food, you force your body to start its digestive work, and this produces a calming effect.

Negative emotions may lead to a feeling of emptiness or an emotional void. Food is believed to be a way to fill that void and create a false feeling of "fullness" or temporary wholeness, as we considered earlier when referencing attachment to caregivers and what happened with Emma. Emotional hunger can never be satisfied with food because it doesn't do anything about the emotion. It can make you feel good temporarily but afterward, you are left with feelings of guilt, shame, and powerlessness. The emotional needs are addressed. This can be through twelve-step groups, trauma recovery programs, and therapy. Therapy can help with tense tiredness and support learning to recognize patterns of negative thinking that lead to stress. Therapy can also stop negative decision making, which can be the cause of more stress. Two types of therapy help end emotional eating: cognitive behavioral therapy (CBT) and psychodynamic therapy.

CBT is based on the concept that your thoughts, feelings, physical sensations, and actions are interconnected, and that negative thoughts and feelings can trap you in a vicious cycle. CBT aims to help you deal with overwhelming problems in a more positive way by breaking them down into smaller parts. You're shown how to change these negative patterns to improve the way you feel.

With Emma, she maintained a food and mood journal so she could start to understand her food behaviors. She realized she reached for cookies as a reward and wanted ice cream when she felt lonely. By bringing more awareness to these issues, she was able to create a pause and make different choices. For instance, rewarding herself with a bath or calling a friend when she feels lonely. What also helped Emma was psychodynamic therapy.

Psychodynamic therapy stresses the significance of early childhood experiences and how they continue to affect you during adulthood. The theory behind psychodynamic therapy is that human behavior arises from conscious and unconscious motives. The act of talking about problems can help people find ways of understanding how their past influences their present behavior. Questions include, "Is this a habit stemming from childhood?" "Is my social environment affecting my choices?" and "Am I feeling bored or empty inside?"

Therapy and other programs must be combined with being mindful about portion sizes, getting at least seven hours of sleep a night, and choosing a healthy dietary pattern low in highly palatable, low-nutrient foods to cut down on emotional eating.

Emotions vs. feelings

In this chapter, much attention has been paid to emotional eating, but what we haven't explored is the difference between emotions and feelings. Emotions are a biochemical reaction to an event, created by the lower brain regions, namely the amygdala and ventromedial prefrontal cortices. For example, there are universal reactions to certain emotions, such as smiling when you are happy, or widening your eyes when surprised. These are NOT learned reactions to emotions, because the same responses occur in people who are born blind.

A feeling is an emotion that is assigned meaning, there is an interpretation. This requires us to perceive an event, have an emotional reaction, and then make an interpretation about it. Note that feelings are processed in a different part of the brain—the neocortical regions. When it comes to emotional eating, people often assign meaning in advance: "I'm going to be home alone so I know I'll binge" or "Work is going to be stressful and I know I'll want to buy fast food because of that."

Anticipating an eating event is based on previous experience constructed from bodily sensations and interpretations of past events. When they do this, emotional overeaters then start engaging in negative self-talk and recollect autobiographical memories, which refer to the recollection of personally experienced past events. Because of anxiety and fear associated with the future event, bingeing occurs. In her book *How Emotions Are Made: The Secret Life of the Brain* (2017), Lisa Feldman Barrett writes, "When you experience [a feeling] without knowing the cause, you are more likely to treat [the feeling] as information about the world, rather than your experience of the world" (p. 75).

This becomes problematic because it turns into a habit or an automatic or go-to behavior. The habit turns into a compulsion underpinned by a sense of a loss of control. Breaking the habit requires creating new ones, which can be divided into four steps: cue, craving, response, and reward. Charles Duhigg uses these terms in his book, *The Power of Habit* (2012). He wrote (on the book's jacket and his website), "The key to exercising regularly, losing weight, raising exceptional children, becoming more productive … and achieving success is understanding how habits work."

The way you feel is a rich source of information about you; paying attention to it can lead you that much closer to understanding yourself and becoming free. Feelings are a beautiful transparent window into our interior world, and they should not be buried with food or other fillers. Next, we'll look into the link between mental health and nutrition.

The link between mental health and nutrition

Imagine that your diet consists of restricting food in the morning, and by the late afternoon you subsist on coffee and sugar. Your evening meal is fries, eggs, white bread, and more sugary drinks topped off with candy. How do you think you'd feel after eating that way for months? Physically, you'd be malnourished, dehydrated, and on an up-and-down energetic cycle. High-sugar foods can negatively affect your energy levels by causing a spike in blood sugar followed by a crash. Mentally, you'd likely feel depressed or anxious. A prospective study by Knüppel and colleagues (2017) found a diet high in added sugar and processed foods may increase the chances of developing depression. They think that blood sugar swings, neurotransmitter dysregulation, and inflammation may all be reasons for sugar's detrimental effect on mental health. Nutrition is where the physical and social worlds intersect, and it's essential to our physical and mental well-being.

Returning to our imagined diet that was high in sugar and caffeine, we have covered the effects of high sugar, but there are also risks of high caffeine intake. Caffeine-induced anxiety disorder is one of four caffeine-related syndromes listed in the DSM. Extremely high daily intakes of caffeine, defined as 1,000 mg or more per day, have been reported to cause nervousness, jitteriness, and similar symptoms in most people. Anecdotally, you might know not to drink caffeine after a certain time of day because you won't be able to sleep that night, but this effect has also been studied. Drake and colleagues (2013) investigated the effects of 400 mg of caffeine on sleep when taken zero, three, or six hours before bed. They found for all three groups, the time it took participants to fall asleep and the time they spent awake at night increased significantly.

The imagined diet would also lead you to be dehydrated. The lay press says up to 75% of Americans are dehydrated, but that statistic hasn't been proven medically, despite the frequency with which people are hospitalized for the condition. However, what *has* been proven is that people with larger bodies are often under-hydrated. A paper by Chang et al. (2016) found in a study of more than 9,500 people that 32.6% of the sample was inadequately hydrated and that the population for whom that was true had larger bodies.

Water has a direct impact on our mental health and overall wellness. Numerous studies show attention, memory, and mood can be damaged, and physical distress such as headaches, constipation, and kidney problems can result from dehydration. There are also emotional effects. Even being the tiniest bit under-hydrated can affect your mood. When you haven't been drinking enough water, your body starts to trigger different areas of the brain that make you feel more anxious or nervous and can even heighten your emotions. Staying hydrated can prevent the intensity of those enhanced feelings. Similarly, when your body doesn't have enough water, the chemical process in your brain can't run smoothly, and there's a decrease in your serotonin production.

The neurotransmitter serotonin helps regulate sleep, appetite, mood, and inhibits pain. Instead of being primarily located in the brain, about 95% of serotonin is produced in the gastrointestinal tract, and the gastrointestinal tract is lined with a hundred million nerve cells or neurons. It makes sense then that the inner workings of the digestive system don't just help digest food but also guide emotions. This is further reinforced by the communication system between the gut and the brain, which is called the gut–brain axis. Research backs this up. Gesch et al. (2002) wrote an article demonstrating the effect food and dieting patterns have on human behavior by influencing the brain's structural development, neurotransmitters, and functions. They found antisocial behavior in prisons, including violence, is reduced by vitamins, minerals, and essential fatty acids.

In another study involving children, Liu, Raine et al. (2004) demonstrate that malnourished children are more likely to have lower cognitive ability and suffer more psychosocial adversity. Early malnutrition negatively influences brain formation and development. It can also lead to brain dysfunctions and cognitive impairments such as lower IQ and tends to predispose children to future antisocial and violent behaviors (Donnellan, Ge, & Wenk, 2000).

Some studies are more specialized and focus on biomarkers, such as one led by Kivimäki and colleagues (2014) who found a link between persistently elevated levels of the biomarker proinflammatory cytokine interleukin (IL-6) and a contribution to the development of mental disorders. It's worth noting the mental disorders were measured by a questionnaire as opposed to a clinical diagnosis of depression or anxiety, but self-reporting is also a valid form of measurement. A more extensive study of more than 69,000 postmenopausal women by Gangwisch and colleagues (2015) showed those with the highest intakes of added sugars had a significantly greater risk of depression compared to those with the lowest intakes.

Food as an expression of sharing and love

So far, we've examined negative food behaviors, but there are positive food behaviors as well. Miller, Rozin, and Fiske (1988) found sharing food is another form of nonverbal communication. Four types of food sharing create varying degrees of closeness both perceived from the outside and within the relationship: no sharing, sharing voluntarily, sharing with consubstantiation (situations in which your partner eats food that you have already touched), and feeding.

The results indicated sharing food implies a positive/friendly social relationship, and feeding implies a stronger, often romantic relationship.

Perceived from the outside, consubstantiation superimposed on sharing modestly increased judgments of intimacy and closeness of the relationship. Specifically, sharing food that has already had physical contact with someone else increases the romantic judgment from 74% to 90%. Also, feeding someone else shows the strongest sign of intimacy within couples and will lead observers to the assumption of romantic involvement.

Some people would like food to just be fuel, but it's not. It's an expression of love, and it affects our brains and our bodies in both positive and negative ways. It regulates our emotions. For all of these reasons and more, it's important to give food the attention it deserves and to be mindful of not only what we're eating but how we're eating. While it's crucial to understand and address negative food behaviors, it's equally important to recognize and celebrate the positive aspects of our relationship with food. Sharing a meal, cooking for loved ones, and enjoying cultural traditions all contribute to a healthy and fulfilling relationship with food. By fostering positive food experiences and understanding our emotional connections to eating, we can promote a healthier and more balanced approach to our dietary habits.

CHAPTER 6

Stress and its impact on food intake

Beth Frates

Impact of stress on the body

Stress is a hot topic! Everyone is talking about it. The world in which we live is full of stress. The question is, what do people mean when they use that term? In engineering terms, stress is defined as pressure, tension, or force exerted on a material object (Oxford English Dictionary, n.d.). However, in today's vernacular, when people say they are "stressed," they are talking about a state of mental or emotional strain or tension resulting from external or internal pressures. These pressures can create challenges, adversity, and very demanding circumstances. The result of managing these pressures or even thinking about the pressures can be stress. In engineering terms, excessive stress can lead to the deformation of the material object. In medical terms, *chronic* stress can lead to deleterious effects on the body and even the brain.

But not all stress is bad. When talking about mental stress, it is important to recognize that there are two types of stress: eustress and distress. Eustress serves a positive role in promoting alertness, arousal, and motivation. Eustress can also be considered a state of flow in which a person is so involved with the project in front of them that they lose track of time. They are fully engrossed; all consumed. They are engaged, focused, and using their strengths. For surgeons, most are in flow and experiencing eustress in the operating room. Health and wellness coaches are often in flow during coaching sessions when working with clients. This type of eustress is energizing and helps people thrive.

People often respond to stress with a spike in cortisol, which can help them get things done. For example, deadlines make this happen and help people complete projects. Think about what would happen if there were no deadlines for projects. When would they be completed? Would they be completed? In this way, a little dose of stress is motivating and may be considered "good" stress. A mild-to-moderate transient stress increases arousal, alertness, motivation, and synaptic plasticity. The problem arises if the stress persists over a longer period of time or the stressor far exceeds our ability to handle it and we do not return to our rest and digest (parasympathetic mode) state (Kim, Pellman, & Kim, 2015).

There is "bad" stress. This worrisome type of stress is distress, which people usually refer to when they say they are "stressed out." Distress is extreme, ongoing, and unrelenting stress that can lead to negative consequences for the body and brain and is associated with great pain.

Mental stress activates the parasympathetic system via the hypothalamic-pituitary-adrenal (HPA) axis and puts us into flight-fight-freeze mode. That works well when people must flee danger or fight for their lives. In ancient times, humans needed to flee the lion to survive or fight a predator to protect their food or family members. These days, the stressors aren't lions but paperwork, bills, arguments with colleagues, and disturbing posts on social media. Our HPA axis can respond to these situations, such as threats from a lion or predator. Our mind assesses the threat and creates a stress response. Some people may experience a large stress response from a specific situation, while another person will not even elicit the stress response from that same situation. How we handle stress as individuals can also change daily or hourly depending on whether we are sleep-deprived, hungry, or lonely.

Evidence suggests that a prolonged state of distress activates inflammatory cytokines like IL-6 and TNFα and that inflammation might be associated with many chronic conditions like heart disease, metabolic syndrome, obesity, depression, and diabetes. Automatic system dysfunction is proving to be a good predictor of morbidity and mortality of people with type 2 diabetes, and it indicates that diabetes might be caused by stress in addition to unhealthy eating patterns and lack of exercise (Vinik, 2012).

A hormone commonly mentioned when discussing stress is cortisol, which is often labeled the stress hormone. Dealing with stressors will cause the adrenal glands to release cortisol. Cortisol performs multiple useful functions in our body. In addition to increasing the capacity of our body to handle physical threats and increase our physical and mental performance, when necessary it also manages how the body uses carbohydrates, fats, and proteins, increases blood sugar, regulates blood pressure, controls the sleep–wake cycle, and lowers inflammation.

Having low cortisol levels can lead to brain fog, cloudy-headedness, mild depression, low thyroid function, blood sugar imbalances (hypoglycemia), fatigue (especially morning and mid-afternoon), sleep disruption, low blood pressure, lowered immune function, and inflammation (Thau, Gandhi, & Sharma, 2023; WebMD Contributors, n.d.). The body is remarkably in tune and can manage cortisol levels in most cases. If someone has low cortisol, it is usually due to problems with the adrenal glands, often referred to as adrenal insufficiency. Addison's disease and hypopituitarism or a pituitary tumor could be the cause of low cortisol. The body generally regulates cortisol levels through the HPA axis when the pituitary gland and adrenal glands function normally.

High levels of cortisol can occur with Cushing's syndrome, which is a rare condition with a variety of causes, including taking high quantities of corticosteroids to treat other medical conditions, adrenal gland tumors, or other neuroendocrine tumors. These conditions create pathologically high levels of cortisol.

Cortisol levels can rise naturally in response to stressors. They can stay elevated due to hearing about horrifying news stories, experiencing natural disasters, working in challenging environments, living with disruptive family dynamics, or the hustle and bustle of trying to make a living in the twenty-first century. Some of the negative effects of long-term elevated cortisol levels include impaired cognitive performance, sleep disruption, blood sugar imbalances (hyperglycemia), elevated blood pressure, lowered immune function, lower levels of HDL and higher levels of LDL, dampened thyroid function, decreased muscle mass and bone density, and increased abdominal adiposity (strongly correlated with certain health problems). All of that can cause an increased likelihood of developing diabetes, heart attacks, and strokes. In addition, cortisol also increases food cravings, thus influencing our nutrition (DUJS, 2011; Yaribeygi et al., 2017).

Stress and nutrition

As stress is known to influence multiple metabolic processes, it is not surprising that stress impacts a person's food consumption and even digestion. Stress has been shown to disrupt healthy eating patterns by increasing the desire for hyper-palatable foods (foods high in fat, sugar, or both), and elevated cortisol levels seem to be responsible for that disruption (Yau & Potenza, 2013). It is important to note that the relationship also goes in the opposite direction. A survey of food's relationship to perceived stress and depressive symptoms in 3,706 university students has shown that consuming "unhealthy" foods (sweets, snacks, and fast food) was significantly positively associated with perceived stress in females only and depressive symptoms in both males and females. Consuming "healthy" foods (fruits and vegetables) was significantly negatively correlated with perceived stress and depressive symptoms in both sexes (El Ansari, Adetunji, & Oskrochi, 2014).

There is evidence that sugar consumption can have a negative influence on stress-driven, emotional, and addictive behaviors (Jacques et al., 2019). Sugar impacts the human brain's reward system in the ventral tegmental area and nucleus accumbens. Considering that throughout most of human existence, getting enough food was a bigger problem than having too much food, it is understandable that humans are wired to seek energy-dense (high-calorie) foods, and foods full of sugar are at the top of the energy or calorie list.

While people usually think of drugs and their relationship with our reward pathways, in research studies, it has been demonstrated that sugar creates a similar response in the brain to substances like alcohol and opioids (Ahmed, Guillem, & Vandaele, 2013). Over a decade ago, Volkow and colleagues (2013) advocated that obesity may not be the result of a lack of the ability to control food intake but may be partly driven by the addictive influence sugar has on our reward system. Neuroimaging research shows that the addicted brain loses connection to the executive control center (prefrontal cortex, or CEO of the brain) when making decisions (Volkow et al., 2003), making it challenging to control the consumption of addictive substances. Thus, since sugar seems to influence our reward system like addictive substances, consuming sugar can make it difficult for people to use rational decision processes controlled by the prefrontal cortex and resist reaching out for that next sugar fix (Avena, Rada, & Hoebel, 2008) or other highly palatable foods (DelParigi et al., 2005). As prolonged elevated cortisol levels have also been shown to impair cognitive functions, prolonged stress may further impair our decision-making and make us more susceptible to succumbing to cravings for foods high in sugar and fats (Tryon et al., 2013).

Recent research looks deeper into how life stressors such as food insecurity can be contributing factors to the development of type 2 diabetes. Research results demonstrate that increased stress due to food insecurity can have both a direct impact on type 2 diabetes by elevating Hgb A1C as well as an indirect effect through decreased social support and self-care (Walker et al., 2018). Some people experiencing food insecurity may purchase inexpensive food items that are high in calories, thinking that they will meet their calorie needs for the day that way. This leads individuals to purchase fast food, packaged food, and other cheap, unhealthy foods.

Additional research on stress exposure, emotional states, and food intake showed complex food-stress interactions. Stress may influence both the type and quantity of food eaten, and the interaction between food and stress is bidirectional. Increased consumption of highly palatable foods (foods often layered in salt, fat, and sugar) serves as a coping mechanism for managing excess stress. Yet, the long-term effect of highly processed hyper-palatable foods promotes increased physiological and behavioral stress responsiveness. In addition, it seems that the type of stress may modulate the quantity of food intake, with increased social stress increasing food intake. In contrast, intense and more imminent psychological stress (fear response) seems to significantly decrease food intake (Ulrich-Lai et al., 2015). People respond to stress differently, as noted earlier. Some people are more prone to stress eating. Others are more likely to forget about food and focus on the stressful issues.

Stress may influence food cravings. For some people, elevated stress can elevate food cravings, which, in people with a healthy weight, seems to be mainly connected with a rise in cortisol levels, and in people who have overweight and obesity it may have an additional component of raised ghrelin levels that make cravings more intense (Sinha et al., 2019). In addition to encouraging people to desire more hyper-palatable foods, elevated cortisol also shifts metabolism to store fat, making chronic stress one of the main culprits in weight gain (Spencer & Tilbrook, 2011; Vicennati et al., 2009).

Food craving is a complex mechanism and involves many other factors. Other mental causes of cravings include personality (higher impulsivity or higher addictive personality score), eating context (memory and mental connections, like movie + popcorn), and mood (negative moods often spark cravings for comfort foods). Some physical causes of cravings include leptin/ghrelin imbalances (leptin increases satiety or feelings of fullness, and ghrelin increases appetite), hormonal changes due to pregnancy or premenstrual syndrome (PMS), lack of sleep, nutrient-poor diets (low in fiber and protein), poor hydration, unhealthy gut flora, lack of physical activity, highly processed foods, and the frequency at which a person eats the craved food—the less a person eats the craved food, the less he or she craves it (Petre, 2023).

Moreover, not only can stress increase the type and amount of food we crave and then eat, but also food can, in turn, influence our mood. Some foods shown to improve mood are fatty fish, dark chocolate, fermented foods, bananas, oats, berries, nuts and seeds, beans and lentils, and coffee (Davidson, 2020). Unfortunately, other than maybe dark chocolate, it doesn't seem that the foods people crave when stressed are the most helpful foods for improving mood. Therefore, when dealing with heightened periods of stress, there needs to be concentrated and conscious effort to keep one's eating balanced and rich in nutrients and foods that will help in effective coping with stress rather than just temporarily easing the discomfort of stress by resorting to high fat/high sugar "comfort foods." Managing stress with techniques that don't involve food is well advised.

Stress resilience and stress management techniques

The ability to effectively handle stressors is called stress resilience. We can think of resilience as having some level of flexibility and elasticity to recover from the effects of a stressor after it is gone and to return to our homeostasis. All animals experience the activation of the stress response when faced with a stressor; the problem with humans is that they can sometimes remain in a stressed and hyper-vigilant state long after the initial stressor is gone. Also, they can create stressors in their heads that don't exist in reality and treat them as seriously as they would the stress of a lion chasing them. Managing stress is one of those cases where our larger human brain with higher cognitive functions may be more of a hindrance than a help.

For centuries, people have tried to find different ways to deal with stressors and distress, and modern science has investigated some of them. The term often used to denote the opposite of stress is relaxation. In the psychology of stress, to relax can mean to become less tense, tight, or stiff, to stop feeling nervous or worried, or to spend time resting and doing something enjoyable. Dr. Herbert Benson coined the term "Relaxation Response" (Benson, Beary, & Carol, 1974). He defined it as a person's ability to turn on the body's protective mechanisms and help one's body release brain signals and natural chemicals that can help one relieve and counteract the negative effects of stress (Benson, 1985; Mitchell, 2013).

Dr. Benson's progressive relaxation technique included several steps that help lower a person's heart rate, respiratory rate, blood pressure, muscle activity, and muscle tension (Benson & Klipper, 1975). Here are his six steps for the "Relaxation Response."

1. Sit quietly in a comfortable position.
2. Close your eyes.
3. Deeply relax all muscles from feet to face.
4. Breathe through your nose, repeat, "one."
5. Continue for ten to twenty minutes.
6. Do not worry about whether you are successful in achieving a deep level of relaxation. Maintain a passive attitude and permit relaxation to occur at its own pace. When distracting thoughts occur, try to ignore them by not dwelling upon them and return to repeating "one."

Several other practices can be used to elicit the relaxation response, such as deep breathing, yoga, and different mindfulness-based practices.

Sometimes, simple practices like taking a deep breath can be successful in reducing feelings of distress and anxiety (Perciavalle et al., 2017; Vlemincx, Van Diest, & Van den Bergh, 2016). When people are stressed or anxious, their breathing becomes shallow and rapid. Intentionally concentrating on slowing one's breathing pattern and taking deep breaths signals to the body that it can relax and move from sympathetic (flight-fight-freeze) to parasympathetic (rest and digest) mode. It is felt that the exhalation helps to turn on the rest and digest mode or parasympathetic response.

There are many different deep breathing techniques, such as:

- Box Breathing—Inhale for count of 4, Hold for 4, Exhale for 4, Hold for 4, Repeat
- 4-7-8 Breathing—Inhale for count of 4, Hold for 7, Exhale for 8
- Diaphragmatic Breathing—Taking deep breaths by expanding your diaphragm rather than just your chest. Some people consider diaphragmatic breathing to be a type of vagal nerve massage. The vagus nerve is the tenth cranial nerve (X), running from the brain to the gastrointestinal tract. It innervates part of the diaphragm. Thus, by working to use their diaphragm while breathing, a person can help put themselves into the parasympathetic rest and digest response.

No matter which technique one uses, as long as the breaths are kept slow and deep, the practice can be an easy and accessible way to quickly turn down the body's stress response (Bentley et al., 2023; Zaccaro et al., 2018).

Yoga is another often-used relaxation practice. It combines several practices known to help mitigate the stress response: exercise, breathing, and meditative focus. Studies have shown that regular yoga practice influences both psychological mechanisms, such as an increase in positive affect and self-compassion, and physiological mechanisms, such as lower cortisol levels and inhibition of the posterior hypothalamus (Riley & Park, 2015). Yoga seems to be particularly effective in reducing physiological measures of stress, such as waking and evening cortisol levels, ambulatory systolic blood pressure, and resting heart rate, as well as improving other health measures, such as fasting blood glucose, cholesterol levels (Pascoe et al., 2017), and immune function (Eda et al., 2018). Practicing yoga may also be protective when dealing with heightened stress (Franklin, Butler, & Bentley, 2018).

Regarding nutrition, regular yoga practice has been shown to have some potential in managing eating disorders, especially binge eating (McIver, McGartland, & O'Halloran, 2009; McIver, O'Halloran, & McGartland, 2009). The effect is most likely due to yoga promoting better awareness of one's feelings, enhanced connection to one's body, increased self-esteem, and more positive body image, according to studies and the reports of the participants. When considering eating patterns, it is helpful to note that practicing yoga has also been shown to increase fruit and vegetable consumption, lower intake of sugar-sweetened beverages and snack foods, and lower the frequency of fast food consumption in a young adult population (Watts et al., 2018).

Mindfulness can be defined as "the quality or state of being mindful" and "the practice of maintaining a nonjudgmental state of heightened or complete awareness of one's thoughts, emotions, or experiences on a moment-to-moment basis" (Merriam-Webster, n.d.). The key element to successful mindfulness practices is that heightened awareness needs to be nonjudgmental and accompanied by self-compassion.

Mindfulness-based interventions have shown effectiveness in dealing with symptoms of stress, anxiety, and depression, as well as cognitive reactivity (Van der Gucht et al., 2015). Mindfulness meditation can help develop a greater sense of control and be an effective coping mechanism when dealing with life's stressors (Astin, 1997). Frequent meditators report fewer stressors, fewer illness symptoms, fewer symptoms of anxiety and depression, and higher levels of positive affect (Beauchamp-Turner & Levinson, 1992). A review of twenty studies on the effectiveness of mindfulness meditation interventions suggests that those interventions may lower inflammation and promote other healthy immune system functions (Black & Slavich, 2016).

Mindfulness-based stress reduction (MBSR) is the mindfulness-based intervention that has been most commonly used in research. Jon Kabat-Zinn developed the initial MBSR program, first conducted by the Stress Reduction Clinic organized in 1979 at the University of Massachusetts Medical School. He later founded the Center for Mindfulness in Medicine in 1995. He defined mindfulness as "awareness that arises through paying attention, on purpose, in the present moment, non-judgmentally" (Staff, 2017). His eight-week MBSR program aims to empower individuals to respond to life circumstances consciously rather than automatically. It consists of daily meditations and gentle stretching exercises designed to refocus the body's response to stressors outside of one's control (UMass Memorial Health, 2024). Numerous studies confirm the effectiveness of MBSR on stress and burnout reduction, promoting relaxation and sleep, and increased self-compassion and effectiveness in dealing with life stressors (Janssen et al., 2018; Sharma & Rush, 2014). When it comes to nutrition, MBSR has shown some promise in dealing with emotional eating (Levoy et al., 2017), weight loss maintenance (Chumachenko et al., 2021), and modulating stress eating (Torske et al., 2024).

Mindful eating is another mindfulness practice that can promote eating less and eating higher quality (healthier) foods, preventing overeating, and enhancing enjoyment and satisfaction of food. It is described as the art of being present when eating and includes the following steps (Hanh & Cheung, 2010; Harvard T.H. Chan School of Public Health, 2020b; Nelson, 2017):

1. Honor the food—acknowledge where the food comes from, and start your healthy eating process while still acquiring food.
2. Engage all senses—notice the smell, taste, texture, color, and sound of food while eating.
3. Serve in modest portions—avoid overeating and food waste. Use a smaller plate and fill it only once.
4. Savor small bites and chew thoroughly—take your time eating.
5. Eat slowly to avoid overeating—it takes time for satiety cues to activate, and eating slowly will give the body time to signal that it has enough food.
6. Don't skip meals—going too long without food increases the risk of strong hunger that may cause us to eat mindlessly and overeat. Set regular eating times, and plan enough time to enjoy meals.
7. Eat a plant-predominant diet—this incorporates both the health benefits of eating plant-based food and promotes more environmentally conscious eating.

The methods described previously in this chapter are some of the most researched relaxation techniques; however, it is not an all-inclusive list. Some of the other relaxation techniques supported by research are listed below.

- Reconnect with nature:
  - Get out into nature—multiple studies have shown that being in forests (forest bathing) lowers blood pressure (Ideno et al., 2017)
- Lifestyle activities:
  - Exercise—about half of the studies show that increased physical activity and exercise correlate with attenuated response to psychosocial stress (Mücke et al., 2018)
  - Take a time out—taking time off for self-care promotes relaxation and psychological detachment from stressors (Dugan & Barnes-Farrell, 2017)
- Engage in pleasurable activities:
  - Music—listening to music elicits positive emotions and decreases the level of stress (Iyendo, 2016)
  - Laugh—humor and laughter are good coping mechanisms and the act of laughing itself, even without humor, has been linked to chemical changes in the body that may potentially reduce stress (Louie, Brook, & Frates, 2016)
  - Expressive writing—emotionally expressive writing significantly reduces anxiety (Niles et al., 2014)
  - Interacting with pets (American Heart Association, 2022; Barker et al., 2012)
- Other:
  - Chew gum—chewing gum prompts physiological and psychological responses and may reduce stress-related responses (Konno et al., 2016)
  - Checking email less frequently during the day can reduce daily stress levels (Kushlev & Dunn, 2015).

Considering how strongly prolonged stress influences eating habits, choice of foods, metabolic processes, immune system, and overall health, experimenting with different relaxation techniques to find one that works on a personal level is a good investment of time and resources. Stress may be constant in our modern life, but it doesn't mean it cannot be effectively managed.

CHAPTER 7

How mindset and positive psychology influence food preferences and consumption

Beth Frates

Positive psychology concepts

Positive psychology is a branch of psychology that focuses on what is working well in a person's life rather than focusing on the deficits, weaknesses, and problems in a person's life. The goal of positive psychology interventions is not just to alleviate distress and survive but to help individuals grow, improve, and flourish. Martin Seligman, PhD, often regarded as the father of positive psychology, discusses a happy life and what it means with three examples.

A happy life can mean:

The "Pleasant Life" refers to the hedonistic happiness and enjoying pleasant aspects of life.

The "Good Life" focuses on personal strengths and engagement.

The "Meaningful Life" with a focus on the purpose and something greater than ourselves

(Psychology Today contributors, n.d.; Seligman, 2011).

Several positive psychology constructs, such as positive affect, optimism, gratitude, sense of purpose, and self-acceptance, have been assessed for their influence on physical and psychological health (Amonoo et al., 2019; DuBois et al., 2015). The benefits from these positive psychology constructs can come either via the direct influence of positive emotions on physiological and psychological health or through positive psychological constructs promoting engagement and adherence to health behaviors (Celano et al., 2020; Masters et al., 2023).

Gratitude is one of the well-researched positive psychology constructs.

Early research into positive psychology interventions demonstrated the power of gratitude. Dr. Martin Seligman and colleagues conducted a small study with 411 students and compared a placebo exercise to four gratitude exercises (Seligman et al., 2005). The placebo exercise involved writing down early memories, and the four gratitude exercises included 1) a gratitude visit, involving writing and hand delivering a letter of gratitude, 2) three good things in life, involving writing three things that went well each day and their causes, 3) you at your best, involving writing about a time when you were at your best and considering your strengths, and 4) using signature strengths in a new way, inviting the subject to use one of their top five strengths in a new and different way for one week. The signature strengths come from a Values In Action (VIA) character strengths online survey (VIA Institute, 2024), available for free. This is a helpful survey for students, teachers, and learners of all types. The study's results revealed that using signature strengths in a new way and listing three good things daily positively influenced a person by increasing happiness and decreasing depressive symptoms for six months. Writing and personally delivering a letter of gratitude to someone who had not been properly thanked revealed an immediate boost in happiness scores, and the benefits lasted one month (Seligman et al., 2005). These strategies are used today in many classes, including the popular Happiness Course at Yale taught by Dr. Laurie Santos.

Other research studies confirm that counting one's blessings and having a grateful outlook on life events had significantly more positive effects on a person's well-being, especially positive affect, compared to listing one's hassles in life or just writing down neutral accounts of events. People who counted their blessings were more optimistic, felt better about their whole lives, had fewer physical complaints, and spent significantly more time exercising (Emmons & McCullough, 2003). A follow-up study with adults with neuromuscular disease participating in a twenty-one-day gratitude intervention of listing blessings daily resulted in participants reporting having more energy, increased positive mood, more optimism about one's life, a greater sense of connectedness to others, and better sleep duration and quality. This showed that the positive effects of gratitude intervention are not influenced by a person's life circumstances (ibid.).

Other studies have confirmed that gratitude positively influences decreasing depression symptoms, improving sleep, and, by way of improving sleep, also decreasing anxiety (Ng & Wong, 2013). How could gratitude have such a powerful impact on a vital bodily function like sleep? Perhaps it helps reduce stress. Perhaps it relaxes the body and mind. Perhaps it refocuses the brain on positive aspects of life that bring joy and meaning. But where is gratitude expressed or experienced in the brain? This is a complex and complicated question. More and more research is being performed to unravel these types of mysteries. One such study used functional neuroimaging and showed that subjects with more gratitude had higher levels of activity in the hypothalamus, which is a control center for vital functions such as sleep, eating, drinking, stress, and metabolism (Zahn et al., 2009). This is food for thought.

Another important aspect of positive psychology is finding and using personal strengths to promote well-being and facilitate change and growth. One facet of this is focusing on the positive, on what went well, on success rather than on failure or personal weaknesses.

As described by Barbara Frederickson, positive emotions include joy, contentment, serenity, interest, engagement, pride, hope, inspiration, awe, and love. These were identified years ago and are still the topic of medical journal articles today (Roth & Laireiter, 2021). Traditionally, psychology was more focused on negative emotions and how to alleviate the distress they bring. Recently, research has been expanding on the power that positive emotions can have in people's lives and the ways people can encourage and nurture those emotions (Ackerman, 2018).

The broaden and build theory (Fredrickson, 2001), first put forward by Barbara Frederickson, is another positive psychology approach that looks into ways positive affect can increase performance and positive outcomes, including health behaviors and well-being. Positivity brings with it creativity. Positive emotions increase energy, enthusiasm, and receptivity, leading to novel ideas, activities, and relationships. These can then lead to increased stress resilience, enhanced skills, and new knowledge and skills. In turn, this can lead to improved health and greater fulfillment. These end products lead back to more positive emotions, which can set off the positive spiral again with joy, awe, and pride, leading to novel ideas, improved skills, and better health, for example. This is the basis of the broaden and build model.

Frederickson's research into the power of positivity showed that experiencing more positive than negative emotions broadens people's minds, builds their resourcefulness, helps them achieve their goals, and makes them more resilient to adversity. One of the key points of her research is that for this broadening and building effect to happen in people's lives, there is a need to strive to have and create more positive emotions than negative, somewhere between a 3-to-1 to 10-to-1 ratio in favor of positive emotions (Fredrickson, 2009). Interesting that it is not 3-to-0 or 10-to-0. That one negative emotion can create a steadying force for improvement.

The sailboat analogy is sometimes used to describe this. The sail in the boat represents the positive emotions, and the one negative emotion is like the centerboard that helps to keep the person steady. Negative emotions are part of life. They are not to be ignored. People do not have to feel they need to escape from them. Negative emotions come and go like all emotions. They can teach us about ourselves and our lives if we pay attention to them. Striving for more positive than negative emotions daily, especially when collaborating on a work project, is helpful for progress, creativity, and resilience.

People experiencing positive emotions can see the big picture, have wider awareness, see more possibilities, can be more socially connected, and come to better win-win solutions. The success that comes from positive emotions in turn increases positive affect, thus building a positive upward growth loop (Fredrickson & Branigan, 2005). According to Barbara Frederickson, one way to build positivity in our lives is by being open, appreciative, curious, real, sincere, and kind (Fredrickson, 2011).

Being kind also includes being kind to ourselves. Kristin Neff is one of the pioneers in the study of self-kindness and self-compassion. She considers these principles to be one of the best ways to fight paralyzing self-judgment and discourage automatic negative thinking and negative self-talk (Neff, 2015). This aligns well with positive psychology's focus on a person's strengths and what is working well rather than failures. Self-compassion directs people's attention to the inner voice that is listing their positive attributes, encouraging them to continue, and assuring them that they can succeed (i.e., our inner princess or prince), while at the same time challenging and dampening their negative inner voices that criticize and point to all the ways a person can fail (i.e., our inner gremlin).

A person's inner dialogue is important. Speaking to oneself the way he or she would speak to a good friend is key. This is showing self-compassion. People talk to themselves. They may have conversations throughout the day, debating what to do or how to act. To some extent, people can control this. They can identify if that inner voice is harmful, like a gremlin, or helpful, like a coach, prince, or princess. A person can choose to fire the gremlin in their head and hire a positivity coach to help guide them when making decisions or managing mistakes.

Mistakes are part of life. Everyone makes them. Learning how to use mistakes as opportunities to learn and grow will help people be more resilient and productive.

Carol Dweck, PhD, put forward the growth mindset theory. It examines people's beliefs on whether intelligence is malleable or fixed, meaning we cannot change it with effort. People who believe that a person can increase their intelligence or other skills by working on them are labeled as having a "growth" mindset, while those who believe there is nothing they can do to get better are labeled as having a "fixed" mindset. Carol Dweck has a Theories of Intelligence Scale (TOI). People can be on different points in the TOI scale, and there may be interventions that can help people move more toward the "growth" mindset end of the TOI scale. Where one is on the TOI scale might matter in how one handles mistakes, setbacks, and obstacles in all tasks in life, including health behaviors (Dweck, 2008).

One research study on growth mindset examined the difference between a "growth" mindset and a "fixed" mindset in situations where people make mistakes. The researchers in this study used EEGs (electroencephalograms) to examine the brain activity of subjects who were asked to perform a task in which they had a high likelihood of making a mistake, like identifying the middle letter in a string of five letters, such as MMNMM or MMMNM. Test participants were initially given a growth mindset test where higher scores indicated more "growth" mindset. The subjects were also hooked up to EEG monitors to monitor the electrical signals in their brains. When the participants performed the task and made a mistake, two electrical impulses were recorded. The first indicated an acknowledgment of the mistake, and the second corresponded to the brain figuring out what went wrong. Higher brain electrical activity in the second impulse was noted in those subjects with a "growth" mindset. This indicated that their brain was actively engaged in fixing the mistake or doing better the next time, rather than just giving up after a failure. On repeat testing, people who scored higher on the growth mindset scale and showed greater brain electrical activity in that second recorded signal after the mistake performed better on repeat testing (Moser et al., 2011). Thus, with a growth mindset, people are more likely to learn from their mistakes and improve.

Positive psychology and nutrition

There are several different aspects of how a positive mindset can interact with the way people eat and what they eat. Some positive psychology constructs influence the choice of foods, while others influence how people feel about food and how they approach food consumption.

A study on the relationship between the constructs of optimism and gratitude and eating behaviors among people with metabolic syndrome showed directionality. These positive constructs led to healthier eating patterns and reduced negative emotions, thus creating an upward spiral (Carrillo et al., 2022).

A "growth" mindset has been shown to indirectly decrease the risk of developing eating disorders and other unhealthy weight control behaviors, such as body shame, by promoting a future-oriented sense of control over whether one will reach one's goal (Hoyt et al., 2019). In other words, the growth mindset promotes the idea that even if a person encounters failure, there is a possibility of future success. If one has this growth mindset, makes the necessary adjustments, and keeps striving to improve, one can experience increased self-compassion and even ease the distress of being imperfect, especially if one suffers from perfectionism.

Sometimes, the hardest part of having healthy nutrition is sticking with healthy eating practices long-term in the face of life changes and setbacks. Approaching eating with the mindset of healthy foods providing physical and mental health benefits, providing nutrients, vitamins, and minerals necessary for our bodily functions, and providing enjoyment with delicious tastes and textures, rather than in terms of having the mindset that eating healthy foods leads to deprivation and forgoing of pleasure, can be beneficial in the long-term sustainability of healthy eating habits.

The concept of body positivity needs to be discussed when trying to determine how positivity influences food choices and eating patterns. Diet cultures have had body image as the main motivation for what and how people eat. The goal of being thin or skinny prevailed for decades. This led many people to compare themselves to some "ideal body size and shape" created by the media and often promoted by social media influencers. This type of comparison doesn't correlate with a focus on healthy nutrition or optimal health and functionality. Even moderate levels of body dissatisfaction and body concerns are strongly associated with disordered eating. The problem is bigger when the body image one sees as ideal is found in the unrealistic and heavily edited images portrayed by popular culture and social media. Focus on negative feelings about how far one's body is from that "ideal" can promote unhealthy dieting and eating disorders that can endanger the healthy functioning of the body.

In line with focusing on the positive concept of positive psychology, increasing body appreciation may be easier than attempting to decrease body dissatisfaction (Aparicio-Martinez et al., 2019). Increasing body appreciation involves acknowledging the hard work a body does each day by walking up hills, balancing up steps, lifting groceries, and succeeding in complex tasks such as riding a bicycle.

Increasing body positivity and self-esteem may be good ways to empower people. Positive psychology interventions have been used to promote these feelings. Those interventions mostly had a positive impact by increasing the likelihood of engaging in different health behaviors. The intervention of having people imagine their best possible self increased their intent to lose weight, while gratitude interventions increased their intent to exercise, positive affect, and some aspects of body compassion (Dennis & Ogden, 2023).

New movements that promote healthy eating concentrate on body positivity and "gentle nutrition." The focus of this movement is on the positive—what foods will nurture our bodies, and having a healthy and strong body regardless of its shape and size—rather than on the negative feelings about how one's body measures up against some culturally imposed ideal, which often leads to toxic dieting and vilifying certain foods or even entire food groups (Hartley, 2021). Another term connected with this concept is "healthy at every size," moving the approach to nutrition away from weight-centric modalities toward a healthy and well-functioning body focus (Nairn, 2023).

The danger associated with different body shapes and sizes is under further exploration and investigation, with specific attention being paid to nationality in terms of BMI. For example, people who are Asian will have lower cut-off points with respect to BMI categories, and may also have a different distribution of adipose tissue (Jih et al., 2014). Adiposity in the midline or abdominal adiposity is shown to be linked to metabolic factors associated with chronic conditions (Lukács et al., 2019). This is one of the reasons that waist circumference is measured in many medical clinics. Visceral adiposity or fat tissue around the organs is a type that is linked to several chronic conditions, including metabolic disease, cardiovascular disease, and certain cancers (Shuster et al., 2012). It is important to remember that a person can be in the healthy weight BMI category and still be unhealthy (Ding, Chan, & Magkos, 2016). There are ongoing clinical trials to better understand how adipose tissue in people with a healthy weight can contribute to disease (Weill Cornell Medicine, 2015). It is important to consider body composition and acknowledge that having lean muscle mass is a sign of health, regardless of BMI.

The more positive approaches to body image and nutrition have been shown to encourage a healthier approach to food with a positive body connection, defined as having positive feelings about one's body and feeling comfortable in one's body. Self-esteem showed the strongest protective factor against developing disordered eating and eating disorders (Voica et al., 2021). Routine physical activity, consuming foods consistent with a whole food, plant-predominant diet (as described earlier, with the Harvard Healthy Plate as an example), restorative sleep, and stress reduction are ways that people can improve their health at any size. Thus, one can strive for optimal health at all sizes. Someone who is considered skinny or thin also needs to practice these healthy lifestyle behaviors to reach their optimal level of health and wellness. No matter the size or shape of your body, it is important to follow the guidelines for the six pillars of lifestyle medicine discussed in the introduction chapter.

One of the approaches to eating used by the "gentle nutrition" approach is intuitive eating, which focuses on the premise that the body has mechanisms to self-regulate its nutritional needs. Therefore, the focus when eating should be on learning to listen to and understand those internal body cues. The four facets of intuitive eating are unconditional permission to eat, eating for physical rather than emotional reasons, choosing foods that are good for your body, and being attuned to hunger and satiety cues. Intuitive eating is associated with lower levels of concern about body weight and shape, regardless of BMI (Keirns & Hawkins, 2019), less disordered eating, more positive body image, and greater emotional functioning (Bruce & Ricciardelli, 2016). Besides improved body image, intuitive eating has also shown a consistent positive association with lower BMI and better psychological health (Dyke & Drinkwater, 2014). The key to intuitive eating is being in tune with your body and its internal signals. Eating for physical rather than emotional reasons is key and requires people to hone their stress reduction techniques discussed in Chapter 6.

"Positive nutrition" is another term used in this context. It is defined as eating well with a focus on healthy, minimally processed, nutritious foods that nourish our bodies rather than focusing on all the foods and nutrients we should avoid. The Mediterranean diet and lifestyle build one of the main pillars of this approach, which focuses not just on macronutrients but also on all the micronutrients that are necessary for optimal body functioning as well as on other elements of the healthy lifestyle, such as social connection, physical activity, and stress management (Martini et al., 2023).

The connection between food and positive emotions goes both ways. Not only can positive psychological constructs enable us to engage in healthy behaviors, including healthy eating patterns, but healthy food consumption can also promote our feeling of well-being, mostly by increasing positive affect and promoting vitality, energy, and overall physical health (Holder, 2019).

Getting all the nutrients necessary for healthy functioning of the body, including healthy functioning of the brain, is key to mental health and positive affect. Not only can the person's mood affect what foods are craved and consumed, but also what the person eats can strongly affect their mood. This influence is both direct, by determining how the brain functions and the quantity of neurotransmitters synthesized, such as serotonin, and indirect, through healthier functioning of the entire body with healthier food consumption (Firth et al., 2020). Proper functioning of human neurological systems and, by extension, a person's mood requires enough nutrients in the diet that are necessary for building the structure of the brain, such as omega-3 fatty acids, and for the synthesis of neurotransmitters, such as B-vitamins and neurotransmitter precursors, including tyrosine, choline, and tryptophan (Lachance & Ramsey, 2015). The neurotransmitters most often connected to a positive affect are serotonin, dopamine, and endorphins (Dfarhud, Malmir, & Khanahmadi, 2014). Table 7.1 presents some of the nutrients and foods needed for neurotransmitter synthesis.

Microbiome diversity is another mediator between nutrition and physical and mental health. A well-balanced and well-functioning microbiome produces a host of compounds that have been shown, among other things, to improve the immune system, prevent and fight cancers, regulate metabolism, help in maintaining a healthy weight, and mediate brain function and mood (Mohajeri, Brummer et al., 2018; Mohajeri, La Fata et al., 2018). A variety of microorganisms is essential. This comes from eating a variety of whole foods. Several

Table 7.1. Neurotransmitters production and food (created from the information in Gasmi et al., 2022).

Neurotransmitter	*Production*	*Foods to consume*
Serotonin	95% produced in the gut Precursor: Tryptophan	Beans, soy, nuts, seeds, poultry (turkey and chicken), fish (especially salmon), and cheese
Dopamine	Produced in the brain (substantia nigra, ventral tegmental area, and hypothalamus) Precursor: Tyrosine	Avocados, bananas, soy, pumpkin, sesame seeds, poultry, and dairy foods
Endorphins	Produced in the pituitary gland	Chocolate, strawberries, spicy foods, leafy greens, avocados, nuts and seeds

mental health conditions, such as depression, anxiety, bipolar disorder, autism spectrum disorders, and schizophrenia, have been linked to an imbalance of gut microbe communities or microbiome dysbiosis (Xiong et al., 2023). Increasing the intake of foods rich in probiotics, prebiotics, and fiber may help balance the microbiome and thus lead to improved physical and mental health. The main mechanism through which the microbiome affects the physical and mental health of the host is the fermentation of insoluble fibers that result in the production of short-chain fatty acids (SCFA) such as acetate, propionate, and butyrate, as discussed in the lifestyle medicine section of the introductory chapter of this book.

Table 7.2 provides a list of foods that may help create and sustain a healthy microbiome.

Table 7.2. Foods for a healthy microbiome (created from the information in Harvard T.H. Chan School of Public Health, 2017; Pham et al., 2021; Xiong et al., 2023).

Food groups	*Description*	*Foods*
Probiotics	The bacteria most beneficial for mental health and mood come from the lactobacillus family (e.g., Lactobacillus acidophilus, Lactobacillus casei) and bifidobacterium family (e.g., Bifidobacterium bifidum)	Fermented milk products (yogurt, kefir, aged cheese), kimchi, sauerkraut, tempeh
Prebiotics	Indigestible carbohydrates and fibers such as inulin, resistant starches, gums, pectins, and fructooligosaccharides	Raw versions of the following: garlic, onions, leeks, asparagus, Jerusalem artichokes, dandelion greens, bananas, and seaweed Other fruits, vegetables, and whole grains are also good sources of insoluble fibers
Supporting foods	Vitamins (most important: A, B2, B3, C, D, E, and K), phytonutrients	Fruits and vegetables, spices (e.g., Zanthoxylum bungeanum, curcumin, and capsaicin)

Therefore, a diet rich in fiber, vitamins, phytonutrients, and fermented foods and low in processed food, added sugars, and saturated fats has been shown to be beneficial for maintaining a well-balanced and diverse microbiome (Valdes et al., 2018). A Mediterranean diet meets those criteria, and research shows that adhering to such a diet increases diversity and quality of microbiota (Merra et al., 2020; Nagpal et al., 2019).

How we think about food, how we think about our bodies, and how we think about health all impact our eating patterns. With a focus on healthy lifestyles, working to optimize our body's functioning, as well as body composition, with a combination of both strength training and aerobic training (to be discussed in more detail in Chapter 13), striving to enjoy our food, understanding that mishaps are opportunities to learn and grow, and practicing self-compassion, people can enjoy and embody what Dr. Beth Frates calls a "healthy body, peaceful mind, and joyful heart" in *PAVING the Path to Wellness Workbook* (Frates, Tollefson, & Comander, 2021).

CHAPTER 8

The influence of social connections on dietary patterns

Beth Frates

Power of social connections

Connection is defined as something that joins or connects two or more things, the act of connecting two or more things, and a situation in which two or more things have the same cause, origin, goal, etc. (Merriam-Webster, 2024). Dr. Jane Dutton defined connection as "the dynamic, living tissue that exists between two people when there is some contact between them involving mutual awareness and social interaction" (Dutton & Heaphy, 2003). People define words differently, and words conjure up different images for people. Social connections can be viewed as strings that attach one person to another: sometimes, there are many strings connecting two people, and those strings may be really thick, like rope, or very thin, like a shoestring. Strings and ropes come in all different colors, shapes, and sizes. The significance and quality of the connection are also something to consider.

In Maslow's hierarchy of basic psychological needs, social connection is labeled as a sense of belonging and love. The psychological need, as identified by Maslow, is third in his pyramid or hierarchy of needs. The foundation and first layer of the pyramid is a physiological (food and water) need, and on top of that layer is the need for safety (shelter) (Maslow, 1954). In the self-determination theory developed by

Deci and Ryan (Deci & Ryan, 1985), relatedness, described as feeling socially connected to others, is one of three requirements for sustained motivation. The other two are autonomy and competence. Social connection is key in many different psychological theories.

When writing about the power of connection in his book *Connect*, Dr. Edward Hallowell wrote,

"A five-minute conversation can make all the difference in the world if the parties participate actively. To make it work, you have to set aside what you're doing, put down the memo you were reading, disengage from your laptop, abandon your daydream, and bring your attention to bear upon the person you are with. Usually, when you do this, the other person (or people) will feel the energy and respond in kind, naturally." (Hallowell, 1999). This is true to this day.

The Harvard Study of Adult Development is a longitudinal study that initially followed 724 men from Harvard College to determine the psychosocial predictors of healthy aging. Men belonged to two groups: a group of sophomores at Harvard College and a group chosen from an underserved working-class Boston neighborhood. Years after the study started, the participants' wives were also followed. As Dr. Robert Waldinger, a psychiatrist at Mass General Hospital and the third director of this eighty-plus year study, reported in a *Harvard Gazette* article, the surprising finding of the study was that happy relationships and being more socially connected to your family and community have a powerful influence not just on happiness but also on health (Harvard Medical School, n.d.; TED, 2016, 2023; Waldinger & Schulz, 2023). "Those [social] ties protect people from life's discontents, help to delay mental and physical decline, and are better predictors of long and happy lives than social class, IQ, or even genes" (Mineo, 2017).

The opposite of connection is disconnection. The opposite of social connection is social isolation. Social isolation can come in many forms and create different outcomes for people. Loneliness is a subjective experience that one can feel in various social settings. Loneliness is something that people perceive for themselves. It is different for different people. In the same room at the same work event, one person could feel socially connected, and one person could feel lonely. This subjective feeling is a combination of how socially supported one feels in general, how one is experiencing the present moment in time, and the psychological state of the individual, whether they are stressed, depressed, or anxious.

Loneliness can be toxic. Loneliness has been defined as being more isolated from others than one wants to be (Waldinger & Schulz, 2023). The CDC has considered social isolation and loneliness in older adults a serious public health risk for years (Centers for Disease Control and Prevention, 2024a). Considering a 2020 report from the National Academies of Sciences, Engineering, and Medicine (NASEM) that more than one-third of adults aged forty-five and older feel lonely, and nearly one quarter of adults aged sixty-five and older are considered to be socially isolated, loneliness and social isolation are likely to become a serious problem and strain on healthcare resources. The report's findings are that social isolation significantly increases one's risk of premature death from all causes and that the severity of the risk may compare to smoking, obesity, and physical inactivity. Social isolation is associated with 50% increased risk of dementia, 29% increased risk of heart disease, 32% increased risk of stroke, higher rates of depression, anxiety, and suicide, and increased risk of hospitalization (68%) and emergency department visit (57%) (ibid.).

These serious consequences of lack of social connection are not new. There has been research on this topic for decades. For example, a study of coronary artery disease (CAD) patients found that socially isolated patients had a 2.4 times higher risk of cardiac death compared to their more socially connected peers (Brummett et al., 2001). In men, social isolation is comparable to hypertension as a mortality risk factor, and low social network index scores were associated with a risk of mortality at a similar level as smoking (Pantell et al., 2013). In women, the effect was not as strong but still was an important predictor of mortality along with smoking and high blood pressure (ibid.). Social isolation risk is not only comparable to hypertension, but new research has shown that, especially in women, it can also increase the risk of having hypertension (Hosseini et al., 2021). A review on the effects of loneliness and social isolation showed that low quality and quantity of social ties was linked with the progression of CVD, recurrent heart attacks, atherosclerosis, high blood pressure, cancer, delayed cancer recovery, slower wound healing, increased inflammatory markers, and impaired immune function (Umberson & Montez, 2010).

Covid-19 lockdowns and curtailing of social gatherings only increased the problem of social isolation. People were limited to personal contact only with their closest family members for months. People living alone before the pandemic were suddenly removed from social support structures. Therefore, it is unsurprising that research now finds that social distancing measures negatively affect older people's physical and mental health (Sepúlveda-Loyola et al., 2020). Although most of the research on social isolation was done with older age groups, studies have found that social distancing during Covid-19 affected adults of all ages. Young adults reported the highest level of isolation even if they were not necessarily more alone than older adults, and they also felt that their life satisfaction was lowest due to forced social isolation (Clair et al., 2021). This may indicate that loneliness is not a matter of being alone but of the perception and feeling of having fewer social interactions than one wants.

The Covid-19 pandemic changed the face of loneliness or may have exposed factors that contribute to feeling lonely that were not investigated before. A comparison of Cigna's 2021 loneliness research to prepandemic research on loneliness shows that during the pandemic, young adults (age eighteen–twenty-four) reported feeling lonely and being left out twice as often as those over sixty-five. People of underrepresented racial groups and people with lower incomes also felt lonelier during the pandemic than the general population and those of higher income (The Cigna Group, 2021). This may indicate that groups who could depend more on social support and social interactions will be affected more by forced isolation.

As loneliness is subjective, one should not assume that people who are alone are lonely or that those surrounded by people have an adequate level of good-quality relationships and cannot feel lonely. Assessing social relationship levels and relationship quality and satisfaction may need to be added when assessing the overall quality of life, well-being, and potential health risks of any patient.

Research about loneliness has been increasing, and attention on this topic is growing. Dr. Vivek Murthy declared that the United States was experiencing an epidemic of loneliness, which sparked a number of articles and projects to help prevent this situation from worsening (Office of the Surgeon General, 2023).

Social connections can influence multiple factors in a person's life, both negatively and positively. Positive, good-quality social interactions can encourage healthy behaviors (physical activity, nutrition, substance use, sleep, adherence to medical treatments), physical health (cardiovascular, immune system, sugar metabolism), and psychological functioning (stress, depression, resilience, safety, meaning, and purpose). Negative and toxic relationships can sabotage health behaviors and worsen the physical and mental health of an individual. When assessing social connections, one may need to assess not only frequency but also quality and supportive factors of the relationships in a person's life (Holt-Lunstad, 2021).

Considering all the negative effects of loneliness and all the benefits of positive social interactions, "positive social connection" is identified as one of the core six pillars of lifestyle medicine. The significant evidence that quality social support and connectedness can help with maintaining a healthy weight, blood sugar control, with improving cardiovascular health and cancer survival, decreasing depression and post-traumatic stress disorder symptoms, and improving mental health, makes it important for lifestyle medicine practitioners to consider writing social connection prescriptions in the same way as they might do for nutrition or exercise. When prescribing social connection, healthcare professionals can assess social connection quality and patient needs as well as satisfaction with their current social life and, if necessary, make a social connection prescription (Martino, Pegg, & Frates, 2015).

Table 8.1 shows examples of how to use FITT-type lifestyle prescription for social connection.

Table 8.1. Examples of using FITT-type lifestyle prescription for social connection

Elements of social connection prescription	*Description*	*Examples of social connection prescription*
Frequency	What is the quantity of social connection recommended (i.e., daily, weekly, etc.)	***Example 1:*** F: Once a week I: Call a good friend who you haven't heard from in a while T: and talk for 15 minutes T: to catch up and reconnect
Intensity	What quality of interaction is recommended (i.e., more new acquaintances, rekindling old connections, deepening existing close connections)	***Example 2:*** F: Every 2 weeks I: attend a social activity

(*Continued*)

Table 8.1. *(Continued)*

Elements of social connection prescription	*Description*	*Examples of social connection prescription*
Time	How much time to spend on social interactions	T: spend 5 minutes per person talking
Type	That is, family connections, friendships, acquaintances with shared interests, etc.	T: with 5 different new people

Social connections and nutrition

Eating food and socially connecting are two of the most basic human needs, as evidenced in Maslow's hierarchy of needs. Both are essential for our survival. People experience the effects of eating and socially connecting, or the lack thereof, in some of the same brain structures and processes. Humans can crave both food and social interactions in the same way. Mid-brain regions that light up on a functional MRI when people have food cravings also light up when people have been isolated for a while and crave social interaction. Social isolation causes social cravings, similar to how fasting causes food cravings (Tomova et al., 2020). This similarity of processes and effects is not limited only to the brain but extends to the entire body. As already described, a lack of healthy social relationships can have negative consequences for our cardiovascular health, metabolic health, mental health, and immune system, as does a lack of healthy foods. Considering how tightly intertwined these two essential human needs are, it is not surprising that we find a bidirectional influence between food and social connections.

Food and sharing meals with friends and family is a way to facilitate and improve relationships. A review of community programs that worked on promoting better aging and combating social isolation has found that food serves as an effective hook to get people engaged with activities and programs by providing motivation to attend, a welcoming atmosphere, and a common interest in conversation topics (Community Fund, 2019). Communal feasts and family meals are essential parts of human history and social bonding, and those who eat in social settings more often are more engaged with the local community, have more friends, are more trusting of other people, and are more satisfied with life (Dunbar, 2017). Social eating not only improves individual lives but has also been shown to strengthen families and communities (University of Oxford, 2017). Frequent family meals have an inverse association with substance use, disordered eating, violent behavior, depression, and suicidality among adolescents, as well as an increase in their self-esteem and school success (Harrison et al., 2015). The benefit of frequent family meals extends to parents' self-esteem and lower depression levels, and these meals can even help improve the functioning of the entire family (Utter et al., 2018).

Research results indicate that connection may go the other way, too. How people perceive food, how they eat, and how healthy their food choices and eating patterns are can be influenced by the company they are keeping. The influence of social relationships on food preferences and eating habits is particularly pronounced in childhood and youth. It seems that in youth, friends' intake of unhealthy foods may promote their intake of unhealthy foods (van den Broek et al., 2020) and that friends seem to be more influential in prompting unhealthy food consumption vs. healthy food consumption (Anderson Steeves et al., 2016). Only some research shows that parents', especially mothers', intake of healthy foods may promote healthier eating in adolescents (van den Broek et al., 2020) but may not have as much influence at ages nine to fifteen, although parents not offering unhealthy food options correlates with higher healthy eating scores even in that age group (Anderson Steeves et al., 2016).

This influence of social circles on healthy eating continues in adulthood. People living and eating alone, men in particular, have demonstrated lower intake of fruits and vegetables compared to people who eat with others, especially with other members of their family (Conklin et al., 2014).

Humans are social creatures who try to fit in with their social environment and social influences. Peer pressure can influence both the quantity and the choice of food consumed. A review and meta-analysis of forty-two studies on social facilitation of eating shows that people eat more when dining out with friends and family than when eating alone or with strangers or acquaintances. The review concludes that the possible reasons might be that people spend more time eating when in good company and feel it is more appropriate to eat more when in the company of people with whom they feel comfortable (Ruddock et al., 2019).

How closely we relate to the group may moderate how much influence their food choices will have on us. People were more likely to consume portion sizes similar to those eaten by people they considered their "in group" vs. the portion sizes that were consumed by people they related less to (Versluis & Papies, 2016). In addition, in a group of friends, the first person who orders often sets the standard for further food orders of the group. If they order healthier items, their friends who order after them also tend to make healthier choices, and if the first person orders high-calorie items, others are more likely to also order high-calorie items (Ellison, 2014). Social interactions influence food intake, even in anticipation of social engagement. One study showed adult women may eat larger food portions before social gatherings than if they knew their next meal would be eaten alone (Ruddock et al., 2021).

Social influences on food choices and eating extend beyond family and close friend groups. They include culture, religion, community, and societal norms, as well as access to food. As with any health behavior, socio-economical models must be considered when planning interventions and designing infrastructure to support healthy eating (Monterrosa et al., 2020).

The social circles people interact within may correlate not just with what and how much people eat but also with their weight and health. Christakis and Fowler (2013) looked at social networks and how social connections influenced obesity. They mapped social network connections of 1,700 undergraduate students, color-coded people based on gender and BMI status, and noticed that people in the obese and non-obese categories by BMI seemed to be in separate connected clusters. People who had obesity were more likely to be heavily connected with other people who had obesity, and people in the healthy weight range by BMI seemed to be more heavily connected with others in the healthy weight range. What mattered was whether people were socially close, not necessarily geographically close.

There is evidence that suggests if your friend gains weight, you are more likely to gain weight, and the other way around. If you want to lose weight successfully, it is also good to enlist the help of your friends, as social support has been shown to aid healthy eating interventions (Yoshikawa et al., 2021).

Even memories of people we interacted with in the past can influence what we eat. When stressed or isolated, people tend to crave "comfort foods," which conjure up the comfort of home, like macaroni and cheese, chicken noodle soup, mashed potatoes, lasagne, and pasta, like carbonara. Depending on where a person grew up and their family of origin, these comfort foods can vary. Comfort foods often have some sentimental value, and consuming them makes people feel better, regardless of the nutritional value of the food. Those comfort foods connect us with people who have made us feel loved and cared for and can trigger feelings of connection with those people, which in turn may help alleviate our distress (Troisi et al., 2015). While those foods can give us the comfort we crave, we must be careful not to overdo it with high-calorie or unhealthy comfort foods and not use them as the primary method of stress relief. Healthy stress management techniques are described in Chapter 6.

People who share the same social circles can become great helpers or end up sabotaging the efforts of others. If someone is trying to eat healthier, it may be a good practice to get people in their social circles on board along with them. Even if they don't want to go through a change process with the person, it can be beneficial to ensure they are not directly or indirectly sabotaging the person's efforts. Encouraging individuals to talk with their family members or friends about what kind of food they bring into the house and what type of restaurants they eat at can be a simple but powerful practical tip. Eating together is often enjoyed as a bonding activity between family members or friends. Therefore, these conversations about food may sometimes be difficult to initiate. Food can be an emotional topic. Some people may not be happy or supportive of the changes someone else is trying to make. However, that conversation can also be a good test of the quality of the relationship and an indicator of which relationships are supporting, nourishing, and thus should be prioritized.

It pays to invest time in fostering healthy connections: healthy connections with others and healthy connections with food.

CHAPTER 9

Physical activity and its impact on food choices

Beth Frates

Guidelines

- Aerobic physical activity: 150 minutes per week of moderate-intensity physical activity, or 75 minutes per week of vigorous physical activity. For more benefits, up to 300 minutes per week of moderate or 150 minutes per week of vigorous activity.
- Strength training—two times or more per week on nonconsecutive days, working all the major muscle groups each session.
- Flexibility and balance—at least two times per week, engage in activities that increase flexibility and balance.
- Reduce time spent sitting. Try to get up at least once each hour. Even low-intensity activity can reduce some risks of being sedentary (U.S. Department of Health and Human Services, 2018). If someone has prediabetes or diabetes, it is recommended that they stand and move around every half an hour (American Diabetes Association, 2024).

Benefits of regular physical activity and exercise

What is one medicine that is so powerful in maintaining and improving health that it could prevent, treat, and even put into remission dozens of chronic conditions, such as diabetes, hypertension, heart disease, depression, metabolic syndrome, and obesity?

Exercise might well be the answer to this question. From the physical health model perspective, exercise has been shown to help prevent cardiac disease and stroke, reduce blood pressure, reduce cholesterol, control blood glucose, control weight and help prevent obesity, improve stamina, endurance, and cardiovascular fitness, help prevent bone loss, improve sleep, and increase energy (Ruegsegger & Booth, 2018). Exercise is also good for brain and mental health. It has been found to improve mood, reduce tiredness, increase mental alertness and cognitive functions, promote stress relief, increase interest in sex, reduce symptoms of anxiety and depression, and increase self-esteem (Sharma, Madaan, & Petty, 2006). There is research that also supports the use of exercise to prevent Alzheimer's disease (Pahlavani, 2023).

The benefits of exercise on cardiovascular health have been known for a while (Wise, 2010), and most people, when they think about exercise, think about physical health, building muscles, regulating metabolism, and increasing physical stamina. However, new research suggests that the brain may benefit from exercise as much as the body. Recent research has been concentrating on the benefits exercise may have on cognition and finding that it helps improve memory (enlarges hippocampus), multitasking, planning, and inhibition (builds prefrontal cortex) (Voss et al., 2011). Randomized control trials show clear positive effects of aerobic exercise on hippocampus volume, even in older women (Brinke et al., 2015). The hippocampus is part of the limbic system deep within the brain. It is involved with memory consolidation. The ability of aerobic exercise to increase the volume of the hippocampus, even in older people, shows its potential in fighting the onset and progress of dementia.

There are several physiological reasons why physical activity may be good for the brain. Physical activity promotes better cardiovascular and respiratory fitness, which improves brain circulation and oxygenation. Another mechanism might be that exercise increases the production of brain-derived neurotrophic factor (BDNF), which plays an important role in promoting synaptic plasticity (Sleiman et al., 2016). Some people call BDNF "miracle grow" for the brain because it increases neurogenesis, the growth of new neurons. Even a single bout of high-intensity interval training (HIIT) has been shown to increase BDNF in previously sedentary healthy men (Nicolini et al., 2020), showing that any amount of added physical activity can give quick benefits. This connection between physical activity and BDNF production might be mediated by irisin, a myokine secreted by muscles during exercise (Inyushkin et al., 2024). New research is looking further into irisin and its influence on neurological health as a possible factor in the prevention and treatment of numerous neurological diseases (Zhang, Zhang, & Lin, 2022). In addition to its effect on brain health, irisin has also been associated with enhancing metabolic processes such as "browning" of the adipose tissue and glucose homeostasis through influencing the pancreas and liver secretions, muscle energy processing, and appetite regulation (Arhire, Mihalache, & Covasa, 2019).

Another way physical activity influences mental health and mood is by enhancing the production of neurotransmitters such as dopamine, which increases motivation; serotonin, which enhances positive mood; and endorphins, which dull the sensation of pain (Lin & Kuo, 2013).

The American Heart Association recognized a "sedentary lifestyle" as a primary controllable cardiac risk factor (Young et al., 2016). An analysis of thirteen studies investigating the harmfulness of prolonged sitting found that the risk of dying for those who were sitting for more than eight hours a day without physical activity was similar to the risk of dying for those who smoked or were obese (Biddle et al., 2016; Laskowski, 2022). Excessive sitting really can be considered a lethal behavior. People have asked, "Is sitting the new smoking?" A study of 8,800 Australians found that each additional hour of television watched per day translated to an 11% increase in all-cause mortality (Dunstan et al., 2010). It is not just the total length of time spent sitting that matters but also how long you sit without movement breaks. Getting up and moving for at least two to five minutes every hour, preferably every thirty minutes is recommended.

If there is concern about prediabetes and type 2 diabetes, it is necessary to counteract the negative effects of sedentary behavior (Diaz et al., 2017). In fact, people with prediabetes and diabetes are advised to stand and move around (walk, run in place, do squats, or do some other activity) every half an hour. Risks of sedentary behavior include reduced functional capacity, osteoporosis, obesity, anxiety and depression, hypertension, cardiovascular disease, colon cancer, thromboembolic stroke, breast cancer, and type 2 diabetes mellitus (Kesaniemi et al., 2001).

Of special consideration and a sentence that demands your attention is this one. Never go straight from a sedentary lifestyle into vigorous activity, as that often results in cardiovascular events like a heart attack. To prevent injury or cardiovascular events, it is recommended that when starting any exercise program, start low and go slow, gradually increasing exercise time, frequency, and intensity (Garber et al., 2011). Before starting an exercise program, people should contact their primary care provider. If someone has a heart condition, endocrine disorders, or lung problems, they may need further evaluations before beginning any exercise routine.

Considering the extensive influence of physical activity and physical inactivity on all processes in our body, it is essential to counsel patients on their importance. Exercise is medicine, and nutrition is medicine too. It is no wonder that changes in nutrition and exercise are well-proven lifestyle interventions suggested for the treatment of a variety of conditions and for preserving both physical and mental health.

One of Dr. Frates' original quotes is: "You cannot outrun an unhealthy eating pattern, and you cannot feed yourself fitness." Both healthy eating patterns and routine physical activity are essential for optimal health. Considering that the World Health Organization (2024a) found that about 31% of the world's adult population is physically inactive, there is a dire need to make exercise (physical activity) prescription part of routine medical care.

The prescription doesn't need to be an elaborate set of guidelines. Simple recommendations that allow people to fulfill the guidelines in the way that best suits their lives can go a long way. Table 9.1 provides some examples of FITT-type exercise prescriptions.

Table 9.1. Examples of FITT exercise (physical activity) prescription

Elements of physical activity prescription	*Description*	*Examples of exercise prescription*
Frequency	How often you should do the activity	***Example 1:*** F: twice a week
Intensity	At what level you should do the activity	I: at a moderate level T: three set reps for each muscle group
Time	How much time to spend on the activity	T: bodyweight exercises
Type	What type of activity you should do	***Example 2:*** F: five days a week I: moderate level T: thirty minutes per day T: take a walk in nature

Exercise and nutrition

The relationship between exercise and food is complex. The most simplistic view of the relationship between nutrition and physical activity was that one provides energy, and the other is used to expend energy. Many people play one off of the other, meaning they say, "Well, I walked for an hour today, so I can have that cake for dessert."

Historically, exercise has been recommended to lose weight and improve cardiovascular health. New research is finding that one cannot exercise one's way out of an unhealthy eating pattern, both in terms of not being able to create sufficient calorie deficit to lose weight with exercise alone without addressing nutrition (Cox, 2017) and in terms of extremely high levels of exercise may not be able to counteract negative health effects and mortality risk that comes with unhealthy diet (Ding et al., 2022). When someone eats highly processed foods with dyes and chemicals in them, exercise is not going to be able to eliminate all those toxins and their possible effects.

On a positive note, as previously explained, physical activity has multiple health benefits, and some studies have shown that exercise may even promote healthier food choices. A study of sixty-one middle-aged, inactive, and overweight or obese people found that starting to exercise changed their food preferences. They no longer found high-calorie, fatty foods irresistible and had fewer episodes of binge eating. People in the intervention group still liked high-fat foods, but they craved them less. In addition, people in the exercise group also lost weight, while some in the control group (no change in physical activity) gained weight (Beaulieu et al., 2020).

A different study found that taking brisk walks reduced sugary snack cravings in overweight people and attenuated their urge to respond to stressful situations by eating (Ledochowski et al., 2015). Not only does exercise help people to have fewer cravings for unhealthy snacks, it also might help them to make healthier food choices. A group of students who did not diet and exercise were introduced to a fifteen-week exercise program of thirty to sixty minutes of walking three times a week. Although they were told not to change their diet, those who exercised started on their own accord to eat more fruits, vegetables, lean meats, fish, and nuts, and to avoid fried foods, snacks, and soda. The more vigorous and lengthy their exercise was, the more their diet tended to improve (Joo et al., 2019).

Exercise, when performed regularly, has the potential to reduce cravings. However, sometimes, after one bout of exercise, a person may feel like they are hungrier, feel like they want more food, and believe that since they exercised, they can consume more food if they are working on the calories in and calories out tracking methodology. This may have to do with the intensity of exercise. While an intense workout may reduce a person's cravings as the blood has been pulled from the person's gastrointestinal tract and into their large muscles to help them complete the intense activity, which puts them into fight or flight mode, a low- or moderate-intensity exercise may not reduce appetite and may even stimulate it (A. M. Miller, 2017).

Research in animal models has demonstrated that exercise promotes the production of Lac-Phe (N-lactoyl-phenylalanine), a metabolite that suppresses feeding and obesity in mammalian species (Li et al., 2022). Research in humans has demonstrated that over time, exercise may reduce the influence of ghrelin (Vatansever-Ozen et al., 2011). Another research study demonstrated that exercise decreased ghrelin and increased leptin, and it also showed that exercise can change people's appetites and food intake after visualizing certain foods (Gómez Escribano et al., 2017). Many factors, both internal (body fat percentage, fitness level, ability to recognize hunger cues) and external (temperature outside or in studio, city's altitude, woman's menstrual cycle), influence if exercise will decrease or increase appetite (A. M. Miller, 2017).

Interestingly, there is evidence that if someone chooses their exercise routine and exerts autonomy in this way, their energy intake is likely to be significantly lower than someone who had no choice in their exercise activity, and, in addition, those in the no-choice group had a greater intake of "unhealthy" foods in recovery (Beer et al., 2017). The importance of taking a COACH Approach™ to counseling patients about physical activity and giving them autonomy and choice will be covered thoroughly in Chapter 16. Further review of research on physical activity and appetite indicates that there might be many individual factors to consider that make it difficult to create a clear-cut statement on the influence of exercise on hunger levels. Research indicates that those people with higher levels of habitual physical activity are more sensitive to appetite control systems and that long-term regular exercise positively influences energy balance (Dorling et al., 2018).

Physical activity will deplete glycogen stores and may cause dehydration. If people do not fuel their bodies adequately pre-workout, it may lead to bouts of strong hunger cues after exercise. This is a reminder that dehydration and the signal for thirst can sometimes be confused with the signal for hunger. This is also a reminder to hydrate before and during exercising. To elicit the full benefits of exercise, good physical performance during exercise, and prevent adverse effects and injuries, it is important to hydrate and feed one's body properly before and after engaging in physical activity.

Table 9.2 shows some of the recommendations by the American College of Sports Medicine, the Academy of Nutrition and Dietetics, and the Dietitians of Canada (Thomas, Erdman, & Burke, 2016) on proper nutrition for athletic performance.

Some ways to manage the potential appetite increase after exercise include planning healthy meals or snacks post-workout. Before the workout, hydrate well, plan for nutrient-rich, high-fiber carbohydrate

Table 9.2. Proper nutrition for athletic performance

Important nutrients	*Description*
Carbohydrates	Muscles, when active, mostly use glucose for energy (either blood glucose or glycogen storage from the liver). Although some view carbohydrates as negative for fitness, they are necessary for preventing fatigue and fueling muscles pre-, during, and post-exercise. How much carbohydrate is highly individualized to a person and the type of physical activity.
Protein	Protein in the diet is necessary as both a trigger and substrate for the synthesis of contractile and metabolic proteins in the body. To trigger the development of muscle proteins, physical activity is necessary in addition to nutrition. For muscle development, the best time to consume protein is within 2 hours after exercise (early recovery stage). Daily recommendations for protein intake are about 1.2–2.0 grams per kilogram of body mass. During short intensified training, more protein might be beneficial, but long-term, higher than the recommended protein intake isn't effective and may create some adverse health effects.
Fat	It is a necessary part of healthy nutrition and provides energy, essential elements of cell membranes, brain and nerve functioning, and promotes the absorption of fat-soluble vitamins. Recommendations are that saturated fats be limited to less than 10% of daily calorie intake and that the rest be supplied by quality mono- and poly-unsaturated fat sources rich in other micronutrients. Although fat has a high energy value, fat is most effectively used as energy during endurance training. For all other types of exercise, carbohydrates are better energy sources. However, athletes are still encouraged not to reduce their intake of fats below 20% of daily energy intake, as that might limit appropriate nutritional balance.

(*Continued*)

Table 9.2. *(Continued)*

Important nutrients	*Description*
Micronutrients	Micronutrients include vitamins, minerals, and phytonutrients necessary for the normal operation of the human body. Exercise stress may increase the need for micronutrients, especially iron, vitamin D, calcium, and antioxidants. Acute, high-intensity exercise can increase oxidative stress on the body, so a diet rich in antioxidants is best.
Hydration	Proper hydration, including enough water and necessary electrolytes, is always important, especially pre-, during, and post-exercise. Dehydration will not only impact performance but can also be dangerous. Sometimes, feeling hungry after exercise may be due to dehydration, as the body and brain can confuse these two physiologic states.

meals, and avoid saturated fats and too much protein. During exercise, stay hydrated properly by taking small and frequent sips of water, and for longer, high-intensity workouts, add 50–100 calories from carbohydrate snacks every half an hour. After exercise, it is important to fuel the body for proper recovery. It may be good to drink water with a small amount of 100% juice mixed in to quickly add hydration and carbohydrates within twenty to sixty minutes after exercise, and take some protein within the first two hours after exercise (American Heart Association, 2015; Kilroy, 2019).

While exercise may help you achieve and keep a healthy weight, people should be cautious not to over-focus on weight loss as a motivator to continue their exercise. Exercise builds muscle mass and boosts metabolism. Muscle is denser than adipose tissue. People can lose adipose tissue and gain more muscle mass. This will tip the scale to be heavier. So, while people might get fitter and healthier, the scales may not immediately show weight loss. This can be frustrating when someone is just starting a new exercise regime. They must be reminded that they are losing adipose tissue and gaining muscle tissue. Exercise is the best way to alter body composition, and body composition is important. Some people use the belt test to determine how their exercise sessions are going. This means they notice when they are moving their belt one rung, indicating their waist is smaller. The importance of reducing abdominal adiposity was covered in Chapter 7 on mindsets. As a reminder, weight carried in the middle is associated with multiple metabolic conditions. In addition, exercise has many benefits for the body and brain, which are already covered in this chapter. It impacts many of the other pillars. It helps improve sleep. Stress relief is a major benefit that can be experienced with a short walk of five to ten minutes. These are powerful benefits. To stay motivated to keep moving, it is good to focus on all the benefits people gain by engaging in physical activity, such as lower blood pressure, improved insulin sensitivity, increased HDL (good cholesterol), improved bone mineral density, weight control, lower inflammation, better body composition, improved mood, better sleep, improved cognition, increased creativity, reduced stress, and enhanced overall well-being. These were all covered at the beginning of this chapter and are good to review regularly. They can motivate patients and providers alike.

The best type of motivation is intrinsic motivation, which comes from within. Noticing how good people feel after a bout of exercise, likely due to the endorphins, or noticing how people feel more creative after a walk will help them tap into their intrinsic motivators, which will help sustain this healthy behavior. Motivation and behavior change will be covered in detail in Chapter 12.

CHAPTER 10

Substance use and its impact on food choices

Beth Frates

Guidelines

Alcohol

- If you don't drink, don't start.
- If you drink, limit yourself to one standard drink for women and two standard drinks for men. These limitations are for a twenty-four-hour period.
  One standard drink contains roughly 14 grams of pure alcohol, which is equivalent to 12 ounces of regular (5% alcohol content) beer, 5 ounces of wine (about 12% alcohol), or 1.5 ounces of distilled spirits (about 40% alcohol) (National Institute on Alcohol Abuse and Alcoholism (NIAAA, 2025c); USDA & USDHHS, 2020).
  NOTE: The reason why the limit is lower for women doesn't have to do as much with size or weight as previously thought. Women have less alcohol dehydrogenase (ADH) in their stomach linings and thus metabolize only a small amount of alcohol in their stomachs. The rest goes into the bloodstream. Thus, EtOH (ethyl alcohol) in women has about twice the effect as that in men (Mumenthaler et al., 1999).

Caffeine

- 400 milligrams (about four cups of brewed coffee) is considered a safe amount of caffeine for healthy adults to consume daily (USFDA, 2023).
- Pregnant women should limit their caffeine intake to 200 mg a day (about two cups of brewed coffee) (The American College of Obstetricians and Gynecologists, 2023).
- Children under age twelve should not consume any food or beverages with caffeine. Children aged twelve to eighteen should limit their caffeine intake to no more than 100 mg daily (about two or three 12-ounce cans of cola soda) (American Academy of Child and Adolescent Psychiatry (AACAP), 2020).

Tobacco

Tobacco is one of the leading causes of preventable death and health impairment, and no amount of tobacco products is safe for use (World Health Organization (WHO), 2024b).

Psychoactive substances

Only if prescribed by a physician, only for a period, and in doses prescribed.

Marijuana (cannabis) is one of the psychoactive substances that people are starting to access not only as prescription medication but increasingly as a recreational substance due to its legalization in some states in the U.S.A. As of yet, there are no official recommendations on the recreational use of marijuana. In those states in which marijuana is legal, there is increasing concern about its use, including driving while high.

Avoidance of risky substances

Alcohol use

Alcohol is a legal substance, and its use is socially acceptable and even encouraged in many cultures. As research has evolved over the years, the guidelines have changed and may differ from country to country and may even vary depending on which medical specialist is advising. People who drink tend to want to believe that there is a protective effect or a healthy impact that alcohol may be able to provide to the body. They are slow to accept the findings of the most recent research studies, and often find it hard to accept that alcohol is classified as a carcinogen.

- Cardiologists, for years, were basing their recommendations on research that showed some benefits of alcohol on heart health. Indeed, some studies suggest alcohol consumption within the AHA guidelines may reduce the risk of heart disease and ischemic stroke (Elkind et al., 2006; Sacco et al., 1999) and that a polyphenol called resveratrol that is found in red wine has health benefits by helping protect the lining of blood vessels in the heart (Castaldo et al., 2019). Therefore, cardiologists had previously recommended some low-level use of alcohol (especially red wine).
- Oncologists treat cancer, focus on cancer, and are concerned about alcohol and cancer. Recent cancer research has concluded that there is no safe level of alcohol use, and moderate alcohol drinking recommendations cannot be labeled as safe, only as low-risk (NHS, 2022b). Drinking too much alcohol can increase your risk of developing certain cancers, including cancers of the mouth (oral cavity), esophagus, throat (pharynx), voice box (larynx), liver, and breast (National Cancer Institute, 2021).
- There are four ways alcohol can contribute to cancer (Rumgay et al., 2021):
    - Alcohol (ethanol) breaks down into acetaldehyde, which has been shown to damage DNA, increasing the risk of developing cancer.
    - Alcohol increases oxidative stress, which damages DNA, proteins, and cells and increases inflammation, all of which can increase the risk of developing cancer.
    - Alcohol alters levels of multiple hormones, including estrogen, which raises the risk of breast cancer.
- Alcohol damages cells in the mouth and throat, which leads to greater absorption of other carcinogens.

Due to numerous ethical concerns, it would be hard to conduct randomized trials that will give a clear answer to whether alcohol use in any amount is beneficial. In the absence of randomized trials, several studies using human genetic data (i.e., mendelian randomization [MR]) suggest that there is some causal link between any alcohol consumption and an increase in the risk of cardiovascular disease (Holmes et al., 2014; Smith & Ebrahim, 2003). Observational analysis of UK Biobank participants' data suggests that maybe this research discrepancy on the effect of low or moderate use of alcohol on cardiovascular health might be due to confounding factors of light or moderate drinkers also having other, healthier lifestyle choices than abstainers, and cardiovascular benefits may come from observing those other healthy lifestyle habits (Biddinger et al., 2022). There is also the added confounder that in the past, abstainers and nondrinkers were one group, without separating those who abstained or were nondrinkers due to a history of alcohol use disorder.

It is not only chronic alcohol use that can cause problems; even occasional but heavy drinking episodes that involve five or more drinks in about two hours for men and four or more drinks for women, known as binge drinking, can cause significant health problems (National Institute on Alcohol Abuse and Alcoholism (NIAAA, 2025b). Alcohol has also been shown to produce detectable impairments to memory after only a few drinks. As the amount of alcohol increases, so does the level of impairment, and large quantities of alcohol, especially when consumed quickly on an empty stomach, can cause blackouts—intervals of time when the intoxicated person cannot recall what happened.

Chronic alcohol use can cause multiple issues, including Korsakoff psychosis (a chronic and debilitating syndrome characterized by persistent learning and memory problems), Wernicke's encephalopathy (characterized by mental confusion, paralysis of the nerves that move the eyes, and difficulty with muscle coordination), and thiamine (B1) deficiency (Oscar-Berman & Marinkovic, 2003).

Drinking a lot over a long time or too much on a single occasion (binge drinking) can damage the body, causing problems including heart issues (cardiomyopathy, arrhythmias, and high blood pressure), liver issues (steatosis, alcoholic hepatitis, fibrosis, and cirrhosis), neurological issues (neuropathy, stroke, seizures, memory loss, paresthesias, peripheral neuropathy, slower reaction time), pancreatitis, and weakening of the immune system (Obad et al., 2018; Planas-Ballvé et al., 2017). Binge drinking has been shown to slow the body's ability to ward off infections, even up to twenty-four hours after getting drunk (National Institute on Alcohol Abuse and Alcoholism (NIAAA, 2025a). Even a single alcohol binge in young, healthy volunteers transiently impacts neutrophil function (Stadlbauer et al., 2019).

Taking into consideration all the recent research on the negative influence of alcohol, trying to accommodate historical ideas that people still believe about the benefits of moderate alcohol use, and having an understanding of how difficult it is to change social acceptance of alcohol use, current CDC and AHA recommendations try to accommodate different views by recommending no use of alcohol as the best option but allowing for some level of low-risk use, which translates to if you don't drink, don't start. If you choose to drink, limit yourself to one drink per twenty-four-hour period if you are a woman and two drinks per twenty-four-hour period if you are a man.

There is evidence that the culture around alcohol is shifting in the United States. The former surgeon general, Dr. Vivek Murthy, recommended heightening the warning labels on alcoholic beverages to emphasize the risk for cancer. He created an advisory in January 2025 spelling out the risks of drinking alcohol (USDHHS, 2025).

The sustained appeal of alcohol comes from its interaction with the body. Alcohol is an indirect GABA agonist. High levels of GABA cause your body temperature to drop and your heart rate and blood pressure to decrease. GABA is the neurotransmitter that helps us feel relaxed and aids in lowering anxiety and stress, and alcohol binding to GABA receptors also produces that feeling (Okey & Draskovic, 2023). Many say that alcohol helps them socialize, and social connections are important for health. People say it helps them relax, and stress reduction is important for health. However, there are other ways to feel comfortable socially and to relieve stress. Chapter 6 reviews healthy stress reduction techniques.

Unlike tobacco products and other addictive substances that have clear health dangers, alcohol is one of the substances that is socially acceptable and, at some times in history, might have even been recommended for heart health. Therefore, there is a lower entrance barrier for people to use alcohol as a coping mechanism. Many people drink in social settings, so even if they often exceed recommendations, it doesn't feel like a problem to them. They may not realize when they have crossed into substance use disorder territory. Again, in this situation, social connections can either help or hurt people. If people are friends with heavy drinkers, they too may indulge in heavy drinking. Many people who quit drinking also stop going to the bars they used to frequent, and they find new friends with different hobbies like cards, biking, hiking, swimming, pickleball, basket weaving, painting, knitting, photography, or other enjoyable activities. Some people replace their drinking with exercise, which can be a healthy option. However, anything taken to an extreme can become unhealthy.

During the pandemic and all the stressors that came with it, people noticed that they started increasing their alcohol use and became aware that their alcohol use was not just a way to socialize but also a way to handle stress (Grossman, Benjamin-Neelon, & Sonnenschein, 2020). The problem with longer-term alcohol use is that it suppresses natural GABA productions, and while at the beginning, it may help people relax, de-stress, and be less anxious, ultimately, it will lead to higher anxiety and stronger dependence on alcohol to manage mood (Georgetown Behavioral Hospital, 2021; Valenzuela, 1997). In Chapter 11 on sleep, alcohol will be discussed as a sleep disruptor. People often feel that it helps them fall asleep, and it may. Research studies indicate that alcohol decreases REM sleep, which is the stage of sleep that is vitally important for memory consolidation.

Historic stigma and often exaggerated stereotypes that were attached to the term "alcoholic" may make it hard for people to admit to themselves that their alcohol use is becoming harmful, and often confronting family members, friends, colleagues, or even patients about the problem may elicit strong defensive denial. This is where motivational interviewing and the COACH Approach™ are needed. These are discussed in Chapter 12.

Caffeine use

Caffeine is another substance that is socially acceptable and may have some health benefits in addition to its effect of raising alertness and making people feel more energized. Because many people indulge in caffeine shots or multiple cafe lattes to stay awake and to be more productive, it can easily escape people's attention that the amount and frequency of caffeine use in the U.S. is slipping into unhealthy territory for many. Research on the benefits of caffeine is not always clear on whether the benefits are derived from caffeine itself or other compounds in drinks containing caffeine. Phytonutrients, called polyphenols, in coffee, green tea, and dark chocolate may be the primary source of health benefits and not the caffeine itself (LIczbiński & Bukowska, 2022). It is better to consume caffeine in drinks that may have some potential health benefits than in caffeinated sodas and energy drinks, which, in addition to high levels of caffeine, also contain high levels of sugar.

Exceeding recommendations for caffeine may lead to overstimulation of the nervous system (feeling jittery and nervous), increase in blood pressure, dehydration (caffeine is a diuretic), heartburn, and disrupted sleep (Harvard T.H. Chan School of Public Health, 2020a). People with any of those issues are advised to reduce or eliminate their caffeine intake. Caffeine may interfere with calcium absorption, and it may not be advisable for people with a risk of osteoporosis (Heaney, 2002). There is also a strong adverse association between caffeine and pregnancy-related outcomes (may affect DNA methylation and proper fetal growth), and pregnant women are advised not to use it (Ding, Xu, & Lau, 2023). The American College of Obstetricians and Gynecologists recommends that if pregnant women do drink coffee, they limit their caffeine intake to 200 mg a day, which is about two cups of brewed coffee.

Tobacco use

The harmfulness of tobacco use in all its forms is well-researched, and there are many tobacco use cessation programs that can help people quit. Healthcare professionals need to keep in mind that people continue their tobacco use despite knowing all its harms, mainly because of both physical and psychological addiction. Quitting tobacco use can often be a long and involved process and may require helping people find better ways to cope with stress and other issues they may encounter as they stop using tobacco. Motivational interviewing and the COACH Approach™ are essential when counseling people about tobacco use. These topics are covered in Chapter 12.

Psychoactive substances

As recreational cannabis use is slowly becoming legalized across the U.S. and other parts of the world, one is starting to notice more relaxed attitudes about its use. In addition, research on the possible harmful effects of overuse and what constitutes overuse is still lagging. There is an increasing societal acceptance of the use of psychoactive substances, and it can be difficult for both medical professionals and law enforcement to deal with the potential consequences of misuse of substances and substance use disorders. Although people think that smoking cannabis is safer than smoking tobacco, that may not be the case, as people who smoke marijuana often have the same breathing problems and other negative health effects as tobacco users. Cannabis use so far has shown it can cause increased heart rate, brain development impairment in young users or when used during pregnancy, nausea, vomiting, dehydration, worsening symptoms of paranoia, hallucinations, and schizophrenia, and in some people, addiction (National Institute on Drug Abuse (NIDA), 2024). Not using cannabis—unless it is used as a prescription and under the supervision of a physician—for a well-researched health benefit is still the safest recommendation.

Some emerging recommendations to reduce harm from cannabis use include not using it at all during adolescence or pregnancy, using varieties with lower THC and higher CBD:THC ratio, not using synthetic cannabinoids, not using administration that involves inhaling combusted cannabis (edibles can be safer) and especially not inhaling deeply, not using it more than one day per week and not driving impaired (Fischer et al., 2017). Edibles can be dangerous, especially if there are children or young adults who may indulge in them and not know they have cannabis in them or not know the limits.

Substance use disorder

Any substance that impacts the reward system can be problematic. A person using a substance, whether controlled or not, may need psychological and behavioral change intervention to address it fully. Because of the way these substances interact with the brain reward system, addressing substance use problems will rarely be successful when a physician simply points out the problem and then educates the patient on the harm of the substance. More is needed.

Not all substance use meets the criteria of being diagnosed as substance use disorder. According to DSM-5, for something to be considered substance use disorder, the following criteria need to be met:

- Taking the substance in larger amounts or for longer than you're meant to
- Wanting to cut down or stop using the substance but not managing to
- Spending a lot of time getting, using, or recovering from use of the substance
- Cravings and urges to use the substance
- Not managing to do what you should at work, home, or school because of substance use
- Continuing to use it, even when it causes problems in relationships
- Giving up important social, occupational, or recreational activities because of substance use
- Using substances again and again, even when it puts you in danger
- Continuing to use, even when you know you have a physical or psychological problem that could have been caused or made worse by the substance
- Needing more of the substance to get the effect you want (tolerance)
- Development of withdrawal symptoms, which can be relieved by taking more of the substance (Hartney, 2024).

DSM-5 diagnosing criteria are complex and should be done only by trained professionals, but for initial diagnosis purposes, the CAGE Questionnaire can be a friendlier tool (Ewing, 1984). If people score 2 or more on the CAGE Questionnaire (see Table 10.1), that may be an indicator for physicians to initiate the involvement of mental health professionals to help their patients deal with the problem.

Table 10.1. CAGE Questionnaire questions for alcohol use and scoring (created from the information in Ewing, 1984)

CAGE Questionnaire questions for alcohol use and scoring
• Have you ever felt you should cut down on your drinking? • Have people annoyed you by criticizing your drinking? • Have you ever felt bad or guilty about your drinking?

(*Continued*)

Table 10.1 *(Continued)*

- Have you ever had a drink first thing in the morning to steady your nerves or to get rid of a hangover (eye opener)?

Scoring:

- Item responses on the CAGE are scored 0 or 1, with a higher score indicating alcohol problems. A total score of 2 or greater is considered clinically significant.

Substance use and nutrition

Alcohol and nutrition

When considering the influence of alcohol on nutrition, one must take into consideration that alcoholic beverages themselves have caloric and sometimes other nutritional value. We have already discussed that red wine has been considered beneficial due to its phytonutrient content, and some beers are even considered a food staple because of their nutritional content (WebMD, 2022). However, there is a serious risk of cancer with alcohol consumption at any level.

Most alcoholic drinks have a significant sugar content and caloric value, so this needs to be taken into consideration in research on weight loss and management (NHS, 2022a). However, a bigger problem alcohol use may present for weight management is the tendency of people to overeat high-fat meals while drinking, after heavy drinking, and when managing hangover symptoms (Tremblay et al., 1995). Research studies show that when alcohol is consumed before a meal, about 20–25% more calories are consumed at a meal, or about 33% more calories when calories from alcohol are added in (Caton, Bate, & Hetherington, 2007; Harbolic & Stoppler, 2021). Alcohol consumption has been shown to increase abdominal adiposity ("beer belly"), which is implicated in an increased risk of heart disease, high blood pressure, and diabetes (Ryu et al., 2010; Schröder et al., 2007), as discussed in Chapter 7 on mindsets. Studies on college students show that alcohol consumption not only impacted their cognitive performance but also increased their consumption of high-calorie snacks like cookies (Christiansen et al., 2016) and food cravings for unhealthy foods like salty snacks, pizza, hamburgers, also known as "drunk munchies" or "drunchies," while decreasing their intake of nutrient-dense foods like vegetables and fruit (Kruger et al., 2018; Kruger & Kruger, 2015).

This relationship between alcohol and high-fat food intake may be related to loss of inhibition due to an increase of GABA or may be due to the effects of the neuropeptide galanin. Interestingly, galanin's production is enhanced by alcohol and high-fat food use, which in turn also increases the drive to consume more alcohol and fatty foods, thus creating a vicious cycle (Barson, Morganstern, & Leibowitz, 2010). Another mechanism might be that while moderate alcohol consumption raises blood sugar, excessive use of alcohol inhibits glycogenolysis and gluconeogenesis in the liver, which leads to hypoglycemia that can lead to hunger and cravings for high-calorie foods (Kruger et al., 2018). Alcohol also reduces the amount of vasopressin (antidiuretic hormone) and increases urination, which can lead to dehydration (Epstein, 1997), and it has been shown that people often confuse thirst for hunger. Thus, people who drink a lot of alcohol are often dehydrated and may mistake the signal for thirst for the signal for hunger and eat more.

Regardless of the possible reason, drinking alcohol, especially people engaging in heavy drinking or binge drinking, has been associated with poor adherence to healthy food consumption guidelines, with excessive consumption of eggs, meat, and fish but insufficient consumption of fruits and vegetables (Valencia-Martín, Galán, & Rodríguez-Artalejo, 2011). This preference for eggs, meat, and fish may be the body's way of dealing with the negative effects of alcohol on the digestive system, as the amino acid L-cysteine has been shown to reduce the negative effects of acetaldehyde (a metabolite of ethanol and also contained in tobacco smoke) by covalently binding to it and neutralizing its carcinogenicity (Hellström et al., 2017; Sprince et al., 1975). Animal-based food products contain high levels of L-cysteine. Still, considering that high consumption of those foods is implicated in many health issues, it would be beneficial to turn to many plant-based sources of L-cysteine, such as beans, whole grains, nuts, and seeds, to combat the rise in acetaldehyde created by drinking alcohol.

Recent research on alcohol's ability to disrupt healthy microbiota may explain some reasons for the toxic effects alcohol has on the body. As the role of microbiota in multiple functions and metabolic processes in our body emerges, and research shows a correlation between alcohol-related disorders and quantitative and qualitative dysbiotic changes in the intestinal microbiota, future research may find that alcohol's negative effects on the microbiome lie behind many alcohol-related health issues

(Engen et al., 2015). Taking this into consideration, special attention to maintaining the health of microbiota could be beneficial for people with heavy and even moderate alcohol use. Eating food rich in probiotics and prebiotics probably should be discussed with patients with alcohol use-related problems as a way to offset at least some of the damage to their microbiome.

The Mediterranean diet, with its high consumption of fruit, vegetables, whole grains, fish, nuts, and healthy oils, and decreased consumption of meats, is a good option for maximizing the health benefits of food. This diet does allow for a glass of wine with meals, and it may be the healthfulness of the rest of the diet that compensates for any negative effect of alcohol consumption while allowing for the benefits of the phytonutrients contained in wine. It is also worth noting that while there are studies that showed some benefits of low-to-moderate alcohol intake, numerous studies suggest that the negatives of alcohol consumption may outweigh the positives and that those positives may be the result of other healthy lifestyle choices by light-to-moderate drinkers over nondrinkers rather than the fact that they consume alcohol (Biddinger et al., 2022). The dietary guidelines for Americans caution against beginning to drink (or drinking more often) based on potential health benefits (USDA & USDHHS, 2020).

Caffeine and nutrition

Some studies show that caffeine may reduce the amount of food eaten by 10% at breakfast, with effects not lasting throughout the day (Panek-Shirley et al., 2018). Caffeine is a diuretic, especially when consumed in larger doses (Lohsiriwat, Hirunsai, & Chaiyaprasithi, 2011). There is little evidence of caffeine impacting nutrition in other ways as well. The indirect effect is more related to what drink or food is mixed with the caffeine. Some foods containing caffeine, such as coffee, green tea, and dark chocolate, may contain beneficial phytonutrients, while others may come loaded with added sugars and fats. In addition, many people put sugar and cream in their coffees or teas. This is not recommended. People may consume unhealthy food items and drink choices due to their desire for caffeine. In this way, caffeine may contribute to unhealthy nutrition habits. Another way caffeine may negatively affect nutrition is by disrupting sleep and triggering all the effects that lack of sleep or late bedtime may have on food consumption and food choices. Recommendations are to refrain from taking caffeinated drinks at least six hours before bedtime (Drake et al., 2013). As is stated in Chapter 11, caffeine binds to the same receptor as adenosine, and adenosine helps to signal the body to sleep. Thus, caffeine disrupts the sleep process if consumed too close to bedtime, since it has a half-life of four to six hours.

Tobacco use and nutrition

The influence of tobacco use, especially smoking, on the body's nutrition is multifaceted. Smoking has been shown to cause lower levels of vitamins C and B-carotene in blood plasma, bioavailability of selenium, and lower levels of vitamin E in the tissue of smokers, while at the same time, smokers have been shown to have a lower intake of fruits and vegetables, which could counteract those nutrients deficiencies (Preston, 1991). Smokers have often been shown to eat fewer meals, fewer calories, less nutritious foods (Stefanikova et al., 2009), and have a higher intake of fast food and overall more unhealthy nutrition (Heydari et al., 2014). This pattern of less food intake and using smoking for stress coping might be a reason why many people gain weight when they stop smoking and may go back to smoking as a way to control weight and stress (Bush et al., 2016). Stopping tobacco use has multiple health benefits, and successful tobacco cessation programs may also need to include developing healthy nutrition habits and better stress-coping practices, which may help with contracting possible negatives.

Marijuana (cannabis) and nutrition

It is a popular view that the use of cannabis products increases food cravings, especially cravings for highly palatable food items (high-fat and high-sugar foods). As the use of cannabis is increasing, there is research that shows that consumption of cannabis increases levels of the hunger hormone ghrelin, which is especially pronounced with the oral intake of cannabis (Farokhnia et al., 2020). Smoking marijuana has been shown to increase daily calorie consumption by 40% (Foltin, Fischman, & Byrne, 1988). While the research is not yet clear whether cannabis use causes weight gain, some THC-based medications are currently used to help HIV, cancer, and anorexia nervosa patients gain weight (Examine, 2024).

Substances like alcohol, caffeine, tobacco, and marijuana impact human physiology in many ways, including the sleep-wake cycle and hunger signals. Paying attention to the use of substances, how much a person uses, and when they use the substance is beneficial information. Are they using the substances for stress relief, to help them sleep, to keep them awake, or to numb themselves? Depending on the answers, different interventions are recommended. A referral to a mental health professional or an addiction specialist may be the most appropriate way to manage issues with risky substances. Evaluating a person's use of substances is part of a lifestyle medicine practice. It is crucial to help people adopt and sustain healthy eating patterns.

CHAPTER 11

Sleep and food choices: What we eat when we are sleepy

Beth Frates

Guidelines

Sleep recommendations from the National Sleep Foundation (Hirshkowitz et al., 2015):

- 7–9 hours of good quality sleep for 18-year-olds and older
- 8–10 hours for 14–17-year-olds
- 9–11 hours for 6–13-year-olds
- 10–13 hours for 3–5-year-olds
- 11–14 hours for 1–2-year-olds
- 12–15 hours for 4–11-month-olds
- 14–17 hours for 0–3-month-olds.

Importance of sleep

Modern lifestyles have ignored the importance of sleep. Functioning with a minimum number of hours of sleep is exalted as a badge of honor. Only recently has quality sleep been gaining more attention, especially for its role in preventing and treating chronic diseases. Multiple studies show that not getting the recommended amount of sleep regularly can cause numerous issues. Sleeping less than five hours a night increases the risk of death from all causes by about 15% (US Institute of Medicine Committee on Sleep Medicine and Research, 2006). Lack of sleep affects proper brain function, cognitive abilities, and emotional regulation, impacts the immune system, every major system in our body, and metabolic processes, increases the chance of developing chronic illnesses, and, over time, dramatically lowers a person's quality of life (Medic, Wille, & Hemels, 2017). Lack of sleep can impact our mood, outlook on life, productivity, creativity, sociability, relationships, exercise levels, and eating patterns (IMCSMR, 2006).

One serious hazard of lack of sleep is something most people need to consider, especially if they are over sixteen years old and they drive. It is DWD, which stands for driving while drowsy. How do people become drowsy? From a lack of sleep. In a 2013 survey, about 4% of adults in the U.S. reported falling asleep behind the wheel in the past thirty-day period (Centers for Disease Control and Prevention (CDC), 2013). Statistics from 2017 reveal that driving while drowsy was responsible for approximately 91,000 crashes that resulted in 50,000 injuries and almost 800 deaths (NHTSA, n.d.). Impairment in DWD is comparable to that of driving-under-the-influence (DUI) in terms of a person's reaction time. Our reflexes slow down when we drink alcohol, and they slow down when we are sleepy. For example, someone who has been awake for between seventeen and nineteen hours has a similar reaction time to someone with a blood alcohol level (BAC) of 0.05%, and someone who has not slept for twenty-four hours has a reaction time similar to someone with a BAC of 0.1%, which is over the BAC for being legally drunk, at 0.08% (Williamson & Feyer, 2000). When people are inebriated, they often feel like they can drive, and will insist on having their keys when friends try to rationalize with them and tell them they are too drunk to drive. Interestingly, when people are sleep deprived, they may also make this type of irrational decision, thinking that they don't have too far to drive and can make it to their destination.

Despite all the research on the value of sleep for overall health, the National Sleep Foundation reports that 32.6% of adults in the U.S. get less than six hours of sleep, which is an increase from 28.4% in the 2009 report (Suni & Truong, 2023).

To better understand what is necessary to experience restorative sleep, and how lack of sleep may affect our eating habits and the quantity and quality of food consumed, it is important to review the mechanisms that drive the wake-sleep cycle.

Neurobiology of sleep

Normally, in any twenty-four hours, people circulate between about sixteen hours of wakefulness and about eight hours of sleep. Maintaining stable wakefulness and sleep every twenty-four-hour period is crucial for the proper functioning of all physical and mental processes. This sleep-wake cycle is governed by a combination of two mechanisms: sleep-wake homeostasis and the circadian rhythm.

A small number of brain cells are responsible for keeping us awake or asleep. Some cells promote wakefulness, and others promote sleep. Those signals compete for the attention of the cerebral cortex and inhibit each other. Arousal centers that stimulate wakefulness are located in certain areas of the brain stem and the lateral hypothalamus. They produce the neurotransmitter (NT) orexin (a.k.a. hypocretin), which stimulates arousal centers by keeping them active. Orexin also stimulates the cerebral cortex. When signals from orexin are dominant, we are alert, conscious, and capable of complex brain functions and processes.

Neurons that promote sleep are in the area of the anterior hypothalamus called the ventrolateral preoptic area (VLPO), also known as the intermediate nucleus of the preoptic area (IPA). Neurotransmitters released from VLPO neurons—GABA and galanin—inhibit the activity of arousal regions, causing us to pass quickly into the unconscious state of non-rapid eye movement (NREM) sleep (Harvard Medical School, 2021). The VLPO is active during sleep, particularly NREM sleep, and is activated by the substance adenosine (Huang, Urade, & Hayaishi, 2011) and prostaglandin D2 (Urade & Hayaishi, 2011) and inhibited during wakefulness by the arousal-inducing NT norepinephrine and acetylcholine (Ma et al., 2018).

The circadian rhythm

This twenty-four-hour cycle of wakefulness and sleep, as well as other physiological and behavioral rhythms, is often referred to as the circadian rhythm. The internal master clock, also called *zeitgeber* (GER: time-giver), regulates the circadian rhythm. A small group of neurons in the hypothalamus called the suprachiasmatic nucleus (SCN) controls this sleep-wake cycle as well as many other physiological and behavioral rhythms occurring over a twenty-four-hour period. The SCN is influenced by light, especially blue light which is 470 nm wavelength. Melatonin also influences the SCN, helping to induce sleep. When sunlight stimulates retinal ganglion cells (RGC) behind the eyes, they produce the photo-pigment melanopsin. During the daytime, melanopsin "signals" to the SCN, which in turn induces the pineal gland to suppress melatonin production and secretion, and thus promotes wakefulness (Kohsaka & Bass, 2009; Pilorz et al., 2016)

Homeostatic sleep drive process

On the sleep-inducing side of the wake-sleep cycle, adenosine plays a crucial role. Adenosine is produced by the degradation of adenosine triphosphate (ATP), the molecule that serves as the "energy currency" for the body's cellular functions. Neurons and glial cells are particularly heavy producers of ATP, especially during wakefulness. High cell activity causes adenosine to build up, which triggers non-REM sleep (the period when the brain is less active), thus placing the brain and the body into the recovery phase, during which glycogen stores are rebuilt. Adenosine is constantly degraded by the enzyme adenosine deaminase, and adenosine production decreases quickly during sleep. Eventually, by morning, adenosine levels decrease to a point that is favorable for awakening (Bjorness & Greene, 2009).

With every waking hour, the homeostatic sleep drive strengthens. This strengthening is not directly measurable as a quantity, but experts think that it results from the level of brain activity during wakefulness. One hypothesis suggests that the build-up in the brain of adenosine, a by-product of energy consumption by cells, promotes the sleep drive. The fact that both adenosine and sleep drive increase during wakefulness and dissipate during sleep suggests a possible link between the two (Huang, Urade, & Hayaishi, 2011).

Figure 11.1 gives a graphic presentation of the interplay between the homeostatic sleep drive, circadian rhythm drive, and twenty-four-hour wake-sleep cycle (Deboer, 2018).

When we consider the wake-sleep cycle and how it correlates with the body's use and storage of energy, it is quite clear why sleep is crucial for the normal functioning of all body systems, including the nervous system. The mechanism is mediated through adiponectin, a protein hormone produced and secreted exclusively by adipocytes (fat cells) during sleep

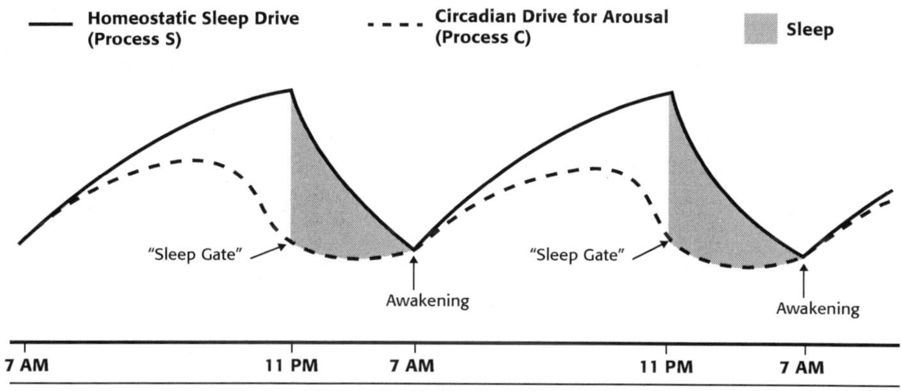

Figure 11.1. Homeostatic sleep drive and circadian rhythm interplay in sleep-wake cycle (used with permission from: Frates, B., Bonnet, J. P., Joseph, R., & Peterson, J. A. (2021). *Lifestyle Medicine Handbook: An Introduction to the Power of Healthy Habits* (2nd edn). Monterey, CA: Healthy Learning).

that regulates the metabolism of lipids and glucose (Sawamoto et al., 2016). Adiponectin influences the body's response to insulin (Havel, 2002), and it has anti-inflammatory effects on the cells lining the walls of blood vessels called endothelial cells (Ebrahimi-Mameghani et al., 2015). Studies have shown a dose-response relationship between short sleep duration and metabolic syndrome (Iftikhar et al., 2015). See Table 11.1.

Table 11.1. Day-night pattern of metabolic functions (created from the information in Covassin, Singh, & Somers, 2016)

Nighttime (Sleep–rest–fasting)	*Daytime (Wakefulness–activity–feeding)*
Adipose tissue: Lipolysis, fatty acid oxidation, leptin secretion	**Adipose tissue:** Lipogenesis, fatty acid esterification, adiponectin secretion
Brain: Growth hormone, melatonin secretion	**Adrenal gland:** Cortisol secretion
Muscle tissue: Oxidative metabolism	**Muscle tissue:** Glycolytic metabolism, fatty acid uptake
Liver: Gluconeogenesis, glycogen breakdown	**Liver:** Glycogen synthesis, cholesterol synthesis
Pancreas: Glucagon secretion	**Pancreas:** Insulin secretion
	Stomach: Ghrelin secretion

Many research studies emphasize the importance of getting enough quality sleep, and the timing of that sleep also matters. The full benefits of sleep are derived when people get their sleep at night. The presence of light when we sleep can disrupt the quality of sleep and its health-promoting function. A study of 40,000 women investigating, among other variables, whether women sleep with a light on nearby or in the same room found that those who slept with a light or television on in the room were 17% more likely to have gained eleven pounds or more during the study (Park et al., 2019). These findings might present some problems for shift workers, who often cannot get their sleep time during the night, and may suggest that it is important to recreate nighttime conditions with pitch dark when they go home in the morning. For this reason, night shift workers are encouraged to create nighttime conditions if they want to get restorative sleep during the day.

Sleep hygiene

With all the parameters we examined that influence and promote sleep, the following list of sleep hygiene steps is recommended (Cleveland Clinic, 2024; Suni & Rosen, 2009):

- Creating cave-like settings as sleeping environments promotes good quality sleep. That includes keeping it quiet (if the environment is noisy, use ear plugs), cool (60–70°F, 15–19°C), and dark. The sweet spot with temperature is 67°F (19°C), but people must experiment to determine what works best.
- Have regular sleep time and bedtime routines.
- De-stress and relax before sleep. Do some deep breathing or relaxing activities, and avoid activities that will increase arousal.
- Avoid blue wavelength (400–490 nm) light emitted by electronic screens, monitors, tablets, smartphones, televisions, light bulbs that are fluorescent, and compact fluorescent lights (CFL), which are more energy efficient. Blue wavelength light blocks melatonin production and secretion from the pineal gland. The recommendation is to avoid using electronic screens for at least two hours before sleep or to turn on sleep mode on devices that support it.

- Cultivate healthy daily habits such as healthy nutrition, physical activity, exposure to sunlight during the daytime, not smoking, and avoiding or limiting alcohol consumption. Alcohol disrupts REM sleep. Many people wake up in the middle of the night after drinking alcohol, and they have trouble falling back to sleep.
- Stop using caffeinated products at least four-to-six hours before sleep. Caffeine binds to the same receptor as adenosine but has the opposite effect. It has a four-to-six hour half-life and will disrupt the homeostatic drive for sleep. Caffeine metabolism varies, and some people are more sensitive to its effects.
- Don't eat for at least three hours before sleep, especially not heavy meals or meals that can cause heartburn, such as spicy foods, citrus fruits, fatty foods, fried foods, or carbonated beverages.
- Regular exercise promotes sleep, but it is good to avoid vigorous exercise too close to bedtime.

Nutrition and sleep

The relationship between food, eating, and sleep is complex and bidirectional. Sleep affects multiple metabolic processes in our body. Since both sleep and food impact our physical and mental energy levels, it is not uncommon that if one of those energy sources is neglected, our body will try to compensate with an increased desire for the other. Thus, lack of sleep may make us feel that we need to compensate for this low energy with increased food consumption, and lack of proper nutrition may make us tired and sleepy, which may prompt us to nap or sleep early to help us increase our energy.

Research on the intersection between sleep, food, and metabolism is multidimensional. Sleep deprivation has been shown to have multiple metabolic and endocrine effects, including an increase in cortisol, impairment of carbohydrate tolerance (increasing the risk for diabetes), disturbance in energy balance, and acceleration of the aging process (Copinschi, 2005).

Table 11.2 summarizes some of the research on sleep and nutrition interactions.

Table 11.2. Sleep and nutrition research summary

Sleep and hormones

- Sleep deprivation impacts hunger regulation hormones: ghrelin increases, fueling appetite (Schmid et al., 2008), and leptin decreases, also fueling appetite (Taheri et al., 2004). Leptin is the hormone that suppresses hunger and increases satiety or feeling full.
- Too little sleep triggers a cortisol spike. This stress hormone signals your body to conserve energy to fuel your waking hours (Hirotsu, Tufik, & Andersen, 2015). Chronically elevated cortisol levels prompt the body to store more adipose tissue, especially in the abdominal area, and to be more inclined to use other soft tissue, such as muscles, as energy. Thus, sleep-deprived dieters lose more muscle and gain adipose tissue, which promotes obesity (Marniemi et al., 2002).
- Within just four days of insufficient sleep, your body's ability to process insulin, a hormone needed to change sugar, starches, and other food into energy, is disrupted. Insulin sensitivity drops by over 30% (Broussard et al., 2012).

Sleep and weight

- A study following 21,469 adults aged twenty-plus for three years showed that people sleeping less than five hours per night were more likely to gain weight and become obese, while those with seven to eight hours of sleep were more successful in weight management (Kobayashi et al., 2012).
- When weight is lost under sleep deprivation conditions, it is more likely that the decrease in pounds comes from losing fat-free tissue rather than fat deposits. Dieters who cut their sleep to five and a half hours for a fourteen-day period lost weight, but compared to dieters who slept eight and a half hours, the amount of weight they lost from fat dropped by 55%. Their loss of fat-free body mass (muscle mass) increased by 60%. They also felt hungrier and less satisfied after meals, and their energy was zapped compared to those with adequate sleep (Nedeltcheva et al., 2010).

Lack of sleep influence on food intake

- Sleep insufficiency was associated with a significantly higher desire for high-calorie foods, which are known to contribute to weight gain. The magnitude of food cravings was proportional to the severity of sleep loss (Greer, Goldstein, & Walker, 2013).
- Study participants who slept only four hours ate 300 extra calories compared to those who got nine hours of rest (St-Onge et al., 2011).
- People with limited sleep showed increased activity in brain areas that view food as a positive reward, making them more vulnerable to overeating (St-Onge et al., 2012).

(*Continued*)

Table 11.2. *(Continued)*

- Sleep restriction (especially moving the bedtime later) increased late-night snacking, and people were more likely to choose high-energy snacks (Nedeltcheva et al., 2009).
- After a night of sleep deprivation, people ate about 14% larger meals than the people who had a full night's sleep, and about 16% of the food consumed was snack-type foods (vs. 6% of the food consisting of snack food in people who had a full night's sleep) (Hogenkamp et al., 2013).
- A review of studies on partial sleep deprivation and food consumption consistently showed that lack of sleep increased appetite and energy (food) consumption (Shlisky et al., 2012).
- Sleep restriction causes an amplified increase in endocannabinoid levels and a more active endocannabinoid system, which regulates mechanisms of food intake, lipid synthesis and turnover, and glucose metabolism in muscle cells. This increase in endocannabinoids also coincides with an increased desire for highly palatable foods (a.k.a. munchies). Sleep-deprived people choose snacks with two-times higher fat content than those with sufficient sleep (Hanlon et al., 2016).
- Lack of sleep impairs the function of the prefrontal cortex and decision-making capabilities, which leads to poor-decision making in multiple areas of life, including healthy eating (Harrison & Horne, 2000).

Food and eating habits influence on sleep

- **Heartburn:** Big meals may induce and exacerbate acid reflux, resulting in heartburn that can make it harder to get quality sleep (Vela et al., 2014). Heartburn may be more likely if overeating involves certain foods that can cause indigestion, such as spicy foods, fatty foods, and chocolate (Nisar et al., 2019).
- **Eating large meals** with certain foods can also disrupt sleep by increasing body temperature, which runs counter to the body's typical process of cooling down during sleep (S. J. Edwards et al., 1992).
- **Eating within three hours of your bedtime** increases the likelihood of sleep disruptions, and that risk may be even greater if you overeat at dinner (McHill et al., 2017).

If you could pick the right foods to help you get the best sleep possible, would you? And if you knew which foods would hinder your restful slumber, would you avoid them?

Table 11.3 gives a summary of foods that promote sleep and those we should avoid, especially before sleep time (St-Onge et al., 2016).

Table 11.3. Foods to include and foods to avoid for a good night's sleep

Foods that promote sleep

- Foods rich in tryptophan (precursor to serotonin and melatonin) dairy products, nuts, seeds, bananas, honey, eggs, turkey (Hartmann, 1982).
- Tart cherry: one week of tart cherry juice supplementation increased urinary melatonin concentrations, total sleep time, and sleep efficiency compared to placebo (Howatson et al., 2012).
- Minerals and vitamins: magnesium (almonds, bananas), calcium, B6—helps the body process tryptophan (poultry, fish, chickpeas, bananas), B3—extends REM cycle and limits instances of waking up mid-sleep (beets, pork, poultry, peanuts) (Ji, Grandner, & Liu, 2017; Lichstein et al., 2007).
- High-glycemic carbohydrate-rich foods (Afaghi, O'Connor, & Chow, 2007) complement dairy foods by increasing the level of tryptophan in the blood. Perfect late-night snacks: a bowl of cereal and milk, yogurt and crackers, or bread and cheese, warm oatmeal (it's soft and soothing; it has calcium, magnesium, phosphorus, and potassium). Of note, make sure the portions are small.
- Herbal teas:
    - Chamomile tea is non-caffeinated and may help with relaxation; drink it cold or lukewarm (Srivastava, Shankar, & Gupta, 2010). The mechanism may be through GABA, a naturally occurring amino acid that works as a neurotransmitter. It inhibits certain brain signals and decreases activity in the nervous system, leading to relaxation. Apigenin, a flavonoid found in chamomile, binds to benzodiazepine receptors GABA A in the brain.
    - Lavender—it is a flowering plant in the mint family. Studies suggest that lavender produces slight relaxing and calming effects when inhaled, as in aromatherapy, and it can also be used as a tea (Koulivand, Khaleghi Ghadiri, & Gorji, 2013).
- Fermented foods: total microbiome diversity was positively correlated with increased sleep efficiency and total sleep time and was negatively correlated with wake after sleep onset. There are also positive correlations between total microbiome diversity and interleukin-6, a cytokine previously noted for its effects on sleep (Smith et al., 2019).

  Fermented foods such as kefir, yogurt, fermented cheeses, sauerkraut, kombucha, kimchee, pickles, and miso are full of probiotics and help increase microbiome diversity.

(*Continued*)

Table 11.3. *(Continued)*

- Melatonin supplement: there is no recommended dietary allowance (RDA) for melatonin. Regarding melatonin supplements, some experts recommend a dosage of around 0.5–3 grams for sleep-related issues. Higher doses may cause daytime drowsiness.
- Food with high levels of melatonin: tart cherries (one of the best sleep aids), goji berries, eggs, milk, nuts (pistachios and almonds), fish (better source of melatonin than other meats—best is oily fish like salmon or sardine). Fish and nuts are also strong sources of omega-3 fatty acids that can enhance the brain's secretion of melatonin (Kuehn, 2022).
- Mediterranean style diet—this is associated with adequate sleep duration and fewer insomnia symptoms (Castro-Diehl et al., 2018).
- Meal quantity: a small snack is best if you feel you must eat before bed. Little food in your stomach may help you sleep. However, big meals can make it difficult to fall asleep.

Foods that disrupt sleep

- Heartburn-causing foods: certain foods are associated with heartburn, and it is best to avoid them before bedtime. These foods include tomatoes, citrus fruits, garlic, onions, chocolate, coffee, other caffeinated products, alcohol, and peppermint.
- High-protein and high-fat foods: protein-rich, high-fat foods are harder to digest and are a poor choice for bedtime snacks. Warm milk or a small slice of whole-grain bread with almond butter may work better.
- Caffeine binds to the same receptor as adenosine and has the opposite effect—it increases cell activity and adrenaline production. It has a half-life of four to six hours, so it is best not to have any caffeine-containing drinks or foods for at least six hours before bedtime. This includes coffee (even decaffeinated coffee), chocolate, tea, etc. (Drake et al., 2013; O'Callaghan, Muurlink, & Reid, 2018).
- Water before bedtime: it is good to stay hydrated, but large quantities of water shortly before bed may promote going to the bathroom during the night and disrupt sleep
- Alcohol: it may help you fall asleep faster, but you may experience frequent awakenings, less restful sleep, headaches, night sweats, and nightmares. It also reduces REM sleep. If you're consuming alcohol in the evening, balance each drink with a glass of water to dilute the alcohol's effects. For a good night's sleep, the best bet is to avoid alcohol for four to six hours before bedtime (Ebrahim et al., 2013).

Getting restful sleep is critical for your health. Set yourself up for sound sleep by paying attention to how much caffeine you consume, if you drink alcohol, and what you eat. There are foods that will disrupt your sleep by potentially giving you heartburn. And there are foods that may help you fall asleep. Knowing how the lifestyle medicine pillar of sleep influences the pillar of nutrition is important. Sustaining a healthy eating plan involves paying attention to your sleep.

CHAPTER 12

Empowering healthy eating patterns

Beth Frates

Healthy eating statistics

Regarding healthy eating, as already summarized in the introductory chapter of this book, a few basic recommendations have the highest value, such as adding whole foods like vegetables and fruits to each meal. Following the Healthy Eating Plate, half the plate is full of fruits and vegetables, a quarter is full of whole grains, and the other quarter is full of healthy proteins. In addition, it is best to avoid ultra-processed foods and sugar-sweetened beverages. Avoid trans fats, and eliminate or reduce saturated fat intake to less than 10% of daily energy value.

People struggle to reach basic healthy eating recommendations. For example, in the U.S., a 2017–18 survey found that only one-third of adults met the recommendations for limiting saturated fat (Bowman & Clemens, 2022). While evidence of the benefits of a whole-food, plant-based diet and especially high consumption of fruit and vegetables is mounting, a study in 2019 found that only 12.3% of U.S. adults met the fruit intake recommendations of two or more items, and only 10% met vegetable intake recommendations of three or more (Lee, 2022). The situation is not better in the rest of the world, as analysis of World Health Organization (WHO) data showed that the average vegetable intake in the population in 88% of world countries is below the recommendations

(Kalmpourtzidou, Eilander, & Talsma, 2020). Vegetables do not fall into the category of common foods people crave, and many people state that the main reason for low consumption is that they just do not like them. Conversely, lifestyle-induced noncommunicable diseases and resulting disability and deaths are becoming predominant in today's health landscape (World Health Organization, 2020). People need to learn how to prepare and cook vegetables with spices and herbs so that they are nutritious and delicious. The focus needs to be on making healthy foods scrumptious. Improving cooking skills and bringing the joy of cooking back into the home will also help.

With the staggering statistics shared above about fruit and vegetable consumption, something must be done. There is a significant amount of research focusing on theories and interventions that can be effective in promoting healthy eating and other healthy behaviors to reverse lifestyle-induced chronic disease trends.

Using food as medicine, providing prescriptions for produce, and prescribing medically tailored meals is becoming a focus for many organizations in the United States. These efforts require change on the part of the healthcare professional to use food as medicine. This is an important change. Changing society and making the healthy choice the easy choice is ultimately the most important change to make. People make choices each day. The goal is to empower people to create lifestyle patterns that align with the six pillars of lifestyle medicine no matter where they live, work, or play. That takes getting to know the patient or person by asking questions and listening, having patience for the change process, and practicing the COACH Approach™.

Behavior change theories for lifestyle changes

Counseling patients on healthy lifestyles is not the same as telling them what medication to take. Changing lifestyle behaviors requires different skills, including listening, guiding, working on resolving barriers, motivating, empowering, cocreating, setting goals, and other behavior change and coaching techniques.

One of the researchers who has made significant efforts to study behavior change for healthy lifestyles is behavioral epidemiologist Dr. Karen Glanz, a professor and the director of the Center for Health Behavior Research at the University of Pennsylvania.

Her studies found that the following four behavior change models were most effective for addressing health behavior changes (Glanz, Rimer, & Viswanath, 2015).

1. *Health Belief Model (HBM)*
   The HBM theorizes that people's beliefs about whether or not they are at risk for a disease or health problem and their perceptions of the benefits of taking action to avoid it influence their readiness to take action (Glanz & Bishop, 2010; Glanz, Rimer, & Viswanath, 2015).
2. *Transtheoretical Model of Change (TTM)*
   This model states that in the process of behavior change, there are five possible stages people can be in: precontemplation, contemplation, preparation, action, and maintenance. The stage of change the person is in will inform what behavior change tools and techniques are best suited to help move the person to the next stage. The progress through the stages is often not one-directional, and this model also recognizes that people experience relapses in behavior (Prochaska & Velicer, 1997; Prochaska, Redding, & Evers, 2002). People can be in action and fall back into contemplation. They can move from contemplation to action. This is not a step-by-step process, and the distinctions between the different stages can be a little gray.

   Table 12.1 gives a basic summary of the stages of change and counseling strategies that are effective for each of the stages:

Table 12.1. Stages of change description and counseling strategies

Stage of change	*Description*	*Counseling strategies*
Pre-contemplation	Not ready or willing to change	• Express empathy • Share a story about someone who was in a similar situation and was successful with change, if they express an interest in hearing it • Ask them what they need to be in place to even start to think about a change • Ask how you can help them in this moment • Ask if they could benefit from other services like social work, mental health, health coach, or nutrition counseling depending on their situation

(*Continued*)

Table 12.1. *(Continued)*

Stage of change	*Description*	*Counseling strategies*
Contemplation	Contemplating change, still weighing the pros and cons of change	• Work on decisional balance with the patient • Ask about the pros and cons of change • Ask how important the change is to the patient on a scale of zero to ten, with ten being the most important (if they answer five, ask why they said five and not two) • Ask how confident they are that they could make the change on a scale of zero to ten (if they say seven, ask what it would take to change that answer to an eight) • Explore their motivations for change
Preparation	Have realized the pros of change outweigh the cons, and have started to plan for the change	• Review any obstacles they see in their way • Brainstorm solutions around any obstacles • Ask what needs to be in place to start healthy behavior • Ask what resources would help them get started • Ask what support system they need in place to get started • Ask if there is someone who can join them in the journey or help keep them accountable
Action	Doing the new healthy behavior for six months or less	• Identify the benefits the person is experiencing from engaging in healthy behavior • Ask the patient what keeps them motivated • Ask the patient if they foresee any obstacles in the future, like a vacation or change in job • Ask the patient what is helping them stay on track and how they are keeping themselves accountable (this could be an app, a log with pen and paper, a scale, a pedometer, or many other measuring devices) • Ask what their goals are for the future

(*Continued*)

Table 12.1. *(Continued)*

Stage of change	*Description*	*Counseling strategies*
Maintenance	Doing the new healthy behavior for over six months	• Ask if the patient has considered being a mentor for someone just starting the behavior they are engaging in • Ask if they have put variety into their plan to keep them motivated in the long term • Ask what benefits they have noticed since performing the healthy behavior • Ask what motivated them to keep going • Ask what obstacles they may see in the future • Ask what their goals are for the future.

The stages are not linear. People can be in maintenance and fall into contemplation due to life circumstances, like the birth of a child, the death of a parent, the loss of a job, the purchase of a new home, and so many other factors. It is important to remember there is no time line for movement from one stage to the next. People progress on their own time line. The healthcare professional aware of these stages can target their counseling to meet people where they are, in the stage they are currently experiencing. Table 14.1 provides examples.

3. *Social Cognitive Theory (STC)*

   This is a social learning theory described by Albert Bandura (2010). It explains human behavior in terms of a three-way, dynamic, reciprocal model in which personal factors, environmental influences, and behavior continually interact. This theory combines several cognitive, behavioristic, and emotional models of behavior change that can be used in counseling interventions for disease prevention and management. Some of the most-used concepts and interventions include behavior modeling, behavior rehearsal, reinforcements, self-control, self-efficacy, goal setting, self-monitoring, and accountability. The key construct of STC is reciprocal determinism, postulating that a person can be both an agent for change and a responder to change. Also, changes to the person's environment can be used to further health behaviors.

4. *Social Ecological Model of Change*
   This model acknowledges several factors that influence a person and the effectiveness of a person's behavior change. These factors need to be combined to ensure the long-lasting success of behavior changes, and they include individual factors, such as knowledge, attitude, and skills; interpersonal factors, such as social networks; organizational factors, such as environment and ethos; and community factors, such as cultural values, norms, and public policy (Bronfenbrenner, 1977). When designing health-behavior change interventions and programs, all of these factors need to be addressed to succeed.

   It is essential that behavior change counseling be culturally sensitive. It is important to know the patient's background, heritage, and exposure to family traditions. Taking into account the Social Determinants of Health (SDoH) will help ensure that the recommendations shared will be in alignment with the patient's current life circumstances (see Figure 12.1).

Figure 12.1. Social Determinants of Health (U.S. Department of Health and Human Services: Free copyright permission. Figure source: USDHHS, 2024).

The Social Determinants of Health (SDoH) include:

- Economic stability
- Education access and quality
- Healthcare access and quality
- Neighborhood and built environment
- Social and community context

If a healthcare professional tells a patient to walk thirty minutes a day for five days a week, but there are no safe sidewalks or spaces to walk, this advice is not that helpful. Exploring the patient's home environment, work environment, and neighborhood is important so that any recommendations are tailored specifically to that person and their situation. Recommending that people consume five servings of fruits and vegetables is a solid suggestion, but knowing where the patient can obtain free produce is essential for this recommendation to become a reality. If no grocery stores supply fresh fruits and vegetables, then a discussion about the value of frozen fruits and vegetables is critical. Frozen fruits and vegetables are healthy options. Canned fruit in water—not corn syrup or sweetened juice—can also be healthy, as can canned vegetables. Canned foods may be high in salt, sugar, or added fat.

All of the theories described in this section are employed in one way or another in coaching interventions for implementing successful and long-lasting lifestyle changes.

Coaching conversations in lifestyle medicine

Collaborating with a patient through coaching conversations differs from telling a patient what to do with direct advice. Traditional healthcare providers mostly approach a patient from the point of view of an expert, which works well in most situations when treatment is urgent and acute, depends solely on their expertise, or requires only the short-term involvement of the patient. However, chronic diseases are becoming more prevalent, and the best line of treatment involves lifestyle changes, which require more effort and long-term involvement from the patient. The classical EXPERT Approach™ is not efficient or effective for chronic conditions that require long-term approaches and behavior

Table 12.2. Difference between the Expert Approach™ and the Coach Approach™ (used with permission from Healthy Learning (Frates et al., 2021))

EXPERT Approach™	*COACH Approach™*
• Treats patients • Educates • Relies on the skills and knowledge of expert • Strives to have all the answers • Focuses on the problem • Advises	• Helps patients help themselves • Builds motivation, confidence, and engagement • Relies on patient self-awareness and insights • Strives to help patients find their own answers • Focuses on what is working well • Collaborates

change. Adding a COACH Approach™ to the treatment mix will elicit better results. Table 12.2 shows differences between the EXPERT Approach™ and the COACH Approach™ (Frates et al., 2011).

There is a mnemonic for the COACH Approach™ and one for the EXPERT Approach™. If someone is working to empower another person to adopt and sustain healthy lifestyles, using the skills and characteristics in the COACH Approach™ mnemonic will be useful (Frates et al., 2019).

C—Curiosity
O—Openness
A—Appreciation
C—Compassion
H—Honesty

Many healthcare professionals need to use the EXPERT Approach™, especially in the case of emergencies and urgent care (ibid.).

E—Examine
X—X-ray and/or other radiologic studies and labs
P—Plan the treatment by using and analyzing all the information collected
E—Explain the treatment and the protocol
R—Repeat the instructions to the patient and family
T—Tell the patient what to do and what not to do

These are two different ways of being. They are both necessary in medical care. One is for acute care, and the other is for helping people manage their chronic conditions through lifestyle change.

Some studies have looked into communication styles that elicit change in the patient even in the short time physicians spend with a patient, which is sometimes only ten minutes. The study looked at three different communication strategies to encourage patients to engage in more physical activity. One group of physicians spent twenty minutes advising patients on the health benefits of exercise, explaining the risks of not exercising, and making current exercise recommendations. Another group of physicians spent the same twenty minutes negotiating and collaborating with patients by asking patients if they knew the benefits of exercise, finding out what level of physical activity the patients were currently doing, discussing the patients' barriers to better physical activity, brainstorming how to get around those barriers, and helping patients set their own goals for physical activity. The third group of physicians was a control group that just did normal physical exams, sometimes talking about physical activity and sometimes not at all.

At a twelve-month checkup, the study looked at the self-reported physical activity levels as a primary observed variable. The brief negation group showed the biggest improvement in increased minutes of physical activity per week between these three groups (Hillsdon et al., 2002). So the best use of those twenty minutes was collaborating and discussing increasing physical activity levels, not advising and telling the patient what to do.

Effective health and wellness coaching techniques and strategies

Research on the effectiveness of coaching in promoting healthy behavior changes is evolving. The following five landmark randomized control trials provide a brief overview of the positive effect coaching can have on cardiovascular disease, type 2 diabetes, asthma, and pain management. These studies were the foundational ones that helped to bring health and wellness coaching into academic medicine, and with time, it is slowly becoming part of mainstream medicine, with some health coaches serving on the lifestyle medicine healthcare team in clinics and hospitals in the U.S.

A study by Vale and colleagues (2003) conducted on 792 cardiovascular patients, with half assigned to a group with just usual care and the other half assigned to usual care plus coaching for change, showed substantially better improvements in total cholesterol measures in patients who were in a group with coaching intervention (–21 mg/dL) vs. those who were in usual care alone (–7 mg/dL). A Yale Nursing School pilot study on the effectiveness of a six-month nurse-coaching intervention for a group of women with type 2 diabetes showed women in the intervention group had better diet self-management, less diabetes-related distress, higher satisfaction with care, and trends of better exercise and BMI management (Whittemore et al., 2004). Another six-month coaching intervention for fifty-six diabetic patients improved patients' medication adherence, decreased their HbA1c, and, according to self-reporting by patients, lowered their perceived stress, improved their mood, and improved their exercise frequency (Wolever & Dreusicke, 2016). A two-year coaching intervention for parents of children with asthma showed a reduced rehospitalization rate in the coached group (36.5%) vs. the control group (59.1%) (Fisher et al., 2009). One twenty-minute coaching session on pain management among cancer patients at the two-week follow-up showed improved pain severity in the group that received coaching vs. the group that just had traditional pain management treatment (Oliver et al., 2001). Although this foundational body of research on coaching had some limitations in sample size, long-term follow-up, and lack of consistency in coaching practice, some common threads emerged. These studies showed that having a one-on-one relationship that encourages collaboration and negotiation between a health professional and a patient, and promoting goal setting and setting accountability, can help adherence to prescribed treatments and improve patient satisfaction with the treatment. Although health coaching is underresearched and underreported in the medical literature, there are elements of coaching, such as motivational interviewing and goal setting, which are more researched and are becoming more mainstream in medicine.

Research into health and wellness coaching (HWC) and its elements is expanding, and researchers have compiled and analyzed the developing data. One such systematic review found 219 articles related to HWC, 150 of which were data-driven research articles, and sixty-nine provided positive commentary on practical application (Sforzo et al., 2018). Creating such compendiums helps coaching and medical professionals easily find and access information on HWC and solidify definitions and parameters of HWC.

In that compendium article, HWC was defined as a client- or patient-centered process that assumes a working relationship/partnership develops between the patient and clinician to advance healthy lifestyle behavior change using tools such as nonjudgmental dialogue, goal setting, and accountability (ibid.).

Analyzing this body of research to find out how HWC and its tools can be applied to improving nutrition, physical activity, and other health behaviors yields some common practices and guidelines. A systematic review of nutrition and diet counseling methods finds cognitive behavioral therapy (CBT), motivational interviewing (MI), self-monitoring, meal replacement, and structured meal plans most effective. Goal setting, problem solving, and social support are other promising strategies that may need more attention (Spahn et al., 2010). Meta-analysis of randomized control trials with behavior change interventions for patients with type 2 diabetes showed improvements in both Hb1Ac and BMI. Most effective interventions included instructions and demonstrations on how to perform behavior, behavioral practice/rehearsal, action planning, and supervised and group sessions (Cradock et al., 2017). Another meta-analysis of interventions to increase self-efficacy for physical activity in obese patients adds time management, prompt self-monitoring, and planning for social support and social change to the list of effective behavior change techniques (Olander et al., 2013). Studies on nutrition behavior change interventions in older adults found that identifying barriers and problem solving for those barriers, as well as planning for social support and social changes, were the most effective techniques (Lara et al., 2014). Analysis of studies with long-term follow-up again found that goal setting and self-monitoring, including setting appropriate progress measurements and feedback, are successful for both short- and long-term change. In addition to techniques, this analysis also found that person-centered, autonomy-supporting approaches, such as motivational interviewing, usually yielded long-lasting results (Samdal et al., 2017). Autonomous motivation, self-efficacy, and self-regulation skills are confirmed in other research also to be good predictors of positive outcomes in weight and physical activity management (Teixeira et al., 2015).

In summary, goal setting, action planning, problem solving around barriers, social support, modeling behavior, behavioral rehearsal, self-monitoring and measuring of progress, receiving constructive feedback, support of autonomous motivation, and strengthening of self-efficacy are the most successful behavior change strategies and techniques. Conversely, one of the often applied strategies that has shown to have little effectiveness is financial motivators (Spahn et al., 2010). Specifically, when looking at the management of obesity in children, reward motivators, information about the negative consequences of behavior, and social comparison were ineffective (Martin, Chater, & Lorencatto, 2013).

The five-step cycle of behavior change

When working with patients on behavior change, a physician must utilize different tools instead of diagnostic technologies like MRIs, CTs, lab tests, angiograms, medications, injections, or surgery. One powerful road map for coaching is the five-step cycle of behavior change. According to this model, five elements need to be included for a fruitful process of behavior change. Figure 12.2 shows the elements of that coaching cycle (Frates, 2015; Frates et al., 2011).

1. Empathy is the capacity to understand, be sensitive to, and feel the feelings, thoughts, and experiences of another (Merriam-Webster, 2024). Empathy is part of the therapeutic relationship and has been identified as an essential ingredient in patient-centered counseling, as described by Carl Rogers since 1957. Rogers writes about the importance of empathy, "The therapist experiences an empathic understanding of the client's internal frame of reference and endeavors to communicate this experience to the client" (Rogers, 1957). Coaching is not therapy, but coaches can learn a great deal from the way that therapists build connections with their clients and communicate in a patient-centered approach.

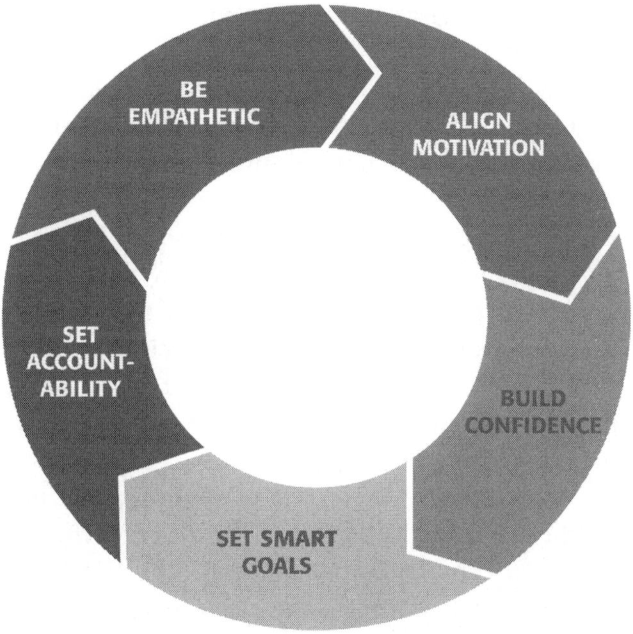

Figure 12.2. Five-step cycle of behavior change (used with permission from: Frates, B., Bonnet, J. P., Joseph, R., & Peterson, J. A. (2021). *Lifestyle Medicine Handbook: An Introduction to the Power of Healthy Habits* (2nd edn). Monterey, CA: Healthy Learning).

The keys to empathy are building a caring relationship, trusting and being trustworthy, listening deeply, reflecting, and being nonjudgmental, respectful, supportive, positive, optimistic, and genuinely curious. Showing empathy can go a long way, as research shows that chronic disease (type 2 diabetes) management is better in patients whose physicians scored higher on the empathy scale (Hojat et al., 2011).

Daniel Goleman (2011) identified three different types of empathy:

- Cognitive—"I know how you see things; I can take your perspective."
- Emotional—"I feel with you." Basis for rapport and chemistry.
- Empathic need—"I sense you need some help and I spontaneously am ready to give it."

2. In successful health coaching, coaches must access all three types, especially the last one. The only way to provide an "empathic need" to someone is to be fully present and mindful of the human being

in front of you. The healthcare professional must be undistracted, focused, open, and available.

3. Another good skill in building empathy and rapport is active listening. Listening can happen at three levels: level 1, or internal listening, where awareness is turned to internal monologue; level 2, or focused listening, where the focus is on another person; and level 3, or global listening, where all senses are used to better understand what is being said (Whitworth et al., 2007). Engaging in focused and global listening helps the patient or client feel heard, and that is a basis for developing trust and eliciting their willingness to share and listen to what they are being taught. Coaches think about generous listening and deep listening. Listening is a powerful communication skill.
4. Align motivation. Once there is a relationship of trust and the patient or client is comfortable answering the open-ended questions and engaging in conversation about their life's priorities, purpose, and values, motivation for change can be further explored and strengthened. Research has shown autonomous motivation is the best for eliciting and sustaining change.

   Motivational interviewing techniques are a good tool to use for evoking change talk. Miller and Rollnick (2023, p. 29) defined motivational interviewing as

   > ... a collaborative, goal-oriented style of communication with particular attention to the language of change. It is designed to strengthen personal motivation for and commitment to a specific goal by eliciting and exploring the person's own reasons for change within an atmosphere of acceptance and compassion.

   The underlying spirit of motivational interviewing is compassion, acceptance, collaboration, and evocation. During a motivational interview, a clinician focuses on promoting the client's welfare and prioritizing the client's needs. Miller and Rollnick emphasize that clinicians must honor the client's self-worth, internal perspective, unique strengths, and right to self-direction or autonomy. In addition, the process must be one of partnership and not coercion (Miller & Rollnick, 2023).

The focus is on change talk. Change talk comprises sentences and words illuminating the need for change and highlighting the possibility of change. The opposite is sustain talk, which is about staying the same. The clinician wants to elicit change talk when using motivational interviewing.

The change talk can be brought forward by focusing on positive emotions and experiences, like previous successes and personal strengths, that were used to accomplish past goals. That positive mindset and framing can help build self-efficacy and move them toward applying those strengths and lessons learned to current goals. As mentioned in Chapter 9 on mindsets, positivity can also help increase creativity.

Other motivational interviewing techniques that can be used in evoking change talk are known by the acronym OARS: Open-ended questions, Affirmations, Reflective listening, and Summarizing (ibid.). Using motivational interviewing has shown effectiveness in several medical care settings, with the most promising areas being lowering death rate, body weight, alcohol and tobacco use, and sedentary behavior, and improving self-monitoring and confidence in change (Lundahl et al., 2013).

After using motivational interviewing to engage the patient, focusing them on the behavior they are willing and ready to change, and evoking change talk to enhance motivation and align motivation, the patient is ready to make concrete plans (Crum, Leibowitz, & Verghese, 2017). Engaging, focusing, evoking, and aligning need to come before setting the goal. However, another important step before goal setting is building confidence. One of the problems encountered by healthcare professionals working to help people with behavior change is that they move to goal setting too early. Behavior change is a process, and it takes careful attention and time. Patience is key.

5. Building confidence is tied in with the concept of self-efficacy, the person's belief in their ability to change their behavior. One of the qualities that need to be developed for building confidence is the "growth mindset," the belief that one's intelligence and abilities can improve with practice (Dweck, 2008, 2015). If people think their abilities are

limited to what they are born with, which is termed a "fixed mindset," the first failure and setback may discourage them from continuing change. If they believe that with additional effort, they can improve, they will view mistakes and setbacks not as failures but as learning opportunities. This was reviewed in Chapter 7 on mindsets. Other elements that can help build self-efficacy are identifying people's strengths, developing a feeling of mastery by remembering past successes through a series of small achievements toward the goal, social support with encouragement by others, and seeing how others who are in similar situations have achieved the same goal (i.e., behavior modeling) (Pekmezi, Jennings, & Marcus, 2009).

Different questions to ask when helping to build confidence are:

- What are your strengths?
- How have you used your strengths to reach goals in the past?
- How can you use your strengths to help you reach this goal?
- In the past, how have you been successful with reaching goals?
- If I were to ask your friends what makes you unique, what would they say?

6. Set SMART Goals. The SMART acronym stands for Specific, Measurable, Action-oriented, Realistic, and Time-sensitive and is based on Edwin Locke's goal setting theory (Locke & Latham, 2006).

   This is a common acronym. The S, M, and T are consistent in the different variations of this acronym. However, the A and R are not consistent. Often the A stands for achievable, and the R stands for relevant. With goal setting in the business arena, where Edwin Locke originally developed his theory, making goals achievable and relevant to an employee or manager was critical. The goals in business are often about the profits and bottom line of the company. However, with coaching, the business is the person's life and health. So, the R does not need to be relevant. By definition, the patient or client is making the goal or cocreating it with the coach. Thus, it will be relevant to the patient because they developed it, not a manager, a doctor, or someone else. With coaching, the R is often realistic. The coach wants to make sure the patient or client can be successful. And the A is actionable for coaching because, with coaching, we do want to focus on taking action; even small steps toward change. Goal setting can provide a source of motivation, guidelines, and steps for reaching the desired outcome, as well as a sense of accomplishment, which can strengthen self-efficacy and motivation for further change. One sound methodology for goal setting is to have long-term and mid-term goals as guiding principles toward the final vision. However, the main focus should be on a series of short-term, achievable goals that can produce frequent motivating dopamine reward bursts. In addition, reaching goals gives people a sense of pride and thus can help increase serotonin.

7. Set accountability. Accountability can be set up in several ways, such as checking back with patients, using a buddy system to have them report to a friend, and using different self-monitoring strategies, including logging, applications, and tracking devices. Designing the right measurements for a given behavior may be useful. Still, one may need to be careful not to develop measuring myopia and not reduce people down to just numbers. To have an effective measurement system is helpful. However, do not let the number on the measuring tool become the target of change itself. One example of a problem with measuring is over-focusing on dropping numbers on the scale and losing weight. This misses the main point of behavior change.

There is a validated assessment tool that reviews all the pillars of lifestyle medicine called the Lifestyle Medicine Behavior Health (LMBH) Scale (Pangalangan et al., 2024). This tool can be used with patients to get a baseline of their lifestyle behaviors. Asking patients to fill this out annually can be eye-opening for patients and providers alike. It is the only assessment tool that covers all six pillars, and it has been validated. It can be downloaded on the website www.pavingwellness.org, which is a nonprofit dedicated to helping patients adopt and sustain healthy lifestyles. Other assessment tools and questionnaires specific to the patient's goals can be used for tracking.

The goals of eating healthily, having adequate physical activity, and gaining cardiovascular fitness are powerful and will help prevent, treat, and may even put into remission several chronic conditions. The behaviors are important and healthful even if the scale does not reveal a drop in weight. With healthy eating, one might need to be careful that over-focusing on the quality and quantity of food does not develop into problematic eating, limiting eating and social interactions, or even debilitating eating disorders.

There is a balance to life. A coach helps clients keep balance and keep moving forward. As Albert Einstein said, "Life is like riding a bicycle. To keep your balance, you must keep moving" (Einstein, 1930). SMART goals and accountability to them keep people moving forward. With the growth mindset, patients and clients are more open to trying new things, because they realize that any mishap is an opportunity to learn and grow.

Empowering people to adopt and sustain healthy lifestyles takes time, patience, perseverance, creativity, and compassion. However, it can be done. When coaching people, remember to use the COACH Approach™. The mnemonic COACH stands for Curiosity, Openness, Appreciation, Compassion, and Honesty.

CHAPTER 13

The psychology of product branding

Stelios Kiosses

Golden Arches. The swoosh. Chances are, you immediately thought of the brands these symbols represent. Branding is the way a customer perceives a company—for better or worse. It's the complete visual identity of a company, but ultimately, branding is about emotions and the feelings that are transmitted to the ideal customer. This matters because people make choices based on emotions, and brands appeal to emotions by creating trust. A brand strengthens the impact of all messages, and it's more than just a trademark, logo, or label—branding is a mark of promise, and can have a huge effect on the company, organization, person, country, and the world. That mark goes back to the etymology of "brand." The word derives from Old Norse, a Viking language in Scandinavia until the fourteenth century. *Brandr* meant "to burn," and later in history, the word came to identify the process of marking things—cattle, criminals, or slaves, for example—with a hot iron.

Today, branding is still about burning, but now the consumers are the cattle, and the marks are sustained psychologically. Brands today are created not in the world of matter but in the minds of people. Some interesting statistics: Research indicates that the average person is exposed to between 4,000 and 10,000 advertisements daily, requiring repeated exposure to marketing messages—often cited as seven to ten times—before they become memorable (Webtribunal.net, 2023).

Branding seems to have fostered a culture of irrationality in which the answers to our most precious and intimate needs for love, meaning, and identity have become projected and mediated through brands. Consumers keep running on the spinning wheel of desire—what Arthur Schopenhauer referred to as the "wheel of Ixion"—endlessly pursuing new desires. Ixion was a king in Greek mythology who tried to seduce Zeus's wife Hera. He was punished for this crime by being bound to a great fiery wheel that spun for eternity, and so his suffering was eternal. According to Schopenhauer, people can never be happy, and if we think we are happy, it is just a temporary state of not suffering. It's a closed circle that is very difficult to break, and not everybody can do that, which is why we are on a spinning wheel of Ixion.

Brands also intentionally keep us on the spinning wheel of Ixion. If we remain unaware of the psychological and mythological dimensions of brands, we risk having our emotions held captive by them, or more pessimistically, being coopted by them into a colonized psychological state in which a part of our self and our desires stays projected onto their shiny surfaces. On a practical level, brands plan for obsolescence such that consumers *have* to buy new versions of their products. On a psychological level, we continue to be fed in our collective unconscious through the symptoms or relief of fragmentation, dissociation, and cognitive dissonance.

Branding and the psyche

When your psyche wishes at any price to escape a feeling of disintegration and/or is constantly searching for a sense of identity or belonging, that is called fragmentation. Brands play off fragmentation by offering a community for us to become part of. There's a "tribe" that temporarily relieves anxiety and tension. Think about the iPhone and Android. There are heated arguments about which is better, with people vehemently arguing for one over another. Why? Because there's an identity wrapped up with each device that "says" something about you, the consumer.

Dissociation involves a disconnect between reality and perception, often manipulated by brands to create a hyperreal experience where the symbol or image becomes more significant than the reality it represents. Brands like Disney create worlds where the experience and emotional gratification offered are far removed from everyday reality. That leads consumers to associate the brand with an idealized version of life. This manipulation of reality helps brands maintain a strong emotional grip on their consumers.

The dissociation process is best described by George Orwell in his book *1984*: "If one is to rule, and to continue ruling, one must be able to dislocate the sense of reality." Brands seem to have been constructed to lead our libido astray by stimulating and promising emotional gratification that is never satisfied other than illusorily. French philosopher Jean Baudrillard described this as "hyperreality," where the sign, image, and symbol become more real than reality. Coca-Cola's branding goes beyond selling a beverage; it sells an experience and a lifestyle associated with happiness and social connections. The brand's advertising often depicts idealized scenes of joy and togetherness, creating a hyperreal image that consumers aspire to. Other examples of hyperreality include the following:

- A sports drink flavor that doesn't exist ("wild ice zest berry")
- A plastic Christmas tree that looks better than a real Christmas tree ever could
- Instagram and TikTok filters
- Entertainment news programming and supermarket tabloids
- Portraying foods in advertisements that don't exist.

The food you see in commercials isn't edible. Steam comes from a heated cotton ball that is placed behind the food. Glue is used as a substitute for milk because it lasts longer in shoots. Wax is added to sauce so color pops and ice cream is typically made out of Play-Doh or mashed potatoes so it doesn't melt. You can't even eat the food that's being shown to you.

The last way brands feed into our unconscious is through cognitive dissonance. This describes the discomfort experienced when two cognitions are incompatible with each other. A cognition is a piece of knowledge, such as a thought, attitude, personal value, or behavior. In 1957, psychologist Leon Festinger stated human beings always try their level best to have internal consistency, meaning that their beliefs, thoughts, and opinions match their actions, behavior, and attitude to avoid mental tension of any kind. If dissonance, discomfort, or inconsistency of any kind is experienced, we tend to feel psychological discomfort and strive hard to reduce it, or to avoid it altogether. Advertisers try to paint a picture that your life isn't complete without their product or service. Many use cognitive dissonance to point out the inconsistencies between the idealized version of you and the real-life you. You experience dissonance because you want to see yourself in that idealized way.

Brands often use cognitive dissonance to their advantage by creating marketing strategies that highlight the dissonance before offering their product as a resolution. For example, a health-conscious consumer might experience dissonance when tempted by fast food; a brand like McDonald's might alleviate this by marketing healthier menu options, thus resolving the dissonance and retaining the customer.

Also consider the marketing strategies of tobacco companies. Smokers experience dissonance knowing the health risks but continue to smoke. Brands often mitigate this by emphasizing filtered cigarettes or "healthier" alternatives, thus providing a mental loophole for the consumer to reduce their discomfort without changing their behavior.

Another common example of cognitive dissonance is the rationalization that takes place when people "cheat" on their diets. How many times have you committed to healthy eating when a doughnut or another unhealthy food item threatened to take you off course? Maybe you thought, "Eh, it's only one muffin. I'll skip lunch today to make up for the calories." Or you tell yourself, "It's not actually that many calories," or "My diet will start on Monday." You want to think of yourself as a healthy eater, and so you rationalize your behavior when you aren't eating in that way.

Here's a clinical example of cognitive dissonance. A client who is overweight has been advised by her physician to follow a certain diet and exercise to reduce any possible health risks. The diet includes completely removing junk food. She knows why changing her diet is important, yet she keeps binging on cakes and burgers. She tells herself, "It's OK. Cheating once in a while is allowed!" "I'll just exercise extra tomorrow and work this off," or "The doctor is being unfair, my diet doesn't really have to be this strict." By telling herself this, she reduces the dissonance she feels when she doesn't eat healthily, and adds new cognitions that support her conflicting behavior and will outweigh her original belief about the need for a diet change.

Brand archetypes

Brands don't only evoke emotions, they also tell stories via mass and social media that follow certain archetypal structures or root metaphors. Archetypes are universal narratives of expression associated with ideas and images found in myths, legends, folktales, and religions across cultures and generations. There are twelve primary brand archetypes.

The Innocent is happy, optimistic, and pure. Examples of brands that use this archetype are Coca-Cola and Dove. The Innocent appeals to consumers' desire for simplicity and happiness. You see this in Coca-Cola's advertising, which often features happy, smiling people enjoying Coke. This can evoke positive emotions in consumers and create positive associations with the brand.

With Dove, there's an added layer of mythology, as the soap brand was named after Aphrodite, the goddess of beauty and love; the dove was her symbol. The message from the company, which is reinforced by the logo, is that if you use their soap, your skin will look beautiful and smoother.

The Explorer is adventurous, ambitious, and daring. Examples include Jeep and Patagonia. The Explorer connects with consumers' urge to explore and discover.

The Sage displays wisdom, intelligence, and knowledge. Examples are Google and the BBC. These brands appeal to those seeking truth and learning.

The Hero shows courage, determination, and bravery. Examples are Nike (the Greek goddess of victory!) and Adidas. The hero inspires consumers to overcome challenges and achieve greatness.

The Outlaw is rebellious, disruptive, and revolutionary. Examples of this archetype in brands are Harley-Davidson and Virgin. The archetype resonates with those who challenge the status quo.

The Magician is a visionary, someone who is imaginative and innovative. We see the Magician in Apple and Disney, both of which appeal to consumers' desire for transformation and making dreams come true.

The Lover is passionate, intimate, and sensual. Examples are Victoria's Secret and Chanel. Brands using this archetype appeal to those who value relationships and beauty.

The Jester is fun, playful, and humorous. Examples include M&Ms and Old Spice. These brands connect with consumers looking for joy and entertainment.

The Everyman is relatable, down-to-earth, and friendly. Examples include IKEA and Budweiser. This archetype appeals to people who value belonging and acceptance.

The Caregiver is compassionate, nurturing, and protective. Examples of this brand archetype include Johnson & Johnson and UNICEF. The Caregiver archetype resonates with people who value care and support.

The Ruler is authoritative, commanding, and controlling. Examples of this archetype in brands are Mercedes-Benz and Rolex. Both brands appeal to those who value power and status.

The Creator is similar to the Magician, but more than being imaginative, the Creator is also artistic and wants to support others with their creativity and self-expression. Examples of brands that do so are Adobe and LEGO.

It's not only that brands use character archetypes—they also draw from mythology, as we see with Nike but also Starbucks. The Starbucks logo uses a twin-tailed siren from Greek mythology, and according to Greek mythology, the twin-tailed sirens were beautiful but dangerous sea creatures who used their beauty and melodious music to lure sailors to their deaths.

Another example is Versace. The company's logo is Medusa's head, which is full of snakes in place of hair. Medusa could turn anyone who looked at her to stone, and she was transformed into a beast by Athena. However, it was also believed that anyone who fell in love with Medusa couldn't flee from her, and that is also the message of the fashion brand.

The psychology of color in branding

Just as companies think about mythology with their brands to stimulate the unconscious, they are also thoughtful about which colors to use. For instance, red is associated with excitement, energy, passion, and urgency. Seeing the color red increases the heart rate, stimulates appetite, and is often used to attract impulse buyers. Coca-Cola uses red to evoke feelings of excitement and energy, which align with its branding message of happiness and refreshment. Target and Netflix also use red to create a sense of urgency and excitement.

Blue is associated with trust, loyalty, dependability, and calmness. It conveys a sense of security and reliability and is often used by tech and financial companies, such as Facebook and American Express.

Yellow conveys happiness, optimism, and cheerfulness. It stimulates mental activity and attracts attention, but too much yellow can cause anxiety. You'll notice that IKEA and Nikon use yellow to grab attention and convey positivity and clarity, but both logos are tempered with other colors. Also, yellow is particularly effective at drawing in window shoppers. Flash sale signs often use both red, to convey urgency, and yellow, to grab attention.

The color green is associated with growth, tranquility, health, and nature. It evokes feelings of calmness and serenity and is often used by eco-friendly and health-related brands. The color also suggests wealth and stability. You'll notice that Whole Foods uses green to highlight its connection to health and environmental consciousness.

Orange signals creativity, enthusiasm, and warmth. It conveys friendliness and confidence. It's often used to appeal to younger audiences and encourage impulse purchases. Nickelodeon uses orange to reflect creativity and fun, while Home Depot uses it to suggest affordability and value.

Long considered the color of royalty—because it was a difficult and expensive color to produce—purple signals luxury, wisdom, and spirituality. It implies high quality and exclusivity and is often used by luxury and creative brands. Hallmark uses purple to appeal to its predominantly female audience and convey a sense of sophistication. Cadbury uses purple to convey luxury and indulgence.

Black is associated with power, sophistication, and elegance. It creates a sense of authority and luxury and is often used in high-end products. Examples are Chanel and Nike, both of which use black to convey sophistication and timelessness to enhance their brand's perception of quality and prestige.

The color white is associated with purity, simplicity, and cleanliness. It evokes feelings of openness and clarity and is often used in minimalist and modern designs. For instance, Apple uses white to communicate simplicity and innovation and to create a sleek and modern brand identity. With so much thought and research put into influencing us, it's difficult sometimes to judge which recommendations come from careful studies and which are based on oversimplifications, gut feelings, and hidden personal or commercial agendas. It has been estimated that the typical American makes up to 200 food decisions a day, and research suggests that most of them are reactive and made without much thought. That's in part because companies start targeting people when they're children, and so decisions become automatic and long-running.

Food decisions start early

Take the example of McDonald's. Locations have a playground in bright primary colors. The food is sweet, salty, and fatty, which you eat with your fingers. There are tie-in toys with the "Happy Meal" to further entice children to beg their parents for a Happy Meal. Why? Because brand loyalty can be established by the age of two! Market research has found that children can recognize a brand logo before they can recognize their own name. In a study of thirty-eight Australian preschool children of three to nearly five years old, McAlister and Cornwell (2010) revealed that while they cannot read yet, they often knew exactly which logo corresponded to which brand, including those for fast food chains (McDonald's) and entertainment companies (Disney and Warner Brothers). McDonald's was the most recognized brand, with nearly 93% of children correctly identifying the restaurant chain by its golden arches.

This early loyalty is critical for fast food brands because it can influence children's taste preferences and consumption patterns for life. Studies have shown that children are more likely to prefer the taste of foods if they are associated with a familiar and trusted brand, such as McDonald's. An experimental study (Robinson et al., 2007) involving children of "3.5 to 5.4" years old found they preferred the taste of identical foods and beverages when they believed they were from McDonald's compared to when they were in unbranded packaging.

Connell, Brucks, and Nielsen (2014) demonstrated how this can persist into adulthood. Study participants viewed images of characters that would have been widely advertised when they were children. The results showed that when people are exposed to advertising using characters before age thirteen, they develop positive long-term feelings toward the characters and the brand's nutrition for years to come.

In the case of McDonald's, it's not only the mascot Ronald McDonald that creates a positive feeling—it's the logo itself. The M stands for McDonald's, but the rounded "m" represents mummy's mammaries, according to the design consultant and psychologist Louis Cheskin. In the 1960s, McDonald's was prepared to abandon the logo, but Cheskin successfully urged the company to maintain this branding with its Freudian symbolism of a pair of nourishing breasts. He was a very strong supporter of Freud's theory on how sexuality drives all aspects of human behavior and argued that the maternal association with the breasts would be what persuaded customers to eat at McDonald's instead of eating homemade food. In part, he was right, also because this long-time positive association with junk food brands can lead people to prefer junk food over healthier food options and thus can contribute to unhealthy eating habits later in life. Some people thus assume that fast-food branding and advertising are the reason many people have gained weight and why the population is physically bigger now than ever before. But is fast food really to blame?

The real culprit behind weight gain

Body shape and size are complicated. A whole host of factors go into whether a person is gaining weight—stress, poor sleep, medication, hormone changes, an imbalanced gut microbiome, and more. It is not mathematically possible for 15–18% of calories coming from fast-food restaurants to cause 67% of the population to be overweight. Too much fast food is partly responsible for fatness in America and the world, but it may also be that we are just eating too much food in general.

Portion sizes for fast food have increased over the last fifty years, but portion sizes have increased across the board at all restaurants, and in the home environment, over the same period. The more food we see in front of us, the more food we are likely to eat. Vending machines reach out to us with their bright graphics. Food images are everywhere, enticing us to eat and eat more. Foods high in calories, fat, salt, and sugar seem to increase our desire to eat more food rather than satisfy our hunger. Branding plays a powerful role in shaping consumption patterns, especially when it comes to high-calorie, high-sugar foods and beverages. Companies such as Coca-Cola and PepsiCo have developed marketing strategies that associate their products with positive emotions, personal identity, and social connection. For instance, Coca-Cola's "Share a Coke" campaign used personalized names on bottles to encourage sharing and social engagement. Research has shown that such branding tactics can significantly influence consumer behavior, particularly among young people. Harris, Schwartz, and Brownell (2009) found that marketing and brand exposure increase children's preferences for sugary drinks and snacks, while Andreyeva, Kelly, and Harris (2011) linked food advertising exposure to increased consumption of energy-dense products. These strategies, while commercially effective, have raised public health concerns due to their potential contribution to the overconsumption of added sugars—a risk factor for obesity, type 2 diabetes, and other diet-related diseases (Malik et al., 2010).

Snack food companies like Frito-Lay and Doritos use branding to create a sense of excitement and indulgence around their products. This can encourage overconsumption of unhealthy snack foods, often high in calories, fat, and salt.

Where are the ethics in branding? Especially when targeting vulnerable populations such as children, we as a society seem to be in an "anything goes" phase. This has some very serious consequences though, as we're seeing. In the short term, companies are profiting and improving their bottom line, but in the long term, people are harmed when ethics fly out the window. There must be a balance between effective branding and responsible marketing practices. Companies can succeed if they take into account the well-being of their consumers. And especially with the rise of social media, brands are not able to get away with the things they were before, because their actions and any repercussions become public.

Social media and modern branding

Social media has become an indispensable tool in modern branding because it provides businesses a platform to engage directly with their audience, build brand awareness, and foster community. The immediacy and accessibility of social media allow brands to interact with their customers in real time and help to create a dynamic and engaging brand presence. Consistent and strategic use of social media can significantly enhance brand visibility and credibility.

Due to direct engagement and real-time interaction, brands can respond to customer inquiries, address complaints, and participate in conversations about their products and services in a very public way.

This real-time interaction not only improves customer satisfaction but also builds trust and loyalty. The converse is also true—real-time interaction, if it's callous, poorly handled, or counter to what the company claims to care about, can turn customers off. Brands can directly affect customer retention not based on the product itself but on how they're presenting themselves on social media. This is why consistent messaging across all social media channels is crucial for reinforcing brand identity and values. While maintaining consistency, brands must also adapt their strategies to the evolving dynamics of each platform and its audience. That means tailoring content to fit the specific style and format of each social media site, such as short-form videos for TikTok or professional updates for LinkedIn. Also, the tone and language of each social media site is different. What goes viral on TikTok likely will not fly on LinkedIn.

Another big difference in modern branding? The role of influencers, user-generated content, and viral marketing. Influencer marketing leverages the reach and credibility of social media personalities to amplify brand messages. By partnering with influencers who resonate with their target audience, brands can tap into established communities and gain authenticity. Influencers can create content that aligns with the brand's voice and values, helping to attract a wider audience and boost engagement.

User-generated content (UGC) encourages customers to create content related to the brand, such as reviews, photos, and videos, which can significantly enhance brand perception. UGC provides genuine testimonials and social proof, making the brand more relatable and trustworthy. Featuring UGC on the brand's social media channels can also foster a sense of community and belonging among customers, further strengthening brand loyalty.

Lastly, what every brand hopes to achieve is viral marketing. Viral marketing campaigns aim to create content that is highly shareable and resonates deeply with the audience. These campaigns can rapidly increase brand visibility and awareness by leveraging the power of social media shares and interactions. Successful viral marketing often involves creative, humorous, or emotionally impactful content that encourages users to share it with their network, thereby expanding the brand's reach organically. It's essentially free advertising that puts a brand in the public eye—for better or worse. Where will branding evolve from here? It's hard to say, but given how society is trending, it's likely AI, personalization, and sustainability will be involved. Gen Z in particular cares about personalization, sustainability, and ethics.

One study by Bain & Company and Depop (Levato & Colacchio, 2021) found that when it comes to daily life, 90% of Gen Z participants reported making changes in their daily lives to live more sustainably. They also have a different view as to what sustainability means. Petro (2022) found that not only does Gen Z think sustainability means products made from recycled, sustainable, and naturally harvested fibers and materials, but close to 50% also take into account sustainable manufacturing when defining what sustainable products are, showing their awareness of sustainable materials and supply chains.

Tidswell (2023) reports that social values also matter to Gen Z. In one survey, 75% of them stated they want to see brands ensuring employee and consumer safety. Tidswell also reports in another survey that 60% of respondents considered brands' commitments to diversity and inclusion when making purchasing decisions. Lastly, 70% were influenced by fair wages when choosing where to spend their money. Brands would do well to take these concerns into consideration because otherwise, they might find themselves obsolete.

We are all influenced by branding whether we recognize it or not. By being more conscious of archetypes, the psychology of color, and how companies manipulate consumers, we will all be able to make better choices in our daily lives that align with our values. This applies not only to food but to everything.

CHAPTER 14

Gastrophysics: An introduction

Charles Spence

Introduction

One of the most disturbing indicators concerning the state of culinary nutrition here in the U.K. is the sheer amount of junk food that is sold in hospitals. The last thing that one would expect to see in those institutions dedicated to the health and well-being of those they look after would be vending machines stuffed full of sugary confectionary. However, that is exactly what one finds (Speir, 2016)! The fact of the matter is though that hospital food concessions are highly profitable. For example, the hospital branch of Gregg (a popular bakery chain in the U.K.) is the second busiest in the land (Williams, 2015). At the same time, however, suggestions that fast food companies should be banned from selling junk food in hospitals have fallen on deaf ears (Spencer & White, 2015), presumably because of the profits involved (Anon., 2016; Campbell & Johnson, 2016). In fact, three decades ago, Ritzer (1993) was already complaining about the presence of McDonald's in North American hospitals.

Flavor expectations and flavor experiences

It is generally assumed that the provision of healthy and nutritious food is something of a luxury within the (health)care system. As Tyler Cowen

(2012) writes in *An Economist Gets Lunch*, no one expects the food to taste good in hospital, and so it doesn't. Several decades of research have demonstrated just how profoundly our expectations influence taste, flavor, and food quality ratings. This is perhaps best illustrated by those studies in which the same prepared meals are served to those in different environments. Ratings are often significantly lower when the same food is served in the context of a prison or hospital, say, than they are in the context of a hotel dining room (J. S. A. Edwards et al., 2003). The power of expectation to bias people's food experiences may also help to explain why it is that at one fancy Swiss neuro-rehabilitation center that I visited a few years ago (https://cereneo.ch/), they were unable to provide food to match what the patients, and their families (many of whom came from the Middle East), might have eaten at home, much though they tried. This was surprising, inasmuch as one of the Michelin-starred kitchens in the hotel attached to the center was used to prepare the patients' food.

Could this be a version of the well-known Provencal Rose Paradox (see Spence, 2017a; Spence & Piqueras-Fiszman, 2014)? This refers to the observation that the same wine tastes much better on one's summer holiday in the Mediterranean than back home on a cold winter's night. Considering the problem in such a light leads to the suggestion that simply changing the name of the dish and/or the environment in which it is presented might do more to enhance the patient's experience of the food than merely tweaking the recipe (see Bell et al., 1994, for evidence supporting this suggestion). The lowered mood of patients and their worried families likely also negatively affected their rating of the food they were served, though that may be something that is much harder to fix. For example, a "mental palate cleanser," such as the mooing plastic cow, is used to playfully elevate the guests' mood prior to eating in Denis Martin's Swiss restaurant (https://denismartin.ch/; see Spence, 2017a; Spence & Piqueras-Fiszman, 2014) would presumably not be appropriate, given the gravity of the situation that is likely facing those concerned.

Gastrophysics: Focusing on the food

Using ice cream as a vehicle for nutrient delivery

One of the areas that we have been working on in recent years relates to the design of nutritionally enhanced ice creams, based on seeing my mother's unfortunate decline from Alzheimer's a few years ago. For the last half-year or so, about the only thing that anyone could get her to eat was ice cream (cf. Cockroft, Spillett, & Duell, 2016). This was surprising, inasmuch as I don't remember her eating, or especially liking, ice cream before. It may be that my mother (like many other octogenarians) was functionally anosmic (this being the technical term for someone who is unable to smell). Indeed, the scientific evidence suggests that the elderly on medication (which is, after all, the majority of them) may need as much as twelve times as much salt in a bowl of tomato soup to achieve the same taste sensation as they did when they were younger (Stevens et al., 1991). In my mother's case, the cold temperature perhaps provided a salient sensory cue in the absence of any input from the chemical senses (Eccles et al., 2013).

Chef Jozef Youssef developed a range of healthy ice creams designed to have familiar flavors for those in their later years (see also Casas et al., 2012). In this case, the flavors included Heinz cream of tomato soup, prawn cocktail, and bone marrow (Spence, Navarra, & Youssef, 2019; Spence & Youssef, 2021). Using protein powders and a PacoJet (https://pacojet.com/en-GB/),[1] the chef was able to achieve a wonderfully creamy texture without the need for fat. That said, the cost of these machines (c. £5,000) is likely to place them out of the league of all but the most well-funded care establishments. However, as soon as the ice creams started to appear, we realized that there was a danger of "disconfirmed expectation" (Yeomans et al., 2008). For instance, Yeomans and colleagues have already shown how pink ice creams that don't taste sweet (i.e., of strawberry) can all too easily lead to a negatively valenced disconfirmation of expectation response (see Piqueras-Fiszman & Spence, 2015; Spence, 2017a). As such, we were careful to clearly name and describe the flavors in advance.

Tackling the problem of metal mouth

Many patients undergoing chemotherapy suffer from "metal mouth" , the lingering unpleasant taste sensation elicited when eating and drinking (Reith & Spence, 2020; Ruiz-Ceamanos, Spence, & Navarra, 2022).

[1] This is a modernist or molecular gastronomy piece of culinary equipment. However, looking back, it is interesting to note "sous vide" (Baldwin, 2012), which is currently popular among many of the top chefs, is a technique that first emerged in Switzerland in the 1960s as a way of preserving and sterilizing the food served in hospitals. The technique was further refined in 1967 by French chef Pralus in his restaurant in Roanne.

While the physiological causes of this condition have yet to be figured out, there is nevertheless scope to consider why metallic couldn't be turned into a desirable taste/flavor sensation, perhaps if it were first experienced outside of a likely negatively valenced healthcare situation. After all, if stinky French cheese, not to mention stinky tofu, can be made desirable, I wonder if there are any taste/flavor sensations that are necessarily, fundamentally, and unalterably unpleasant? My challenge to chefs is therefore to consider whether it would be possible to develop a delicious metallic-forward menu. After all, metallic sometimes does pop up as a desirable flavor characteristic when, for example, pairing champagne and oysters (https://archivio.letitwine.com/en/oysters-and-champagne-match-not-made-heaven/).

Gastrophysics: Focusing on the "everything else"

Patients eat first with their eyes

It was Apicius (c. 1st century) who first suggested that we eat with our eyes. A large body of contemporary cognitive neuroscience and marketing research supports the Roman gourmand's early suggestion (Spence et al., 2016). For example, even something as simple as balanced central plating of food (when compared to unbalanced asymmetric plating) can lead to a marked difference in people's perception of, and willingness to pay for, even a very standard plate of food (Michel et al., 2015). Unfortunately, however, the visual presentation of food in many U.K. hospitals is frightfully bad (see Poulter, 2017, for a few examples), with little, if any, care (or thought) seemingly being given to the presentation of the patient's food in the setting of (health)care. Relevant here is the fact that simply improving the visual presentation of a meal has been shown to increase food intake (and to decrease readmission rates) among hospitalized patients (Navarro et al., 2016).

An emerging body of research demonstrates that the color of plateware can not only enhance the visibility of hospital food for those with visual deficits (see Spence, 2017a, 2017b) but can even modify the taste/flavor of the food (see Piqueras-Fiszman et al., 2012, for early findings; and Spence, 2018, for a review of the burgeoning literature in this area). For example, in one U.K. hospital study, the effects of introducing new plateware were pretty dramatic. In particular, simply switching from the standard white to high contrast blue plates led to those elderly and weak patients taking part in the intervention consuming nearly a third more food (Adams, 2013). While such results are undoubtedly promising, and fit within the broader literature on gastrophysics, one always needs to be careful to look out for the Hawthorne effect (McCambridge, Witton, & Elbourne, 2014). This is the name given to the phenomenon that any behavioral changes resulting from a given intervention might be caused by the study group in question appreciating that someone is taking an interest in them, rather than necessarily being a result of the experimental intervention, whatever that might happen to be. It would be good to see longer-term follow-up studies to better understand how long the effects last.

The art and science of food naming and description

It has long been known that the way in which a dish is described on the menu or meal sheet can exert a profound effect over people's food choices as well as their sensory-discriminative and hedonic response to it (Spence, 2017a; Spence & Piqueras-Fiszman, 2014). For instance, when some bright spark came up with the idea of renaming Patagonian toothfish as Chilean sea bass some years ago, sales of this healthy, nutritious, and reasonably sustainable fish increased by 1,200% in the U.K., North America, and Australia. A recent series of studies has demonstrated that customers in North American canteens were significantly more likely to choose the vegetable options if they were given an appealing sensory description rather than a health-related description (Turnwald et al., 2019; Turnwald, Boles, & Crum, 2017; Turnwald & Crum, 2019).

Noise, music, and soundscapes at mealtimes

Noise is a well-recognized problem that will be familiar to anyone who has spent time on the wards as a patient. Not only does it stop patients from getting the sleep they need to aid recovery, it can also interfere with the perception and enjoyment of food at mealtimes (cf. Alamir & Hansen, 2021). At the same time, music and nature soundscapes (such as the sounds of the sea) have been used to help calm agitated psychiatric patients and lead to their consuming more (Goddaer & Abraham, 1994; see also Spence & Keller, 2019). Intelligent acoustic interventions can, in other words, improve the patient's mealtime well-being in hospital dining environments (Mathiesen et al., 2021).

Commensality

Eating is a fundamentally social activity (Pliner & Bell, 2009; Spence, Mancini, & Huisman, 2019). According to the results of one NHS study that took place across six hospital trusts, having an assistant give elderly patients an extra meal a day halved their chances of dying while in hospital (Patel, 2019). Addressing the more social aspects of eating (and drinking), it is intriguing to see how one French hospital opened a bar in their palliative care unit, funded largely by donations from the drinks industry (Newton, 2014).[2] Once again, such an open-minded approach would seem to recognize that eating and drinking are fundamentally social activities, and as Brillat-Savarin once noted, *'The pleasures of the table, belong to all times and all ages, to every country & to every day; they go hand in hand with all our other pleasures, outlast them, and remain to console us for their loss'* (Brillat-Savarin, 1825b). The trend may be catching on, with a local pub opening in a care home for the elderly in Tewkesbury a few years ago (Burrows, 2017).

Conclusions

The principal contribution of the emerging study of the science of gastrophysics (Spence, 2017a) to culinary nutrition is to help emphasize the "everything else" beyond the food itself (though this is, of course, also important) that influences the experience of eating and drinking. This includes everything from the plateware to plating (i.e., visual presentation), and from the cutlery (Michel, Velasco, & Spence, 2015) through to the background music/noise (see Spence & Youssed, 2021). The suggestion that "The pleasures of the table reside mainly in the mind not the mouth" (Spence, 2017a, 2017b) is likely to be just as true of those who find themselves eating in a (health)care facility as for anyone else.

---

[2] This, note, is a little different from the U.K. hospital, mentioned by Jamie Goode (2005, pp. 190–196) where, following a heart attack, patients are prescribed two glasses of red wine per day.

Contrasting with the negative synopsis of junk food in hospitals with which I started, there are signs that a focus on culinary nutrition really can work. For instance, just take the headline of an article that appeared in the British press a few years ago concerning Hinchingbrooke Hospital, Huntingdon: "Is this hospital a miracle cure for the NHS? It has a Michelin chef, happy patients and is run by doctors and nurses. And shock, horror, it's operated for the state-at a profit-by a private firm" (see Jones, 2014). Ultimately, I would argue that gastrophysics offers the exciting opportunity to nudge people towards eating more healthily and/or more sustainably, no matter what their status in life (Spence & Youssef, 2016). And while the focus in this brief review has been very much on the use of gastrophysics insights to benefit culinary nutrition in the adult and elderly sections of the population, similar approaches are also being trialed with younger children (Youssef et al., 2022). For example, in one ongoing project, we have been working with an international hospital for children with cancer in Barcelona. My colleagues have already redesigned the meal tray experience, introducing playfully decorated paper sheets to enliven the plastic meal trays, and using fast food packaging to make the kids think differently about the food that they are served.[3] The preliminary results look promising.

[3] Note here that already by seven years of age children judge that burgers taste better if they believe that they come from McDonald's (Robinson et al., 2007).

CHAPTER 15

Practical gastronomy and developing taste and flavor in cooking

Neil Rippington

Introduction

Taste and flavor are central to the culinary arts, contributing significantly to the sensory experience of eating. Developing a sophisticated palate and the ability to create balanced, flavorful dishes is a journey that combines scientific understanding, practical skills, and artistic intuition. This chapter explores the key components and strategies for developing taste and flavor in cooking, with references to culinary science, professional practices, and sensory analysis.

Understanding taste and flavor

Taste and flavor, though often used interchangeably, refer to distinct sensory experiences. Taste is detected by taste buds on the tongue. Flavor, on the other hand, is a more complex perception that combines taste with aroma, texture, and temperature, as well as psychological and contextual factors (McGee, 2004).

When we talk about taste, we are referring specifically to the five basic categories of taste that are known and recognized. Four tastes were initially determined, with a fifth identified more recently.

The initial four basic tastes:

Sweet Typically derived from sugars, sweet flavors are often associated with energy-rich foods.

Sour Acidity, found in citrus fruits and fermented products. The acidity of citrus fruits is used to brighten and balance other flavors.

Salty Salt enhances overall flavor, including sweetness, and counterbalances bitterness. Think of the enhancement of caramel with salt to make salted caramel.

Bitter Often a warning signal of toxins, bitterness in small amounts can add complexity to dishes.

With the later introduction of:

Umami Known for its savory taste, umami is present in meats, cheese, and fermented products, contributing depth and richness (Yamaguchi & Ninomiya, 2000).

The discovery of umami

At the beginning of the twentieth century, Japanese chemist and Tokyo Imperial University professor of chemistry Kikunae Ikeda noted that an unidentified taste quality, distinct from the four basic tastes (sweet, salty, sour, and bitter) was present in many appetizing foods. He detected this taste most clearly in soups and in "dashi" (a Japanese stock) prepared from kelp (*konbu*) or dried skipjack (*katsuobushi*), both of which are commonly used in traditional Japanese cooking. Subsequently, Ikeda investigated the constituents of the dried konbu and discovered the taste to be contributed by the glutamate it contained. He named this taste "umami" (Kurihara, 2009).

Umami translates as "pleasant savory taste," often described as brothy or meaty. The umami taste is found in foods that contain a high level of the amino acid glutamate. Umami-rich foods include Parmesan cheese, seaweed, miso, soy foods, mushrooms, savory stocks, and products such as yeast extract (often used as a breakfast spread on toast).

The discovery of umami in areas of the Western diet stems from many of the sensory qualities from cooked meats (animal fats) when compared to Japanese cuisine, which is generally lower in fats and more reliant on "dashi." In the West, Brillat-Savarin, in his classic 1825 treatise *The Physiology of Taste*, proposed the name "osmasome" to identify the essence of a meaty taste, but was not able to isolate the key substance, as later identified by Ikeda.

The tongue as the tasting organ: A brief history of the taste map

This taste map was created following research in 1901 by German scientist David Hanig (Hanig, 1901). His results were generally in order, but the differences in sensitivity were subtle. Many people in the trial reported the four basic tastes on many parts of the tongue, yet the results were misrepresented due to a mistranslation of Hanig's findings and conclusions. Surprisingly, the flawed and oversimplified taste map, in its various forms, has survived the test of time and has been used for the last century as a teaching tool identifying specific sections of the tongue as major taste receptacles, appearing in hundreds of texts, guides and publications.

Later, in 1942, American Harvard psychologist and professor Edwin Boring created a new chart giving the impression that the differences were significant in the various regions of the tongue. Work since,

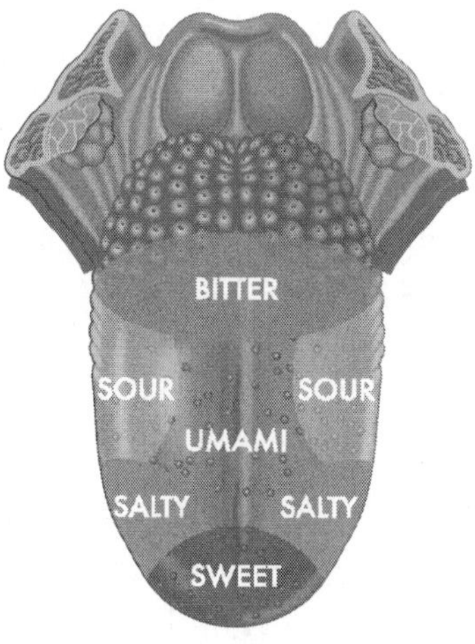

Figure 15.1. The taste map

however, including that of University of Pittsburgh scientist Dr. Virginia Collins in 1974, suggests that the map was oversimplistic, with far too many taste buds to consider. Collins found that all tastes can be detected anywhere there are taste receptors around the tongue, on the soft palate at the back roof of the mouth, and even in the epiglottis.

Interestingly, nearly all life-forms have a sense of taste—the ability to recognize chemicals in their environment to distinguish whether an item might be nutritious or dangerous. Taste and smell, the chemical senses, were the first senses to evolve. Moths have taste receptors on their wings, flies have them on their knees, tarantulas taste with their feet, and octopi taste with their whole body, including their eyelids.

Humans also have taste receptors in several unexpected parts of the body. For example, we have taste receptors in our pancreas, liver, and testicles. When we inhale something noxious, we have taste receptors in our lungs that send a signal to the brain to make us cough to expel harmful contents. We have taste receptors in our nose that help fight infections, and taste receptors in our gut that influence our perception of food. The taste receptors in our gut also tell the brain whether we should keep eating and when to stop, and it is believed that disturbances in the signaling pathways of these receptors play a role in the development of diet-induced illnesses, from irritable bowel syndrome to diabetes. However, only the taste receptors located inside the 5,000 (and up to 20,000 for supertasters) taste buds on the tongue and, perhaps surprisingly, taste buds that are located on the roof of the mouth and in the throat, are hooked up to the cortex in the brain that gives us the perception of what we call taste.

In addition to the five basic tastes, there have been proposals for other sensations to be considered as additional basic tastes, including fatty, crisp, cool, spicy, and astringent. However, scientific evidence supporting their status as basic tastes remains limited.

Smell, taste, and flavor—the difference

The sense of smell can be critical in life events, including avoiding predators, finding receptive mates, recognizing terrain, and locating food. However, compared to other species, smell in humans appears to play a lesser role in survival, especially when compared to our reliance on vision and hearing. Nevertheless, our smell can significantly impact our pleasures. The loss of smell (please try the experiment below) affects our sense of taste and can lead to decreased appetite.

Our smell can also recapture memories, as described in the classic novel *Remembrance of Things Past* (*À la recherche du temps perdu* in the original French, literally translating as *In Search of Lost Time*) (Proust, 1927). This nostalgic experience is often referred to as the "Proust Phenomenon," after author Marcel Proust describes a scene from a long-forgotten scent of madeleines and lime-blossom tea and the recollection of a forty-year-old memory of emotions and settings.

"Smell and taste form a single sense, of which the mouth is the laboratory, and the nose is the chimney" wrote Jean Althelme Brillat-Savarin (1755–1826). Brillat-Savarin was a French lawyer, politician, and the author of the then-groundbreaking book *Physiologie du goût*, translated as *The Physiology of Taste* (1825a). This apt quote is taken from his culinary reminiscences and reflections on the craft and science of eating and the art of cookery. It emphasizes the importance of the nose in the consumption (and hopefully) enjoyment of eating (Shepherd, 2012).

Brillat-Savarin identified the important role of smell in taste but did not differentiate between taste as a single sense and flavor as a combined sense of smell and taste. The close relation between smell and taste has obscured the dominant role of smell.

The enjoyment of eating food is a complex sensory experience involving multiple senses, including taste, smell, and texture. Among these, the sense of smell plays a crucial role, and it is experienced through two different pathways: orthonasal and retronasal olfaction.

Try this simple experiment

- Place a small amount of powdered/ground cinnamon at the tip of a teaspoon. Using your forefinger and thumb on one hand, squeeze your nostrils to block them. With the other hand, place the cinnamon on your tongue. Describe what you can taste. What is happening in the mouth?

Most people answer with responses ranging from "nothing" to "dry" and a "gritty" sensation. Some may refer to a slight heat.

- Next, release the forefinger and thumb from the nostrils and breathe in through the nose. Describe what happens now.

Practically everyone responds with "Wow, a burst of cinnamon." The mouthfeel changes completely.

Olfaction

Orthonasal olfaction refers to the detection of odors through the nostrils. When we smell food before it enters our mouth, orthonasal olfaction is in action. This initial aroma can set expectations and trigger anticipatory pleasure, influencing how much we will enjoy the food once we start eating it. For example, pleasant smells can stimulate appetite and enhance the desire to eat. The olfactory epithelium is structurally adapted to function as a sensory system. It comprises three distinct cell types: basal cells, olfactory sensory neurons, and sustentacular (or supporting) cells, sensing environmental chemicals and odorants (Moon, Jun Yoo, & Soo Han, 2014).

The aroma of food can set expectations about its flavor, which can affect the overall eating experience. For instance, the smell of freshly baked bread can evoke positive emotions and enhance the anticipation of its taste. Orthonasal olfaction can influence our choices of food. Aromas perceived as pleasant can attract us to certain foods, while unpleasant smells can deter us.

Retronasal olfaction, alternatively, occurs when volatile compounds released from food in the mouth travel up the back of the throat to the nasal cavity. This pathway is activated during chewing (maceration) and swallowing, playing a critical role in the perception of flavor. Retronasal olfaction integrates with taste to create the perception of flavor. While taste buds on the tongue detect basic tastes (sweet, sour, salty, bitter, umami), the complex flavors we experience come largely from retronasal olfaction.

The combination of taste and smell through retronasal olfaction is essential in the enjoyment of food. Without it, food can taste bland

and uninteresting. For example, when someone has a cold and their nasal passages are blocked, they often report that the food lacks flavor. This was also a commonly reported symptom during the Covid-19 global pandemic. Retronasal olfaction allows us to perceive complex flavors and subtle nuances in food, such as the richness of a curry or the delicate flavors in a fine wine.

The interaction between orthonasal and retronasal olfaction

Both pathways work together to enhance the overall eating experience. The initial orthonasal smell can set up expectations, which are either confirmed or adjusted by the retronasal olfaction as we eat. The sense of smell is closely linked to memory and emotion. Orthonasal and retronasal olfaction can evoke memories and emotional responses, adding layers of enjoyment and satisfaction to eating. Understanding the importance of orthonasal and retronasal olfaction can have practical applications in various fields: Orthonasal and retronasal olfaction are fundamental to the enjoyment of food. They work together to create a rich, multisensory experience beyond simple taste, influencing our appetite, food choices, and overall enjoyment of eating. Dishes can be enhanced to provide appealing aromas, taste and flavor profiles, heightening the overall dining experience.

Aromatic compounds, detected by the olfactory system, significantly influence flavor perception. Herbs, spices, and cooking methods like grilling or roasting can enhance aromatic complexity. Texture and mouthfeel, including factors like creaminess, crunchiness, and tenderness, form a crucial role in the enjoyment of food. The temperature of food can affect the release of aromatic compounds and the perception of taste (Spence, 2017a).

Can we smell sweetness?

Strawberries have much less sugar than blueberries but are consistently rated much sweeter. This is because strawberries have so many more volatiles, around 360 compared to blueberries, which have 38. Strawberries also contain fewer carbohydrates and sugar than blueberries, although blueberries are higher in fiber. Blueberries contain double the quantity of sugars and carbs as strawberries, although the sweet aroma of strawberries leads many people to assume they are higher in sugar (sweetness).

The Maillard reaction: Enhancing the flavors of food

The Maillard reaction, named after French chemist Louis-Camille Maillard, is a chemical reaction between amino acids and reducing sugars upon heating. This reaction is responsible for the complex flavors, aromas, and browning observed in various cooked foods, contributing significantly to the sensory qualities that make food appealing. The Maillard reaction is a cornerstone of culinary science, impacting everything from the crust of a seared steak to the rich flavor of roasted coffee.

The mechanism of the Maillard reaction

The Maillard reaction begins with condensing an amino group from an amino acid and a carbonyl group from a reducing sugar. This initial step forms what is referred to as a "Schiff Base," which rearranges to produce Amadori compounds. These intermediates undergo further complex reactions, including rearrangements, fragmentations, and polymerizations, leading to various flavor compounds and brown pigments known as melanoidins (Chandra, Bharagava, & Rai, 2008). This sounds very complicated, but it is a form of caramelization where the amino acids in proteins interact with sugars, eliciting a range of pleasurable aromas and flavors.

The Maillard reaction produces several flavor compounds, including aldehydes, ketones, and heterocyclic compounds. These compounds contribute to the depth and complexity of flavors in cooked foods:

1. Aldehydes and ketones: These compounds impart sweet and floral notes. For example, furfural, derived from the degradation of sugars, contributes sweet, almond-like aromas.
2. Pyrazines: These are responsible for roasted, nutty, and earthy flavors, common in baked goods, coffee, and roasted meats.

3. Thiazoles and oxazoles: These sulphur-containing compounds contribute to the development of meaty and savory notes, enhancing the umami profile of foods.

The Maillard reaction in culinary applications

The Maillard reaction is crucial in many culinary techniques and food preparations. In bread and pastry, the Maillard reaction occurs at the crust, creating desirable golden-brown colors and complex flavors. The reaction enhances the sensory appeal of baked goods, not only in the appealing appearance of the items but in the tempting aromas of freshly baked products.

In roasting and grilling, when meats and vegetables are exposed to high heat, the Maillard reaction produces a flavorful crust, enhancing taste and aroma. The reaction creates a variety of volatile compounds that contribute to the characteristic flavor of roasted foods. This is similar in seared and grilled meats where the Maillard reaction develops the savory crust. The interaction between proteins and sugars at high temperatures forms a flavorful exterior, textural development, and contrast, alongside mouthwatering aromas.

The roasting of coffee beans and cocoa also results in the Maillard reaction, essential for developing the rich, complex flavors and aromas of coffee and chocolate. The reaction transforms simple sugars and amino acids into a spectrum of flavor compounds.

While the Maillard reaction is fundamental for flavor development, it also produces compounds that may have health implications. Advanced glycation end-products (AGEs), formed during the Maillard reaction, are linked to aging and chronic diseases when consumed in excess. However, moderate consumption as part of a balanced diet is generally considered safe.

The Maillard reaction is a pivotal process in the culinary world, enhancing cooked foods' textures, flavors, aromas, and appearance. Understanding and controlling this reaction allows chefs and food scientists to optimize the sensory qualities of a wide range of foods. While there are health considerations to be mindful of, the Maillard reaction remains an essential tool for creating delicious and appealing food. The Maillard reaction remains a testament to the intricate science behind cooking, turning simple ingredients into complex and enjoyable culinary experiences.

Techniques for developing taste and flavor

Good food comes from good ingredients, but with so many ingredients carrying such a wide range of properties, it becomes a complex scenario.

High-quality, fresh ingredients usually provide superior flavors. Seasonality and sourcing from reputable suppliers will provide a solid foundation to enhance the taste of dishes. Nature is the original flavorist, and balancing the five basic tastes is fundamental. For example, adding a touch of sweetness to a sour dish can create harmony, while a bit of acidity can enliven a rich, fatty dish. In the culinary arts, a simple mixture of sugar (or honey, maple syrup) and vinegar, known as a "gastric," boiled to a liquid and added in small quantities can provide excellent balance, particularly in meat- and tomato-based sauces.

Developing depth in dishes involves layering flavors through different cooking techniques and ingredient combinations. Patterson and Aftel (2018) discuss the four layers of flavor. Rule 1 describes how similar ingredients need a contrasting flavor. Too much harmony becomes safe and a little boring. Dishes need a counterpoint to punctuate a dish. Adding different notes through the controlled addition of herbs and spices adds aromatic and flavor complexity. Understanding their properties and how they interact is crucial. For example, cumin adds warmth and depth, while basil provides fresh, sweet notes.

On the contrary, Rule 2 describes how contrasting ingredients need a unifying flavor, a bridge. In the example of a cauliflower dish with cumin seed and browned butter, the flavors are rich and intense; however, the use of browned butter unites the cauliflower and cumin, and the addition of lime zest cements the bridge. Its fresh green note locks both ingredients and balances the flavors.

This dish needs acidity for balance. The lime zest provides spark, performing almost like a herb, but the deep and savory flavors benefit from another counterpoint. Lime juice on its own will diminish the savory qualities achieved. Acidity diminishes umami and dilutes concentration. To take this further, lime juice is added to Greek yoghurt for a bright, sharp accompaniment. This provides relief without undermining the flavors of the cauliflower.

Rule 3 demonstrates how heavy flavors need a lifting note. For example, a parsley-lemon gremolata for a pot roast, or a pinch of citrus to lift and lighten a pudding. The biggest roles in a dish tend to be played by the heaviest, densest flavors, but they do not necessarily contribute to making the dish distinctive or memorable.

Rule 4 illustrates how light flavors need to be grounded; they need a platform from which to perform.

The use of bases from vegetables, broths, sauces, and umami-rich ingredients provides the grounding for a delicate and delicious combination.

Marinating proteins or vegetables allows flavors to penetrate deeply, while infusing oils or liquids with herbs and spices can add subtle, nuanced flavors. Continuous tasting and adjustment during cooking are vital to ensure the dish is heading in the right direction. Professional chefs often rely on their palate to make incremental adjustments and adjust seasonings, particularly at the end of the preparation and cooking before serving guests.

Terpenes and phenols

Terpenes and phenols are crucial in delivering flavors in food due to their distinct chemical properties and interactions with our sensory receptors. Terpenes are a diverse class of organic compounds produced by plants and some insects. They are responsible for the aromatic qualities of many herbs, fruits, and spices. Here are a few examples of how they contribute to flavor:

Aroma and fragrance

Limonene: Found in citrus fruits, delivers a fresh, zesty aroma.

Pinene: Present in pine needles and herbs like rosemary, offers a piney, resinous scent.

Myrcene: Common in hops and bay leaves, has a musky, earthy fragrance.

Terpenes interact with our taste receptors and enhance the perception of flavors. For example, the terpenes in basil amplify the savory taste of a tomato-based sauce. Terpenes work synergistically with other flavor compounds to create complex flavor profiles. This interaction can enhance the overall sensory experience of the food.

Their counterpart, phenols, are a class of chemical compounds consisting of a hydroxyl group (-OH) bonded directly to an aromatic hydrocarbon group. They are known for their antioxidant properties and their contribution to flavor enhancement.

Phenolic compounds like tannins contribute astringency and bitterness in foods and beverages such as wine, tea, and chocolate. Phenols have antioxidant properties, which help to preserve food and add a depth of flavor. For example, the phenols in olive oil contribute to its distinct peppery and bitter notes. Phenolic compounds add complexity to flavors. In coffee, phenols contribute to the rich, roasted flavor. In smoked foods, phenolic compounds from the smoke impart a deep, smoky flavor.

Both terpenes and phenols are abundant in herbs and spices. For example, thyme contains thymol (a phenol) and linalool (a terpene), contributing to dishes with its unique flavor. Citrus fruits are rich in terpenes like limonene and phenolic compounds like flavonoids, providing a vibrant, complex flavor profile. The phenolic compounds in tea and wine contribute significantly to their flavor, aroma, and mouthfeel, creating a rich sensory experience.

Terpenes and phenols play essential roles in flavor delivery in foods. Terpenes primarily contribute to aroma and flavor enhancement, while phenols add astringency, bitterness, and complexity. Together, these compounds create the diverse and rich flavors we experience in various foods and beverages.

Conclusion

Sensory analysis involves systematic evaluation of food using the senses. This scientific approach helps us to understand how different factors affect taste and flavor perception (Stone, & Sidel, 2004). Developing a refined palate requires practice and exposure. Tasting a wide variety of foods, noting their flavors, and understanding the role of different ingredients and techniques can enhance one's ability to discern subtle differences.

Traditional cuisines offer a wealth of knowledge about flavor combinations and cooking techniques that have been refined over centuries. Exploring these traditions can provide inspiration and a deeper understanding of flavor development. While tradition is important, innovation drives the culinary arts forward. Experimenting with new ingredients, techniques, and flavor pairings can lead to unique and memorable dishes (Spence, 2017a).

Developing taste and flavor in cooking is a multifaceted process that combines scientific principles, sensory skills, and creative expression. By understanding the components of taste and flavor, employing effective techniques, and continuously training the palate, we can create dishes that are not only balanced and harmonious but also rich and complex. Both tradition and innovation play pivotal roles in this ongoing journey of culinary exploration. Happy cooking!

CHAPTER 16

Cutlery: The science and sensory experience

Neil Rippington

Introduction

As the Earth's human population reaches 8 billion, we remain fairly evenly split in terms of the number of people who eat using chopsticks, knives and forks, or from the hands.

Why is it that, culturally and historically, we have adapted to the daily custom of eating in such different ways? Why is it considered rude or uncouth to eat with our hands in certain cultures and circumstances, yet it is viewed as perfectly normal and acceptable in others?

Chopsticks are used by billions of people around the world, particularly in many East Asian countries. The Chinese are believed to have been using chopsticks since at least 1200 BC, spreading their use throughout Asia, and into countries including Cambodia, Korea, Vietnam, and Japan. Interestingly, in Thailand, a combination of cutlery and chopsticks is used, depending on the dishes being served.

The early use of chopsticks was mainly as apparatus in cooking. A population explosion across China saw resources stretched, and cooks began preparing food into smaller pieces to speed up the cooking time and to utilize less fuel. The dishes, as presented, matched perfectly to the use of chopsticks. It was, indeed, a match made in heaven!

While there have been radical changes to crockery and plateware in recent times, it has not been the same for cutlery. This suggests an opportunity for further innovation to deliver a more experiential offering at the table. This is explored later in the chapter.

The psychology and power of tradition and perceived social etiquette

To demonstrate the significance of tradition and perceived social etiquette, I refer to two examples from the worlds of a novelist and a TV entertainment show. In Martel's magical realism book *Life of Pi* (2001), set during a period of troubled times in India, a young boy, Pi, finds himself on a journey to start a new life in Canada. At the end of an epic journey to reach his new home, Pi describes his first dining experience. Although a fictional tale, the paragraph provides a powerful insight to the hurtful consequences someone can cause through a lack of understanding and awareness of another person's cultural norms. (Not to mention diabolical customer service!)

> The first time I went to an Indian restaurant in Canada I used my hands and/or fingers. The waiter looked at me critically and said, "Fresh off the boat, are you?"
>
> I blanched. My fingers, which a second before had been my taste buds savouring the food a little ahead of my mouth, became dirty under his gaze. They froze like criminals caught in the act. I didn't dare lick them. I wiped them gently on my napkin.
>
> He had no idea how deeply those words wounded me. They were like nails being driven into my flesh. I picked up the knife and fork. I had hardly ever used such instruments. My hands trembled. My sambar lost its taste.

On a lighter note, I refer to a classic sitcom series. In the episode "The Pledge Drive" of the U.S. TV sitcom *Seinfeld* (Seinfeld & David, 1994), the writers provide hilarious scenes of the cast eating chocolate bars and doughnuts using knives and forks rather than directly from the hands, as would be expected. The show humorously makes fun of the "haughty" superiority and the sophisticated nature of "society types" and how this leads to others following suit to keep up with trends and appearances. The clips strike very clear, and funny, examples to demonstrate how conditioned we can become in terms of our eating practices and norms, and how we develop our perceptions of others when they are not behaving as we have become accustomed to or expect.

So how do we determine when it is OK to eat with our hands or when we should be using knives and forks, or perhaps chopsticks? Who is right or wrong? Why is it that, in the Western world, children at the point of weaning are taught to eat using forks and spoons and then to become proficient in the use of the knife and fork? Is this a reflection of our evolution from savage times to a point where social conditioning and expectations make it seem a shameful activity to touch food using our hands? As the French philosopher Rambourg (2013) states, "The hand is natural, the fork is cultural."

Does great cooking result in the best dining experiences?

Michelin star chefs, including Michael Caines, MBE, and Gordon Ramsey, OBE, support the concept that great cooking can speak for itself (Ellis, 2009). Caines (in Sanson, 2017) discusses the importance of seasonality of ingredients, the detail and technique in the preparation and the beautiful cooking, and argues that there are too many examples of "messing about with food of late and too many concepts."

While top-quality ingredients and highly skilled cooking undoubtedly contribute to a positive dining experience, scientific research coined as gastrophysics, a blend of experimental psychology and cognitive science, has provided evidence that the pleasures of eating are not just about the physical and molecular properties of food or drink. It suggests that flavor is a perception (not a sensation) created in our brains (not in our mouths) informed by the integration of information coming from all our senses.

Vision, touch, olfaction, audition and, of course, taste, all play a role in moderating our experience of foods. Eating is one of the most multisensory experiences, yet, when designing foods, we mostly think of what happens in the mouth: through texture, aromatic complexity, taste, balance, and temperature. While these aspects play a fundamental role, the "everything else," such as expectations, atmosphere, and social conventions, model our experiences much more than we imagine.

Amid the complexity of food experience, when it comes to designing flavor, there is one approach that is rarely acknowledged and probably from which there is most to gain in terms of quality of ritual, purpose, and enjoyment: the tools we use to serve from and bring food to the mouth. Indeed, cutlery impacts our enjoyment much more deeply than we think, and its influence is broad, affecting taste perception, value perception, attention, and the way we engage with the food.

Does food taste better when eaten from the hands?

The skin is the body's largest organ and is our sensory organ for touch. Current research indicates there are many olfactory receptors in the skin (Drew, 2022), and not only restricted to the nose.

Consider the experience of heat caused by the stimulation of hot and cold receptors. The skin contains a variety of nerve endings, combinations of which respond to particular types of pressures and temperatures. The thousands of nerve endings in the skin respond to the four basic sensations: pressure, heat, cold, and pain.

A more conscious and calm state of mind may support optimal digestion and better assimilation of nutrients. When eating from the hands and fingers, the body is in sync with the food compared to eating with a fork or spoon. As the skin contains a variety of nerve endings, combinations of which respond to particular types of pressures and temperatures, the senses are working in line with one another—integrating the senses to give rise to multisensory flavor.

Despite the cultural and historical views and circumstances of the Western use of the knife and fork, there are exceptions to the rule. Take McDonald's and the other fast-food giants, serving millions of meals each day, which are eaten … with the hands. No cutlery in sight! Could this success be because such restaurants provide an environment where adults and children can indulge in their food with their bare hands? Other examples include pizza, a staple in Italy, and fish and chips eaten wrapped in paper (used to be yesterday's newspaper, but this had to stop for contamination reasons) in the U.K.

Although there will be a divide in the answers to the question as to whether these dishes should be eaten with the hands or with a knife and fork, practically all Italian consumers (at least the ones I have met) would tell you that pizza is always eaten with the hands! They believe that the outcome is just more delicious when eaten this way than it could ever be using a knife and fork! Some of the world's most popular foods (pizza, burgers, fajitas, fish and chips) are eaten with the hands.

Touch is on trend!

Many of the world's Michelin-starred restaurants are incorporating several courses that are eaten with the fingers (Spence, 2017a). Touch is the largest and earliest-developing of our senses, accounting for 16–18% of body mass. Yet regardless of trend, in many parts of the world, including Africa, the Middle East, and the Indian sub-continent, billions of people eat with their hands every day.

Ayurveda (Jaiswal & Williams, 2017) is one of the world's oldest healing systems, originating in the Indian subcontinent in the second century BC. Ayurveda translates as the "science (or knowledge) of life." Its principles come from the observation of nature, defining every person as a unique receptacle of five elements: earth, fire, water, air, and space. Hence, we have a distinctive body constitution influencing our health.

In India, people eat with their hands as an expression of the act of connecting with food, which is perhaps more meaningful when considered more deeply. Beyond providing nutrition to the body, it is believed that eating with the hands also feeds the mind and the spirit. Touching food can contribute to a deeper connection through texture, smell, and taste, which creates a more enhanced sensory experience. Think back to the pizza!

The five elements symbolize everything that exists on Earth, and it is believed that, using the fingers and hands, there is a more natural connection to our existence. Eating with our hands creates harmony between the food and our energy, allowing greater assimilation of this life force.

What do science and nutrition say about it?

Eating with the hands can be beneficial to our muscles and blood circulation (Hegde et al., 2018). Selecting food with our fingers animates specific muscles that are not often stimulated.

Eating from the hands can help prevent overeating and poor digestion. Using fingers constrains us to eat more slowly, primarily as there is an increased interaction with the food in the process and generally smaller quantities involved in each food-to-mouth movement.

Research suggests that the brain needs approximately twenty to thirty minutes to receive the information that we are becoming satiated (full to the point of termination). Hence, if time is taken during consumption and not rushed (MacDonald, 2010), it is more likely that one will be satisfied (feeling satiated) with less. Please note, however, that this is a generalized finding, and there are many individual factors that contribute to feeling satiated, including physical fitness, weight, and other health-related factors (see Benelam, 2009).

However, eating consciously and mindfully means that we give full attention to what is present and in front of us. As we focus on our food more mindfully, it can notably enhance our awareness and experience of different textures, tastes, temperatures, etc., although if we become distracted (by a film, sports on TV, playing video games, etc.), this can lead to mindless eating and its consequences: inadequate mastication, poor digestion, and potential weight gain in the longer term.

The digestion process begins before ingesting anything. We have all experienced mouthwatering moments before a morsel of food enters our mouths. During this process, our brain is sending signals to prepare the digestion process, as saliva contains the enzymes needed to break down the food we are anticipating.

Awareness of our five senses would be a great start in our journey to well-being, because sight, smell, and touch help us in the preparation of healthy digestion. The nerve endings in our fingers receive information about what we are about to eat—from its texture, feel, and temperature. Such messages are transmitted to the brain, and then to the digestive system to produce adequate digestive juices.

Finally, there is evidence emerging of more play and toddlers' groups in the U.K. encouraging children to eat with their hands and experiment by eating foods from different food groups, with less emphasis on teaching them to use cutlery. This will allow children to experiment and learn for themselves, encouraging them to eat and explore. It is also important to allow oxygen into the mouth/nose (olfaction) to enhance flavor and experience texture, sound, and crunch, so perhaps less emphasis is needed on having to eat with one's mouth fully closed! (Another debate!)

Design

Eating is one of the most multisensory experiences we enjoy (or sometimes not) on a daily basis. We eat with our five major senses, using our eyes, ears (crunch!), touch, smell (olfaction) and, of course, our taste. It could be argued that further senses are also deployed in terms of proprioception (our movement), thermoception (temperature), and even pain (e.g., chilli burn), forming additional experiences in the process of eating.

Nevertheless, much of the design process, with the design intention of eating well, focuses on the food quality, its texture, flavor, balance, temperature, aroma, etc. Of course, each of these aspects is vitally important and, when achieved, will contribute to a positive experience utilizing aspects of the senses described in the above.

However, what about the other characteristics and contributors that form part of the process? Crockery, in terms of design, shape, size, color, and material, has made many innovative developments from the standard white china plate, the innovative styles rippling down from the Michelin superstar chefs through the lower echelons of the industry and into retail and the domestic kitchen.

Is this the same for cutlery? Perhaps not so much! However, we must also remember that cutlery is not always in the form of a knife and fork, or chopsticks, or crockery in the form of a plate, bowl, or piece of slate. There are many occasions when we eat directly from the packaging, for example, when eating chips directly from the bag (crisps in the U.K.), or popcorn.

Cutlery with texture

The lips and tongue are among the body's most sensitive skin sites. However, delivering food to these areas using cold, steel knives and forks is limited in increasing additional sensitivity or experience. Plastic cutlery perhaps even less so! Where there have been radical changes to crockery and plateware, this has not been to the same degree for cutlery.

This suggests an innovative opportunity to deliver a more experiential offering at the table. There are examples of designers innovating cutlery to add more sensory mouthfeel. Innovations include cutlery and spoons designed with textured surfaces and in different shapes to add another dimension and sensation in the mouth, lips, and tongue.

As previously discussed, many trends and developments are disseminated to the mainstream via chefs to the general public.

Perhaps at some time in the future when you eat lamb (carnivores only), might you tuck in using a knife and fork wrapped in wool?

Does the weight of cutlery matter?

In an experiment conducted by Michel, Velasco, and Spence (2015), diners at a large dinner were served the same food. However, half of them dined with banquet cutlery and the other half with canteen cutlery.

Unaware of the manipulation, diners were asked to rate:

- How flavorful they find the food
- How beautifully presented and plated they thought it was
- How much would they pay for it

In summary, the ratings were significantly higher from customers given the banquet cutlery. People were willing to pay 15% more for their food, found it to be more delicious, and found the presentation more beautiful.

But why? The shape and overall design of the two different cutlery sets were very similar. The weight of the banquet cutlery, however, was three times heavier than the cheaper counterpart.

This also seems to apply if you are flying supersonic! Since every gram counts, and plastic is not an option, designers were deployed to develop stylish new extra-lightweight cutlery for the fully "first-class" service offered when flying by Concorde. The designers created beautiful cutlery from titanium. The set was exquisite to look at, yet it was lighter than any cutlery used previously. All criteria were met, and everyone was happy?

Not quite! During trials, feedback was overwhelmingly negative. Passengers simply did not like it. It just didn't feel right. The range was never introduced, and the project was closed.

"Affective ventriloquism," as described by Spence (2017a), discusses the potential of textured cutlery/packaging, with the intention of enhancing the natural taste of the contents. Designers, including Naoto Fukasawa, worked with food manufacturing companies to produce packaging to replicate its contents. Examples included fruit juices to look and feel exactly like the fruits from which they are made/flavored.

Perhaps the production costs were too high, as such products have yet to reach the wider market. However, the packaging is highly realistic and promotes a natural, nutritious, and healthy perception of the contents in a way that a glass bottle cannot. There is also the tactile link between the feel of the product and its anticipated contents.

Following from the above more generally, is the receptacle important when we are drinking? Why should it make a difference? How would you feel drinking tea from a wine glass or a champagne flute? Imagine the appearance of an ice-cold beer in a frosted glass on a sunny day, or the way that cola is advertised poured over ice to amplify the fizz and freshness. Get the receptacle and conditions wrong and the drink loses a significant part of its appeal, although the drink itself has not changed in its physical properties.

Why does it seem more important, and arguably more enjoyable, to drink from the right vessel? The vessel forms part of the experience. For example, all the major beer-producing companies have glasses designed for their products, arguably to enhance the consumption experience but also with the branding/logos visible. Restaurants, hotels, and pubs/bars are often supplied (according to their contracts) with glasses to serve the branded product in the assigned glass, promoting the "whole product," not just the element consumed. However, occasionally during busy times, and perhaps due to breakages, this doesn't always happen, and the product is not quite the same!

Color

How does color impact what we taste and our wider perceptions? Here are a few examples. Following changes to carbonated drink (soda) packaging (i.e., the cans), findings concluded that consumers found the taste of the drinks had changed also. In an experiment undertaken by the brand 7-Up, the predominantly green packaging (linking lime as one of the main flavors) was adjusted to include more yellow (leaning more towards lemon). Following a taste test, consumers concluded that the taste from the revised 7-Up was indeed stronger in lemon than the 7-Up in the traditional green can, although the actual recipe had not been adjusted (Samuel, 2010).

Supporting these findings, in 2011, Coke launched a white Christmas Coke can, featuring polar bears and links to global warming awareness. However, large numbers of consumers were confused and convinced that the recipe and taste had changed.

The Coke corporation was concerned with the level of complaints to the point that the company replaced the white cans with the original red cans within a few weeks of the campaign launch.

Another example of the importance of color to the general public is evident through the pandemonium caused by crisp (potato chip) packaging in the U.K., through the non-conforming actions of the company Walkers Crisps. Research commissioned by YouGov (2016) established that the British public considered the appropriate color for a bag of cheese and onion flavor crisps as green. However, despite a petition in 2013 by rival company, Golden Wonder, who first launched the iconic flavor in green packets in the early 1960s, calling on all makers to package flavors in the same colored packaging, Walkers remains the only major brand to package their cheese and onion crisps (the U.K.'s favorite flavor) in blue packaging.

Blue packaging is used for salt and vinegar crisps by all other major brands, but Walkers use green packaging for their salt and vinegar crisps. How confusing for the poor crisp consumers! Notably, the only group sampled that differed in this view was the eighteen to twenty-four age group (born between 1992 and 1998), suggesting a well-considered marketing strategy in which Walkers Crisps deployed the services of Gary Lineker, one of England's all-time footballing icons and the most highly paid presenter in the BBC, as the comical figurehead of their advertising campaign during this period.

To test the influence that color can have on people, whether through the product itself or the cutlery/packaging used in the product delivery, try a simple experiment with some friends at home. Have a "blind" tasting of red and white wine, or mix the popcorn/crisp (potato chip) packaging to see if there is any reaction.

Take this a step further. It might be more fun if you can adjust the colors and flavors of the samples—e.g., white wine presented as red (adjusted with food coloring, or by using red tinted glasses), or jellies that are red but flavored with vanilla. The red color will suggest fruit, such as strawberry or raspberry, but the vanilla will be a familiar flavor.

Color can also contribute to sensation transference and how the senses transfer expectations to the food you are about to eat. We form expectations and judgments when considering the colors of food. Black, for example, is an indicator of how color can affect appetite negatively. Think of a squid ink pasta dish or risotto. No matter how delicious the dish might be, it doesn't look quite right for many people. The color is not naturally associated with food.

This is like blue, as so few foods are naturally blue. Blue foods do not tend to whet the appetite. This differs significantly from how the appearance of a light blue sky or crystal-clear blue sea can make us feel calm and relaxed. In contrast, if we consider the healthiness we relate to other colors, such as green, which is associated with nutritious fresh green vegetables, the vibrancy of red in fresh red fruits, or the vitality of orange, we have natural perceptions of the colors and expectations of our food.

An element of the research by Harrar and Spence (2013), investigating how the taste of food is affected by color, revealed that the taste of yoghurt differed according to the color of the cutlery. However, these effects appeared dependent on the color of the food as well. This suggests that color contrast may have been partially responsible for the observed effects, but also that the color of the food or the cutlery may have impacted separately.

As the saying goes, "You don't get a second chance at making a first impression." To a degree, this conveys the power of branding and our unconscious associations with products. However, there is another famous saying, "Don't judge a book by its cover."

Conclusions

The general use and style of the knife and fork have not changed significantly in comparison to other developments in food and drink. We already use a multitude of different-sized and shaped cutlery, from a teaspoon to a dessert spoon and a tablespoon, or perhaps a butter knife, a fish knife, or a steak knife. However, these examples are more about tackling the food or drink concerned than how the cutlery functions in a sensory capacity. This suggests an opportunity for innovation, particularly when considering the sensory and hedonic experiences that development in this area could bring: textured cutlery, for example, adding further dimensions to the eating experience.

Conversely, it could be argued that there is no requirement for innovation at all, particularly if our natural cutlery, our fingers and hands, are used more often to enjoy the sensory experiences this form of eating can bring. Eating with the hands is a growing trend and becoming more prominent as courses of tasting menus are developed by some of the world's leading chefs in their Michelin-starred restaurants (Spence, 2017a). Furthermore, it is interesting to note that in the Western world, where the use of the knife and fork is the custom, some of the most popular foods are in fact eaten with the hands—think burgers, pizzas, sandwiches/wraps, fish and chips, and confectionery.

The diffusion of chopsticks in Chinese culture is attributed to the Confucian philosophy emphasizing harmony as the basis for civil order. According to the rules of this philosophy, knives and other sharp objects have no place at the table. Such items are considered dangerous (used for killing) and unsuitable for the table, a place of peace and harmony. In China and other regions of the Far East, chopsticks remain the cutlery of choice. Since their inception thousands of years ago, chopsticks were first utilized as tools in cooking before becoming cutlery used by individuals during a meal. Their use remains highly significant and engrained in the culture of these countries.

Going forward, there is also the opportunity to consider more inclusive "cutlery" solutions for those who may have difficulties engaging with food (e.g., blindness) and how cutlery can be designed to provide a tactile experience for the consumer. From a sustainability and waste avoidance perspective, there are emerging examples of products designed to reduce environmental damage from the disposal of single-use cutlery, crockery, and packaging. For example, the use of edible cutlery and crockery.

Science fiction and a few infamous historical claims predicted that we will obtain all our nutritional and calorific requirements at some point in the future by eating a few pills. We would not require cutlery for that, and how much fun would that be? (Not many mouths watering at that thought, either!) Fortunately, this appears highly unlikely, particularly trying to cram two thousand calories plus into a few pills.

Eating is so much more than simply ingesting nutrients and supplying the body with energy: it is one of the most important aspects of our being. Eating has social, educational, and cultural dimensions, and if we have the pleasure of sharing a meal, we have an excellent reason to continue to use cutlery in whatever its form, today and in the future.

CHAPTER 17

Food sustainability and ethical eating: How to feed the world without breaking it!

Neil Rippington

Introduction

Planet Earth has never been an equitable place in terms of the access individuals have to its resources, some of which are essential to our health, well-being, and ultimately our lives. Food is one of these essential resources, and it appears as a regular feature in our daily routines, supplying us with the energy, vitamins, and minerals we need to function, grow, heal, and repair as we navigate the opportunities and challenges life presents us and we endeavor its journey. However, there is a growing number of people suffering from hunger. In 2020, between 720 million and 811 million people worldwide were suffering from hunger, roughly 161 million more than in 2019 (United Nations, 2022).

Today, the world faces some of its most pressing challenges in the form of protecting the planet for the benefit of future generations and the millions of species that occupy its lands and seas. Human beings have made a devastating impact on the health of the planet, and our actions will contribute significantly to its future health, and the health of all species dependent on the resources the planet produces for us to live healthily as a global community.

When considering our food choices, we are making ethical and sustainable decisions, whether consciously or not. There is a complexity to modern food systems that integrates politics, economics, and culture, as well as human, animal, and environmental health. Our food choices not only contribute to our own health and the health of our children, but they also impact those employed in food production, the welfare of animals, and the health of the planet and its oceans.

To find solutions to the issues raised above, we need to find ways to produce nutritious and high-quality food in sufficient volumes to feed everyone, but in a way that is environmentally sustainable and considerate to the planet and all the species who share life on it.

Increasing food production for a growing population

On November 15th 2022, the world population reached 8 billion people, a milestone in human development. The current world population of 8.2 billion is expected to reach 8.6 billion in 2030, 9.8 billion in 2050 and 11.2 billion in 2100 (United Nations, 2019). Land forms 29% of the Earth's surface, and of that, 71% is habitable. 46% of the habitable land, approximately 9.5% of the Earth's surface area, is used for agriculture (see Figure 17.1).

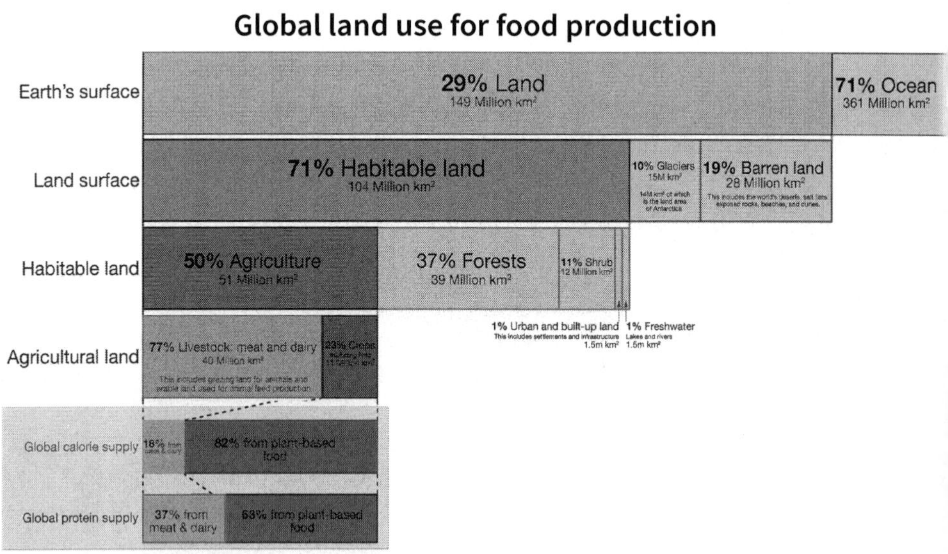

Figure 17.1. Land use definitions for agricultural and non-agricultural land cover (Ritchie, Rosado, & Roser, 2019). *OurWorldinData.org*. Retrieved from: https://ourworldindata.org/land-use

During the majority of the time that humans have inhabited Earth, its lands were predominantly made up of forests and grasslands. It is only during the last few centuries that this has changed so intensely, with wild habitats being transformed into agricultural land. Estimates suggest that one thousand years ago, less than 4% of the world's habitable land area was used for farming. Today, nearly half of the Earth's habitable land is used for agricultural purposes (Ellis et al., 2010).

The diagram above illustrates the breakdown of our planet's total land area, representing only 29% of the Earth's surface. Of this, approximately 10% is covered by glaciers, and a further 19% is uninhabitable land (e.g., desert, salt flats, beaches, dunes, and exposed rocks). The remaining, habitable, land consists of 38% forest, 11% grasslands, 1% freshwater coverage, and 1% urban development, including cities, towns, villages, roads, and other human infrastructure. Note the definition of urbanized land differs according to the research methodology. This ranges from below 1% to 3% (see Liu et al., 2014).

There is also an unequal distribution of land use between livestock and crops for human consumption. Combining pastures used for grazing with land used to grow crops for animal feed, livestock accounts for 77% of global farming land, and while livestock takes up most of the world's agricultural land, it only produces 18% of the world's calories and 37% of total protein consumption (Poore & Nemecek, 2018).

Agricultural activities through the farming of livestock, waste management, energy use, and biomass burning all contribute to methane (CH_4) emissions. Other activities, such as fertilizer use, are the primary source of N_2O emissions, and the conversion of forests, grasslands, and other carbon "sinks" into cropland or pasture results in carbon dioxide (CO_2) emissions. Agriculture generates 13,500,000,000 tonnes of CO_2-equivalent annually—fifty times more than the mass of all humans on earth (ibid.).

The expansion of agriculture has been one of humanity's largest impacts on the environment. It has transformed habitats and is one of the greatest pressures for biodiversity. In 2025, more than 47,000 species evaluated are threatened with extinction on the International Union for Conservation of Nature and Natural Resources (IUCN) Red List, a staggering 28% of all known species (IUCN, 2025). In 2019, agriculture was listed as a threat for 85% of the threatened species listed (Ritchie,

2019). While agriculture alongside land conversion and overharvesting is identified as a primary driver of extinction risk, the IUCN is asking countries to rethink agricultural and conservation policies to help protect biodiversity while delivering food for humanity (IUCN, 2024).

With such a warning to the world's biodiversity, the threat to so many species, coupled with the increasing population and number of people suffering from hunger, presents a huge problem for the world, although we do have the resources, technology, and capabilities to solve these problems.

The global Millennium Ecosystem Assessment (MA) methodology (Ash et al., 2010) focused on linkages between ecosystem services and human well-being and the influence of direct and indirect drivers of change. Over the past fifty years, humans have changed ecosystems more rapidly and extensively than in any comparable period in human history, largely to meet rapidly growing demands for food, fresh water, timber, fiber, and fuel. This has resulted in a substantial and largely irreversible loss in the diversity of life on Earth.

The changes that have been made to ecosystems have contributed to substantial net gains in human well-being and economic development, but these gains have been achieved at growing costs in the form of the degradation of many ecosystem services, increased risks of nonlinear changes, and the exacerbation of poverty for some groups of people. These problems, unless addressed, will substantially diminish the benefits that future generations obtain from ecosystems.

Finding long-term sustainable and equitable solutions

The United Nations Sustainable Development Goal 2 is about creating a world free of hunger by 2030. In 2020, a staggering 2.4 billion people, more than 30% of the world's population, were moderately or severely food insecure, lacking regular access to adequate food.

As the global population grows and incomes rise across the developing world, overall food demand is predicted to increase by more than 50% by 2050, and demand for animal source foods (ASF) by nearly 70% (World Resources Institute, 2019). Despite the rise in veganism and vegetarianism, as developing countries become more affluent, the demand for animal source foods is rising. Yet today, almost one billion people remain undernourished as local agricultural systems fail to provide enough nutritious food, and economic factors prevent equitable distribution of available food.

The arable land needed to produce a fixed quantity of crops is calculated as arable land divided by the crop production index (PIN). This index is the sum of crop commodities (minus crops used for animal feed) weighted by commodity prices. This is measured as an index relative to 1961 (where 1961 = 1 and 2020 = 0.29). This shows that during the last fifty years, we have been capable of producing more than three times more crops (such as cereal and grain), although this has been largely achieved through the use of fertilizers, pesticides, crop breeding, and intensification. The amount of food per person has increased, and the cost has decreased, yet transportation and access remain huge barriers.

Nevertheless, the evidence is there to show that we can reduce these impacts, both through dietary changes, by substituting some meat with plant-based alternatives, and through technological advances. Crop yields have increased significantly in recent decades, meaning we have spared a lot of land from agricultural production globally, essentially to produce the same crop yields as in 1961, with only 30% of the farmland now required. With solutions from both consumers and producers, we have an important opportunity to restore some of this farmland back to forests and natural habitats.

Fish and seafood as a vital food source

Our oceans are at the point of industrialized fishing, and there is much evidence and debate as to the damage overfishing is causing, and the detrimental impact this is having on the marine ecosystem and the number of extinct and endangered species as a consequence. Aquatic products (largely fish, aquatic mollusks, and crustaceans) have a critical role in the food system, providing nearly 3 billion people with at least 15% of their animal protein intake (Godfray et al., 2010). Fish yields have increased tremendously, in a similar way to food production on land between 1960 and 2015, but not all has come from the sea.

Aquaculture is the farming of aquatic organisms, including fish, mollusks, crustaceans, and aquatic plants. "Capture fisheries" production is the volume of wild fish catches landed for all commercial, industrial, recreational, and subsistence purposes (FAO, 2022). In many regions, aquaculture, or fish farming, has been successful from a food source and economic perspective. If this was replicated in areas of the world suffering food poverty and/or a lack of access, it could bring significant benefits. Technical advances in hatchery systems, feeds and feed delivery systems, and disease management could all increase output. Future gains may also come from better stock selection, larger-scale production technologies, aquaculture in open seas and larger inland water bodies, and the culture of a wider range of species. The long production cycle of many species (typically six to thirty-six months) requires a financing system capable of providing working capital as well as offsetting risk.

From a cautious perspective, aquaculture has the potential to cause harm to the environment due to the release of organic effluents or disease treatment chemicals into water bodies; indirectly, through its dependence on industrial fisheries to supply feeds, and by acting as a source of diseases or genetic contamination for wild species. Efforts to reduce these negative externalities and increase the efficiency of resource use—the fish-in-fish-out ratio (Tacon & Metian, 2008)—have been spurred by the rise of sustainability certification programs, though these mainly affect only higher-value sectors. Gains in sustainability could come from concentrating on lower-level species and in integrating aquatic and terrestrial food production, for example by using waste from the land as food and nutrients. It will also be important to take a more strategic approach to site location and capacity within catchment or coastal zone management units.

However, to compare production values, in 1960, capture fisheries produced 35 million tonnes of fish globally compared to only 2 million tonnes in aquaculture. By 2015, capture fisheries had grown to 94 million tonnes, a significant growth, but overshadowed massively by the growth of aquaculture to 106 million tonnes (Ritchie & Roser, 2021).

Food availability and access

Food availability is a measure of the sufficient supply of food for all people consistently. Availability depends on food production quantities and reserves. However, this alone does not ensure food security for all communities and/or individuals. Food security also requires access, a measure of the resources people have to acquire food. Access is dependent on availability but also on physical and economic access. Food distribution, or where food is located, the local environment, mobility, and access to transportation and time determine physical access. The cost of food aligned to the funds available to spend on food also determines an individual's economic access to food (Powell et al., 2012).

The issues are exacerbated by several social and economic factors, creating further difficulties for people in less affluent areas, whether in developing countries or in the poorer regions within developed countries. Such areas are often depleted of options in terms of access to and availability of nutritious food at affordable prices.

The term "food desert" describes urban and rural communities with limited or no access to healthy food options. Such communities may not have access to shops and stores selling fresh, highly nutritious produce. Additionally, people may not have access to personal vehicles or effective public transportation to travel to fresh food retailers.

"Food swamp" is a term used to describe communities with access to a range of limited food options, such as takeaways, fast-food restaurants, and stores selling limited, and often expensive, food and drink supplies, many of which are highly processed. These outlets are likely to sell processed foods high in sugar, salt, and trans and saturated fats. Food swamps have been found to have a greater impact on obesity than food deserts (Cooksey-Stowers, Schwartz, & Brownell, 2017). There is a call that the term "food apartheid" should be used over "food desert" or "food swamp," as these terms suggest natural environments, not human-made ones.

Food waste

It is estimated that approximately one-third of the food produced for human consumption is lost during the farming process or wasted at the retail and consumer levels (Fanzo & McLaren, 2020), and of the roughly 4 billion tonnes of food produced each year, approximately 1.2–2 billion tonnes are wasted. This is valued at $1 trillion and would be sufficient to feed 3 billion people, exceeding the number of people currently suffering from hunger (Igini, 2023).

How food is wasted depends on the region and country. In Europe and North America, most of the food waste is in the hands of retailers and consumers (Willett et al., 2019). In sub-Saharan Africa and

South and Southeast Asia, more food is lost on farms with significant spoilage of fruits, vegetables, root crops, and some animal source foods. Wasting food wastes resources, as does wasting 1.4 billion hectares of land and 250 km^3 of blue water to produce uneaten food (ibid.).

Global food waste also amounts to 3.3 gigatons of CO_2 equivalents. A study by Neff, Kanter, and Vandevijvere (2015) examined how wasting food also wastes nutrients. Findings concluded that food waste of fruits and vegetables in the U.S.A. contained significant quantities of key nutrients that could have helped millions of people meet their daily recommended intakes

Reducing waste

Roughly 30–40% of food in both the developed and developing world is lost to waste, though the causes are very different (Nellemann, 2009). In the developing world, losses are due mainly to the absence of food chain infrastructure, and to lack of knowledge or investment in storage technologies on the farm, although data is scarce. For example, in India, it is estimated that 35% to 40% of fresh produce is lost because neither wholesale nor retail outlets have cold storage. Even with rice grain, which can be stored more readily, as much as a third of the harvest in Southeast Asia can be lost after harvest to pests and spoilage (World Economic Forum, 2023).

By contrast, in the developed world, pre-retail losses are much lower, but those arising at the retail, food service, and home stages of the food chain have grown dramatically in recent years. Food in developed countries has been relatively cheap, at least for many domestic consumers, which reduces the incentives to avoid waste. In the period circa 1990–2010, consumers became accustomed to purchasing foods of the highest cosmetic standards, and hence retailers discarded many edible yet only slightly blemished products.

Commercial pressures can encourage waste. For example, the food service industry frequently uses "supersized" portions as a competitive lever, while "buy one get one free" offers have the same function for retailers. There is evidence that the perceived "extra value" by the consumer adds to food waste, as it is not consumed due to oversized portions, or the food is not used in time before it becomes unsafe to eat. In both examples, the consumer has purchased more than they need. Litigation and lack of education on food safety have led to a reliance on "use-by dates" whose safety margins often mean that food fit for consumption is discarded. In some developed countries, unused food goes to landfills rather than being redirected as animal feed or compost because of legislation to control disease.

Different strategies are required to tackle the two types of waste. In developing countries, public investment in transport infrastructure would reduce the opportunities for spoilage, while better-functioning markets and the availability of capital would increase the efficiency of the food chain, for example by allowing the introduction of cold storage (though note this has implications for greenhouse emissions) (WRAP, 2008). Existing technologies and best practices need to be spread by education and extension services, and market and finance mechanisms are required to protect farmers from having to sell at peak supply, leading to gluts and wastage. There is also a need for continuing research in post-harvest storage technologies. Improved technology for small-scale food storage in poorer contexts is a prime candidate for the introduction of state incentives for private innovation, with the involvement of small-scale traders, millers, and producers.

Since the Covid-19 pandemic, food prices have only risen. If they were to continue to do so, there would likely be a decrease in the volume of waste produced by consumers in developed countries. Waste may also be reduced by alerting consumers to the scale of the issue, as well as to domestic strategies for reducing food loss. Promotion, education, and possibly legislation may also reduce waste in the food service and retail sectors. Legislation, such as that on sell-by dates and swill that has inadvertently increased food waste, should be reexamined within a more inclusive competing risks framework. Reducing developed-country food waste is particularly challenging, as it is so closely linked to individual behavior and cultural attitudes to food.

Economic sustainability

The cost of food disproportionately impacts the poor because they spend a higher proportion of their income on food, with poor households in low-income countries spending 50–80% of their household budget on food (FAO, 2011).

Evidence from high-income countries indicates that healthier diets are generally more expensive, with healthier diets costing about

$1.50 more per day (Rao et al., 2013). Additionally, healthier diets are more expensive per calorie than diets with lower nutritional quality (Darmon & Drewnowski, 2015). Vegetables and fruits are prohibitively expensive for many, as discussed in the section referring to access and availability. Globally, the price of a basic diet, which only meets caloric needs, often exceeds daily wages. Therefore, many can only afford the least healthy food, low in nutrient density and high in sodium, sugar, and unhealthy fats (Aggarwal, Monsivais, & Drewnowski, 2012).

As incomes increase across the globe, it is projected that three billion more people will enter the defined "middle class" by 2030. Analysis from 187 countries found that higher incomes are associated not only with higher consumption of healthy foods but also with a substantially increased consumption of unhealthy food items, indicating that the links between socio-economic status and diet quality are complex (Imamura et al., 2015). As incomes rise, diets are adapting from those centered on traditional staples to more diverse foods. This is generating increased demand for animal source foods; processed, packaged foods; and takeaway foods (Ranganathan et al., 2016). High-income countries such as the U.S.A. already have high demands for ASFs, and in countries including China, India, and Brazil, where incomes are increasing, there has been a parallel increase in demand for meat and ASFs (Tilman & Clark, 2014).

The food environment has influenced how we access, prepare, and consume food, including the increasing power of retailers, particularly supermarkets, as well as restaurants, chefs, and influencers. Social media shapes desires, competition, and food choices. While some of the world still purchases food from local, informal markets, food is increasingly being purchased in larger markets and has traveled longer distances, sometimes from distant parts of the world. These purchasing patterns have been influenced by increased urbanization, income growth, and expansion of food processing, distribution, and retail (Lu & Reardon, 2018).

The return to local, organic, and seasonal produce

Ideally, we would all have access to local, organic, and seasonal produce. However, there is the contradiction that food produced locally can be significantly more expensive than food produced thousands of miles away. In previous generations, before the developments of transportation and technology, food was sourced more locally, leading to the cultures and traditions of regional cuisine.

The development of supermarkets and hypermarkets, with global purchasing power and infrastructures designed on huge scales and to maximize profit, have made it extremely difficult for local producers to compete from a selling price perspective. The operating costs (labor, equipment, overheads, meeting legal requirements, etc.) and scales of production are not comparable and therefore push local food prices higher than supermarket equivalents.

From a quality perspective, food produced and bought locally is likely to be seasonal, fresher, and arguably more nutritious and flavorsome. However, the price of food is a significant factor when making purchasing decisions, particularly if money is scarce.

Purchasing cheaper, mass-produced food might be kinder to the pocket, but it comes at a cost to the local economy and the planet. If demand for local food increases, supply is likely to rise and become more efficient, prices will come down, and the local economy will benefit. This is an ethical and economic dilemma. Once again, buying local food is often by the more affluent in society, as they can afford it.

A recipe for change

How do we generate between 50% and 70% more food without using any more land, not compromising biodiversity, and with minimal/zero greenhouse gas (GHG) emissions?

The challenge of creating a sustainable food future involves balancing several competing needs. By 2050, the world must feed many more people, do so more nutritiously, and ensure that agriculture contributes to poverty reduction through inclusive economic and social development, all while reducing greenhouse gas (GHG) emissions, loss of habitat, freshwater depletion and pollution, and other environmental impacts of farming.

The evidence suggests that everyone, from governments, corporate retailers, business owners/hoteliers/restaurateurs, educators, and us all as individuals, has to play their part in contributing towards meeting the challenges ahead. It is no small task!

Pursuing any of these goals to the exclusion of the others is likely to fail to achieve any of them. Creating a sustainable and ethical food future is possible, but there is no silver bullet.

CHAPTER 18

The restaurant journey: From booking to departure

Neil Rippington

Canapés: Before we begin

Is there a typical journey?

The desire or need to eat in a restaurant is multifaceted. It can come from necessity: being away from home and needing to use a restaurant for sustenance. It may also stem from a desire to eat in a highly reputable restaurant with a famous chef and a raft of accolades.

What are the considerations and decision-making processes when deciding where to eat? It might start with the occasion. It could be a business meeting, a reunion, a date, a family celebration, a catch-up with close friends … the list goes on!

Following these initial considerations, many other factors come into play, including:

- What is the likely cost? Is it affordable? Is it within a preferred personal budget?
- What type of food is served? Is there enough variety for the group of diners? Who is eating? What are their preferences, likes, and dislikes?
- What is the style of service? Is it relaxed, formal, or somewhere in between?
- What are the travel implications?

- Which day of the week is best suited to the occasion?
- What time of the day is best to dine?
- What clothing is best to wear?
- What is the atmosphere going to be like? Will it be bustling and loud or tranquil and private?
- Will the restaurant cater for the needs of each diner?

Whatever the occasion, there will be a sequence of events, or a journey of experiences as each guest navigates, or is navigates or is navigated through the dining experience. Getting all these steps or processes right, in terms of the customers' positive experience and meeting their anticipated expectations, is the challenge that restaurateurs face, often impacting the success and longevity of the business.

Starters: Perceptions and first impressions

In terms of a dining experience, a perception or expectation can be gained through recommendations, reviews, social media platforms, promotions in journals, television shows or perhaps through the reputation and profile of the chef. Zhang et al. (2010) discuss the importance of electronic word of mouth (EWOM) in today's digital world, and this supports the premise that consumers are already forming judgments and perceptions before they make purchasing decisions. The power of social media cannot be underestimated in both the positive and negative impact it can make on a business, leading to the adaptation of services and implementation of others (see Lee et al., 2022). The significance is massive!

Yet an impression is gained through the interaction and experience of the product and service, and all that this entails. Where is the first point of consumer contact? It could be through an app or website, a phone call, or by walking through the entrance of the restaurant. If things go wrong at this stage, the journey is, probably, at its end before it begins! However, for the sake of the chapter and the journey, we will assume that the reservation has gone through, whether made months in advance or as a last-second decision on a whim.

The phrase, "You only get one chance to make a first impression" is simple but accurate, and an impression is made within the opening seconds of interaction (see Willis & Todorov, 2006). Applying this to a restaurant setting, a first impression is based on several factors, often happening and homogenized into just a few moments. We will take in the visuals and the physical environment, the décor, the quality of fixtures, cleanliness, etc., and include the personal interaction with the person/host responsible for our welcome to the establishment. Although seemingly a straightforward process, this person is representing the business and therefore setting the first of many standards that form an association with the restaurant. This is the first face of the business, and a warm and genuine welcome has a great part to play in terms of making guests feel relaxed, yet excited, in terms of their expectations and anticipation for the rest of the journey.

It is spontaneous to soak up the atmosphere of the establishment. This is happening naturally, often without deep and conscious consideration, as we consider aspects of design and the environmental atmosphere, including the:

- Ambience
- Ambient temperature
- Scent
- Sound (and volume/noise level)
- Decoration
- Color scheme
- Furniture
- Lighting and the level of illumination
- Degree of comfort
- Size and shape
- Layout of seating
- Artifacts (pictures, ornaments, other features)
- Views (internal and external)
- Cleanliness.

And this is before starting to observe other aspects of the environment, such as:

- The staff (number of, mix—gender, age, appearance)
- Uniforms (smart/corporate, casual/relaxed, different according to role)
- Other diners (what they are wearing, their demographics—age, dress, couples, groups, etc.)
- How busy is the restaurant? (quiet and almost empty, full and bustling).

We are instinctively programmed as human beings to protect ourselves, and we have many internal "alarm systems" to inform us when things are not as they should be. Cleanliness and good hygiene standards are basic expectations when using restaurants. The sight of a dirty, messy kitchen is highly off-putting for many, making the difference in the consumer decision-making process as to whether to utilize a restaurant's services. We associate such conditions with the potential of contaminated food and the risk of illness from food poisoning or the spread of harmful bacteria. Psychologically, such environments provide little confidence in terms of professionalism, and this will often impact our mindset before any food is served.

Similarly, the condition and maintenance of facilities such as restrooms/toilets are highly important to restaurant consumers. Having clean and functional facilities can say a great deal about the establishment and its leadership in managing the customer journey. Regardless of the positioning of a restaurant, whether a low-cost, fast-food outlet through to a restaurant serving haute cuisine at much higher prices, such fundamental aspects of hygiene and cleanliness should be a given.

In a study by Alonso and O'Neill (2010) focusing on restaurant customers' ideal dining experiences, 16.2% of the comments referred to the restaurant's cleanliness as an element pertaining to the style of the establishment. Restaurateurs therefore must realize and understand that customers are surrounded by forms of communication informing them and developing their perceptions. Communication is everywhere in the restaurant environment, through our interactions and informed by our senses; through our sight, touch, sound, and smell, from which we form quality assessments and judgments.

Intermediate course: Service

The importance of service in the restaurant journey cannot be understated. In a world of developing virtual reality (VR) and artificial intelligence (AI), there is much discussion about the potential that robots and technological developments can bring to various industries. There is certainly a novelty factor in the use of robots in the food service industry, but there is much to support the human interaction between the guest and those responsible for the delivery of high-quality and memorable experiences (Choi et al., 2019; de Kervenoael et al., 2020; El-Said & Al Hajri, 2022). When dining out, which is the more important, great food or great service? Both would be ideal, but can one survive without the other? Can one remedy the other?

There are proficiencies that skilled personnel can bring to the dining experience that are intuitive to the scenario and form the very nature of hospitality. Guests want to feel welcome and valued. Acknowledgment of guests is a simple signal but so often overlooked. A gesture to show awareness of a guest's presence provides consumer confidence and reassurance that they are present in the scenario and of the staff's imminent attention. Ultimately, a guest wants to be seen.

In the modern service industry, IT can eradicate some areas of potential weaknesses in the delivery of products and services. For example, digital menus produce real-time information that can often be delayed in the traditional communications between a service provider and a customer. For example, if a product is out of stock but appears on a printed menu, it is the role of the service staff to inform the guest that this is the case. This may create some disappointment if the guest had selected, and therefore anticipated, a dish prior to ordering. They will also be asked to make another choice. Worse still is the scenario where service staff are unaware of the item being out of stock, proceeding to take an order and then having to return to the guest to let them know that their choice is unavailable. This also adds to a further time delay and can impact the whole group experience. Groups dining together expect dishes to be served at the same time, adding enjoyment and social connection when eating together. However, this is not always the case when service communications and processes falter, as many of us will have experienced at some point.

A digital menu will automatically remove items that are not in stock and, if well managed, will be ready to replace the item with another product. The consumer will see the menu in real time and be unaware of the movement of dishes and products. They will view what is live and available. Furthermore, a digital menu does not require the human interaction that is required in the ordering process, hence making the process much quicker during peak times when service staff can be stretched to cover all bases.

In an age where consumer information is partially driven by informed choice, trends, and current issues, it is also becoming legislated in some respects. For example, the identification of allergens is now demanded in many countries, as consumers with allergies must be confident that the food they are consuming is safe for them to eat. Cases of anaphylaxis, a severe, potentially life-threatening allergic reaction that can develop rapidly, will be avoided if this is adhered to, although there are still cases reported where mistakes have been made. It is also becoming a legal requirement in many countries to provide calorific values and traffic lights, which are RAG-rated (red, amber, green) systems to indicate key components of dishes and products, indicating fat, saturates, sugars, and salt. Although it is not currently a requirement to have this information on printed menus, it is becoming a requisite to be able to provide customers with this type of information on request, so the information must be readily available. This is a similar situation with more detailed nutritional information, covering key sources of nutrients such as the composition of fats, protein, and carbohydrates.

Menu information is now going further, with some menus detailing the CO_2 emissions generated in the production of dishes. More restaurants, including some of the major brands, are attempting to lower CO_2 emissions created by purchasing food locally and seasonally. It is becoming integral in marketing strategies by engaging consumers and encouraging them to make ethical and sustainable food choices.

However, there is the argument that consumers, particularly when enjoying a luxury treat or perhaps celebrating a specific occasion, do not want to have this type of information in front of them, potentially affecting their food choices and distracting attention from the purpose of the event. Consumers have reported feelings of guilt and being put off dishes that they would have selected if this information had not been presented. This also has the potential to dampen the celebratory spirit of the occasion. Having the option to request this type of data, particularly in the high-end dining market, is therefore perhaps the most appropriate, giving consumers the option as to how much information they want at the time and on the occasion.

Human interaction with guests often goes further in terms of food and drink choices. AI has the potential to recommend dishes based on the information (data) collected, but the recommendations from staff, particularly experienced and highly knowledgeable staff such as sommeliers, can provide highly personalized and specific recommendations, contributing to the overall meal experience. AI, no matter how far it develops and how accurate it becomes, is not human, and there will always be that divide between our relationships with people and those with advanced and developing technologies.

Main course: Personalization and experience triggers

Personalization doesn't have to be complex and expensive. The coffee shop brand Starbucks personalizes the experience of all its customers every day by asking for the name of the customer before making their coffee. The customer's name is written on the cup, and once the drink is prepared, the customer is called by their name and handed their personalized order. Simple, but highly effective!

At the highest of echelons, New York restaurateur of the world-renowned and three-Michelin-starred 11 Madison Park, Will Guidara, changed his philosophy to personalization and customer experience after serving a two-dollar hot dog to a table of four foodies enjoying a gastronomic tour of the city. He created a personalized experience for the group after overhearing their conversation in which they stated the only thing they had missed during their visit was an authentic New York City hot dog. Guidara immediately sourced a hot dog from a local street vendor. After persuading the chef to serve it, the chef cut it neatly into four even slices and served it with some neatly applied relishes and garnishes to raise the aesthetics of the humble product. Upon service, the gesture produced such a positive and overwhelming reaction that Guidara began pursuing what he has gone on to describe as "unreasonable hospitality," seeking ways to create extraordinary experiences and the creation of personal and powerful memories for guests (see Guidara, 2022).

Personalization and attention to customer preferences are also important when seeking advice from service staff. For example, consumers can feel overwhelmed and under a little pressure when presented with a substantial wine list, perhaps with many unknown wines, alongside prices stretching their intended budget. Pricing can add, even though unintended, pressure. In such positions, many consumers do not want to select the cheapest wine on the menu due to the "perception" this may attach, and although not necessarily the case, they may start to look at wines slightly above this point. This can add a "decoy" effect, placing high-margin wines (those with higher profit) slightly above the cheapest on the list, as customers in such positions are likely to select wines in this category.

However, the role of a (good) sommelier is to consider a customer's requirements from their preferences in terms of wines, grape varieties, and styles they have enjoyed in the past, and to make suggestions matched to the foods a customer has selected. In many cultures, particularly Mediterranean countries, wine is considered a food in many respects as opposed to a drink. Wine is recognized as a component of the meal, rather than something additional to it. The sommelier should therefore look at the complementary or in some cases contrasting features of a wine that are likely to pair well with the food selection. Above all, recommendations should be within the customer's budget; a sommelier should not put them in an uncomfortable position by recommending wines beyond this. Of course, in the contemporary industry, there is now a greater emphasis and growing trend in the service of non-alcoholic drinks, and the same emphasis in terms of the food-matching process in the service of "zero" wines, beers, cocktails, etc., to be enjoyed while complementing food during the dining experience.

The rapid developments in AI and data collection have made personalization a reality at all levels of the industry. Buying patterns and usage of products provide opportunities for companies to utilize this data and "pop-up" with offers that consumers are likely to be interested in, in line with previous buying behaviors. AI can support service, personalization, and even deliver finished products. However, this is difficult to compare to the feeling that exceptional service and personalization produce when delivered from one human to another. Hospitality is ultimately a process of human interaction and the joy felt when we receive excellent service and personalization. Furthermore, hospitality organizations with disengaged employees, effectively offering less interest and aspects of personalization for their customers, tend to be less productive and possess lower customer loyalty than companies with a high-engagement culture (Harter, 2018; Sims, 2015). This suggests that it is in everyone's interest that the relationships between service staff and customers are actively encouraged.

The importance of the environment

The environment has an enormous impact on the dining experience. The most lavish and luxurious facilities with expensive fixtures and fittings do not guarantee the most memorable and enjoyable dining experience. Of course, such surroundings, linked to excellent food and service, can deliver wonderful experiences, often as a treat or special occasion. However, when many people are asked to share their favorite or most memorable dining experiences, they refer to a huge range of circumstances, such as sitting on a beach, eating from a street vendor, or a scene more connected to the people with whom they were dining.

"Servicescape" is a model developed by Bitner (1992) to emphasize the impact of the physical environment in which a service process takes place. The servicescape model aims to analyze the behavior of people within the service environment to design surroundings that achieve goals in terms of desired behavioral responses. In a restaurant setting, such behaviors include an obvious enjoyment of the experience such that the customer returns on repeated occasions and is also likely to refer and recommend the use of the restaurant to others or through personal reviews.

For consumers visiting a service provider, the service environment is the first aspect of the service that is perceived by the customer, and it is at this stage that consumers are likely to form impressions of the level of service they will receive. Bitner defines a servicescape as "the environment in which the service is assembled and in which the seller and customer interact, combined with tangible commodities that facilitate performance or communication of the service" (Booms & Bitner, 1981, pp. 47–51). In other words, the servicescape refers to the nonhuman elements of the environment in which service encounters occur.

Research conducted by Heung and Gu (2012) unveils the relationship between restaurant atmospherics and dining satisfaction and behavioral intentions. The results revealed restaurant atmospherics to have a significant influence on guest dining satisfaction and their behavioral intentions, particularly their intentions to return and spread positive word-of-mouth reviews and their willingness to pay more.

Al-Kilani and El Hedhli (2021) also discuss the importance of perceived restaurant authenticity, in terms of design, ambience, and social factors as exogenous antecedents affecting restaurant authenticity dimensions. This includes the dining experience, atmospherics, restaurant attachments, and patronage. These dimensions are linked to a positively influenced restaurant attachment, which in turn positively predicts restaurant patronage.

The summary is a view that collectively designed servicescape and "experiencescape" will create lasting memories and emotional connections with customers (Dedeoglu et al., 2018). Such pleasures and experiences reside in the mind, after all, not in the moment.

Dessert: The proof of the pudding is in the eating

What happens when we are presented with a plate of food? The usual process includes a series of quality checks. Does the dish look good? Is it what was expected or perhaps more? Are the aromas pleasant? Is the temperature appropriate (hot, cold, ambient?), etc. Has the dish passed these simple tests?

Next comes the taste test. The initial morsels enter the mouth and the analysis of flavors and textures begins. Is it delicious, or perhaps at the other end of the scale, or somewhere in between?

If food quality is acceptable, we tend to continue, depending on a series of variables. For example, as a wedding guest, would you send a meal back if the quality was not quite right? Perhaps not? However, there may be circumstances where we feel fully justified, as consumers, to return meals that have quality issues. This is highly dependent on circumstances alongside a range of personal considerations and characteristics as to how we might respond or react.

It is natural beyond these initial checks to relax and enjoy the social aspects of dining, enjoying the occasion, the company of our fellow diners, and the general atmosphere. The theory of the primacy and recency effect, alongside "duration neglect," also suggests that we tend to recall more details at the beginning (primacy) and end (recency) of events and struggle to record accurate accounts of proceedings in between (the duration neglect). It is suggested, therefore, that chefs and restaurateurs should be mindful of this and meet the challenge of ensuring that all aspects of the meal occasion have memorable and high-quality interactions, particularly when delivering tasting menus of many courses (see Muñoz et al., 2018).

Value judgments are personal and not straightforward. For example, the same consumer can enjoy a high-cost experience and feel they have received value for money, but on another occasion feel they have not received value for money for a meal at a much lower price point. This applies vice versa. The price may be linked to expectations, but it is not a guarantee of value or even perceived quality.

Many factors drive consumers to pay premium prices for gastronomic experiences. This can range from our appreciation of innovative, high-quality, and technically crafted dishes to more materialistic and hedonistic associations—the exclusivity of dining in the best restaurants, for example (Kiatkawsin & Han, 2019). However, it is also the people who interact as an integral part of this process, and at every level of the industry, who play such a pivotal role in the delivery of products, services, and experiences. Long may this continue!

CHAPTER 19

The importance of chefs and their influence on eating patterns

Neil Rippington

Introduction

Chefs play a pivotal role in shaping the culinary landscape, influencing the types of food we consume and our broader eating patterns. This chapter explores chefs' historical and contemporary significance, examining their impact on health trends, sustainability, and culinary innovation.

The chapter investigates recent historical developments and how a relatively small number of people, in this case chefs, can influence remarkable change in the development of cuisine.

Chefs and their roles

Have you ever considered why a chef's jacket is like that of a doctor?

In the past, when medicine was far less advanced, chefs or cooks played a part similar to that of doctors today. However, instead of medicine, they used healthy meals to boost the health of their patients. This is why the chef's job is so important; they have a responsibility to provide healthy, nutritious, and recuperative food.

In 1765, a French chef, A. M. Boulanger, opened a dining space in Paris where several soups were prepared for the guests to choose from. These soups were called "soupe restaurante": a restorative soup made from many vegetables. From this, the word "restaurant" developed into what it is today. At that time, a restaurant was a place where people could restore their bodies by eating a lot of vegetables. The word "restaurant" originates from the French *restaurer*, meaning "to recover." It is derived from the Latin *restaurare*, which translates as "remake," "rebuild," and "renew."

However, using food to restore the body is not a new concept, and dates back much further than 1765. The Greek physician Hippocrates (460–370 BC), considered the "father of modern medicine," is most renowned for his quote, "Let food be thy medicine, and medicine be thy food." This underpins the origin of the Hippocratic Oath for doctors.

Ironically, despite the huge developments in science and technology, we currently live in a time when most of the world's illnesses and diseases are attributed to poor diets and eating patterns.

Brief overview of eating patterns

Through the course of the last several decades, the rate of obesity has progressively increased and is now one of the leading causes of death worldwide. In 2016, the World Health Organization reported 1.9 billion adults as overweight and 650 million as obese. Modern eating habits, processed foods, and global issues related to poor diet, including obesity and food-related diseases, present the most serious medical concerns to our species.

Chefs, therefore, have an important role. They can help to determine the market. They can improve development and influence trends and eating patterns.

Historical context

The profession of chefs has evolved significantly over the centuries. In the past, chefs primarily catered to the elite, but their influence has since permeated all levels of society. This section traces the historical development of the chef's role and its impact on eating habits.

The oldest collection of recipes to survive from antiquity, *De Re Coquinaria* ("The Art of Cooking"), is attributed to Marcus Gavius Apicius (AD 14–37), the famed Roman epicure who flourished during the reign of Emperor Tiberius.

Apicius was renowned for his love of food. He was a gourmand responsible for organizing extravagant dinner parties, funded by the imperial court, to feed and entertain foreign dignitaries. These elaborate affairs offered Apicius and the court the opportunity to showcase the finest Roman cuisine.

In more recent history, the professional chef has risen from the lowest rungs of social status to celebrity prestige. The rise in status of the chef is remarkable. From slaves or indentured servants in the earliest days of colonial America (J. Miller, 2018) to the early European chefs, cooking for the kings and queens of Europe (Antonin Carême, for example), the eminence of leading chefs today is in sharp contrast to the past. This is investigated in further detail in the next section.

The recent evolution of the chef's profession

French cuisine, throughout modern history, has earned global respect and admiration. France enjoys an amazing natural larder and has benefited from such resources. France enjoys a mixed climate bordering northern Europe in the north of the country, with its cooler climate and the cold-water seas of the English Channel, contrasting with the warmer climate of the Mediterranean in the south. France has forests, mountains, rivers and lakes, seas and oceans, and a wealth of nutrient-rich farmland, providing a terrific foundation for haute cuisine and resulting in a country with great pride in its culinary history.

France is renowned for its cuisine worldwide. Just the word "France" conjures associations with food for many people. Regardless of the globalization of foods from around the world and the massive growth in travel during recent decades, French cuisine remains a key influencer in the development of others. However, not all has been smooth in the development of French cuisine. When a paradigm shifts, we all go back to zero—or do we?

Trends and innovations occur in all walks of life. We recently entered a digital age and are experiencing changes in advancing technologies, including artificial intelligence (AI). Such huge social shifts are often affected by a relatively small number of people. This is the same in the culinary world. The developments from leading chefs become the norm in the wider world of hospitality a few years down the line and later filter into the domestic environment.

Historical influence of chefs on eating habits

Suppose the most renowned chefs and those making the most significant innovations are at the top of the culinary pyramid. In this scenario, those below look for inspiration, often replicating their methods and ingredients. From a relatively small number of primary developers and leaders, a larger group is inspired. From chefs and the world of professional cooking, this filters down to the public over time, as innovations and products are not immediately known and people would not know immediately how to use the techniques and products in their cooking. Therefore, the higher echelons of gastronomy function as teachers, providing their metaphorical students with a world of new possibilities.

Classical French cuisine

Modern gastronomy, as we know it, emerged as a field in the first half of the nineteenth century. Institutional change arose with the advent of restaurants and codified culinary knowledge. The French Revolution of 1789 undermined the institutional logic of the *ancien régime* cuisine and the associated role identity of the chef.

Antonin Carême (1784–1833), a chef who worked in the houses of great patrons, pioneered the effort to systematize the principles of modern cuisine. Carême took the idea of the chef as an artist from *ancien régime* cuisine and created a vision of *grande cuisine* as both an art and a science. Another iconic figure in this evolution was Auguste Escoffier (1845–1935). Escoffier worked in the kitchens of fashionable hotels that had been established in the major cities of Europe, notably by César Ritz (Ritz, Savoy).

If Carême's books (see Kelly, 2005) constituted the Old Testament, Escoffier's *Le guide culinaire* (1903a, translated in English by Cracknell & Kaufmann in 2013), became the New Testament forming the body of what came to be known as "French classical cuisine." This book remains a central text in the training of professional cooks today, as well as contributing to many other books and resources. Escoffier introduced a new kitchen organizational structure, the "partie" system, which is still in use in kitchens throughout the world today.

Escoffier wrote down dishes in the order of presentation (*service à la russe*) and developed the first à la carte menu. "In a word, cookery, whilst continuing to be an art, will become scientific and will have to submit its formulas which very often are still too empirical, to a method and precision which leaves nothing to chance" (Escoffier, 1903b, preface).

This was introduced in five dimensions, useful to help in understanding the institutional logic and role identity of classical cuisine. The dimensions were: culinary rhetoric, rules of cooking, the archetypal ingredients used, the role of the chef, and the organization of the menu (Fischler, 1989). Dishes were also regularly associated with names of places, noblemen, events, or characters (e.g., Vichy, Wellington, Paris-Brest, Pavlova).

French classical cuisine relied on conformation. Dishes consisted of the same ingredients cooked in the same way with the same garnishes. Chefs could not divert from these regulations. For example, Tournedos Rossini consisted of a fillet steak (cut from the central section of the fillet of beef) placed on a *croûte* (large crouton), topped with a seared slice of foie gras, and served with Madeira sauce and freshly shaved truffle. Chefs could not deviate from these components. If the dish did not contain these ingredients and steps, it did not qualify to be named Tournedos Rossini. All dishes were registered, and therefore, creativity and freedom were limited for the chefs, regardless of their standing and reputation. These dishes became strong brands related to cultural identity. They stand the test of time, in the same way that an Irish stew or Lancashire hotpot, for example, identifies the cultural identity of the dish in British cuisine.

Menus were long and highly structured in format. Each dish was categorized into its section: hors d'oeuvres (single/variés), soups, eggs, farinaceous, entré, relevé, entremets, savory, etc. This created huge inventories and required significant labor. Processes were often lengthy, involving many steps, transforming and metamorphosing the ingredients to some degree, also losing their lightness and freshness. Another striking difference in comparison to the standing of chefs today was to be seen in the dining ritual. Today, celebrity chefs are known to us through mass media. Many leading chefs have eponymous restaurants, and others have strong associations to the restaurant where the public is aware of the chef concerned.

In French classical cuisine, the ritual was outside the plate and the power was in the restaurant (front-of-house). The maître d'hôtel/maître d' (head waiter) and their team served dishes from silver flats, gueridon trolleys, soup tureens, and dessert trolleys. Dishes such as steak Diane would be prepared and flambéed in front of customers, and lights dimmed as a baked Alaska (omelette soufflé surprise) was flamed and paraded through the restaurant to the guests concerned. The drama and theater belonged to the restaurant, while the chefs were rarely seen, working behind the scenes, preparing dishes for front-of-house personnel to showcase. The delivery of such classic menus was also time-consuming, as the lengthy menus and so many courses created a long consumption period.

The revolution: The shift to nouvelle cuisine

In the eyes of the leading chefs, a growing movement was beginning to suggest that French classical cuisine lacked technical autonomy. These leading chefs, with the highest level of skills and technical ability, became frustrated with the rigidity and regulation demanded. Culinary icons began to lead the defection from "classical" to "nouvelle" cuisine, and this movement of elite chefs led to social change.

Chefs became the "lead actors," the influencers of the new movement. Nouvelle cuisine was an "anti-school" alongside other movements in the arts, film, theater, and literature (in 1968 France was on the verge of a revolution, battling against authoritarian systems). Nouvelle cuisine was promoted from within by those with more credentials than influences from outside the craft. These experts started the attack on existing logic to enhance professional control.

The term "nouvelle cuisine" was coined by two food critics, Henri Gault and Christian Millau, in France in 1973. This nouvelle cuisine (new cuisine) was formed upon ten new commandments based on truth and transparency, lightness and simplicity, imagination and freshness. Service was via the plate, and the power shifted from the maître d' in the restaurant to the chef in the kitchen. The consumption period became shorter and inventories smaller, emphasizing fresh, seasonal products.

The leading chefs became innovators with new identities and logic. They wanted guests to "enjoy the shock of the new." They aimed to explore culinary innovation and simplicity. The innovation of dishes gained increased influence from overseas, for example, from the fresh approach in Japan to the increased use of spices and the exploration of exotic traditions.

Missing from the above are a whole host of influences, most notably where this new style of cooking came from. There was little precedent in France for the lightly cooked, lightly sauced, yet intricately plated dishes, what the late writer and critic Josh Ozersky called "tweezer food," before it appeared suddenly and decisively in France in the 1960s (McCarron, 2017).

A great deal of nouvelle cuisine's innovations paralleled classical aspects of Japanese dining, especially the movement's emphasis on shorter cooking times; minimalist, playful plating; and a focus on extracting the essential aspects of an ingredient, rather than transforming it. Perhaps not coincidentally, from the time that French chefs began visiting Japan (and Japanese chefs began training in France) in the mid-1960s, fine dining has become increasingly like Japan's most formal dining tradition, Kaiseki.

Kaiseki is most easily defined as Japanese haute cuisine, but like many translations, that equivalence leaves out key context. As previously discussed, European haute cuisine descended from royal court banquets, whereas Kaiseki's cultural legacy is tied both to the dining habits of the elite and the Zen Buddhist tradition, highlighting the rustic and the seasonal as a meditation on impermanence.

The "lead actors" influencing and at the heart of the movement in France were among the most respected and renowned chefs, including:

- Paul Bocuse
- Michel Guerard
- Pierre Troisgros
- Alain Chapel.

Each of these chefs held the coveted three Michelin stars, and all were awarded the "Meilleur Ouvrier de France," a national award presented by the president of France. Below is a simple example of the power of influence as highlighted by chef Troisgros.

> You need to know the context to understand the story of the famous dish "L'escalope de saumon à l'oseille" [Escalope of salmon with sorrel]. We were in a very creative period, with the nouvelle cuisine, new journalists, new cooking techniques ... I remember it was in 1970. I presented the recipe to the Culinary Academy. It was refused, it was too easy! Yet afterwards, the recipe spread. We were sickened and appalled by the plagiarism.
>
> But you know, Coco Chanel once said, "Sad is the day when I won't be plagiarized anymore."
>
> It was great if my colleagues mentioned our dish, like my friend Paul (Bocuse) did; nobody could ignore its inventors, the creators (Troisgros, interview with Monin, Roanne, January 25, 2001, in Rao, Monin, & Durand, 2003).

The new movement ...

The term "molecular gastronomy" was coined by physicist Nicolas Kurti in 1992. It gave people trying to make sense of menus from leading chefs with dishes such as grain-mustard ice cream and white chocolate with caviar, or palate cleansers cooked in "liquid nitrogen," an easy label. However, the term created artificial barriers. "Molecular" suggested complicated, and "gastronomy" made it sound elitist. However, the biggest development was in "sensory design." No longer was eating out about putting food in our mouths and deciding whether it was pleasant or not; eating became a multisensory experience. Its roots blended tradition with innovation, food science, and technology.

The leading chefs at this point included Ferran Adria of El Bulli, Heston Blumenthal of The Fat Duck, Thomas Keller of the French Laundry and Per Se, and food scientist and writer Harold McGee. The group produced a statement on the "new cookery" (Adria et al., 2006).

Three basic principles guide our cooking: excellence, openness, and integrity.

1. Cooking values tradition, builds on it, and along with tradition is part of the ongoing evolution of our craft.

This suggests selecting from the entire planet's ingredients, cooking methods, and traditions, and draws on all human knowledge in the exploration of what it is possible to do with food and the experience of eating.

2. We embrace innovation—new ingredients, techniques, appliances, information, and ideas—whenever it can make a real contribution to our cooking.

This emphasizes that novelty is not pursued for its own sake. The chefs accept the use of modern thickening agents, sugar substitutes, enzymes, liquid nitrogen, sous vide, dehydration, and other non-traditional means, but these do not define the cooking.

They represent a few of the many tools that chefs are fortunate to have available as they strive to make delicious and stimulating dishes. Similarly, the disciplines of food chemistry and food technology are valuable sources of information and ideas for all cooks. Even the most straightforward traditional preparations can be strengthened by an understanding of the ingredients and methods, and chemists have been helping cooks for hundreds of years.

3. We believe that cooking can affect people in profound ways and that a spirit of collaboration and sharing is essential to true progress in developing this potential.

The principle here is that the act of eating engages all the senses as well as the mind. Preparing and serving food could therefore be the most complex and comprehensive of the performing arts.

With development comes the concern of the risk of terrible things being done to food in the name of innovation (and due to imitation). There is the danger that technology overtakes the value of the dish. Many people (chefs included) often miss the point of new approaches. These elite chefs emphasize their beliefs, values, and commitments to be sincere, and do not simply follow the latest trend. They acknowledge that they (the lead actors of today) have a part to play in "the history of tomorrow."

Challenges and future directions: Innovation, sustainability, and modern eating patterns

Despite their significant influence, chefs face numerous challenges, including maintaining sustainable practices in operations and adapting to changing consumer preferences. Looking ahead, the culinary world is likely to see increased emphasis on ethical dining and technological integration.

Chefs today are increasingly focusing on healthy eating, promoting dishes that are not only delicious but also nutritious. This shift reflects broader societal trends towards wellness and preventive healthcare.

Sustainability has become a key concern in the culinary world. Chefs are at the forefront of advocating farm-to-table practices, reducing food waste, and promoting local and seasonal ingredients.

The Green Star was introduced in 2021 to highlight restaurants at the forefront of the industry when it comes to their sustainable practices. These establishments offer dining experiences that combine culinary excellence with outstanding eco-friendly commitments. They are a source of inspiration both for keen foodies and the wider hospitality industry.

Every Green Star restaurant is different and works in its unique way, but all make a difference to the world around them and act as role models to us all. Many work directly with growers, farmers, and fishermen; foraging in hedgerows and woodlands; growing plants and rearing animals; and using regenerative methods such as no-dig vegetable gardens and successional cover crop growing. They also often go beyond environmental considerations to address issues related to ethics and well-being, as well as contributing to local, national, or global charitable and educational projects.

There is no specific formula for awarding a Green Star, as every restaurant and its surrounding region has a unique set of conditions. The Michelin inspectors are simply looking for those at the top of their game when it comes to their sustainable practices. They consider things such as the provenance of the ingredients; the use of seasonal produce; the restaurant's environmental footprint; food waste systems; general waste disposal and recycling; resource management; and the communication between the team and the guests about the restaurant's sustainable approach.

Culinary innovation and its impact on the wider society

Innovation in the kitchen is driven largely by chefs who continuously experiment with new techniques and ingredients. This spirit of creativity not only enhances the dining experience but also sets new standards and trends in the food industry.

Innovation, however, is often created by first reflecting on what has gone before and by delving into history. Examples of chefs who have built complete concepts that respect and celebrate history include Grant Achatz, whose menu at Next, Chicago, titled "Paris, 1906," celebrated the cooking of Auguste Escoffier. Another example is Dinner by Heston Blumenthal, in London, where the menu lists dates and historical references next to each dish. The story of Dinner began in the late 1990s with Blumenthal's fascination with historic gastronomy. The savory ice creams of the late 1800s, the theater of the Tudor dining experiences, and the dishes of *Alice's Adventures in Wonderland* all resonated with his unique approach to cooking. Examining the contributions of prominent chefs provides insight into their broader impact. For instance, chef Alice Waters is renowned for pioneering the "Farm-to-Table Movement," while Spanish chef Ferran Adrià, of the renowned El Bulli restaurant (closed 2011) near Roses, in the northeast of Spain, revolutionized culinary techniques.

Chefs have made significant impacts on the world's nutrition, not just by creating innovative dishes but also by advocating for healthier eating, sustainable practices, and food education. Chefs, through their work in the culinary arts, have increasingly formed connections with psychologists, social scientists, nutritionists, farmers, and policymakers. These interdisciplinary collaborations are vital in addressing complex food, health, and sustainability issues, and creating a holistic approach to food

Chefs collaborate with psychologists to understand the sensory and emotional experiences of eating. Such collaboration has led to menus that are not only delectable to consume but also evoke emotions and/or memories. Research in this area includes how different flavors, textures, and presentations can influence mood and psychological well-being (Myhrvold, Young, & Bilet, 2021). For example, the collaboration between chef Heston Blumenthal, psychologists, engineers, and food scientists at The Fat Duck in Bray, U.K., explored how sound and other sensory inputs affect the dining experience (Spence, 2017).

Social scientists study the cultural, social, and economic contexts of food, and chefs often work with them to understand the societal implications of food choices, such as how food can promote community and social justice or how food trends reflect broader cultural shifts. A powerful example is provided by food activist, Carlo Petrini. In 1986, in response to the rapid growth of fast food and the health concerns around its rising consumption, Petrini protested the building of a McDonald's restaurant near the Spanish Steps in Rome. Soon after, Petrini founded the international "Slow Food Movement," renouncing not only fast food but also the increasing pace of life. Issuing a manifesto, the movement called for the safeguarding of local economies, the preservation of indigenous gastronomic traditions, and the creation of a new kind of ecologically aware consumerism committed to sustainability. This movement also emphasizes biodiversity, often partnering with anthropologists and sociologists to promote these values globally (Petrini, McCuaig, & Waters, 2003).

Nutritionists and dietitians also work closely with chefs to create meals that are not only delicious but also nutritionally balanced. This collaboration is crucial in settings like schools, hospitals, and restaurants focused on health-conscious dining. In hospitals, chefs and nutritionists collaborate to create meal plans for patients that meet specific dietary needs while also being appetizing. Programs including "Healthy Kitchens, Healthy Lives," a collaboration between the Culinary Institute of America and the Harvard T.H. Chan School of Public Health, bring chefs and nutritionists together to promote healthy cooking practices, bridging nutrition science, healthcare, and the culinary arts.

Chefs often partner with local farmers to source fresh, seasonal, and sustainable ingredients. These relationships support local economies and ensure chefs have access to high-quality produce. In turn, chefs can influence farming practices by demanding certain types of produce, promoting biodiversity, and supporting organic and sustainable farming methods.

Chef restaurateur Alice Waters is the pioneer of the Farm-to-Table Movement. Her restaurant, Chez Panisse in Berkeley, California, focuses on using fresh, local, and organic ingredients. The Farm-to-Table Movement embodies collaboration, pioneering direct sourcing from local farmers, influencing the wider culinary world and supporting sustainable agriculture. Waters has been a strong advocate for sustainable agriculture and has promoted the integration of healthy food into school programs through her "Edible Schoolyard Project."

Chef Dan Barber is another leading voice in the sustainable food movement. His restaurants, Family Meal at Blue Hill and Blue Hill at Stone Barns, emphasize the importance of sourcing food locally and sustainably. Barber's book, *The Third Plate* (Barber, 2014), explores the future of food and agriculture, advocating a more holistic approach to eating. René Redzepi, the chef behind Noma in Copenhagen, revolutionized Nordic cuisine by focusing on foraging and locally sourced ingredients. His approach emphasizes the nutritional and environmental benefits of eating locally and seasonally.

Chefs are increasingly engaging with policymakers to influence food policy, advocating changes that support sustainable food systems, food security, and public health. They may work on campaigns to reduce food waste, promote local food systems, and address food inequality.

Chef José Andrés is not only known for his culinary expertise but also for his humanitarian work. Through his nonprofit organization, World Central Kitchen, Andrés has provided meals in disaster-stricken areas around the world. His efforts highlight the critical role chefs can play in addressing food security and nutrition during crises. Andrés is an advocate for food policy changes and better food systems worldwide. His work highlights the critical role chefs can play in influencing food policy.

British chef Jamie Oliver, who rose to fame as the "Naked Chef," has also been a vocal advocate for healthy eating, particularly in schools. His campaign to improve school meals in the U.K. led to significant changes in government policies. Oliver has also worked on various initiatives to educate the public on healthy eating and the importance of home cooking and enjoying meals with family and friends.

Massimo Bottura, chef of Osteria Francescana, Modena, Italy, has used his three-Michelin-star platform to combat food waste. Through his nonprofit organization, Food for Soul, Bottura has opened community kitchens around the world that use surplus food to feed those in need, promoting both sustainability and nutrition.

These chefs have gone beyond the kitchen to influence how we think about food, nutrition, and sustainability, impacting global food practices and policies.

Conclusion

In conclusion, chefs have a profound impact on our eating patterns, shaping them through health-conscious choices, sustainable practices, and culinary innovations. Their role continues to evolve, reflecting and driving changes in the way we approach food.

The rise of TV cooking shows and social media platforms has turned chefs into cultural icons. Television programs like *MasterChef* and platforms like Instagram have given chefs a global stage to influence eating patterns and food preferences. Chefs are not simply cooks. Over time, they have been labeled as doctors (think "soupe restaurante"), celebrities, influencers, innovators, activists, teachers, nutritionists, and even historians.

In principle, chefs can choose from the entire planet's ingredients, cooking methods, and traditions, and draw on all human knowledge to explore what it is possible to do with food and the experience of eating.

After all, the world's culinary traditions are collective, cumulative inventions, a heritage created by hundreds of generations of cooks. Tradition is the base that all cooks who aspire to excellence must know and master. An open approach builds on the best that tradition has to offer.

A few final quotes on the influence of chefs on eating patterns …

> "The discovery of a new dish does more for the happiness of the human race than the discovery of a star"—Jean Anthelme Brillat-Savarin (1783–1833), *The Physiology of Taste: Or Meditations on Transcendental Gastronomy* (1825a).

> "When it comes to food, every day is a school day."

And …

> "Great food is built from great ingredients"—Neil Rippington (and many others, I expect).

And although not from a chef, a fitting one to finish:

> "Fashions change, but style endures."—Coco Chanel (Barry, 1965).

In the culinary field, trends and fashions do indeed change, but style and traditional processes continue to provide the foundations for great cooking and the enjoyment of eating.

CHAPTER 20

Reign of the fat heads: The evolutionary advantage of human brain development

Kimberley Wilson

The human body, when compared to those of other members of the kingdom *Animalia*, is, frankly, not very impressive. We can't fly. We're not particularly strong. And it takes us several months to even learn how to walk. In a physical head-to-head against many other animals we would, more often than not, be found decidedly lacking. Where we are the heavyweights of the animal kingdom, though, is when it comes to the brain, in particular the size of our brains *in proportion to our body size*. The largest land mammal, the African elephant, has a brain that is 0.1% of its overall body weight. Our closest primate relative, the chimpanzee's brain weighs in at 0.8%. The human brain, in contrast, makes up around 2% of our body weight. This matters because brains are, metabolically, very expensive to run. So much so that that 2% is the single biggest contributor to basal metabolic rate, comprising 20% of utilized energy when the body is at rest. Our brains are much bigger than would be predicted by our body size and shape. Neurologically speaking, we are commuting in a gas-guzzling tank, while the African elephant it getting around town on a bicycle.

To minimize the threat of a brain energy crisis (i.e., the organism not being able to acquire sufficient energy to fuel the brain), there is usually an evolutionary trade-off between an animal's body size and its brain. Hence the elephant's large body and tiny brain volume. However, rather than a smaller body, our species benefited from two key adaptations: one physical and one cultural. First, humans are able to store more body fat than other primates. A male bonobo chimp, for example, has 0.005% body fat, while a human male varies between 12% and 20%. This portable energy source reduces the amount of time we have to spend looking for and eating food. This frees up time for the second crucial adaptation: culture. In this case, the cultural practice of cooking our food helped to liberate more energy and nutrients from it, giving us more opportunity to contemplate, to explore. To think.

However, it is not solely the *amount* of available energy that is a limiting factor for brain size. Neurons are constructed from specific materials, long-chain fats, that we cannot synthesize endogenously. These fats (and other nutrients important for brain development) are abundant in the marine food web (fish, seafood, seaweed). This factor explains why the next group of animals with a high brain–body ratio are the cetaceans (whales, dolphins, and porpoises) who feed on these food sources daily. And it points, along with other evidence, to seafood having played a significant role in the human diet during our evolutionary history. For a significant proportion of our development as a species, we were coastal and lakeshore dwellers. Fossil analysis indicates that, compared to Neanderthals, seafood comprised 10–50% of the diet for early modern humans (Bradbury, 2011). This diet, rich in marine foods, provided an abundance of preformed DHA (as well as other key brain nutrients like iodine and choline) that propelled the development and complexity of our brains. Simply, our species' brain development was fueled by fish. Consequently, today, we continue to need regular amounts of it for optimal brain health.

Yet population nutrition surveys in the U.K. and other Western countries indicate that our consumption of these brain-building nutrients is worryingly low. If these nutrients are indeed essential for proper brain development and function, we would expect, then, that inadequate consumption would manifest in neurological impairment at both the individual and population levels. And, indeed, that is what we are starting to see in our growing rates of neurodegenerative disease, mental ill-health, and alarmingly, our declining IQ.

The Flynn Effect

Named after the IQ researcher James Flynn, the Flynn Effect is the observation that, for the majority of the twentieth century, global IQ scores have progressively increased. However, starting in the late twentieth century, worrying trends in global IQ began to be reported. For the first time since records began, IQ scores in Western countries like Germany (Pietschnig & Gittler, 2015), Norway (Bratsberg & Rogeberg, 2018), Denmark (Teasdale & Owen, 2005), and Australia (Flynn & Shayer, 2018) started to decline. High IQ scores in the U.K. were "decimated." What could be behind this assault on our IQ?

What is IQ?

IQ is a measure of cognitive capacities such as working memory, verbal comprehension, processing speed, reasoning, knowledge, and visual-spatial processing. Early IQ tests and their outcomes are well-documented for their lack of validity and their misuse by eugenicists to justify prejudicial policies. A full discussion of the early abuse of this science is outside of the scope of this chapter. What we do know is that today and within Western cultures, IQ test scores predict a range of academic and workplace outcomes, including a strong correlation with lifetime earnings. Furthermore, good performance on one part of an IQ test, say verbal reasoning, correlates to good performance on another feature like working memory. This relationship between performance on varied domains of cognition is described as the "general factor" and seems to be a feature of executive function.

Executive function—those higher order capacities such as reasoning, impulse control, goal-directed behavior, and social cognition, are coordinated by the prefrontal cortex (PFC). So, a well-operating PFC can more efficiently coordinate the executive functions that underlie the general factor of IQ. A well-operating PFC is a well-connected PFC. For example, an innovative imaging study by Dubois et al. published in 2018 found that individual intelligence could be predicted from patterns of resting state brain activity, with the degree of connectivity predicting 20% of the variance in intelligence. The better the connectivity, the higher the IQ.

Broadly speaking then, being born with more connections in your brain is a good thing. And adequate nutrition during gestation is the foundation of healthy neuronal architecture. In animal models, mouse pups born to mothers that were deprived of DHA during gestation had a 50% reduction in neurite growth in the hippocampus (Cao et al., 2009). They also showed deficits in long-term potentiation, the neuronal process underlying learning and memory. In short, insufficient DHA during pregnancy led to impaired learning in offspring. But do we see the same thing in humans?

Studies that compare the brain development or cognitive performance of infants born to mothers who had differing levels of essential fatty acid intake during pregnancy show remarkable similarities to the animal data. For example, Hibbeln and colleagues (2007) found a dose-response relationship between maternal fish consumption and IQ. A study of over 1,500 Dutch mother-child pairs by Zou et al. (2021) found that maternal fatty acid status at mid-pregnancy was associated with offspring gray- and white-matter volumes: the higher the mother's blood levels of omega-3, the greater her child's brain volume at age ten. Another research team (Morton et al., 2020) scanned the brains of ninety-two one-month-old babies (born to term) and analyzed the brain imaging data against a range of nutrients in the mother's diet. They too found a positive correlation between the mothers' intake of omega-3 fats and the volume of the prefrontal lobes of the babies' brains (the highest concentration of DHA in the human brain is found in the PFC). These differences were found not to be correlated with the mother's race, education level, or the household income.

Adequate omega-3 during the period of brain development has a dose-dependent relationship to overall and regional brain volumes, and connectivity. But in the enterprise that is your brain, DHA is not the only nutrient in town. Other key compounds, also deficient in the Western or Standard American Diet, help to explain our gradually declining brain health and function.

Iodine

The World Health Organization (2007) deems iodine deficiency "the single most important preventable cause of brain damage" worldwide. This is because iodine is required to produce thyroid hormones, which initiate the development of the brain in utero, determining neuronal density. Iodine deficiency during pregnancy and early life leads to permanently suppressed IQ. Extreme iodine deficiency causes severe physical and mental impairment.

A 2013 study by Bath et al. looked at child IQ as a function of maternal iodine status during the first trimester of pregnancy. They identified two things: first was a dose-dependent relationship between maternal iodine and measure of child IQ and reading ability: the higher the iodine, the higher (better) the cognitive scores. Second, and of concern, was that iodine deficiency in women in early pregnancy was the norm, with 67% of women having mild to moderate deficiency during the first twelve weeks of pregnancy.

Rich sources of iodine (and omega-3 DHA) include oily fish, seaweed, and seafood. Notably, in the U.K., both child and adult intakes of oily fish fall far below recommended levels.

Choline

Another nutrient, long-known to be important for brain development and signal transmission is choline, the derivatives of which form part of brain cell membranes and participate in the one-carbon cycle essential for DNA synthesis and gene expression. It is also a major constituent of the neurotransmitter and neuromodulator acetylcholine, which as well as its role in cognition (particularly learning, memory, and attention) is the principal neurotransmitter of the parasympathetic nervous system. It may also protect the developing fetus from neural tube defects such as spina bifida. Choline is designated "conditionally essential" during pregnancy. Though small amounts of choline can be produced in the liver through the action of phosphatidylethanolamine N-methyltransferase (PEMT), this endogenous production is insufficient for the body's needs, and choline must be topped up through dietary intake. During pregnancy, a very large amount of choline is delivered to the baby, indicating that it plays a crucially important role in fetal development. In animal studies, choline supplementation improves the formation of blood vessels in the placenta and the quality of placental blood flow, crucial to the supply of nutrients to the developing offspring. In humans, it is considered critical for normal brain development during pregnancy. However, research establishes that it also remains important throughout lactation, weaning, and early childhood.

But we have a problem. The choline Adequate Intake measure (U.S.) for pregnant women (450mg p/d) was based on the amount for non-pregnant women + 25mg, a value itself extrapolated from just *one* study conducted on *men* and looking specifically at liver disease. We really have very little experimental data on which to determine the RDA for choline for pregnant women.

One illuminating paper from the U.S. by Bahnfleth et al. (2021) highlights the urgent need for more evidence on the adequate amount of choline for *optimal brain development during pregnancy*. In this study, women were randomized into two groups of choline supplementation during the third trimester of pregnancy. One group received a supplement of the recommended adequate intake of choline (450mg p/d). The second group received more than twice that amount: 930mg per day. Seven years later, the researchers revisited the families and assessed the children on tests of attention. When they compared performance, the children of the mothers who received the higher dose of choline were better able to sustain attention longer and with greater accuracy. Of course, the ability to pay attention goes further than being able to perform well in laboratory settings. Simply put, children who can pay attention do better in school. The ability to pay attention is a predictor of scholastic performance in literacy, vocabulary, and math above the contribution of IQ (McClelland et al., 2007; Metallidou et al., 2016). That is, school performance isn't just about being naturally gifted but also how well you can stay focused on the problem at hand. Though this was a small trial of just twenty children, it is consistent with other clinical trials and animal data; increased maternal choline intake during pregnancy is associated with long-term improved cognition in offspring. Furthermore, it indicates that the current Adequate Intake recommendations might well be far from adequate for the needs of pregnant women. For those of us in the U.K. and Europe, currently the European Food Safety Authority recommends 480 and 520mg p/d of choline for pregnant and lactating women, respectively, around half the amount shown to be beneficial in recent studies. Of further concern is that a recent analysis of dietary intake undertaken by Vennemann et al. (2015) indicated that habitual consumption of choline in adults was below the recommended levels, at 291–468 mg/d.

The Western diet

The diet that drove the development of our impressive brains is, however, for most people in Western countries, not the diet we are consuming. In the U.K. (Dicken, Qamar, & Batterham, 2023) and U.S. (Juul et al., 2022), 50% of the diet is comprised of ultra-processed foods (UPF). These industrialized products are typically made of ingredients that have gone through significant industrial processing, such as refined flours, starches, hydrolyzed proteins, and invert sugar syrups. They also often contain additives such as flavorings, emulsifiers, preservatives, treatment, and anti-caking agents. Crucially, what is typically lost in the production of UPF is fiber, essential fats, and micronutrients (vitamins and minerals).

The more our diets are made up of UPF, the lower our daily nutrient intake. A 2015 Brazilian study by Louzada et al. (2015) that assessed the diets of over 32,000 individuals over the age of ten showed that the consumption of UPF was inversely correlated to the intake of vitamins B12, vitamin D, vitamin E, niacin (B3), pyridoxine (B6), copper, iron, phosphorus, magnesium, selenium, and zinc. A more recent Mexican study of 10,000 people aged over one year conducted by Marrón-Ponce et al. (2023) found the same thing; the higher the consumption of UPFs, the lower the intake of B vitamins, vitamins C and E, and minerals. In a cohort of Columbian children, omega-3s, vitamins A, B12, C, and E, calcium, and zinc were found to be lower (Cornwell et al., 2017).

As UPFs begin to displace more nutrient-dense whole foods, we are starting to see evidence of negative effects on brain and mental health. A 2021 study by Hayhoe et al. of more than 8,000 UK children, published in the *BMJ Nutrition, Prevention & Health*, found an association between higher consumption of fruits and vegetables and self-reported mental well-being. For secondary school children, they saw a linear or dose-responsive pattern, that is, for each extra portion of fruit and veg consumed (measured up to "five or more"), their mental well-being score went up. When the results were adjusted to account for confounding factors such as alcohol consumption, smoking status, household income markers, such as whether they had their own bed, and adverse events, such as bullying or not feeling safe at home, the association held.

In a longitudinal study by Jacka et al. (2015) that looked at the brains of older people over the course of four years, there was a direct relationship between diet quality and hippocampal size; the healthier the diet, the larger the area of the brain's memory center. A separate study by Stevenson et al. (2020) showed that these negative effects on the brain emerge *within days* on a Western UPF diet. In this study, 110 healthy people, who typically ate a nutritious diet, were asked to eat a Western-type diet for just a week. Within that week, they were asked to eat two Belgian waffles for breakfast on four of the days and consume a takeaway meal twice. Compared to a control group, the Western-style diet group suffered impairments in hippocampal-dependent learning and memory, and poorer appetite control. The declines in learning and memory correlated to the degree of impaired appetite control, indicating that damage to the hippocampus underlined these changes. Returning to a healthy diet reverses these changes.

Eating ourselves to extinction

Our large, complex brains are what have distinguished us as a species. The development of culture, and language as a means of disseminating that culture, has allowed us to overcome our relative physical weaknesses to become the dominant species on the planet. That dominance, though, seems to have facilitated our hubris. We have come to believe that we can live *independently* of nature and that we can thrive outside of the conditions in which we evolved. Those conditions include close social relationships, access to green space, regular and varied physical activity, clean air, and a minimally processed, diverse, fiber- and omega-3-rich diet. Indeed, the steady improvement in IQ seen in most of the twentieth century was attributed to better quality of and increased access to education, reduced exposure to neurotoxins such as lead, and better nutrition. Sadly, it is now apparent that diet is the biggest threat to our physical and mental health.

Today, poor diet is the leading cause of death globally (GBD 2017 Diet Collaborators, 2019). A recent global review found that diets low in wholegrains and fruits, and high in sodium, red meat, processed meat, trans fat, and sugar-sweetened beverages account for more deaths than tobacco. This assessment looked at the contribution of diet to cardiovascular-related deaths, cancers, and diabetes. But what about the brain? If our diets are having such a deleterious effect on our hearts and physical health, why would we imagine that the brain is not also suffering these harms? Of course, it is.

Cardiovascular diseases do not only damage the blood vessels of the peripheral body. There are around 400 miles of blood vessels in the brain supplying oxygen, glucose, and nutrients to our highly metabolically active neurones. Diets that harm cardiovascular health damage the brain too.

High consumption of sugar-sweetened beverages confers risk of unhealthy weight gain and type 2 diabetes. Type 2 diabetes significantly increases dementia risk. Conversely, polyphenols in fruits help to keep blood vessels flexible, increasing brain perfusion and improving cognitive function. The microbial by-products of wholegrain fiber fermentation—short-chain fatty acids—actively protect the integrity of the blood–brain barrier. Elders who reported eating leafy greens daily had brains that were eleven years "younger" compared to peers with poorer diets.

We are, day by day, eating our way to poorer physical and neurological health. Ultra-processed and fast foods are aggressively marketed to children and adolescents and offered as a "solution" for busy adults and new parents. But these are not the foods that foster brain development or promote cognitive reserve. These so-called solutions are, in fact, a significant driver of our growing global brain health problems.

CONCLUSION

Culinary psychology—uniting food, mind, and health

Stelios Kiosses, Beth Frates, and Neil Rippington

This book, as introduced by chef Andreas Antona's inspiring Preface, delves into the deep connections between our culinary practices and psychological well-being. Through the combined efforts of the three authors, Stelios Kiosses, Beth Frates, and Neil Rippington, alongside contributors Kimberley Wilson and Professor Charles Spence, we have explored how food influences our emotions, behaviors, and health.

Our journey has highlighted the transformative power of culinary experiences—from their role in personal health to their impact on social and cultural norms. Andreas' reflections underscore the importance of integrating culinary art with medical science, advocating a holistic approach to health that values food's psychological benefits alongside its nutritional properties.

Eating and drinking is an activity that, if fortunate, we partake in daily. Food and drink have also been central to celebrations and marking occasions throughout history. From birthdays, weddings, and religious ceremonies to celebrating successes and socializing with friends and family, a meal is often the event that brings us together. Eating delicious food is, for many of us, one of life's pleasures, and exploring foods from other cultures and regions provides us with an exciting and exploratory insight to new foods, dishes, and concepts.

How we move our bodies, with whom and how we socialize, how often we feel stressed and how we de-stress, what we eat and drink, how much we eat and drink, how much we sleep, and how well we sleep—all have an impact on our culinary practices and the food we choose. The six pillars of lifestyle medicine were reviewed and discussed in detail with regard to culinary psychology processes.

Appreciating the food ecosystem, the resources required in food production, and the need to feed a growing population bring significant challenges. Food provides nourishment and nutrition, helps us to grow, and keeps us healthy. However, a poor diet can lead to the opposite, contributing to illness, disease, and other medically related issues, including depression, fatigue, and poor mental health. Food and drink are complex, interesting, and absorbing subjects. The more we appreciate the effect the subject has on our lives, the more informed our food- and drink-related choices can be.

This collaboration among diverse experts has enriched our understanding and emphasized the potential of culinary psychology to foster healthier, more mindful eating practices. This multidisciplinary approach enhances individual well-being and addresses broader public health challenges.

As we reflect on the insights shared throughout this book, we invite readers from all backgrounds—whether culinary professionals, healthcare providers, or anyone interested in the psychology of eating—to embrace the principles of culinary psychology. By understanding the emotional and psychological impacts of our dietary choices, we can improve both our physical health and our mental resilience.

In conclusion, we hope that this book serves as a valuable resource for those seeking to explore the intricate relationships between diet, psychology, and wellness. Let it inspire you to think critically about how your food choices affect your life and to advocate for a greater integration of nutritional and psychological knowledge in your communities.

References

Ackerman, C. E. (2018, November 8). What is positive and negative affect? Definitions + scale. *PositivePsychology.Com*. https://positivepsychology.com/positive-negative-affect/ (last accessed 29 October 2025).

ACLM (2024a). American College of Lifestyle Medicine. https://lifestylemedicine.org/ (last accessed 29 October 2025).

ACLM (2024b). A whole food, plant-based plate. *American College of Lifestyle Medicine*. https://learning.lifestylemedicine.org/sites/default/files/media/2025-07/ACLM-PlateGraphic-Adult24%20%281%29_0.pdf (last accessed 29 October 2025).

ACLM (2025). Six ways to take control of your health. *American College of Lifestyle Medicine*. https://portal.lifestylemedicine.org/common/Uploaded%20files/PDFs/Practice%20Resources/Patient%20Education/ACLM-6-ways-to-take-control-of-your-health-2021.pdf (last accessed 29 October 2025).

Adams, S. (2013). How to rescue NHS food? Put it on a blue plate: Simple switch has helped elderly and weak patients eat nearly a third more. *Daily Mail Online*. http://dailymail.co.uk/news/article-2520058/How-rescue-NHS-food-Put-blue-plate-Simple-switch-helped-elderly-weak-patients-eat-nearly-more.html (last accessed 29 October 2025).

Adria, F., Blumenthal, H., Keller, T., & McGee, H. (2006, December 10). Statement on the "new cookery." *The Guardian*.

Afaghi, A., O'Connor, H., & Chow, C. M. (2007). High-glycemic-index carbohydrate meals shorten sleep onset. *American Journal of Clinical Nutrition, 85*(2): 426–430. https://doi.org/10.1093/ajcn/85.2.426

Aggarwal, A., Monsivais, P., & Drewnowski, A. (2012). Nutrient intakes linked to better health outcomes are associated with higher diet costs in the US. *PLoS One, 7*(5). https://doi.org/10.1371/journal.pone.0037533

Ahmed, S. H., Guillem, K., & Vandaele, Y. (2013). Sugar addiction: Pushing the drug-sugar analogy to the limit. *Current Opinion in Clinical Nutrition and Metabolic Care, 16*(4): 434–439. https://doi.org/10.1097/MCO.0b013e328361c8b8

Alahmari, L. A. (2024). Dietary fiber influence on overall health, with an emphasis on CVD, diabetes, obesity, colon cancer, and inflammation. *Frontiers in Nutrition, 11*: 1510564. https://doi.org/10.3389/fnut.2024.1510564

Alamir, M. A., & Hansen, K. (2021). The effect of type and level of background noise on food liking: A laboratory non-focused listening test. *Applied Acoustics, 172*: 107600. https://doi.org/10.1016/j.apacoust.2020.107600

Al-Kilani, S., & El Hedhli, K. (2021). How do restaurant atmospherics influence restaurant authenticity? An integrative framework and empirical evidence. *Journal of Retailing and Consumer Services, 63*: 102729. https://doi.org/10.1016/j.jretconser.2021.102729

Alonso, A. D., & O'Neill, M. A. (2010). Consumers' ideal eating out experience as it refers to restaurant style: A case study. *Journal of Retail & Leisure Property, 9*(4): 263–276. https://doi.org/10.1057/rlp.2010.9

Alt, K. W., Al-Ahmad, A., & Woelber, J. P. (2022). Nutrition and health in human evolution—past to present. *Nutrients, 14*(17): 3594. https://doi.org/10.3390/nu14173594

American Academy of Child and Adolescent Psychiatry (AACAP) (2020). Caffeine and children. https://aacap.org/AACAP/Families_and_Youth/Facts_for_Families/FFF-Guide/Caffeine_and_Children-131.aspx (last accessed 29 October 2025).

American College of Obstetricians and Gynecologists, The (2023). Moderate caffeine consumption during pregnancy. https://acog.org/clinical/clinical-guidance/committee-opinion/articles/2010/08/moderate-caffeine-consumption-during-pregnancy (last accessed 29 October 2025).

American Diabetes Association (2024). Breaking sitting streaks. https://diabetes.org/health-wellness/fitness/break-sitting-streak#:~:text=The%20Standards%20of%20Medical%20Care,people%20with%20type%202%20diabete (last accessed 29 October 2025).

American Heart Association (2015). Food as fuel before, during, and after workouts. *www.Heart.Org.* https://heart.org/en/healthy-living/healthy-eating/eat-smart/nutrition-basics/food-as-fuel-before-during-and-after-workouts (last accessed 29 October 2025).

American Heart Association (2022). New survey: 95% of pet parents rely on their pet for stress relief. http://newsroom.heart.org/news/new-survey-95-of-pet-parents-rely-on-their-pet-for-stress-relief (last accessed 29 October 2025).

American Heart Association (2024). Saturated fat. https://heart.org/en/healthy-living/healthy-eating/eat-smart/fats/saturated-fats (last accessed 29 October 2025).

Ames, J. M. (1998). Applications of the Maillard reaction in the food industry. *Food Chemistry, 62*(4): 431–439. https://doi.org/10.1016/s0308-8146(98)00078-8

Amonoo, H. L., Barclay, M. E., El-Jawahri, A., Traeger, L. N., Lee, S. J., & Huffman, J. C. (2019). Positive psychological constructs and health outcomes in hematopoietic stem cell transplantation patients: A systematic review. *Biology of Blood and Marrow Transplantation, 25*(1): e5–e16. https://doi.org/10.1016/j.bbmt.2018.09.030

Anderson Steeves, E., Jones-Smith, J., Hopkins, L., & Gittelsohn, J. (2016). Perceived social support from friends and parents for eating behavior and diet quality among low-income, urban, minority youth. *Journal of Nutrition Education and Behavior, 48*(5): 304–310, e1. https://doi.org/10.1016/j.jneb.2015.12.014

Andreyeva, T., Kelly, I. R., & Harris, J. L. (2011). Exposure to food advertising on television: Associations with children's fast food and soft drink consumption and obesity. *Economics & Human Biology, 9*(3): 221–233. https://doi.org/10.1016/j.ehb.2011.02.004

Anki (2023, August 22). Halal food in Islam: Understanding its meaning and significance. *ReligiousFacts.com*. https://religionsfacts.com/halal-food-in-islam-understanding-its-meaning-and-significance/ (last accessed 29 October 2025).

Anon. (2016, January 18). NHS to slap "sugar tax" on hospital cafes and snacks. *Daily Mail Online*. http://dailymail.co.uk/wires/pa/article-3404243/NHS-slap-sugar-tax-hospital-cafes-snacks.html (last accessed 29 October 2025).

Aparicio-Martinez, P., Perea-Moreno, A.-J., Martinez-Jimenez, M. P., Redel-Macías, M. D., Pagliari, C., & Vaquero-Abellan, M. (2019). Social media, thin-ideal, body dissatisfaction and disordered eating attitudes: An exploratory analysis. *International Journal of Environmental Research and Public Health, 16*(21): 4177. https://doi.org/10.3390/ijerph16214177

Apicius (c. 1st century). *Cooking and Dining in Imperial Rome*. J. D. Vehling (Trans.). Chicago, IL: University of Chicago Press, 1936.

Arhire, L. I., Mihalache, L., & Covasa, M. (2019). Irisin: A hope in understanding and managing obesity and metabolic syndrome. *Frontiers in Endocrinology, 10*: 524. https://doi.org/10.3389/fendo.2019.00524

Armstrong, G. L., Conn, L. A., & Pinner, R. W. (1999). Trends in infectious disease mortality in the United States during the 20th century. *Journal of the American Medical Association, 281*(1): 61–66 https://doi.org/10.1001/jama.281.1.61

Arsalidou, M., Vijayarajah, S., & Sharaev, M. (2020). Basal ganglia lateralization in different types of reward. *Brain Imaging and Behavior, 14*(6): 2618–2646. https://doi.org/10.1007/s11682-019-00215-3

Ash, N., Blanco, H., Brown, C., Garcia, K., Henrichs, T., Lucas, N., Raudsepp-Hearne, C., Simpson, R. D., Scholes, R. J., Tomich, T. P., Vira, B., Zurek, M., & Ranganathan, J. (2010). *Ecosystems and Human Well-being: A Manual for Assessment Practitioners*. Washington, DC: Island.

Astin, J. A. (1997). Stress reduction through mindfulness meditation. Effects on psychological symptomatology, sense of control, and spiritual experiences. *Psychotherapy and Psychosomatics, 66*(2): 97–106. https://doi.org/10.1159/000289116

Avena, N. M., Rada, P., & Hoebel, B. G. (2008). Evidence for sugar addiction: Behavioral and neurochemical effects of intermittent, excessive sugar intake. *Neuroscience and Biobehavioral Reviews, 32*(1): 20–39. https://doi.org/10.1016/j.neubiorev.2007.04.019

Bahnfleth, C. L., Strupp, B. J., Caudill, M. A., & Canfield, R. L. (2021). Prenatal choline supplementation improves child sustained attention: A 7-year follow-up of a randomized controlled feeding trial. *FASEB Journal, official publication of the Federation of American Societies for Experimental Biology, 36*(1). https://doi.org/10.1096/fj.202101217r

Baldwin, D. E. (2012). Sous vide cooking: A review. *International Journal of Gastronomy and Food Science, 1*(1): 15–30. https://doi.org/10.1016/j.ijgfs.2011.11.002

Bandura, A. (2010). Social-cognitive theory. In: *An Introduction to Theories of Personality* (7th edn.). Hove, UK: Psychology Press.

Barber, D. (2014). *The Third Plate: Field Notes on the Future of Food*. New York: Penguin.

Barker, R. T., Knisely, J. S., Barker, S. B., Cobb, R. K., & Schubert, C. M. (2012). Preliminary investigation of employee's dog presence on stress and organizational perceptions. *International Journal of Workplace Health Management, 5*(1): 15–30. https://doi.org/10.1108/17538351211215366

Barrett, L. F. (2017). *How Emotions Are Made: The Secret Life of the Brain*. Boston, MA: Houghton Mifflin Harcourt.

Barry, J. (1965). McCall's, An interview with Chanel [interview with Gabrielle Chanel]. New York: McCall.

Barson, J. R., Morganstern, I., & Leibowitz, S. F. (2010). Galanin and consummatory behavior: Special relationship with dietary fat, alcohol and circulating lipids. *Experientia Supplementum*, *102*: 87–111.

Bath, S., Steer, C., Golding, J., Emmett, P., & Rayman, M. (2013). Effect of inadequate iodine status in UK pregnant women on cognitive outcomes in their children: Results from the Avon Longitudinal Study of parents and children (ALSPAC). *The Lancet*, *382*(9889): 331–337. https://doi.org/10.1016/s0140-6736(13)60436-5

Beauchamp-Turner, D. L., & Levinson, D. M. (1992). Effects of meditation on stress, health, and affect. *Medical Psychotherapy: An International Journal*, *5*: 123–131.

Beaulieu, K., Hopkins, M., Gibbons, C., Oustric, P., Caudwell, P., Blundell, J., & Finlayson, G. (2020). Exercise training reduces reward for high-fat food in adults with overweight/obesity. *Medicine and Science in Sports and Exercise*, *52*(4): 900–908. https://doi.org/10.1249/MSS.0000000000002205

Beer, N. J., Dimmock, J. A., Jackson, B., & Guelfi, K. J. (2017). Providing choice in exercise influences food intake at the subsequent meal. *Medicine and Science in Sports and Exercise*, *49*(10): 2110–2118. https://doi.org/10.1249/MSS.0000000000001330

Bell, R., Meiselman, H. L., Pierson, B. J., & Reeve, W. G. (1994). Effects of adding an Italian theme to a restaurant on the perceived ethnicity, acceptability, and selection of foods. *Appetite*, *22*(1): 11–24. https://doi.org/10.1006/appe.1994.1002

Benelam, B. (2009). Satiation, satiety and their effects on eating behaviour. *Nutrition Bulletin*, *34*(2): 126–173. https://doi.org/10.1111/j.1467-3010.2009.01753.x

Benson, H. (1985). Stress, health, and the relaxation response. In: W. D. Gentry, H. Benson, & C. J. de Wolff (Eds.), *Behavioral Medicine: Work, Stress and Health* (pp. 15–32). Dordrecht, the Netherlands: Springer Netherlands. https://doi.org/10.1007/978-94-009-5179-2_2

Benson, H., Beary, J. F., & Carol, M. P. (1974). The relaxation response. *Psychiatry*, *37*(1): 37–46. https://doi.org/10.1080/00332747.1974.11023785

Benson, H., & Klipper, M. Z. (1975). *The Relaxation Response*. New York: HarperCollins, 2009.

Bentley, T. G. K., D'Andrea-Penna, G., Rakic, M., Arce, N., LaFaille, M., Berman, R., Cooley, K., & Sprimont, P. (2023). Breathing practices for stress and anxiety reduction: Conceptual framework of implementation guidelines based on a systematic review of the published literature. *Brain Sciences*, *13*(12): 1612. https://doi.org/10.3390/brainsci13121612

Benton, D. (2007). The impact of diet on anti-social, violent and criminal behaviour. *Neuroscience and Biobehavioral Reviews, 31*(5): 752–774. https://doi.org/10.1016/j.neubiorev.2007.02.002

Biddinger, K. J., Emdin, C. A., Haas, M. E., Wang, M., Hindy, G., Ellinor, P. T., Kathiresan, S., Khera, A. V., & Aragam, K. G. (2022). Association of habitual alcohol intake with risk of cardiovascular disease. *JAMA Network Open, 5*(3): e223849. https://doi.org/10.1001/jamanetworkopen.2022.3849

Biddle, S. J. H., Bennie, J. A., Bauman, A. E., Chau, J. Y., Dunstan, D., Owen, N., Stamatakis, E., & van Uffelen, J. G. Z. (2016). Too much sitting and all-cause mortality: Is there a causal link? *BMC Public Health, 16*: 635. https://doi.org/10.1186/s12889-016-3307-3

Bitner, M. J. (1992). Servicescapes: The impact of physical surroundings on customers and employees. *Journal of Marketing, 56*(2): 57–71. https://doi.org/10.1177/002224299205600205. JSTOR 1252042. S2CID 220606844

Bjorness, T. E., & Greene, R. W. (2009). Adenosine and sleep. *Current Neuropharmacology, 7*(3): 238–245. https://doi.org/10.2174/157015909789152182

Black, D. S., & Slavich, G. M. (2016). Mindfulness meditation and the immune system: A systematic review of randomized controlled trials. *Annals of the New York Academy of Sciences, 1373*(1): 13–24. https://doi.org/10.1111/nyas.12998

Booms, B. H., & Bitner, M. J. (1981). Marketing strategies and organisation structures for service firms. In: J. Donnelly & W. R. George (Eds.), *Marketing of Services*. Chicago, IL: American Marketing Association.

Bowman, S. A., & Clemens, J. C. (2022). Saturated fat and food intakes of adults: What we eat in America, NHANES 2017–2018. In: *FSRG Dietary Data Briefs*. United States Department of Agriculture (USDA). http://ncbi.nlm.nih.gov/books/NBK588575/.

Bradbury, J. (2011). Docosahexaenoic acid (DHA): An ancient nutrient for the modern human brain. *Nutrients, 3*(5): 529–554. https://doi.org/10.3390/nu3050529

Bratman, S. (1997). Health food junkie. *Yoga Journal*, September/October: 42–50.

Bratsberg, B., & Rogeberg, O. (2018). Flynn effect and its reversal are both environmentally caused. *Proceedings of the National Academy of Sciences, 115*(26): 6674–6678. https://doi.org/10.1073/pnas.1718793115

Brillat-Savarin, J. A. (1825a). *The Physiology of Taste: Meditations on Transcendental Gastronomy*. New York: Liveright, 1970.

Brillat-Savarin, J. A. (1825b). *Physiologie du goût [The Philosopher in the Kitchen / The Physiology of Taste]*. Brussels: J. P. Meline. Reprinted 1884 as *A Handbook of Gastronomy*. A. Lalauze (Trans.). London: Nimmo & Bain.

Brillat-Savarin, J. A. (1825c). *The Physiology of Taste, or, Meditations on Transcendental Gastronomy*. M. F. K. Fisher (Trans.). New York: Vintage, 2011.

Brinke, L. F. T., Bolandzadeh, N., Nagamatsu, L. S., Hsu, C. L., Davis, J. C., Miran-Khan, K., & Liu-Ambrose, T. (2015). Aerobic exercise increases hippocampal volume in older women with probable mild cognitive impairment: A 6-month randomised controlled trial. *British Journal of Sports Medicine, 49*(4): 248–254. https://doi.org/10.1136/bjsports-2013-093184

Brones, A. (2018, May 7). Karen Washington: It's not a food desert, it's food apartheid. *Guernica*. https://guernicamag.com/karen-washington-its-not-a-food-desert-its-food-apartheid/ (last accessed 29 October 2025).

Bronfenbrenner, U. (1977). Toward an experimental ecology of human development. *American Psychologist, 32*(7): 513–531. https://doi.org/10.1037/0003-066X.32.7.513

Broussard, J. L., Ehrmann, D. A., Van Cauter, E., Tasali, E., & Brady, M. J. (2012). Impaired insulin signaling in human adipocytes after experimental sleep restriction: A randomized, crossover study. *Annals of Internal Medicine, 157*(8): 549–557. https://doi.org/10.7326/0003-4819-157-8-201210160-00005

Brown, E. N. (2016, June 13). Five years and $500 million later, USDA admits that 'food deserts' don't matter. *Reason*. https://reason.com/2016/06/13/500-million-later-usda-on-food-deserts/ (last accessed 29 October 2025).

Bruce, L. J., & Ricciardelli, L. A. (2016). A systematic review of the psychosocial correlates of intuitive eating among adult women. *Appetite, 96*: 454–472. https://doi.org/10.1016/j.appet.2015.10.012

Brummett, B. H., Barefoot, J. C., Siegler, I. C., Clapp-Channing, N. E., Lytle, B. L., Bosworth, H. B., Williams, R. B., & Mark, D. B. (2001). Characteristics of socially isolated patients with coronary artery disease who are at elevated risk for mortality. *Psychosomatic Medicine, 63*(2): 267–272. https://doi.org/10.1097/00006842-200103000-00010

Burrows, T. (2017, September 19). Cheers to that! Care home opens up its own PUB dubbed the "Caring Arms" with beer taps and shelves of whiskey and sherry to remind residents of their youth. *Daily Mail Online*. http://dailymail.co.uk/news/article-4898740/Care-home-opens-PUB-dubbed-Caring-Arms.html (last accessed 29 October 2025).

Bush, T., Lovejoy, J. C., Deprey, M., & Carpenter, K. M. (2016). The effect of tobacco cessation on weight gain, obesity and diabetes risk. *Obesity (Silver Spring, MD), 24*(9): 1834–1841. https://doi.org/10.1002/oby.21582

Campbell, D., & Johnson, P. (2016, January 17). NHS chief to introduce sugar tax in hospitals to tackle UK obesity crisis. *The Guardian*. http://theguardian.com/society/2016/jan/17/nhs-sugar-tax-hospitals-tackle-uk-obesity-crisis-simon-stevens (last accessed 29 October 2025).

Cao, D., Kevala, K., Kim, J., Moon, H.-S., Jun, S. B., Lovinger, D., & Kim, H. Y. (2009). Docosahexaenoic acid promotes hippocampal neuronal development and synaptic function. *Journal of Neurochemistry, 111*(2): 510–521. https://doi.org/10.1111/j.1471-4159.2009.06335.x

Caporuscio, J. (2019, March 30). What are the most healthful oils? *Medical News Today*. https://medicalnewstoday.com/articles/324844 (last accessed 29 October 2025).

Carrillo, A., Feig, E. H., Harnedy, L. E., Huffman, J. C., Park, E. R., Thorndike, A. N., Kim, S., & Millstein, R. A. (2022). The role of positive psychological constructs in diet and eating behavior among people with metabolic syndrome: A qualitative study. *Health Psychology Open, 9*(1): 20551029211055264. https://doi.org/10.1177/20551029211055264

Casas, F., León, C., Jovell, E., Gómez, J., Corvitto, A., Blanco, R., Alfaro, J., Ángel Seguí, M., Saigí, E., Massanés, T., Sala, C., Librán, A., & Arcusa, A. (2012). Adapted ice cream as a nutritional supplement in cancer patients: Impact on quality of life and nutritional status. *Clinical & Translational Oncology, 14*(1): 66–72. https://doi.org/10.1007/s12094-012- 0763-9

Castaldo, L., Narváez, A., Izzo, L., Graziani, G., Gaspari, A., Di Minno, G., & Ritieni, A. (2019). Red wine consumption and cardiovascular health. *Molecules, 24*(19): 3626. https://doi.org/10.3390/molecules24193626

Castro-Diehl, C., Wood, A. C., Redline, S., Reid, M., Johnson, D. A., Maras, J. E., Jacobs, D. R., Shea, S., Crawford, A., & St-Onge, M.-P. (2018). Mediterranean diet pattern and sleep duration and insomnia symptoms in the multi-ethnic study of atherosclerosis. *Sleep, 41*(11): zsy158. https://doi.org/10.1093/sleep/zsy158

Caton, S. J., Bate, L., & Hetherington, M. M. (2007). Acute effects of an alcoholic drink on food intake: Aperitif versus co-ingestion. *Physiology & Behavior, 90*(2–3): 368–375. https://doi.org/10.1016/j.physbeh.2006.09.028

Caughron, J. R. (2016). An examination of food insecurity and its impact on violent crime in American communities. *All Theses*. 2565. https://tigerprints.clemson.edu/all_theses/2565 (last accessed 29 October 2025).

Celano, C. M., Beale, E. E., Freedman, M. E., Mastromauro, C. A., Feig, E. H., Park, E. R., & Huffman, J. C. (2020). Positive psychological constructs and health behavior adherence in heart failure: A qualitative research study. *Nursing & Health Sciences, 22*(3): 620–628. https://doi.org/10.1111/nhs.12704

Centers for Disease Control and Prevention (CDC). (1999). *Achievements in Public Health, 1900–1999: Control of Infectious Diseases*. https://cdc.gov/mmwr/preview/mmwrhtml/mm4829a1.htm (last accessed 29 October 2025).

Centers for Disease Control and Prevention (CDC). (2013). Drowsy driving—19 states and the District of Columbia, 2009–2010. *MMWR. Morbidity and Mortality Weekly Report*, *61*(51–52): 1033–1037.

Centers for Disease Control and Prevention (CDC) (2024a, May 15). Health effects of social isolation and loneliness. https://www.cdc.gov/social-connectedness/risk-factors/index.html (last accessed 7 December 2025).

Centers for Disease Control and Prevention (CDC) (2024b). Diet/nutrition. *National Center for Health Statistics.* https://cdc.gov/nchs/fastats/diet.htm (last accessed 29 October 2025).

Chandra, R., Bharagava, R. N., & Rai, V. (2008). Melanoidins as major colourant in sugarcane molasses-based distillery effluent and its degradation. *Bioresource Technology*, *99*(11): 4648–4660. https://doi.org/10.1016/j.biortech.2007.09.057

Chang, T., Ravi, N., Plegue, M. A., Sonneville, K. R., & Davis, M. M. (2016). Inadequate hydration, BMI, and obesity among US adults: NHANES 2009–2012. *Annals of Family Medicine*, *14*(4): 320–324. https://doi.org/10.1370/afm.1951

Choi, Y., Choi, M., Oh, M., & Kim, S. (2019). Service robots in hotels: Understanding the service quality perceptions of human-robot interaction. *Journal of Hospitality Marketing & Management*, *29*(6): 613–635. https://doi.org/10.1080/19368623.2020.1703871

Christakis, N. A., & Fowler, J. H. (2013). Social contagion theory: Examining dynamic social networks and human behavior. *Statistics in Medicine*, *32*(4): 10.1002/sim.5408. https://doi.org/10.1002/sim.5408

Christiansen, P., Rose, A., Randall-Smith, L., & Hardman, C. A. (2016). Alcohol's acute effect on food intake is mediated by inhibitory control impairments. *Health Psychology: Official Journal of the Division of Health Psychology, American Psychological Association*, *35*(5): 518–522. https://doi.org/10.1037/hea0000320

Chumachenko, S. Y., Cali, R. J., Rosal, M. C., Allison, J. J., Person, S. J., Ziedonis, D., Nephew, B. C., Moore, C. M., Zhang, N., King, J. A., & Fulwiler, C. (2021). Keeping weight off: Mindfulness-based stress reduction alters amygdala functional connectivity during weight loss maintenance in a randomized control trial. *PLoS ONE*, *16*(1): e0244847. https://doi.org/10.1371/journal.pone.0244847

Cigna Group, The (2021). The loneliness epidemic persists: A post-pandemic look at the state of loneliness among U.S. adults. *The Cigna Group Newsroom*. https://newsroom.thecignagroup.com/loneliness-epidemic-persists-post-pandemic-look (last accessed 29 October 2025).

Clair, R., Gordon, M., Kroon, M., & Reilly, C. (2021). The effects of social isolation on well-being and life satisfaction during pandemic. *Humanities and Social Sciences Communications*, *8*(1): 1–6. https://doi.org/10.1057/s41599-021-00710-3

Clapp, M., Aurora, N., Herrera, L., Bhatia, M., Wilen, E., & Wakefield, S. (2017). Gut microbiota's effect on mental health: The gut-brain axis. *Clinics and Practice*, *7*(4): 987. https://doi.org/10.4081/cp.2017.987

Cleveland Clinic (2024). Sleep hygiene tips for a better night's rest. *Cleveland Clinic*. https://health.clevelandclinic.org/sleep-hygiene (last accessed 29 October 2025).

Cockroft, S., Spillett, R., & Duell, M. (2016, March 17). "Our life was full of laughter until the last 48 hours when he slipped into sleep": Paul Daniels's tearful wife Debbie McGee reveals he spent his final days eating his favourite Magnum ice creams and singing Beatles songs. *Daily Mail Online*. http://dailymail.co.uk/news/article-3496494/Magician-Paul-Daniels-died-home-aged-77.html (last accessed 29 October 2025).

Community Fund (2019). Ageing better: The role of food in building connections and relationships. https://tnlcommunityfund.org.uk/media/documents/ageing-better/Ageing-Better-Role-of-Food-in-Building-Connections-and-Relationships.pdf?mtime=20200622114244&focal=none (last accessed 29 October 2025).

Conklin, A. I., Forouhi, N. G., Surtees, P., Khaw, K.-T., Wareham, N. J., & Monsivais, P. (2014). Social relationships and healthful dietary behaviour: Evidence from over-50s in the EPIC cohort, UK. *Social Science & Medicine*, *100*(100): 167–175. https://doi.org/10.1016/j.socscimed.2013.08.018

Connell, P. M., Brucks, M., & Nielsen, J. H. (2014). How childhood advertising exposure can create biased product evaluations that persist into adulthood. *Journal of Consumer Research*, *41*(1): 119–134. https://doi.org/10.1086/675218

Cooke, L., Wardle, J., Gibson, E. L., Sapochnik, M., Sheiham, A., & Lawson, M. (2004). Demographic, familial and trait predictors of fruit and vegetable consumption by pre-school children. *Public Health Nutrition*, *7*(2): 295–302. https://doi.org/10.1079/PHN2003527

Cooksey-Stowers, K., Schwartz, M. B., & Brownell, K. D. (2017). Food swamps predict obesity rates better than food deserts in the United States. *International Journal of Environmental Research and Public Health*, *14*(11): 1366.

Cooper, D. (2017, March). What is food justice? *Dara Cooper*. http://daracooper.com/food-justice-blog--more/what-is-food-justice (last accessed 29 October 2025).

Copinschi, G. (2005). Metabolic and endocrine effects of sleep deprivation. *Essential Psychopharmacology*, *6*(6): 341–347.

Cornwell, B., Villamor, E., Mora-Plazas, M., Marin, C., Monteiro, C. A., & Baylin, A. (2017). Processed and ultra-processed foods are associated with lower-quality nutrient profiles in children from Colombia—corrigendum. *Public Health Nutrition*, *21*(1): 254–254. https://doi.org/10.1017/s1368980017001963

Covassin, N., Singh, P., & Somers, V. K. (2016). Keeping up with the clock: Circadian disruption and obesity risk. *Hypertension (Dallas, TX, 1979)*, *68*(5): 1081–1090. https://doi.org/10.1161/HYPERTENSIONAHA.116.06588

Cox, C. E. (2017). Role of physical activity for weight loss and weight maintenance. *Diabetes Spectrum : A Publication of the American Diabetes Association*, *30*(3): 157–160. https://doi.org/10.2337/ds17-0013

Cowen, T. (2012). *An Economist Gets Lunch: New Rules for Everyday Foodies*. New York: Plume.

Cradock, K. A., ÓLaighin, G., Finucane, F. M., Gainforth, H. L., Quinlan, L. R., & Ginis, K. A. M. (2017). Behaviour change techniques targeting both diet and physical activity in type 2 diabetes: A systematic review and meta-analysis. *International Journal of Behavioral Nutrition and Physical Activity*, *14*(1): 18. https://doi.org/10.1186/s12966-016-0436-0

Cronin, P., Joyce, S. A., O'Toole, P. W., & O'Connor, E. M. (2021). Dietary fibre modulates the gut microbiota. *Nutrients*, *13*(5): 1655. https://doi.org/10.3390/nu13051655

Crum, A. J., Leibowitz, K. A., & Verghese, A. (2017). Making mindset matter. *British Medical Journal*, *356*: j674. https://doi.org/10.1136/bmj.j674

Dahl, W. J., & Stewart, M. L. (2015). Position of the Academy of Nutrition and Dietetics: Health implications of dietary fiber. *Journal of the Academy of Nutrition and Dietetics*, *115*(11): 1861–1870. https://doi.org/10.1016/j.jand.2015.09.003

Darmon, N., & Drewnowski, A. (2015). Contribution of food prices and diet cost to socioeconomic disparities in diet quality and health: A systematic review and analysis. *Nutrition Reviews*, *73*(10): 643–660. https://doi.org/10.1093/nutrit/nuv027

Davidson, K. (2020). Mood food: 9 foods that can really boost your spirits. *Healthline*. https://healthline.com/nutrition/mood-food (last accessed 29 October 2025).

Deboer, T. (2018). Sleep homeostasis and the circadian clock: Do the circadian pacemaker and the sleep homeostat influence each other's functioning?

Neurobiology of Sleep and Circadian Rhythms, *5*: 68–77. https://doi.org/10.1016/j.nbscr.2018.02.003

Deci, E. L., & Ryan, R. M. (1985). Intrinsic motivation and self-determination in human behavior. *Springer US*. https://doi.org/10.1007/978-1-4899-2271-7

Dedeoglu, B. B., Bilgihan, A., Ye, B. H., Buonincontri, P., & Okumus, F. (2018). The impact of servicescape on hedonic value and behavioral intentions: The importance of previous experience. *International Journal of Hospitality Management*, *72*: 10–20.

de Kervenoael, R., Hasan, R., Schwob, S., & Goh, E. (2020). Leveraging human-robot interaction in hospitality services: Incorporating the role of perceived value, empathy, and information sharing into visitors' intentions to use social robots. *Tourism Management*, *78*: 104042. https://doi.org/10.1016/j.tourman.2019.104042

DelParigi, A., Chen, K., Salbe, A. D., Reiman, E. M., & Tataranni, P. A. (2005). Sensory experience of food and obesity: A positron emission tomography study of the brain regions affected by tasting a liquid meal after a prolonged fast. *NeuroImage*, *24*(2): 436–443. https://doi.org/10.1016/j.neuroimage.2004.08.035

Dennis, A., & Ogden, J. (2023). The effect of body-focused positive psychology interventions on behavioural intentions, body esteem, and body compassion. *International Journal of Applied Positive Psychology*, *9*(2): 455–472. https://doi.org/10.1007/s41042-023-00134-1

Depoortere, I. (2014). Taste receptors of the gut: Emerging roles in health and disease. *Gut*, *63*(1): 179–190. https://doi.org/10.1136/gutjnl-2013-305112

de Vos, W. M., Tilg, H., Van Hul, M., & Cani, P. D. (2022). Gut microbiome and health: Mechanistic insights. *Gut*, *71*(5): 1020–1032. https://doi.org/10.1136/gutjnl-2021-326789

Dfarhud, D., Malmir, M., & Khanahmadi, M. (2014). Happiness & health: The biological factors—systematic review article. *Iranian Journal of Public Health*, *43*(11): 1468–1477.

Diaz, K. M., Howard, V. J., Hutto, B., Colabianchi, N., Vena, J. E., Safford, M. M., Blair, S. N., & Hooker, S. P. (2017). Patterns of sedentary behavior and mortality in U.S. middle-aged and older adults: A national cohort study. *Annals of Internal Medicine*, *167*(7): 465–475. https://doi.org/10.7326/M17-0212

Dicken, S. J., Qamar, S., & Batterham, R. L. (2023). Who consumes ultra-processed food? A systematic review of sociodemographic determinants of ultra-processed food consumption from nationally representative samples. *Nutrition Research Reviews*, *37*(2): 416–456. https://doi.org/10.1017/s0954422423000240

Ding, C., Chan, Z., & Magkos, F. (2016). Lean, but not healthy: the "metabolically obese, normal-weight" phenotype. *Current Opinion in Clinical Nutrition and Metabolic Care*, *19*(6): 408–417. https://doi.org/10.1097/MCO.0000000000000317

Ding, D., Buskirk, J. V., Nguyen, B., Stamatakis, E., Elbarbary, M., Veronese, N., Clare, P. J., Lee, I.-M., Ekelund, U., & Fontana, L. (2022). Physical activity, diet quality and all-cause cardiovascular disease and cancer mortality: A prospective study of 346,627 UK Biobank participants. *British Journal of Sports Medicine*, *56*(20): 1148–1156. https://doi.org/10.1136/bjsports-2021-105195

Ding, Q., Xu, Y.-M., & Lau, A. T. Y. (2023). The epigenetic effects of coffee. *Molecules*, *28*(4): Article 4. https://doi.org/10.3390/molecules28041770

Donnellan, M. B., Ge, X., & Wenk, E. (2000). Cognitive abilities in adolescent-limited and life-course-persistent criminal offenders. *Journal of Abnormal Psychology*, *109*(3): 396–402. https://doi.org/10.1037/0021-843X.109.3.396

Dorling, J., Broom, D. R., Burns, S. F., Clayton, D. J., Deighton, K., James, L. J., King, J. A., Miyashita, M., Thackray, A. E., Batterham, R. L., & Stensel, D. J. (2018). Acute and chronic effects of exercise on appetite, energy intake, and appetite-related hormones: The modulating effect of adiposity, sex, and habitual physical activity. *Nutrients*, *10*(9): 1140. https://doi.org/10.3390/nu10091140

Drake, C., Roehrs, T., Shambroom, J., & Roth, T. (2013). Caffeine effects on sleep taken 0, 3, or 6 hours before going to bed. *Journal of Clinical Sleep Medicine: JCSM: Official Publication of the American Academy of Sleep Medicine*, *9*(11): 1195–1200. https://doi.org/10.5664/jcsm.3170

Drew, L. (2022). Olfactory receptors are not unique to the nose. *Nature*, *606*(7915): S14–S17. https://doi.org/10.1038/d41586-022-01631-0

DuBois, C. M., Lopez, O. V., Beale, E. E., Healy, B. C., Boehm, J. K., & Huffman, J. C. (2015). Relationships between positive psychological constructs and health outcomes in patients with cardiovascular disease: A systematic review. *International Journal of Cardiology*, *195*: 265–280. https://doi.org/10.1016/j.ijcard.2015.05.121

Dubois, J., Galdi, P., Paul, L., & Adolphs, R., (2018). A distributed brain network predicts general intelligence from resting-state human neuroimaging data. *Philosophical Transactions of the Royal Society B: Biological Sciences*, *373*(1756): 20170284. https://doi.org/10.1098/rstb.2017.0284

Dugan, A. G., & Barnes-Farrell, J. L. (2017). Time for self-care: Downtime recovery as a buffer of work and home/family time pressures. *Journal of Occupational and Environmental Medicine*, *59*(4): e46–e56. https://doi.org/10.1097/JOM.0000000000000975

Duhigg, C. (2012). *The Power of Habit: Why We Do What We Do in Life and Business*. New York: Random House.

DUJS (2011). The physiology of stress: Cortisol and the hypothalamic-pituitary-adrenal axis. *Dartmouth Undergraduate Journal of Science*. https://sites.dartmouth.edu/dujs/2011/02/03/the-physiology-of-stress-cortisol-and-the-hypothalamic-pituitary-adrenal-axis/ (last accessed 29 October 2025).

Dunbar, R. I. M. (2017). Breaking bread: The functions of social eating. *Adaptive Human Behavior and Physiology*, *3*(3): 198–211. https://doi.org/10.1007/s40750-017-0061-4

Dunstan, D. W., Barr, E. L. M., Healy, G. N., Salmon, J., Shaw, J. E., Balkau, B., Magliano, D. J., Cameron, A. J., Zimmet, P. Z., & Owen, N. (2010). Television viewing time and mortality: The Australian diabetes, obesity and lifestyle study (AusDiab). *Circulation*, *121*(3): 384–391. https://doi.org/10.1161/CIRCULATIONAHA.109.894824

Dutko, P., Ver Ploeg, M., & Farrigan, T. (2012). Characteristics and influential factors of food deserts. *U.S. Department of Agriculture*. https://ers.usda.gov/webdocs/publications/45014/30940_err140.pdf (last accessed 29 October 2025).

Dutton, J. E., & Heaphy, E. D. (2003) The power of high-quality connections. In: K. Cameron & J. Dutton (Eds.), *Positive Organizational Scholarship: Foundations of a New Discipline* (pp. 262–278). Oakland, CA: Berrett-Koehler.

Dweck, C. S. (2008). *Mindset: The New Psychology of Success*. New York: Penguin Random House. https://penguinrandomhouse.com/books/44330/mindset-by-carol-s-dweck-phd/ (last accessed 29 October 2025).

Dweck, C. S. (2015, September 23). Carol Dweck revisits the "growth mindset." *Education Week*. https://edweek.org/leadership/opinion-carol-dweck-revisits-the-growth-mindset/2015/09 (last accessed 29 October 2025).

Dyke, N. V., & Drinkwater, E. J. (2014). Review article: Relationships between intuitive eating and health indicators: Literature review. *Public Health Nutrition*, *17*(8): 1757–1766. https://doi.org/10.1017/S1368980013002139

Ebrahim, I. O., Shapiro, C. M., Williams, A. J., & Fenwick, P. B. (2013). Alcohol and sleep I: Effects on normal sleep. *Alcoholism, Clinical and Experimental Research*, *37*(4): 539–549. https://doi.org/10.1111/acer.12006

Ebrahimi-Mameghani, M., Mohammadi, S., Arefhosseini, S. R., Fallah, P., & Bazi, Z. (2015). Adiponectin as a potential biomarker of vascular disease. *Vascular Health and Risk Management*, *11*: 55–70. https://doi.org/10.2147/VHRM.S48753

Eccles, R., Du-Plessis, L., Dommels, Y., & Wilkinson, J. E. (2013). Cold pleasure. Why we like ice drinks, ice-lollies and ice cream. *Appetite*, *71*: 357–360. https://doi.org/10.1016/j.appet.2013.09.011

ECU Physicians (2018). The NOVA Food Classification System. https://ecuphysicians.ecu.edu/wp-content/pv-uploads/sites/78/2021/07/NOVA-Classification-Reference-Sheet.pdf (last accessed 29 October 2025).

Eda, N., Ito, H., Shimizu, K., Suzuki, S., Lee, E., & Akama, T. (2018). Yoga stretching for improving salivary immune function and mental stress in middle-aged and older adults. *Journal of Women & Aging*, *30*(3): 227–241. https://doi.org/10.1080/08952841.2017.1295689

Edwards, J. S. A., Meiselman, H. L., Edwards, A., & Lesher, L. (2003). The influence of eating location on the acceptability of identically prepared foods. *Food Quality and Preference*, *14*: 647–652. https://doi.org/10.1016/S0950-3293(02)00189-1.

Edwards, S. J., Montgomery, I. M., Colquhoun, E. Q., Jordan, J. E., & Clark, M. G. (1992). Spicy meal disturbs sleep: An effect of thermoregulation? *International Journal of Psychophysiology: Official Journal of the International Organization of Psychophysiology*, *13*(2): 97–100. https://doi.org/10.1016/0167-8760(92)90048-g

Einstein, A. (1930, February 5). Life is like riding a bicycle. [Letter to his son, Eduard.]

El Ansari, W., Adetunji, H., & Oskrochi, R. (2014). Food and mental health: Relationship between food and perceived stress and depressive symptoms among university students in the United Kingdom. *Central European Journal of Public Health*, *22*(2): 90–97. https://doi.org/10.21101/cejph.a3941

Elkind, M. S. V., Sciacca, R., Boden-Albala, B., Rundek, T., Paik, M. C., & Sacco, R. L. (2006). Moderate alcohol consumption reduces risk of ischemic stroke. *Stroke*, *37*(1): 13–19. https://doi.org/10.1161/01.STR.0000195048.86810.5b

Ellis, E. C., Goldewijk, K. K., Siebert, S., Lightman, D., & Ramakutty, N. (2010). Anthropogenic transformation of the biomes, 1700 to 2000. *Global Ecology and Biogeography* [preprint], *19*: 589–606. https://doi.org/10.1111/j.1466-8238.2010.00540.x

Ellis, R. (2009). Gordon Ramsay quotes about cooking. *A-Z Quotes*, *A*. https://azquotes.com/author/12069-Gordon_Ramsay/tag/cooking (last accessed 15 May 2023).

Ellison, B. (2014). "I'll have what he's having": Group ordering behavior in food choice decisions. *Food Quality and Preference*, *37*: 79–86. https://doi.org/10.1016/j.foodqual.2014.04.012

El-Said, O., & Al Hajri, S. (2022). Are customers happy with robot service? Investigating satisfaction with robot service restaurants during the COVID-19 pandemic. *Heliyon*, *8*(3). https://doi.org/10.1016/j.heliyon.2022.e08986

Emmons, R. A., & McCullough, M. E. (2003). Counting blessings versus burdens: An experimental investigation of gratitude and subjective well-being in daily life. *Journal of Personality and Social Psychology, 84*(2): 377–389. https://doi.org/10.1037//0022-3514.84.2.377

Engen, P. A., Green, S. J., Voigt, R. M., Forsyth, C. B., & Keshavarzian, A. (2015). The gastrointestinal microbiome: Alcohol effects on the composition of intestinal microbiota. *Alcohol Research: Current Reviews, 37*(2): 223–236.

Epstein, M. (1997). Alcohol's impact on kidney function. *Alcohol Health and Research World, 21*(1): 84–92.

Escoffier, A. (1903a). *Le guide culinaire. Aide mémoire de cuisine.* Paris: Bibliothèque Professionnelle.

Escoffier, A (1903b). *Escoffier: Le guide culinaire.* H. L. Cracknell & R. J. Kaufmann (Trans.) New York: Routledge, 2013.

Eskine, K. J., Kacinik, N. A., & Prinz, J. J. (2011). A bad taste in the mouth. *Psychological Science, 22*(3): 295–299. https://doi.org/10.1177/0956797611398497.

Esposito, K., Giugliano, F., Maiorino, M. I., & Giugliano, D. (2010). Dietary factors, Mediterranean diet and erectile dysfunction. *Journal of Sexual Medicine, 7*(7): 2338–2345. https://doi.org/10.1111/j.1743-6109.2010.01842.x

Ewing, J. A. (1984). Detecting alcoholism. The CAGE questionnaire. *Journal of the American Medical Association, 252*(14): 1905–1907. https://doi.org/10.1001/jama.252.14.1905

Examine (2024). The science behind munchies: Cannabis and your appetite. *Examine.com.* https://examine.com/articles/cannabis-munchies/ (last accessed 29 October 2025).

Fanzo, J., & McLaren, R. (2020). An overview of the ethics of eating and drinking. *Handbook of Eating and Drinking*, pp. 1095–1115. New York: Springer International. https://doi.org/10.1007/978-3-030-14504-0_82

FAO (2011). The state of food insecurity in the World 2011: How does international price volatility affect domestic economies and food security? Rome: Food and Agriculture Organization of the United Nations.

FAO (2022). *The State of World Fisheries and Aquaculture 2022. Towards Blue Transformation*. Rome, FAO.

Farokhnia, M., McDiarmid, G. R., Newmeyer, M. N., Munjal, V., Abulseoud, O. A., Huestis, M. A., & Leggio, L. (2020). Effects of oral, smoked, and vaporized cannabis on endocrine pathways related to appetite and metabolism: A randomized, double-blind, placebo-controlled, human laboratory study. *Translational Psychiatry, 10*(1): 1–11. https://doi.org/10.1038/s41398-020-0756-3

Ferretti, F., Mariani, M., & Sarti, E. (2021). Is the development of obesogenic food environments a self-reinforcing process? Evidence from soft drink consumption. *Globalization and Health, 17*(1): 91. https://doi.org/10.1186/s12992-021-00735-y

Festinger, L. (1957). *A Theory of Cognitive Dissonance*. Redwood City, CA: Stanford University Press.

Firth, J., Gangwisch, J. E., Borsini, A., Wootton, R. E., & Mayer, E. A. (2020). Food and mood: How do diet and nutrition affect mental wellbeing? *British Medical Journal, 369*: m2382. https://doi.org/10.1136/bmj.m2382

Fischer, B., Russell, C., Sabioni, P., van den Brink, W., Le Foll, B., Hall, W., Rehm, J., & Room, R. (2017). Lower-risk cannabis use guidelines: A comprehensive update of evidence and recommendations. *American Journal of Public Health, 107*(8): e1–e12. https://doi.org/10.2105/AJPH.2017.303818

Fischler, C. (1989). La Cuisine Selon Michelin. *Nourritures, Autrement, 108*. Paris.

Fisher, E. B., Strunk, R. C., Highstein, G. R., Kelley-Sykes, R., Tarr, K. L., Trinkaus, K., & Musick, J. (2009). A randomized controlled evaluation of the effect of community health workers on hospitalization for asthma: The Asthma Coach. *Archives of Pediatrics & Adolescent Medicine, 163*(3): 225–232. https://doi.org/10.1001/archpediatrics.2008.577

Fisher, J. O., & Birch, L. L. (2002). Eating in the absence of hunger and overweight in girls from 5 to 7 y of age. *American Journal of Clinical Nutrition, 76*(1): 226–231. https://doi.org/10.1093/ajcn/76.1.226

Flynn, J. R., & Shayer, M. (2018). IQ decline and Piaget: Does the rot start at the top? *Intelligence, 66*: 112–121. https://doi.org/10.1016/j.intell.2017.11.010

Folkvord, F., & Hermans, R. C. J. (2020). Food marketing in an obesogenic environment: A narrative overview of the potential of healthy food promotion to children and adults. *Current Addiction Reports, 7*(4): 431–436. https://doi.org/10.1007/s40429-020-00338-4

Foltin, R. W., Fischman, M. W., & Byrne, M. F. (1988). Effects of smoked marijuana on food intake and body weight of humans living in a residential laboratory. *Appetite, 11*(1): 1–14. https://doi.org/10.1016/s0195-6663(88)80017-5

Food Foundation, The (2020). *The Broken Plate* [annual report].

Franklin, R. A., Butler, M. P., & Bentley, J. A. (2018). The physical postures of yoga practices may protect against depressive symptoms, even as life stressors increase: A moderation analysis. *Psychology, Health & Medicine, 23*(7): 870–879. https://doi.org/10.1080/13548506.2017.1420206

Fraser, G. E., Strahan, T. M., Sabaté, J., Beeson, W. L., & Kissinger, D. (1992). Effects of traditional coronary risk factors on rates of incident coronary events in a low-risk population. The Adventist Health Study. *Circulation, 86*(2): 406–413. https://doi.org/10.1161/01.cir.86.2.406

Frates, E. (2015). The Five Step Collaboration Cycle: A tool for the doctor's office. *International Journal of School and Cognitive Psychology, 2*: 1–5. https://doi.org/10.4172/ijscp.1000144

Frates, E., Bonnet, J. P., Joseph, R., & Peterson, J. A. (2019). *The Lifestyle Medicine Handbook: An Introduction to the Power of Healthy Habits.* 2nd edn. Monterey, CA: Healthy Learning, 2020.

Frates, E., Moore, M., Lopez, C., & McMahon, G. (2011). Coaching for behavior change in psychiatry. *American Journal of Physical Medicine & Rehabilitation / Association of Academic Physiatrists, 90*: 1074–1082. https://doi.org/10.1097/PHM.0b013e31822dea9a

Frates, E., Tollefson, M., & Comander, A. (2021). *PAVING the Path to Wellness: A Guide to Thriving With a Healthy Body, Peaceful Mind, and Joyful Heart.* Monterey, CA: Healthy Learning.

Frattaroli, J., Weidner, G., Merritt-Worden, T. A., Frenda, S., & Ornish, D. (2008). Angina pectoris and atherosclerotic risk factors in the multisite cardiac lifestyle intervention program. *American Journal of Cardiology, 101*(7): 911–918. https://doi.org/10.1016/j.amjcard.2007.11.039

Fredrickson, B. L. (2001). The role of positive emotions in positive psychology. The broaden-and-build theory of positive emotions. *American Psychologist, 56*(3): 218–226. https://doi.org/10.1037//0003-066x.56.3.218

Fredrickson, B. L. (2009). *Positivity: Groundbreaking Research Reveals How to Embrace the Hidden Strength of Positive Emotions, Overcome Negativity, and Thrive.* New York: Crown Archetype.

Fredrickson, B. L. (2011). Are you getting enough positivity in your diet? *Greater Good.* https://greatergood.berkeley.edu/article/item/are_you_getting_enough_positivity_in_your_diet (last accessed 29 October 2025).

Fredrickson, B. L., & Branigan, C. (2005). Positive emotions broaden the scope of attention and thought-action repertoires. *Cognition & Emotion, 19*(3): 313–332. https://doi.org/10.1080/02699930441000238

Frongillo, E. A., Nguyen, H. T., Smith, M. D., & Coleman-Jensen, A. (2017). Food insecurity is associated with subjective well-being among individuals from 138 countries in the 2014 Gallup World Poll. *Journal of Nutrition, 147*(4): 680–687. https://doi.org/10.3945/jn.116.243642

Gabor, G. (n.d.). 12 brand archetypes: How to use them for your business. *Learn.g2.com.* Retrieved July 13, 2024, from https://learn.g2.com/brand-archetypes

Gangwisch, J. E., Hale, L., Garcia, L., Malaspina, D., Opler, M. G., Payne, M. E., Rossom, R. C., & Lane, D. (2015). High glycemic index diet as a risk factor for depression: Analyses from the Women's Health Initiative. *American*

Journal of Clinical Nutrition, 102(2): 454–463. https://doi.org/10.3945/ajcn.114.103846

Garber, C., Blissmer, B., Deschenes, M., Franklin, B., Lamonte, M., Lee, I.-M., Nieman, D., & Swain, D. (2011). Quantity and quality of exercise for developing and maintaining cardiorespiratory, musculoskeletal, and neuromotor fitness in apparently healthy adults: Guidance for prescribing exercise. *Medicine and Science in Sports and Exercise, 43*: 1334–1359. https://doi.org/10.1249/MSS.0b013e318213fefb

Gasmi, A., Nasreen, A., Menzel, A., Gasmi Benahmed, A., Pivina, L., Noor, S., Peana, M., Chirumbolo, S., & Bjørklund, G. (2022). Neurotransmitters regulation and food intake: The role of dietary sources in neurotransmission. *Molecules, 28*(1): 210. https://doi.org/10.3390/molecules28010210

Gaudichon, C., & Calvez, J. (2021) Determinants of amino acid bioavailability from ingested protein in relation to gut health. *Current Opinion in Clinical Nutrition and Metabolic Care, 24*(1): 55–61.

GBD 2017 Diet Collaborators (2019). Health effects of dietary risks in 195 countries, 1990–2017: A systematic analysis for the global burden of disease study 2017. *The Lancet, 393*(10184): 1958–1972. https://doi.org/10.1016/s0140-6736(19)30041-8

Georgetown Behavioral Hospital (2021, May 6). GABA and alcohol: How drinking leads to anxiety. https://gbhoh.com/gaba-and-alcohol-how-drinking-leads-to-anxiety/ (last accessed 29 October 2025).

Gerrard, J. (2005). The Maillard Reaction: Chemistry, biochemistry and implications by Harry Nursten. *Australian Journal of Chemistry, 58*(10): 756. https://doi.org/10.1071/ch0505_br

Gesch, C. B., Hammond, S. M., Hampson, S. E., Eves, A., & Crowder, M. J. (2002). Influence of supplementary vitamins, minerals and essential fatty acids on the antisocial behaviour of young adult prisoners. Randomised, placebo-controlled trial. *British Journal of Psychiatry: The Journal of Mental Science, 181*: 22–28. https://doi.org/10.1192/bjp.181.1.22

Gharby, S. (2022). Refining vegetable oils: Chemical and physical refining. *Scientific World Journal*, 6627013. https://doi.org/10.1155/2022/6627013

Gillum, F., & Williams, C. (2009). Associations between breast cancer risk factors and religiousness in American women in a national health survey. *Journal of Religion and Health, 48*(2): 178–188. https://doi.org/10.1007/s10943-008-9187-9

Giousmpasoglou, C., Brown, L., & Cooper, J. (2019). The role of the celebrity chef. *International Journal of Hospitality Management, 85*:102358. https://doi.org/10.1016/j.ijhm.2019.102358

Giugliano, F., Maiorino, M. I., Di Palo, C., Autorino, R., De Sio, M., Giugliano, D., & Esposito, K. (2010). Adherence to Mediterranean diet and sexual function in women with type 2 diabetes. *Journal of Sexual Medicine, 7*(5): 1883–1890. https://doi.org/10.1111/j.1743-6109.2010.01714.x

Glanz, K., & Bishop, D. B. (2010). The role of behavioral science theory in development and implementation of public health interventions. *Annual Review of Public Health, 31*: 399–418. https://doi.org/10.1146/annurev.publhealth.012809.103604

Glanz, K., Rimer, B. K., & Viswanath, K. (2015). *Health Behavior: Theory, Research, and Practice*. Hoboken, NJ: John Wiley & Sons.

Goddaer, J., & Abraham, I. L. (1994). Effects of relaxing music on agitation during meals among nursing home residents with severe cognitive impairment. *Archives of Psychiatric Nursing, 8*(3): 150–158. https://doi.org/10.1016/0883-9417(94)90048-5

Godfray, H. C. J., Beddington, J. R., Crute, I. R., & Haddad, L. (2010). Food security: The challenge of feeding 9 billion people. *Science, 327*(5967): 812–818. https://doi.org/10.1126/science.1185383

Golden, N. H., & Mehler, P. S. (2020). Atypical anorexia nervosa can be just as bad. *Cleveland Clinic Journal of Nutrition, 87*(3): 172–174. https://doi.org/10.3949/ccjm.87a.19146

Goleman, D. (2011). *The Brain and Emotional Intelligence: New Insights*. Northampton, MA: More Than Sound.

Golomb, B. A., Evans, M. A., White, H. L., & Dimsdale, J. E. (2012). Trans fat consumption and aggression. *PloS One, 7*(3): e32175. https://doi.org/10.1371/journal.pone.0032175

Gómez Escribano, L., Gálvez Casas, A., Escribá Fernández-Marcote, A. R., Tárraga López, P., & Tárraga Marcos, L. (2017). Review and analysis of physical exercise at hormonal and brain levels, and its influence on appetite. *Clinica E Investigacion En Arteriosclerosis: Publicacion Oficial De La Sociedad Espanola De Arteriosclerosis, 29*(6): 265–274. https://doi.org/10.1016/j.arteri.2017.04.002

González Olmo, B. M., Butler, M. J., & Barrientos, R. M. (2021). Evolution of the human diet and its impact on gut microbiota, immune responses, and brain health. *Nutrients, 13*(1): 196. https://doi.org/10.3390/nu13010196

Goode, J. (2005). *Wine Science*. London: Mitchell Beazley.

Grand View Research (2025). Culinary tourism market size, share & trends analysis report by activity (culinary trails, cooking classes), by booking mode (tour operators, direct travel), by tourist type, by region, and segment forecasts, 2024–2030. https://grandviewresearch.com/industry-analysis/culinary-tourism-market-report (last accessed 22 May 2025).

Greer, S. M., Goldstein, A. N., & Walker, M. P. (2013). The impact of sleep deprivation on food desire in the human brain. *Nature Communications, 4*: 2259. https://doi.org/10.1038/ncomms3259

Grossman, E. R., Benjamin-Neelon, S. E., & Sonnenschein, S. (2020). Alcohol consumption during the COVID-19 pandemic: A cross-sectional survey of US adults. *International Journal of Environmental Research and Public Health, 17*(24): 9189. https://doi.org/10.3390/ijerph17249189

Grosso, G., Pajak, A., Marventano, S., Castellano, S., Galvano, F., Bucolo, C., Drago, F., & Caraci, F. (2014). Role of omega-3 fatty acids in the treatment of depressive disorders: A comprehensive meta-analysis of randomized clinical trials. *PloS One, 9*(5): e96905. https://doi.org/10.1371/journal.pone.0096905

Guidara, W. (2022). Will Guidara: The secret ingredients of great hospitality. *TED Talk*. https://ted.com/talks/will_guidara_the_secret_ingredients_of_great_hospitality (last accessed 18 October 2023).

Gunders, D. (2013, October). The dating game: How confusing food date labels lead to food waste in America. *NRDC*. https://nrdc.org/resources/dating-game-how-confusing-food-date-labels-lead-food-waste-america (last accessed 29 October 2025).

Gundersen, C., & Ziliak, J. P. (2015). Food insecurity and health outcomes. *Health Affairs (Project Hope), 34*(11): 1830–1839. https://doi.org/10.1377/hlthaff.2015.0645

Hallowell, E. M. (1999). *Connect*. New York: Pantheon.

Hanh, T. N., & Cheung, L. (2010). *Savor: Mindful Eating, Mindful Life*. New York: HarperCollins.

Hanig, D. P. (1901). Zur Psychophysik des Geschmackssinnes [On the psychophysics of taste]. *Philosophische Studien, 17*: 576–623.

Hanks, A. S., Just, D. R., & Wansink, B. (2013). Smarter lunchrooms can address new school lunchroom guidelines and childhood obesity. *Journal of Pediatrics, 162*(4): 867–869. https://doi.org/10.1016/j.jpeds.2012.12.031

Hanlon, E. C., Tasali, E., Leproult, R., Stuhr, K. L., Doncheck, E., de Wit, H., Hillard, C. J., & Van Cauter, E. (2016). Sleep restriction enhances the daily rhythm of circulating levels of endocannabinoid 2-arachidonoylglycerol. *Sleep, 39*(3): 653–664. https://doi.org/10.5665/sleep.5546

Harbolic, B. K., & Stoppler, M. C. (2021). Alcohol and nutrition. *MedicineNet*. https://medicinenet.com/alcohol_and_nutrition/article.htm (last accessed 29 October 2025).

Hardman, C. A., Christiansen, P., & Wilkinson, L. L. (2016). Using food to soothe: Maternal attachment anxiety is associated with child emotional eating. *Appetite*, *1*(99): 91–96. https://doi.org/10.1016/j.appet.2016.01.017

Harrar, V., & Spence, C. (2013). The taste of cutlery: How the taste of food is affected by the weight, size, shape, and colour of the cutlery used to eat it. *Flavour*, *2*(1). https://doi.org/10.1186/2044-7248-2-21

Harris, J. L., Schwartz, M. B., Brownell, K. D.(2009). Marketing foods to children and adolescents: A review of industry expenditures, activities, and self-regulation. New Haven, CT: Yale Rudd Center for Food Policy & Obesity.

Harris, W. S., Mozaffarian, D., Rimm, E., Kris-Etherton, P., Rudel, L. L., Appel, L. J., Engler, M. M., Engler, M. B., & Sacks, F. (2009). Omega-6 fatty acids and risk for cardiovascular disease. *Circulation*, *119*(6): 902–907. https://doi.org/10.1161/CIRCULATIONAHA.108.191627

Harrison, M. E., Norris, M. L., Obeid, N., Fu, M., Weinstangel, H., & Sampson, M. (2015). Systematic review of the effects of family meal frequency on psychosocial outcomes in youth. *Canadian Family Physician*, *61*(2): e96–e106.

Harrison, Y., & Horne, J. A. (2000). The impact of sleep deprivation on decision making: A review. *Journal of Applied Experimental Psychology*, *6*(3): 236–249. https://doi.org/10.1037//1076-898x.6.3.236

Harrison Green, M. (2016, March 24). Forget Nutraloaf—Prisoners are growing their own food [Review of *Forget Nutraloaf—Prisoners Are Growing Their Own Food.*] *YES! Magazine*. https://yesmagazine.org/democracy/2016/03/24/forget-nutraloaf-prisoners-are-growing-their-own-food (last accessed 29 October 2025).

Harter, J. (2018). Employee engagement on the rise in the U.S. *Gallup*. https://news.gallup.com/poll/241649/employeeengagement-rise.aspx (last accessed 29 October 2025).

Hartley, R. (2021). *Gentle Nutrition: A Non-diet Approach to Healthy Eating.* Las Vegas, NV: Victory Belt.

Hartmann, E. (1982). Effects of L-tryptophan on sleepiness and on sleep. *Journal of Psychiatric Research*, *17*(2): 107–113. https://doi.org/10.1016/0022-3956(82)90012-7. PMID: 6764927

Hartney, E. (2024). The symptoms used to diagnose substance use disorders. *Verywell Mind*. https://verywellmind.com/dsm-5-criteria-for-substance-use-disorders-21926 (last accessed 29 October 2025).

Harvard Medical School (2021). Science of sleep: How is sleep regulated? / *Sleep Medicine*. https://sleep.hms.harvard.edu/education-training/public-education/sleep-and-health-education-program/sleep-health-education-48 (last accessed 29 October 2025).

Harvard Medical School (2024). When it comes to protein how much is too much? *Harvard Health Publishing*. https://health.harvard.edu/nutrition/when-it-comes-to-protein-how-much-is-too-much (last accessed 29 October 2025).

Harvard Medical School (n.d.). Harvard second generation study. *Harvardstudy*. Retrieved July 23, 2024, from https://adultdevelopmentstudy.org

Harvard T.H. Chan School of Public Health (2012). The truth about fats: The good, the bad, and the in-between. *Harvard Health*. https://health.harvard.edu/staying-healthy/the-truth-about-fats-bad-and-good (last accessed 29 October 2025).

Harvard T.H. Chan School of Public Health (2017, August 16). The microbiome. *The Nutrition Source*. https://nutritionsource.hsph.harvard.edu/microbiome/ (last accessed 29 October 2025).

Harvard T.H. Chan School of Public Health (2020a, July 30). Caffeine. *The Nutrition Source*. https://nutritionsource.hsph.harvard.edu/caffeine/ (last accessed 29 October 2025).

Harvard T.H. Chan School of Public Health (2020b, September 14). Mindful eating. *The Nutrition Source*. https://nutritionsource.hsph.harvard.edu/mindful-eating/ (last accessed 29 October 2025).

Harvard T.H. Chan School of Public Health (2023). Healthy eating plate. *The Nutrition Source*. https://nutritionsource.hsph.harvard.edu/healthy-eating-plate/ (last accessed 29 October 2025).

Harvard University (n.d.). Langar: The communal meal. *Pluralism.org*. https://pluralism.org/langar-the-communal-meal (last accessed 29 October 2025).

Hauser, M. E., McMacken, M., Lim, A., & Shetty, P. (2022). Nutrition—An evidence-based, practical approach to chronic disease prevention and treatment. *Journal of Family Practice*, *71*(1 Suppl Lifestyle).

Havel, P. J. (2002). Control of energy homeostasis and insulin action by adipocyte hormones: Leptin, acylation stimulating protein, and adiponectin. *Current Opinion in Lipidology*, *13*(1): 51.

Hayhoe, R., Rechel, B., Clark, A. B., Gummerson, C., Smith, S. J., & Welch. A. A. (2021). Cross-sectional associations of schoolchildren's fruit and vegetable consumption, and meal choices, with their mental well-being: A cross-sectional study. *BMJ Nutrition, Prevention & Health*, *4*(2): 447–462. https://doi.org/10.1136/bmjnph-2020-000205

He, F. J., Nowson, C. A., Lucas, M., & MacGregor, G. A. (2007). Increased consumption of fruit and vegetables is related to a reduced risk of coronary heart disease: Meta-analysis of cohort studies. *Journal of Human Hypertension*, *21*(9): 717–728. https://doi.org/10.1038/sj.jhh.1002212

He, F. J., Nowson, C. A., & MacGregor, G. A. (2006). Fruit and vegetable consumption and stroke: Meta-analysis of cohort studies. *The Lancet, 367*(9507): 320–326. https://doi.org/10.1016/S0140-6736(06)68069-0

Heaney, R. P. (2002). Effects of caffeine on bone and the calcium economy. *Food and Chemical Toxicology: An International Journal published for the British Industrial Biological Research Association, 40*(9): 1263–1270. https://doi.org/10.1016/s0278-6915(02)00094-7

Hegde, S., Nair, L. P., Chandran, H., & Irshad, H. (2018). Traditional Indian way of eating—an overview. *Journal of Ethnic Foods, 5*(1): 20–23. https://doi.org/10.1016/j.jef.2018.02.001

Hellström, P. M., Hendolin, P., Kaihovaara, P., Kronberg, L., Meierjohann, A., Millerhovf, A., Paloheimo, L., Sundelin, H., Syrjänen, K., Webb, D.-L., & Salaspuro, M. (2017). Slow-release L-cysteine capsule prevents gastric mucosa exposure to carcinogenic acetaldehyde: Results of a randomised single-blinded, cross-over study of helicobacter-associated atrophic gastritis. *Scandinavian Journal of Gastroenterology, 52*(2): 230–237. https://doi.org/10.1080/00365521.2016.1249403

Heung, V. C. S., & Gu, T. (2012). Influence of restaurant atmospherics on patron satisfaction and behavioral intentions. *International Journal of Hospitality Management, 31*(4): 1167–1177. https://doi.org/10.1016/j.ijhm.2012.02.004

Heydari, G., Heidari, F., Yousefifard, M., & Hosseini, M. (2014). Smoking and diet in healthy adults: A cross-sectional study in Tehran, Iran, 2010. *Iranian Journal of Public Health, 43*(4): 485–491.

Hibbeln, J. R., Davis, J. M., Steer, C., Emmett, P., Rogers, I., Williams, C., & Golding, J. (2007). Maternal seafood consumption in pregnancy and neurodevelopmental outcomes in childhood (ALSPAC study): An observational cohort study. *The Lancet, 369*(9561): 578–585. https://doi.org/10.1016/s0140-6736(07)60277-3.

Hillsdon, M., Thorogood, M., White, I., & Foster, C. (2002). Advising people to take more exercise is ineffective: A randomized controlled trial of physical activity promotion in primary care. *International Journal of Epidemiology, 31*(4): 808–815. https://doi.org/10.1093/ije/31.4.808

Hippocrates. (n.d.). Hippocrates quotes. *BrainyQuote.* Retrieved August 26, 2024, from https://brainyquote.com/quotes/hippocrates_153531

Hirotsu, C., Tufik, S., & Andersen, M. L. (2015). Interactions between sleep, stress, and metabolism: From physiological to pathological conditions. *Sleep Science, 8*(3): 143–52. https://doi.org/10.1016/j.slsci.2015.09.002. Epub 2015 Sep 28. PMID: 26779321; PMCID: PMC4688585

Hirsch, A. R., & Gruss, J. J. (1999). Olfactory stimuli and their effects on human sexual response. *Journal of Neuropsychiatry, 11*(3): 372–379.

Hirshkowitz, M., Whiton, K., Albert, S. M., Alessi, C., Bruni, O., DonCarlos, L., Hazen, N., Herman, J., Katz, E. S., Kheirandish-Gozal, L., Neubauer, D. N., O'Donnell, A. E., Ohayon, M., Peever, J., Rawding, R., Sachdeva, R. C., Setters, B., Vitiello, M. V., Ware, J. C., & Adams Hillard, P. J. (2015). National Sleep Foundation's sleep time duration recommendations: Methodology and results summary. *Sleep Health, 1*(1): 40–43. https://doi.org/10.1016/j.sleh.2014.12.010

Hogenkamp, P. S., Nilsson, E., Nilsson, V. C., Chapman, C. D., Vogel, H., Lundberg, L. S., Zarei, S., Cedernaes, J., Rångtell, F. H., Broman, J.-E., Dickson, S. L., Brunstrom, J. M., Benedict, C., & Schiöth, H. B. (2013). Acute sleep deprivation increases portion size and affects food choice in young men. *Psychoneuroendocrinology, 38*(9): 1668–1674. https://doi.org/10.1016/j.psyneuen.2013.01.012

Hojat, M., Louis, D. Z., Markham, F. W., Wender, R., Rabinowitz, C., & Gonnella, J. S. (2011). Physicians' empathy and clinical outcomes for diabetic patients. *Academic Medicine: Journal of the Association of American Medical Colleges, 86*(3): 359–364. https://doi.org/10.1097/ACM.0b013e3182086fe1

Holder, M. D. (2019). The contribution of food consumption to well-being. *Annals of Nutrition & Metabolism, 74* (Suppl. 2): 44–52. https://doi.org/10.1159/000499147

Holloway, T. P., Dalton, L., Hughes, R., Jayasinghe, S., Patterson, K. A. E., Murray, S., Soward, R., Byrne, N. M., Hills, A. P., & Ahuja, K. D. K. (2023). School gardening and health and well-being of school-aged children: A realist synthesis. *Nutrients, 15*(5): 1190. https://doi.org/10.3390/nu15051190

Holmes, M. V., Dale, C. E., Zuccolo, L., Silverwood, R. J., Guo, Y., Ye, Z., Prieto-Merino, D., Dehghan, A., Trompet, S., Wong, A., Cavadino, A., Drogan, D., Padmanabhan, S., Li, S., Yesupriya, A., Leusink, M., Sundstrom, J., Hubacek, J. A., Pikhart, H., … InterAct Consortium. (2014). Association between alcohol and cardiovascular disease: Mendelian randomisation analysis based on individual participant data. *BMJ (Clinical Research Ed.), 349*: g4164. https://doi.org/10.1136/bmj.g4164

Holscher, H. D. (2017). Dietary fiber and prebiotics and the gastrointestinal microbiota. *Gut Microbes, 8*(2): 172–184. https://doi.org/10.1080/19490976.2017.1290756.

Holt-Lunstad, J. (2021). The major health implications of social connection. *Current Directions in Psychological Science, 30*: 251–259. https://doi.org/10.1177/0963721421999630

Hosseini, Z., Veenstra, G., Khan, N. A., & Conklin, A. I. (2021). Social connections and hypertension in women and men: A population-based cross-sectional study of the Canadian Longitudinal Study on Aging. *Journal of Hypertension*, *39*(4): 651–660. https://doi.org/10.1097/HJH.0000000000002688

Howatson, G., Bell, P. G., Tallent, J., Middleton, B., McHugh, M. P., & Ellis, J. (2012). Effect of tart cherry juice (Prunus cerasus) on melatonin levels and enhanced sleep quality. *European Journal of Nutrition*, *51*(8): 909–916. https://doi.org/10.1007/s00394-011-0263-7

Hoyt, C. L., Burnette, J. L., Thomas, F. N., & Orvidas, K. (2019). Public health messages and weight-related beliefs: Implications for well-being and stigma. *Frontiers in Psychology*, *10*: 2806. https://doi.org/10.3389/fpsyg.2019.02806

Huang, Z.-L., Urade, Y., & Hayaishi, O. (2011). The role of adenosine in the regulation of sleep. *Current Topics in Medicinal Chemistry*, *11*(8): 1047–1057. https://doi.org/10.2174/156802611795347654

Hung, H.-C., Joshipura, K. J., Jiang, R., Hu, F. B., Hunter, D., Smith-Warner, S. A., Colditz, G. A., Rosner, B., Spiegelman, D., & Willett, W. C. (2004). Fruit and vegetable intake and risk of major chronic disease. *Journal of the National Cancer Institute*, *96*(21): 1577–1584. https://doi.org/10.1093/jnci/djh296

Ideno, Y., Hayashi, K., Abe, Y., Ueda, K., Iso, H., Noda, M., Lee, J.-S., & Suzuki, S. (2017). Blood pressure-lowering effect of *Shinrin-yoku* (Forest bathing): A systematic review and meta-analysis. *BMC Complementary and Alternative Medicine*, *17*: 409. https://doi.org/10.1186/s12906-017-1912-z

Iftikhar, I. H., Donley, M. A., Mindel, J., Pleister, A., Soriano, S., & Magalang, U. J. (2015). Sleep duration and metabolic syndrome. An updated dose-risk meta-analysis. *Annals of the American Thoracic Society*, *12*(9): 1364–1372. https://doi.org/10.1513/AnnalsATS.201504-190OC

Igini, M. (2023). 10 food waste statistics in America. *Earth.Org*. https://earth.org/food-waste-in-america/ (last accessed 10 July 2023).

Imamura, F., Micha, R., Khatibzadeh, S., Fahimi, S., Shi, P., Powles, J., & Mozaffarian, D. (2015). Dietary quality among men and women in 187 countries in 1990 and 2010: A systematic assessment. *The Lancet. Global Health*. https://pubmed.ncbi.nlm.nih.gov/25701991/ (last accessed 10 July 2023).

Institute of Medicine (US) Committee on Sleep Medicine and Research (IMCSMR). (2006). *Sleep Disorders and Sleep Deprivation: An Unmet Public Health Problem*. H. R. Colten & B. M. Altevogt (Eds.). Washington, DC: National Academies Press. http://ncbi.nlm.nih.gov/books/NBK19960/.

Inyushkin, A. N., Poletaev, V. S., Inyushkina, E. M., Kalberdin, I. S., & Inyushkin, A. A. (2024). Irisin/BDNF signaling in the muscle-brain axis and circadian system: A review. *Journal of Biomedical Research*, *38*(1): 1–16. https://doi.org/10.7555/JBR.37.20230133

International Union for Conservation of Nature (n.d.). IUCN red list of threatened species. https://iucnredlist.org/ (last accessed 4 July 2023).

International Union for Conservation of Nature (IUCN) (2024). *Agriculture and conservation: Living nature in a globalised world*. IUCN Flagship Report Series No. 2. Gland, Switzerland: IUCN.

International Union for Conservation of Nature (IUCN) (2025). *The IUCN Red List of Threatened Species*. Version 2025-1. https://iucnredlist.org (last accessed 9 September 2025).

Iyendo, T. O. (2016). Exploring the effect of sound and music on health in hospital settings: A narrative review. *International Journal of Nursing Studies*, *63*: 82–100. https://doi.org/10.1016/j.ijnurstu.2016.08.008

Jacka, F. N., Cherbuin, N., Anstey, K. J, Sachdev, P., & Butterworth, P. (2015). Western diet is associated with a smaller hippocampus: A longitudinal investigation. *BMC Medicine*, *13*(1): 215. https://doi.org/10.1186/s12916-015-0461-x

Jacka, F. N., O'Neil, A., Opie, R., Itsiopoulos, C., Cotton, S., Mohebbi, M., Castle, D., Dash, S., Mihalopoulos, C., Chatterton, M. L., Brazionis, L., Dean, O. M., Hodge, A. M., & Berk, M. (2017). A randomised controlled trial of dietary improvement for adults with major depression (the "SMILES" trial). *BMC Medicine*, *15*: 23.

Jacques, A., Chaaya, N., Beecher, K., Ali, S. A., Belmer, A., & Bartlett, S. (2019). The impact of sugar consumption on stress driven, emotional and addictive behaviors. *Neuroscience and Biobehavioral Reviews*, *103*: 178–199. https://doi.org/10.1016/j.neubiorev.2019.05.021

Jaiswal, Y. S., & Williams, L. L. (2017). A glimpse of Ayurveda—the forgotten history and principles of Indian Traditional Medicine. *Journal of Traditional and Complementary Medicine*, *7*(1): 50–53. https://doi.org/10.1016/j.jtcme.2016.02.002

Janssen, M., Heerkens, Y., Kuijer, W., van der Heijden, B., & Engels, J. (2018). Effects of mindfulness-based stress reduction on employees' mental health: A systematic review. *PloS One*, *13*(1): e0191332. https://doi.org/10.1371/journal.pone.0191332

Ji, X., Grandner, M. A., & Liu, J. (2017). The relationship between micronutrient status and sleep patterns: A systematic review. *Public Health Nutrition*, *20*(4): 687–701. https://doi.org/10.1017/S1368980016002603

Jih, J., Mukherjea, A., Vittinghoff, E., Nguyen, T. T., Tsoh, J. Y., Fukuoka, Y., Bender, M. S., Tseng, W., & Kanaya, A. M. (2014). Using appropriate body mass index cut points for overweight and obesity among Asian Americans. *Preventive Medicine*, *65*: 1–6. https://doi.org/10.1016/j.ypmed.2014.04.010

Jones, D. (2014, May 27). Is this hospital a miracle cure for the NHS? It has a Michelin chef, happy patients and is run by doctors and nurses. And shock, horror, it's operated for the state—at a profit—by a private firm. *Daily Mail Online*. http://dailymail.co.uk/health/article-2641055/Is-hospital-miracle-cure-NHS-It-Michelin-chef-happy-patients-run-doctors-nurses-And-shock-horror-operated-profit-private-firm.html (last accessed 29 October 2025).

Joo, J., Williamson, S. A., Vazquez, A. I., Fernandez, J. R., & Bray, M. S. (2019). The influence of 15-week exercise training on dietary patterns among young adults. *International Journal of Obesity*, *43*(9): 1681–1690. https://doi.org/10.1038/s41366-018-0299-3

Juul, F., Parekh, N., Martinez-Steele, E., Monteiro, C. A. & Chang, V. W. (2022). Ultra-processed food consumption among US adults from 2001 to 2018. *American Journal of Clinical Nutrition*, *115*(1): 211–221. https://doi.org/10.1093/ajcn/nqab305

Kabat-Zinn, J. (1991). *Full Catastrophe Living*. New York: Dell.

Kalmpourtzidou, A., Eilander, A., & Talsma, E. (2020). Global vegetable intake and supply compared to recommendations: A systematic review. *Nutrients*, *12*: 1558. https://doi.org/10.3390/nu12061558

Kashani, L., Raisi, F., Saroukhani, S., Sohrabi, H., Modabbernia, A., Nasehi, A. A., Jamshidi, A., Ashrafi, M., Mansouri, P., Ghaeli, P., & Akhondzadeh, S. (2013). Saffron for treatment of fluoxetine-induced sexual dysfunction in women: Randomized double-blind placebo-controlled study. *Human Psychopharmacology*, *28*(1): 54–60. https://doi.org/10.1002/hup.2282

Katz, D. L., & Meller, S. (2014). Can we say what diet is best for health? *Annual Review of Public Health*, *35*: 83–103. https://doi.org/10.1146/annurev-publhealth-032013-182351

Keirns, N. G., & Hawkins, M. A. W. (2019). The relationship between intuitive eating and body image is moderated by measured body mass index. *Eating Behaviors*, *33*: 91–96. https://doi.org/10.1016/j.eatbeh.2019.04.004

Kelly, I. (2005). *Cooking for Kings: The Life of Antonin Carême: The First Celebrity Chef*. New York: Walker.

Kelly, J., Karlsen, M., & Steinke, G. (2020). Type 2 diabetes remission and lifestyle medicine: A position statement from the American College of Lifestyle Medicine. *American Journal of Lifestyle Medicine*, *14*(4): 406–419. https://doi.org/10.1177/1559827620930962

Kesaniemi, Y., Danforth, E., Jensen, M., Kopelman, P., Lefèbvre, P., & Reeder, B. (2001). Dose-response issues concerning physical activity and health: An evidence-based symposium. *Medicine and Science in Sports and Exercise, 33*: S351–S358.

Khosla, M., Murty, N. A. R., & Kanwisher, N. (2022). A highly selective response to food in human visual cortex revealed by hypothesis-free voxel decomposition. *Current Biology, 32*(19): 4159–4171.e9. https://doi.org/10.1016/j.cub.2022.08.009

Kiatkawsin, K., & Han, H. (2019). What drives customers' willingness to pay price premiums for luxury gastronomic experiences at Michelin-starred restaurants? *International Journal of Hospitality Management, 82*: 209–219. https://doi.org/10.1016/j.ijhm.2019.04.024

Kilroy, D. S. (2019). Eating the right foods for exercise. *Healthline*. https://healthline.com/health/fitness-exercise-eating-healthy (last accessed 29 October 2025).

Kim, E. J., Pellman, B., & Kim, J. J. (2015). Stress effects on the hippocampus: A critical review. *Learning & Memory, 22*(9): 411–416. https://doi.org/10.1101/lm.037291.114

Kivimäki, M., Shipley, M. J., Batty, G. D., Hamer, M., Akbaraly, T. N., Kumari, M., Jokela, M., Virtanen, M., Lowe, G. D., Ebmeier, K. P., Brunner, E. J., & Singh-Manoux, A. (2014). Long-term inflammation increases risk of common mental disorder: A 10-year prospective analysis of the Whitehall II cohort. *Molecular Psychiatry, 19*(1), 134–140. https://doi.org/10.1038/mp.2013.35

Kleinman, R. E., Hall, S., Green, H., Korzec-Ramirez, D., Patton, K., Pagano, M. E., & Murphy, J. M. (2002). Diet, breakfast, and academic performance in children. *Annals of Nutrition & Metabolism, 46 Suppl. 1*(1): 24–30. https://doi.org/10.1159/000066399

Knowler, W. C., Barrett-Connor, E., Fowler, S. E., Hamman, R. F., Lachin, J. M., Walker, E. A., Nathan, D. M., & Diabetes Prevention Program Research Group. (2002). Reduction in the incidence of type 2 diabetes with lifestyle intervention or metformin. *New England Journal of Medicine, 346*(6): 393–403. https://doi.org/10.1056/NEJMoa012512

Knüppel, A., Shipley, M. J., Llewellyn, C. H., & Brunner, E. J. (2017). Sugar intake from sweet food and beverages, common mental disorder and depression: Prospective findings from the Whitehall II study. *Scientific Reports, 7*(1): 1–10. https://doi.org/10.1038/s41598-017-05649-7

Kobayashi, D., Takahashi, O., Deshpande, G. A., Shimbo, T., & Fukui, T. (2012). Association between weight gain, obesity, and sleep duration: A large-scale 3-year cohort study. *Sleep & Breathing = Schlaf & Atmung, 16*(3): 829–833. https://doi.org/10.1007/s11325-011-0583-0

Kohsaka, A., & Bass, J. (2009). Clock genes and metabolic regulation. In L. R. Squire (Ed.), *Encyclopedia of Neuroscience* (pp. 1023–1029). Cambridge, MA: Academic Press. https://doi.org/10.1016/B978-008045046-9.01606-5

Konno, M., Takeda, T., Kawakami, Y., Suzuki, Y., Kawano, Y., Nakajima, K., Ozawa, T., Ishigami, K., Takemura, N., & Sakatani, K. (2016). Relationships between gum-chewing and stress. *Advances in Experimental Medicine and Biology*, *876*: 343–349. https://doi.org/10.1007/978-1-4939-3023-4_43

Koulivand, P. H., Khaleghi Ghadiri, M., & Gorji, A. (2013). Lavender and the nervous system. *Evidence-Based Complementary and Alternative Medicine: eCAM*: 681304. https://doi.org/10.1155/2013/681304

Koven, N. S., & Abry, A. W. (2015). The clinical basis of orthorexia nervosa: Emerging perspectives. *Neuropsychiatric Disease and Treatment*, *11*: 385–394.

Kruger, J., Glassman, J., Knippen, K. L., Glassman, T., & Kruger, D. J. (2018). Drunchies hangover: Heavy episodic drinking and dietary choices while drinking and on the following day. *Californian Journal of Health Promotion*, *16*(1): 79–90. https://doi.org/10.32398/cjhp.v16i1.2127

Kruger, J., & Kruger, D. (2015). The impact of alcohol consumption on food choice among college students. *American Journal of Health Studies*, *30*. https://doi.org/10.47779/ajhs.2015.171

Kuehn, B. M. (2022). Climbing melatonin use for insomnia raises safety concerns. *Journal of the American Medical Association*, *328*(7): 605–607. https://doi.org/10.1001/jama.2022.11506

Kurihara, K. (2009). Glutamate: From discovery as a food flavor to role as a basic taste (umami). *American Journal of Clinical Nutrition*, *90*(3): 719S–722S. https://doi.org/10.3945/ajcn.2009.27462d

Kushlev, K., & Dunn, E. W. (2015). Checking email less frequently reduces stress. *Computers in Human Behavior*, *43*: 220–228. https://doi.org/10.1016/j.chb.2014.11.005

Lachance, L., & Ramsey, D. (2015). Food, mood, and brain health: Implications for the modern clinician. *Missouri Medicine*, *112*(2): 111–115.

Lara, J., Evans, E. H., O'Brien, N., Moynihan, P. J., Meyer, T. D., Adamson, A. J., Errington, L., Sniehotta, F. F., White, M., & Mathers, J. C. (2014). Association of behaviour change techniques with effectiveness of dietary interventions among adults of retirement age: A systematic review and meta-analysis of randomised controlled trials. *BMC Medicine*, *12*: 177. https://doi.org/10.1186/s12916-014-0177-3

Laskowski, E. R. (2022). What are the risks of sitting too much? *Mayo Clinic*. https://mayoclinic.org/healthy-lifestyle/adult-health/expert-answers/sitting/faq-20058005 (last accessed 29 October 2025).

Ledochowski, L., Ruedl, G., Taylor, A. H., & Kopp, M. (2015). Acute effects of brisk walking on sugary snack cravings in overweight people, affect and responses to a manipulated stress situation and to a sugary snack cue: A crossover study. *PLoS One*, *10*(3): e0119278. https://doi.org/10.1371/journal.pone.0119278

Lee, S. H. (2022). Adults meeting fruit and vegetable intake recommendations—United States, 2019. *MMWR. Morbidity and Mortality Weekly Report*, *71*. https://doi.org/10.15585/mmwr.mm7101a1

Lee, W.-L., Liu, C.-H., & Tseng, T.-W. (2022). The multiple effects of service innovation and quality on transitional and electronic word-of-mouth in predicting customer behaviour. *Journal of Retailing and Consumer Services*, 64: 102791. https://doi.org/10.1016/j.jretconser.2021.102791

Levato, F., & Colacchio, F. (2021, June 10). How Gen Z's empathy, awareness, and fluidity are transforming business as usual [review]. *Bain.com*. https://bain.com/insights/how-gen-zs-empathy-awareness-and-fluidity-are-transforming-business-as-usual-webinar/ (last accessed 29 October 2025).

Levoy, E., Lazaridou, A., Brewer, J., & Fulwiler, C. (2017). An exploratory study of mindfulness based stress reduction for emotional eating. *Appetite*, *109*: 124–130. https://doi.org/10.1016/j.appet.2016.11.029

Li, F. (2013). Taste perception: From the tongue to the testis. *Molecular Human Reproduction*, *19*(6): 349–360. https://doi.org/10.1093/molehr/gat009

Li, V. L., He, Y., Contrepois, K., Liu, H., Kim, J. T., Wiggenhorn, A. L., Tanzo, J. T., Tung, A. S.-H., Lyu, X., Zushin, P.-J. H., Jansen, R. S., Michael, B., Loh, K. Y., Yang, A. C., Carl, C. S., Voldstedlund, C. T., Wei, W., Terrell, S. M., Moeller, B. C., … Long, J. Z. (2022). An exercise-inducible metabolite that suppresses feeding and obesity. *Nature*, *606*(7915): 785–790. https://doi.org/10.1038/s41586-022-04828-5

Lichstein, K. L., Payne, K. L., Soeffing, J. P., Heith Durrence, H., Taylor, D. J., Riedel, B. W., & Bush, A. J. (2007). Vitamins and sleep: An exploratory study. *Sleep Medicine*, *9*(1): 27–32. https://doi.org/10.1016/j.sleep.2006.12.009

Lin, L., Allemekinders, H., Dansby, A., Campbell, L., Durance-Tod, S., Berger, A., & Jones, P. J. (2013). Evidence of health benefits of canola oil. *Nutrition Reviews*, *71*(6): 370–385. https://doi.org/10.1111/nure.12033

Lin, T.-W., & Kuo, Y.-M. (2013). Exercise benefits brain function: The monoamine connection. *Brain Sciences*, *3*(1): 39–53. https://doi.org/10.3390/brainsci3010039

Liu, J., Raine, A., Venables, P. H., & Mednick, S. A. (2004). Malnutrition at age 3 years and externalizing behavior problems at ages 8, 11, and 17 years. *American Journal of Psychiatry*, *161*(11): 2005–2013. https://doi.org/10.1176/appi.ajp.161.11.2005

Liu, Z., He, C., Zhou, Y., & Wu, J. (2014). How much of the world's land has been urbanized, really? A hierarchical framework for avoiding confusion. *Landscape Ecology, 29*(5): 763–771. https://doi.org/10.1007/s10980-014-0034-y

LIczbiński, P., & Bukowska, B. (2022). Tea and coffee polyphenols and their biological properties based on the latest in vitro investigations. *Industrial Crops and Products, 175*: 114265. https://doi.org/10.1016/j.indcrop.2021.114265

Locke, E. A., & Latham, G. P. (2006). New directions in goal-setting theory. *Current Directions in Psychological Science, 15*(5): 265–268. https://doi.org/10.1111/j.1467-8721.2006.00449.x

Lohsiriwat, S., Hirunsai, M., & Chaiyaprasithi, B. (2011). Effect of caffeine on bladder function in patients with overactive bladder symptoms. *Urology Annals, 3*(1): 14–18. https://doi.org/10.4103/0974-7796.75862

Louie, D., Brook, K., & Frates, E. (2016). The laughter prescription. *American Journal of Lifestyle Medicine, 10*(4): 262–267. https://doi.org/10.1177/1559827614550279

Louzada, M. L., Martins, A. P., Canella, D. S., Baraldi, L. S., Levy, R. B., Claro, R. M., Moubarac, J. C., Cannon, G., & Monteiro, C. A. (2015). Impact of ultra-processed foods on micronutrient content in the Brazilian diet. *Revista de Saúde Pública, 49*(0): 1–8. https://doi.org/10.1590/s0034-8910.2015049006211

Lu, L., & Reardon, T. (2018). An economic model of the evolution of food retail and supply chains from traditional shops to supermarkets to e-commerce. *American Journal of Agricultural Economics, 100*(5): 1320–1335. https://doi.org/10.1093/ajae/aay056

Lukács, A., Horváth, E., Máté, Z., Szabó, A., Virág, K., Papp, M., Sándor, J., Ádány, R., & Paulik, E. (2019). Abdominal obesity increases metabolic risk factors in non-obese adults: a Hungarian cross-sectional study. *BMC Public Health, 19*(1): 1533. https://doi.org/10.1186/s12889-019-7839-1

Lundahl, B., Moleni, T., Burke, B. L., Butters, R., Tollefson, D., Butler, C., & Rollnick, S. (2013). Motivational interviewing in medical care settings: A systematic review and meta-analysis of randomized controlled trials. *Patient Education and Counseling, 93*(2): 157–168. https://doi.org/10.1016/j.pec.2013.07.012

Ma, S., Hangya, B., Leonard, C. S., Wisden, W., & Gundlach, A. L. (2018). Dual-transmitter systems regulating arousal, attention, learning and memory. *Neuroscience and Biobehavioral Reviews, 85*: 21–33. https://doi.org/10.1016/j.neubiorev.2017.07.009

Maani, I. (2024, January). Could champagne soon stop producing champagne? *NPR.* https://npr.org/2024/01/01/1222380410/grapes-used-in-champagne-may-become-harder-to-grow-because-of-climate-change (last accessed 29 October 2025).

MacDonald, A. (2010, October 19). Why eating slowly may help you feel full faster. *Harvard Health Publishing*. Harvard Medical School.

Maki, K. C., Dicklin, M. R., & Kirkpatrick, C. F. (2021). Saturated fats and cardiovascular health: Current evidence and controversies. *Journal of Clinical Lipidology*, *15*(6): 765–772. https://doi.org/10.1016/j.jacl.2021.09.049

Malik, V. S., Popkin, B. M., Bray, G. A., Després, J.-P., & Hu, F. B. (2010). Sugar-sweetened beverages and risk of metabolic syndrome and type 2 diabetes: A meta-analysis. *Diabetes Care*, *33*(11): 2477–2483. https://doi.org/10.2337/dc10-1079

Marks & Spencer Group (2019). M&S revives its famous "food porn" ad campaign. *The Grocer*.

Marniemi, J., Kronholm, E., Aunola, S., Toikka, T., Mattlar, C.-E., Koskenvuo, M., & Rönnemaa, T. (2002). Visceral fat and psychosocial stress in identical twins discordant for obesity. *Journal of Internal Medicine*, *251*(1): 35–43. https://doi.org/10.1046/j.1365-2796.2002.00921.x

Marrón-Ponce, J. A., Sánchez-Pimienta,T. G., Rodríguez-Ramírez, S., Batis, C., & Cediel, G. (2023). Ultra-processed foods consumption reduces dietary diversity and micronutrient intake in the Mexican population. *Journal of Human Nutrition and Dietetics*, *36*(1): 241–251. https://doi.org/10.1111/jhn.13003

Martel, Y. (2001). *Life of Pi*. Edinburgh, UK: Harcourt.

Martin, J., Chater, A., & Lorencatto, F. (2013). Effective behaviour change techniques in the prevention and management of childhood obesity. *International Journal of Obesity*, *37*(10): 1287–1294. https://doi.org/10.1038/ijo.2013.107

Martini, D., da Costa Ribeiro, H., Gately, P., Mattes, R., Re, R., & Bier, D. (2023). Positive nutrition: Shifting the focus from nutrients to diet for a healthy lifestyle. *Eating and Weight Disorders*, *28*(1): 51. https://doi.org/10.1007/s40519-023-01580-1

Martino, J., Pegg, J., & Frates, E. P. (2015). The connection prescription: Using the power of social interactions and the deep desire for connectedness to empower health and wellness. *American Journal of Lifestyle Medicine*, *11*(6): 466–475. https://doi.org/10.1177/1559827615608788

Maslow, A. H. (1954). *Motivation and Personality* (pp. xiv, 411). New York: Harper & Row.

Masters, K. S., Boehm, J. K., Boylan, J. M., Vagnini, K. M., & Rush, C. L. (2023). The scientific study of positive psychology, religion/spirituality, and physical health. In: E. B. Davis, E. L. Worthington Jr., & S. A. Schnitker (Eds.), *Handbook of Positive Psychology, Religion, and Spirituality* (pp. 329–343). New York: Springer International. https://doi.org/10.1007/978-3-031-10274-5_21

Mathiesen, S. L., Aadal, L., Uldbæk, M. L., Astrup, P., Byrne, D. V., & Wang, Q. J. (2021). Music is served: How acoustic interventions in hospital dining environments can improve patient mealtime wellbeing. *Foods*, *10*: 2590. https://doi.org/10.3390/foods10112590

May, T. (2019, February 1). 9 tons of pangolin scales are seized in Hong Kong. *The New York Times*. https://nytimes.com/2019/02/01/world/asia/pangolin-smuggling-hong-kong.html (last accessed 29 October 2025).

Maybray, B. (2023, July 11). Color psychology: How to use it in marketing and branding. *HubSpot*. https://blog.hubspot.com/the-hustle/psychology-of-color (last accessed 29 October 2025).

McAlister, A. R., & Cornwell, T. B. (2010). Children's brand symbolism understanding: Links to theory of mind and executive functioning. *Psychology and Marketing*, *27*(3): 203–228. https://doi.org/10.1002/mar.20328

McCambridge, J., Witton, J., & Elbourne, D. R. (2014). Systematic review of the Hawthorne effect: New concepts are needed to study research participation effects. *Journal of Clinical Epidemiology*, *67*(3): 267–277. https://doi.org/10.1016/j.jclinepi.2013.08.015

McCarron, M. (2017). The Japanese origins of modern fine dining. *Eater*. https://eater.com/2017/9/7/16244278/japanese-fine-dining-bocuse-tsuji-kaiseki (last accessed 16 August 2024).

McClelland, M. M., Cameron, C. E., Connor, C. M., Farris, C. L., Jewkes, A. M., & Morrison, F. J. (2007). Links between behavioral regulation and preschoolers' literacy, vocabulary, and math skills. *Developmental Psychology*, *43*(4): 947–959. https://doi.org/10.1037/0012-1649.43.4.947

McGee, H. (2004). *On Food and Cooking: The Science and Lore of the Kitchen*. New York: Scribner.

McHill, A. W., Phillips, A. J., Czeisler, C. A., Keating, L., Yee, K., Barger, L. K., Garaulet, M., Scheer, F. A., & Klerman, E. B. (2017). Later circadian timing of food intake is associated with increased body fat. *American Journal of Clinical Nutrition*, *106*(5): 1213–1219. https://doi.org/10.3945/ajcn.117.161588

McIver, S., McGartland, M., & O'Halloran, P. (2009). "Overeating is not about the food": Women describe their experience of a yoga treatment program for binge eating. *Qualitative Health Research*, *19*(9): 1234–1245. https://doi.org/10.1177/1049732309343954

McIver, S., O'Halloran, P., & McGartland, M. (2009). Yoga as a treatment for binge eating disorder: A preliminary study. *Complementary Therapies in Medicine, 17*(4): 196–202. https://doi.org/10.1016/j.ctim.2009.05.002

Medic, G., Wille, M., & Hemels, M. E. (2017). Short- and long-term health consequences of sleep disruption. *Nature and Science of Sleep, 9*: 151–161. https://doi.org/10.2147/NSS.S134864

Mendoza, K., Smith-Warner, S. A., Rossato, S. L., Khandpur, N., Manson, J. E., Qi, L., Rimm, E. B., Mukamal, K. J., Willett, W. C., Wang, M., Hu, F. B., Mattei, J., & Sun, Q. (2024). Ultra-processed foods and cardiovascular disease: Analysis of three large US prospective cohorts and a systematic review and meta-analysis of prospective cohort studies. *The Lancet Regional Health—Americas, 37*: 100859. https://doi.org/10.1016/j.lana.2024.100859

Mentinis, M. (2016). Romanticised chefs and the psychopolitics of gastroporn. *Culture & Psychology, 23*(1): 128–143. https://doi.org/10.1177/1354067x15621477

Merra, G., Noce, A., Marrone, G., Cintoni, M., Tarsitano, M. G., Capacci, A., & De Lorenzo, A. (2020). Influence of Mediterranean diet on human gut microbiota. *Nutrients, 13*(1): 7. https://doi.org/10.3390/nu13010007

Merriam-Webster (2024, July 14). Definition of connection. https://merriam-webster.com/dictionary/connection.

Merriam-Webster (2024, September 18). Definition of empathy. https://merriam-webster.com/dictionary/empathy.

Merriam-Webster (n.d.). Definition of mindfulness. Retrieved July 20, 2024, from https://merriam-webster.com/dictionary/mindfulness

Metallidou, P., Malegiannaki, A. C., Konstantinopoulou, E., & Kiosseoglou, G. (2016). Effects of different functions of attention on school grades in primary school children. *Journal of Education and Human Development, 5*(3): 68–79. https://doi.org/10.15640/jehd.v5n3a8

Michel, C., Velasco, C., Fraemohs, P., & Spence, C. (2015). Studying the impact of plating on ratings of the food served in a naturalistic dining context. *Appetite, 90*: 45–50. https://doi.org/10.1016/j.appet.2015.02.030

Michel, C., Velasco, C., & Spence, C. (2015). Cutlery matters: Heavy cutlery enhances diners' enjoyment of the food served in a realistic dining environment. *Flavour, 4*(1): 26. https://doi.org/10.1186/s13411-015-0036-y

Miller, A. M. (2017). Does exercise make you hungry or suppress your appetite? *US News & World Report*. https://health.usnews.com/wellness/fitness/articles/2017-07-07/does-exercise-make-you-hungry-or-suppress-your-appetite (last accessed 29 October 2025).

Miller, J. (2018). From servant to master: The chef's rise to power in America. Dublin Gastronomy Symposium, Dublin.

Miller, L., Rozin, P., & Fiske, A. P. (1998). Food sharing and feeding another person suggest intimacy; two studies of American college students. *European Journal of Social Psychology*, *28*(3): 423–436. https://doi.org/10.1002/(SICI)1099-0992(199805/06)28:3<423::AID-EJSP874>3.0.CO;2-V

Miller, W. R., & Rollnick, S. (2023). *Motivational Interviewing: Helping People Change and Grow* (Fourth edition). New York: Guilford.

Mineo, L. (2017, April 11). Over nearly 80 years, Harvard study has been showing how to live a healthy and happy life. *Harvard Gazette*. https://news.harvard.edu/gazette/story/2017/04/over-nearly-80-years-harvard-study-has-been-showing-how-to-live-a-healthy-and-happy-life/ (last accessed 29 October 2025).

Minton, E. A., Johnson, K. A., & Liu, R. L. (2019). Religiosity and special food consumption: The explanatory effects of moral priorities. *Journal of Business Research*, *95*: 442–454. https://doi.org/10.1016/j.jbusres.2018.07.041

Mitchell, M. (2013). Dr. Herbert Benson's relaxation response. *Psychology Today*. https://psychologytoday.com/us/blog/heart-and-soul-healing/201303/dr-herbert-benson-s-relaxation-response (last accessed 29 October 2025).

Mohajeri, M. H., Brummer, R. J. M., Rastall, R. A., Weersma, R. K., Harmsen, H. J. M., Faas, M., & Eggersdorfer, M. (2018). The role of the microbiome for human health: From basic science to clinical applications. *European Journal of Nutrition*, *57*(Suppl. 1): 1–14. https://doi.org/10.1007/s00394-018-1703-4

Mohajeri, M. H., La Fata, G., Steinert, R. E., & Weber, P. (2018). Relationship between the gut microbiome and brain function. *Nutrition Reviews*, *76*(7): 481–496. https://doi.org/10.1093/nutrit/nuy009

Mokdad, A. H., Marks, J. S., Stroup, D. F., & Gerberding, J. L. (2004). Actual causes of death in the United States, 2000. *Journal of the American Medical Association*, *291*(10): 1238–1245. https://doi.org/10.1001/jama.291.10.1238

Monterrosa, E. C., Frongillo, E. A., Drewnowski, A., de Pee, S., & Vandevijvere, S. (2020). Sociocultural influences on food choices and implications for sustainable healthy diets. *Food and Nutrition Bulletin*, *41*(2_Suppl.): 59S–73S. https://doi.org/10.1177/0379572120975874

Moon, C., Jun Yoo, S., & Soo Han, H. (2014). Smell. *Encyclopaedia of the Neurological Sciences*, pp. 216–220. https://doi.org/10.1016/b978-0-12-385157-4.00072-5

Morton, S. U., Vyas, R., Gagoski, B., Vu, C., Litt, J., Larsen, R. J., Kuchan, M. J., Lasekan, J. B., Sutton, B. P., Grant, P. E., & Ou, Y. (2020). Maternal dietary intake of omega-3 fatty acids correlates positively with regional brain volumes in 1-month-old term infants. *Cerebral Cortex*, *30*(4): 2057–2069. https://doi.org/10.1093/cercor/bhz222

Moser, J., Schroder, H., Heeter, C., Moran, T., & Lee, Y.-H. (2011). Mind your errors. *Psychological Science, 22*: 1484–1489. https://doi.org/10.1177/0956797611419520

Mosinger, B., Redding, K. M., Parker, M. R., Yevshayeva, V., Yee, K. K., Dyomina, K., Li, Y., & Margolskee, R. F. (2013). Genetic loss or pharmacological blockade of testes-expressed taste genes causes male sterility. *Proceedings of the National Academy of Sciences of the United States of America, 110*(30): 12319–12324. https://doi.org/10.1073/pnas.1302827110

Mosinger, B., Redding, K. M., Parker, M. R., Yevshayeva, V., Yee, K. K., Dyomina, K., Li, Y., & Moxee Marketing. (2022, November 15). The art of influence: How to use color psychology in branding and marketing to connect with your customers and drive sales. *Moxee Marketing*. https://moxeemarketing.com/color-psychology-in-branding-and-marketing/ (last accessed 29 October 2025).

Mottram, D. S. (1998). Flavour formation in meat and meat products: A review. *Food Chemistry, 62*(4): 415–424. https://doi.org/10.1016/s0308-8146(98)00076-4

Mücke, M., Ludyga, S., Colledge, F., & Gerber, M. (2018). Influence of regular physical activity and fitness on stress reactivity as measured with the Trier social stress test protocol: A systematic review. *Sports Medicine (Auckland, N.Z.), 48*(11): 2607–2622. https://doi.org/10.1007/s40279-018-0979-0

Mumenthaler, M. S., Taylor, J. L., O'Hara, R., & Yesavage, J. A. (1999). Gender differences in moderate drinking effects. *Alcohol Research & Health, 23*(1): 55–64.

Muñoz, F., Hildebrandt, A., Schacht, A., Stürmer, B., Bröcker, F., Martín-Loeches, M., & Sommer, W. (2018). What makes the hedonic experience of a meal in a top restaurant special and retrievable in the long term? Meal-related, social and personality factors. *Appetite, 125*: 454–465. https://doi.org/10.1016/j.appet.2018.02.024

Murali, V., & Oyebode, F. (2004). Poverty, social inequality and mental health. *Advances in Psychiatric Treatment 10*: 216–224. https://doi.org/10.1192/apt.10.3.216

Murphy, S. L., Kochanek, K. D., Xu, J., & Arias, E. (2021). Mortality in the United States, 2020. (428; NCHS Data Briefs). *Centers for Disease Control and Prevention*. https://stacks.cdc.gov/view/cdc/112079.

Murphy, S. L., Xu, J., Kochanek, K. D., & Arias, E. (2018). Mortality in the United States, 2017. (328; NCHS Data Briefs). *Centers for Disease Control and Prevention*. https://cdc.gov/nchs/data/databriefs/db328-h.pdf.

Myhrvold, N., Young, C., & Bilet, M. (2021). *Modernist Cuisine: The Art and Science of Cooking*. Bellevue, WA: The Cooking Lab.

Nagpal, R., Shively, C. A., Register, T. C., Craft, S., & Yadav, H. (2019). Gut microbiome–Mediterranean diet interactions in improving host health. *F1000Research*, *8*: 699. https://doi.org/10.12688/f1000research.18992.1

Nairn, R. (2023). Health at every size: A concept to reduce weight-centric thinking and to promote body positivity. *Johns Hopkins University Student Well-Being*. https://wellbeing.jhu.edu/blog/2023/02/20/health-at-every-size/ (last accessed 29 October 2025).

Nanri, A., Kimura, Y., Matsushita, Y., Ohta, M., Sato, M., Mishima, N., Sasaki, S., & Mizoue, T. (2010). Dietary patterns and depressive symptoms among Japanese men and women. *European Journal of Clinical Nutrition*, *64*(8): 832–839.

National Academies of Sciences, Engineering, and Medicine (NASEM) (2020). Social isolation and loneliness in older adults: Opportunities for the healthcare system. Consensus study report. https://nap.nationalacademies.org/catalog/25663/social-isolation-and-loneliness-in-older-adults-opportunities-for-the (last accessed 29 October 2025).

National Cancer Institute (2021, July 14). Alcohol and cancer risk fact sheet. https://cancer.gov/about-cancer/causes-prevention/risk/alcohol/alcohol-fact-sheet (last accessed 29 October 2025).

National Institute on Alcohol Abuse and Alcoholism (NIAAA) (2025a). Alcohol's effects on the body. Retrieved December 7, 2025 from https://www.niaaa.nih.gov/alcohols-effects-health/alcohols-effects-body

National Institute on Alcohol Abuse and Alcoholism (NIAAA) (2025b). Understanding binge drinking. Retrieved December 7, 2025 from, https://www.niaaa.nih.gov/publications/brochures-and-fact-sheets/binge-drinking

National Institute on Alcohol Abuse and Alcoholism (NIAAA) (2025c). What is a standard drink? Retrieved December 7, 2025, from https://www.niaaa.nih.gov/alcohols-effects-health/what-standard-drink

National Institute on Drug Abuse (NIDA) (2024, September). Cannabis (Marijuana). https://nida.nih.gov/research-topics/cannabis-marijuana (last accessed 7 December 2025).

Navarro, D. A., Boaz, M., Krause, I., Elis, A., Chernov, K., Giabra, M., Levy, M., Giboreau, A., Kosak, S., Mouhieddine, M., & Singer, P. (2016). Improved meal presentation increases food intake and decreases readmission rate in hospitalized patients. *Clinical Nutrition*, *35*(5): 1153–1158. http://dx.doi.org/10.1016/j.clnu.2015.09.012

Nedeltcheva, A. V., Kilkus, J. M., Imperial, J., Kasza, K., Schoeller, D. A., & Penev, P. D. (2009). Sleep curtailment is accompanied by increased intake of calories from snacks. *American Journal of Clinical Nutrition*, *89*(1): 126–133. https://doi.org/10.3945/ajcn.2008.26574

Nedeltcheva, A. V., Kilkus, J. M., Imperial, J., Schoeller, D. A., & Penev, P. D. (2010). Insufficient sleep undermines dietary efforts to reduce adiposity. *Annals of Internal Medicine, 153*(7): 435–441. https://doi.org/10.7326/0003-4819-153-7-201010050-00006

Neff, K. (2015). *Self-Compassion: The Proven Power of Being Kind to Yourself.* New York: William Morrow Paperbacks.

Neff, R. A., Kanter, R., & Vandevijvere, S. (2015). Reducing food loss and waste while improving the public's health. *Health Affairs, 34*(11): 1821–1829.

Nellemann, C. (2009). The Environmental Food Crisis: The environment's role in averting future food crises. *A United Nations Environment Programme Rapid Response Assessment.* Arendal, Norway: UNEP/GRID-Arendal.

Nelson, J. B. (2017). Mindful eating: The art of presence while you eat. *Diabetes Spectrum: A Publication of the American Diabetes Association, 30*(3): 171–174. https://doi.org/10.2337/ds17-0015

New International Version (NIV) Bible (1973). *Holy Bible.* New York: Biblica.

Newton, J. (2014, August 1). French hospital plans wine bar to cheer patients' last days. *Daily Mail Online.* http://dailymail.co.uk/news/article-2713390/French-hospital-open-wine-bar-cheer-terminally-ill-patients.html (last accessed 29 October 2025).

Ng, M.-Y., & Wong, W.-S. (2013). The differential effects of gratitude and sleep on psychological distress in patients with chronic pain. *Journal of Health Psychology, 18*(2): 263–271. https://doi.org/10.1177/1359105312439733

NHS (2022a, January 19). Calories in alcohol. *NHS.UK.* https://nhs.uk/live-well/alcohol-advice/calories-in-alcohol/ (last accessed 29 October 2025).

NHS (2022b, January 19). The risks of drinking too much. *NHS.UK.* https://nhs.uk/live-well/alcohol-advice/the-risks-of-drinking-too-much/ (last accessed 29 October 2025).

NHTSA (n.d.). Drowsy driving. *National Highway Traffic Safety Administration.* Retrieved July 16, 2024, from https://nhtsa.gov/risky-driving/drowsy-driving

Nicolini, C., Michalski, B., Toepp, S. L., Turco, C. V., D'Hoine, T., Harasym, D., Gibala, M. J., Fahnestock, M., & Nelson, A. J. (2020). A single bout of high-intensity interval exercise increases corticospinal excitability, brain-derived neurotrophic factor, and uncarboxylated osteocalcin in sedentary, healthy males. *Neuroscience, 437*: 242–255. https://doi.org/10.1016/j.neuroscience.2020.03.042

Niles, A. N., Haltom, K. E. B., Mulvenna, C. M., Lieberman, M. D., & Stanton, A. L. (2014). Randomized controlled trial of expressive writing for psychological and physical health: The moderating role of emotional expressivity. *Anxiety, Stress, and Coping, 27*(1): 1–17. https://doi.org/10.1080/10615806.2013.802308

Nisar, M., Mohammad, R. M., Arshad, A., Hashmi, I., Yousuf, S. M., & Baig, S. (2019). Influence of dietary intake on sleeping patterns of medical students. *Cureus, 11*(2): e4106. https://doi.org/10.7759/cureus.4106

Nolan Brown, E. (2016, June 13). Five years and $500 million later, USDA admits that "food deserts" don't matter. *Reason.com*. https://reason.com/2016/06/13/500-million-later-usda-on-food-deserts/ (last accessed 29 October 2025).

O'Callaghan, F., Muurlink, O., & Reid, N. (2018). Effects of caffeine on sleep quality and daytime functioning. *Risk Management and Healthcare Policy, 11*: 263–271. https://doi.org/10.2147/RMHP.S156404

Obad, A., Peeran, A., Little, J. I., Haddad, G. E., & Tarzami, S. T. (2018). Alcohol-mediated organ damages: Heart and brain. *Frontiers in Pharmacology, 9*: 81. https://doi.org/10.3389/fphar.2018.00081

Office of the Surgeon General (OSG). (2023). Our epidemic of loneliness and isolation: The U.S. Surgeon General's advisory on the healing effects of social connection and community. *US Department of Health and Human Services*. http://ncbi.nlm.nih.gov/books/NBK595227/.

Okey, B., & Draskovic, M. (2023, December 21). What are the effects of alcohol on GABA? *Ardu Recovery Center*. https://ardurecoverycenter.com/alcohol-effects-on-gaba-neurotransmitters/ (last accessed 29 October 2025).

Olander, E. K., Fletcher, H., Williams, S., Atkinson, L., Turner, A., & French, D. P. (2013). What are the most effective techniques in changing obese individuals' physical activity self-efficacy and behaviour: A systematic review and meta-analysis. *International Journal of Behavioral Nutrition and Physical Activity, 10*: 29. https://doi.org/10.1186/1479-5868-10-29

Oliver, J. W., Kravitz, R. L., Kaplan, S. H., & Meyers, F. J. (2001). Individualized patient education and coaching to improve pain control among cancer outpatients. *Journal of Clinical Oncology, 19*(8): 2206–2212. https://doi.org/10.1200/JCO.2001.19.8.2206

Ornish, D., Brown, S. E., Scherwitz, L. W., Billings, J. H., Armstrong, W. T., Ports, T. A., McLanahan, S. M., Kirkeeide, R. L., Brand, R. J., & Gould, K. L. (1990). Can lifestyle changes reverse coronary heart disease? The Lifestyle Heart Trial. *The Lancet, 336*(8708): 129–133. https://doi.org/10.1016/0140-6736(90)91656-u

Ornish, D., Scherwitz, L. W., Billings, J. H., Brown, S. E., Gould, K. L., Merritt, T. A., Sparler, S., Armstrong, W. T., Ports, T. A., Kirkeeide, R. L., Hogeboom, C., & Brand, R. J. (1998). Intensive lifestyle changes for reversal of coronary heart disease. *Journal of the American Medical Association, 280*(23): 2001–2007. https://doi.org/10.1001/jama.280.23.2001

Ortaliza, J., Amin, K., & Cox, C. (2022). COVID-19 leading cause of death ranking. *Peterson-KFF Health System Tracker.* https://healthsystemtracker.org/brief/covid-19-leading-cause-of-death-ranking/ (last accessed 29 October 2025).

Oscar-Berman, M., & Marinkovic, K. (2003). Alcoholism and the brain: An overview. *Alcohol Research & Health, 27*(2): 125–133.

Oxford English Dictionary (n.d.). *Stress, n. Meanings, etymology and more.* Retrieved July 18, 2024, from https://oed.com/dictionary/stress_n

Pahlavani, H. A. (2023). Exercise therapy to prevent and treat Alzheimer's disease. *Frontiers in Aging Neuroscience, 15*: 1243869. https://doi.org/10.3389/fnagi.2023.1243869

Panek-Shirley, L. M., DeNysschen, C., O'Brien, E., & Temple, J. L. (2018). Caffeine transiently affects food intake at breakfast. *Journal of the Academy of Nutrition and Dietetics, 118*(10): 1832–1843. https://doi.org/10.1016/j.jand.2018.05.015

Pangalangan, J., Puma, J., Tollefson, M., & Frates, B. (2024). Development and psychometric evaluation of the Lifestyle Medicine Health Behavior Scale. *American Journal of Lifestyle Medicine*, 15598276241280207. Advance online publication. https://doi.org/10.1177/15598276241280207

Pantell, M., Rehkopf, D., Jutte, D., Syme, S. L., Balmes, J., & Adler, N. (2013). Social isolation: A predictor of mortality comparable to traditional clinical risk factors. *American Journal of Public Health, 103*(11): 2056–2062. https://doi.org/10.2105/AJPH.2013.301261

Park, Y.-M. M., White, A. J., Jackson, C. L., Weinberg, C. R., & Sandler, D. P. (2019). Association of exposure to artificial light at night while sleeping with risk of obesity in women. *JAMA Internal Medicine, 179*(8): 1061–1071. https://doi.org/10.1001/jamainternmed.2019.0571

Parletta, N., Zarnowiecki, D., Cho, J., Wilson, A., Bogomolova, S., Villani, A., Itsiopoulous, C., Niyonsenga, T., Blunden, S., Meyer, B., Segal, L., Baune, B. T., & O'Dea, K. (2017). A Mediterranean-style dietary intervention supplemented with fish oil improves diet quality and mental health in people with depression: A randomized controlled trial (HELFIMED). *Nutritional Neuroscience, 22*(7): 474–487. https://doi.org/10.1080/1028415X.2017.1411320.

Pascoe, M. C., Thompson, D. R., & Ski, C. F. (2017). Yoga, mindfulness-based stress reduction and stress-related physiological measures: A meta-analysis.

Psychoneuroendocrinology, *86*: 152–168. https://doi.org/10.1016/j.psyneuen.2017.08.008

Patel, B. (2019, January 13). Giving elderly patients an extra meal a day can halve their chances of dying in hospital, NHS study finds. *Daily Mail Online*. https://dailymail.co.uk/news/article-6586215/Giving-elderly-patients-extra-meal-day-halve-chances-dying-hospital.html (last accessed 29 October 2025).

Patterson, D., & Aftel, M. (2018). The Art of Flavour: Practices and Principles for Creating Delicious Food. London: Robinson.

Pekmezi, D., Jennings, E., & Marcus, B. H. (2009). Evaluating and enhancing self-efficacy for physical activity. *ACSM's Health & Fitness Journal*, *13*(2): 16–21. https://doi.org/10.1249/FIT.0b013e3181996571

Peng, Y., Gillis-Smith, S., Jin, H., Tränkner, D., Ryba, N. J., & Zuker, C. S. (2015). Sweet and bitter taste in the brain of awake behaving animals. *Nature*, *527*(7579): 512–515. https://doi.org/10.1038/nature15763

Perciavalle, V., Blandini, M., Fecarotta, P., Buscemi, A., Di Corrado, D., Bertolo, L., Fichera, F., & Coco, M. (2017). The role of deep breathing on stress. *Neurological Sciences: Official Journal of the Italian Neurological Society and of the Italian Society of Clinical Neurophysiology*, *38*(3): 451–458. https://doi.org/10.1007/s10072-016-2790-8

Petre, A. (2023). What do food cravings mean? Facts and myths, explained. *Healthline*. https://healthline.com/nutrition/craving-meanings (last accessed 29 October 2025).

Petrini, C., McCuaig, W., & Waters, A. (2003). *Slow Food: The Case for Taste*. New York: Columbia University Press.

Petro, G. (2022, February 21). Gen Z and sustainability: The disruption has only just begun [review]. *Forbes.com*. https://forbes.com/sites/gregpetro/2022/02/18/gen-z-and-sustainability-the-disruption-has-only-just-begun/?sh=3f97e2d23eb7 (last accessed 29 October 2025).

Pham, V. T., Dold, S., Rehman, A., Bird, J. K., & Steinert, R. E. (2021). Vitamins, the gut microbiome and gastrointestinal health in humans. *Nutrition Research (New York)*, *95*: 35–53. https://doi.org/10.1016/j.nutres.2021.09.001

Pietschnig, J., & Gittler, G. (2015). A reversal of the Flynn effect for spatial perception in German-speaking countries: Evidence from a cross-temporal IRT-based meta-analysis (1977–2014). *Intelligence*, *53*: 145–153. https://doi.org/10.1016/j.intell.2015.10.004

Piqueras-Fiszman, B., Alcaide, J., Roura, E., & Spence, C. (2012). Is it the plate or is it the food? Assessing the influence of the color (black or white) and shape of the plate on the perception of the food placed on it. *Food Quality & Preference*, *24*(1): 205–208. https://doi.org/10.1016/j.foodqual.2011.08.011

Piqueras-Fiszman, B., & Spence, C. (2015). Sensory expectations based on product-extrinsic food cues: An interdisciplinary review of the empirical evidence and theoretical accounts. *Food Quality & Preference*, *40*(A): 165–179. http://dx.doi.org/10.1016/j.foodqual.2014.09.013

Pilorz, V., Tam, S. K. E., Hughes, S., Pothecary, C. A., Jagannath, A., Hankins, M. W., Bannerman, D. M., Lightman, S. L., Vyazovskiy, V. V., Nolan, P. M., Foster, R. G., & Peirson, S. N. (2016). Melanopsin regulates both sleep-promoting and arousal-promoting responses to light. *PLoS Biology*, *14*(6): e1002482. https://doi.org/10.1371/journal.pbio.1002482

Planas-Ballvé, A., Grau-López, L., Morillas, R. M., & Planas, R. (2017). Neurological manifestations of excessive alcohol consumption. *Gastroenterologia Y Hepatologia*, *40*(10): 709–717. https://doi.org/10.1016/j.gastrohep.2017.05.011

Pliner, P., & Bell, R. (2009). A table for one: The pain and pleasure of eating alone. In: H. L. Meiselman (Ed.), *Meals in Science and Practice: Interdisciplinary Research and Business Applications* (pp. 169–189). Cambridge: Woodhead.

Poore, J., & Nemecek, T. (2018). Reducing food's environmental impacts through producers and consumers. *Science*, *360*(6392): 987–992. https://doi.org/10.1126/science.aaq0216

Pot, G. K., Battjes-Fries, M. C., Patijn, O. N., van der Zijl, N., Pijl, H., & Voshol, P. (2020). Lifestyle medicine for type 2 diabetes: Practice-based evidence for long-term efficacy of a multicomponent lifestyle intervention (Reverse Diabetes2 Now). *BMJ Nutrition, Prevention & Health*, *3*(2): 188–195. https://doi.org/10.1136/bmjnph-2020-000081

Poulter, S. (2017, March 23). Would YOU eat these meals? Bake Off's Prue Leith backs campaign for hospitals to meet government. *Daily Mail Online*. http://dailymail.co.uk/health/article4342940/BakesPrueLeithbackshospitalfoodcampaign.html (last accessed 29 October 2025).

Powell, L. M., Chriqui, J. F., Khan, T., Wada, R., & Chaloupka, F. J. (2012). Assessing the potential effectiveness of food and beverage taxes and subsidies for improving public health: A systematic review of prices, demand and body weight outcomes. *Obesity Reviews*, *14*(2), pp. 110–128. https://doi.org/10.1111/obr.12002

Prescott, J., & Bell, G. (1994). Cross-cultural studies of Japanese and Australian taste preferences. In: K. Kurihara, N. Suzuki, & H. Ogawa (Eds.), *Olfaction and Taste XI*. Tokyo: Springer. https://doi.org/10.1007/978-4-431-68355-1_122

Prescott, J., Laing, D. G., Bell, G., Yoshida, M., Gillmore, R., Allen, S., Yamazaki, K., & Ishii, R. (1992). Hedonic responses to taste solutions: A cross-cultural study of Japanese and Australians. *Chemical Senses*, *17*(6): 801–809. https://doi.org/10.1093/chemse/17.6.801

Preston, A. M. (1991). Cigarette smoking—nutritional implications. *Progress in Food & Nutrition Science, 15*(4): 183–217.

Prochaska, J. O., & Velicer, W. F. (1997). The transtheoretical model of health behavior change. *American Journal of Health Promotion: AJHP, 12*(1): 38–48. https://doi.org/10.4278/0890-1171-12.1.38

Prochaska, J. O., Redding, C. A., & Evers, K. E. (2002). The transtheoretical model and stages of change. In: K. Glanz, B. K. Rimer, & F. M. Lewis (Eds.), *Health Behavior and Health Education: Theory, Research, and Practice* (3rd edn.) (pp. 99–120). San Francisco, CA: Jossey-Bass.

Proust, M. (1927). *Remembrance of Things Past.* C. K. Scott-Moncrieff & S. Hudson (Trans.) London: Penguin, 2022.

Public Health Institute (n.d.). Farmers Market Initiative: Connecting SNAP participants with healthy food and support. *Public Health Institute.* Retrieved July 2, 2024 from https://phi.org/about/impacts/farmers-market-initiative-connecting-snap-participants-with-healthy-food-support/

Psychology Today contributors (n.d.). Positive psychology. Retrieved August 4, 2024, from https://psychologytoday.com/us/basics/positive-psychology

Rambourg, P. (2013). *Histoire de la cuisine et de la Gastronomie Françaises* [preprint]. https://doi.org/10.3917/perri.rambo.2013.01

Ranganathan, J., Vennard, D., Waite, R., Dumas, P., Lipinski, B., & Searchinger, T. (2016). *Shifting Diets Toward a Sustainable Food Future*. Washington, DC: World Resources Institute. https://doi.org/10.2499/978096295827_08

Ranjbar, H., & Ashrafizaveh, A. (2019). Effects of saffron (*Crocus sativus*) on sexual dysfunction among men and women: A systematic review and meta-analysis. *Avicenna Journal of Phytomedicine, 9*(5): 419–427.

Rao, H., Monin, P., & Durand, R. (2003). Institutional change in Toque Ville: Nouvelle cuisine as an identity movement in French gastronomy. *American Journal of Sociology, 108*(4): 795–843. https://doi.org/10.1086/367917

Rao, M., Afshin, A., Singh, G., & Mozaffarian, D. (2013). Do healthier foods and diet patterns cost more than less healthy options? A systematic review and meta-analysis. *BMJ Open, 3*(12). https://doi.org/10.1136/bmjopen-2013-004277

Rastelli, M., Cani, P. D., & Knauf, C. (2019). The gut microbiome influences host endocrine functions. *Endocrine Reviews, 40*(5): 1271–1284. https://doi.org/10.1210/er.2018-00280

Reith, A. J. M., & Spence, C. (2020). The mystery of "metal mouth" in chemotherapy. *Chemical Senses, 45*: 73–84. https://doi.org/10.1093/chemse/bjz076

Reynolds, A., Mann, J., Cummings, J., Winter, N., Mete, E., & Te Morenga, L. (2019). Carbohydrate quality and human health: A series of systematic reviews and meta-analyses. *The Lancet, 393*(10170): 434–445. https://doi.org/10.1016/S0140-6736(18)31809-9

Riera, C. E., Tsaousidou, E., Halloran, J., Follett, P., Hahn, O., Pereira, M. M. A., Ruud, L. E., Alber, J., Tharp, K., Anderson, C. M., Brönneke, H., Hampel, B., Filho, C. D. M., Stahl, A., Brüning, J. C., & Dillin, A. (2017). The sense of smell impacts metabolic health and obesity. *Cell Metabolism, 26*(1): 198–211.e5. https://doi.org/10.1016/j.cmet.2017.06.015.

Riley, K. E., & Park, C. L. (2015). How does yoga reduce stress? A systematic review of mechanisms of change and guide to future inquiry. *Health Psychology Review, 9*(3): 379–396. https://doi.org/10.1080/17437199.2014.981778 Ritchie, H. (2019). *50% of all land in the world is used to produce food, World Economic Forum.* Available at: https://weforum.org/stories/2019/12/agriculture-habitable-land/ (last accessed 9 September 2025).

Ritchie, H. (2022). Wild mammals make up only a few percent of the world's mammals. *Our World in Data.* https://ourworldindata.org/wild-mammals-birds- biomass (last accessed 31 May 2025).

Ritchie, H., & Roser, M. (2021). Fish and overfishing. *Our World in Data.* https://ourworldindata.org/fish-and-overfishing (last accessed 10 July 2023).

Ritzer, G. (1993). *The McDonaldization of Society: An Investigation into the Changing Character of Contemporary Social Life.* Thousand Oaks, CA: Pine Forge.

Robinson, T. N., Borzekowski, D. L., Matheson, D. M., & Kraemer, H. C. (2007). Effects of fast food branding on young children's taste preferences. *Archives of Pediatrics & Adolescent Medicine, 161*(8): 792–797. https://doi.org/10.1001/archpedi.161.8.792

Rogers, C. R. (1957). The necessary and sufficient conditions of therapeutic personality change. Journal of Consulting Psychology, *21*(2): 95–103. https://doi.org/10.1037/h0045357

Roth, L. H. O., & Laireiter, A. R. (2021). Factor structure of the "Top ten" positive emotions of Barbara Fredrickson. *Frontiers in Psychology, 12*: 641804. https://doi.org/10.3389/fpsyg.2021.641804. PMID: 34054647; PMCID: PMC8162787

Ruddock, H. K., Brunstrom, J. M., Vartanian, L. R., & Higgs, S. (2019). A systematic review and meta-analysis of the social facilitation of eating. *American Journal of Clinical Nutrition, 110*(4): 842–861. https://doi.org/10.1093/ajcn/nqz155

Ruddock, H. K., Long, E. V., Brunstrom, J. M., Vartanian, L. R., & Higgs, S. (2021). People serve themselves larger portions before a social meal. *Scientific Reports, 11*(1): 11072–11072. https://doi.org/10.1038/S41598-021-90559-Y

Ruegsegger, G. N., & Booth, F. W. (2018). Health benefits of exercise. *Cold Spring Harbor Perspectives in Medicine, 8*(7): a029694. https://doi.org/10.1101/cshperspect.a029694

Ruiz-Ceamanos, A., Spence, C., & Navarra, J. (2022). Individual differences in taste and smell perception amongst cancer patients undergoing chemotherapy: A brief review. *Nutrition and Cancer, 74*(6): 1927–1941. http://dx.doi.org/10.1080/01635581.2021.2000625

Rumgay, H., Shield, K., Charvat, H., Ferrari, P., Sornpaisarn, B., Obot, I., Islami, F., Lemmens, V. E. P. P., Rehm, J., & Soerjomataram, I. (2021). Global burden of cancer in 2020 attributable to alcohol consumption: A population-based study. *The Lancet Oncology, 22*(8): 1071–1080. https://doi.org/10.1016/S1470-2045(21)00279-5

Ryu, M., Kimm, H., Jo, J., Lee, S. J., & Jee, S. H. (2010). Association between alcohol intake and abdominal obesity among the Korean population. *Epidemiology and Health, 32*: e2010007. https://doi.org/10.4178/epih/e2010007

Sacco, R. L., Elkind, M., Boden-Albala, B., Lin, I.-F., Kargman, D. E., Hauser, W. A., Shea, S., & Paik, M. C. (1999). The protective effect of moderate alcohol consumption on ischemic stroke. *Journal of the American Medical Association, 281*(1): 53–60. https://doi.org/10.1001/jama.281.1.53

Samdal, G. B., Eide, G. E., Barth, T., Williams, G., & Meland, E. (2017). Effective behaviour change techniques for physical activity and healthy eating in overweight and obese adults: Systematic review and meta-regression analyses. *International Journal of Behavioral Nutrition and Physical Activity, 14*(1): 42. https://doi.org/10.1186/s12966-017-0494-y

Samuel, L. R. (2010). *Freud on Madison Avenue: Motivation Research and Subliminal Advertising in America.* Oxford: University of Pennsylvania Press.

Sánchez-Villegas, A., Toledo, E., de Irala, J., Ruiz-Canela, M., Pla-Vidal, J., & Martínez-González, M. A. (2011a). Fast-food and commercial baked goods consumption and the risk of depression. *Public Health Nutrition, 15*(03): 424. https://doi.org/10.1017/S1368980011001856

Sánchez-Villegas, A., Verberne, L., de Irala, J., Ruíz-Canela, M., Toledo, E., Serra-Majem, L., & Martínez-González, M. A. (2011b). Dietary fat intake and the risk of depression: The SUN Project. *PloS One 6*(1), e16268. https://doi.org/10.1371/journal.pone.0016268

Sánchez-Villegas, A., Verberne, L., de Irala, J., Ruíz-Canela, M., Toledo, E., Serra-Majem, L., & Martínez-González, M. A. (2022). The impact of food advertising on childhood obesity. *APA.org*. https://apa.org/topics/obesity/food-advertising-children#:~:text=Research%20has%20found%20strong%20associations (last accessed 29 October 2025).

Sanson, M. (2017). Michael Caines (cover interview). *Food and Travel Magazine*. https://foodandtravel.com/food/cover-interviews/michael-caines#:~:text='There's%20too%20much%20messing%20about,conduit%20to%20a%20good%20night (last accessed 27 August 2025).

Sawamoto, R., Nozaki, T., Furukawa, T., Tanahashi, T., Morita, C., Hata, T., Nakashima, M., Komaki, G., & Sudo, N. (2016). A change in objective sleep duration is associated with a change in the serum adiponectin level of women with overweight or obesity undergoing weight loss intervention. *Obesity Science & Practice*, *2*(2): 180–188. https://doi.org/10.1002/osp4.32

Schmid, S. M., Hallschmid, M., Jauch-Chara, K., Born, J., & Schultes, B. (2008). A single night of sleep deprivation increases ghrelin levels and feelings of hunger in normal-weight healthy men. *Journal of Sleep Research*, *17*(3): 331–334. https://doi.org/10.1111/j.1365-2869.2008.00662.x

Schoenthaler, S. J. (1983). Diet and crime: An empirical examination of the value of nutrition in the control and treatment of incarcerated juvenile offenders. *International Journal of Biosocial Research*, *4*(1): 25–39.

Schröder, H., Morales-Molina, J. A., Bermejo, S., Barral, D., Mándoli, E. S., Grau, M., Guxens, M., de Jaime Gil, E., Alvarez, M. D., & Marrugat, J. (2007). Relationship of abdominal obesity with alcohol consumption at population scale. *European Journal of Nutrition*, *46*(7): 369–376. https://doi.org/10.1007/s00394-007-0674-7

Seale, S. A., Sherard, T., & Fleming, D. (2010). *The Full Plate Diet: Slim Down, Look Great, Be Healthy!* Austin, TX: Bard.

Searchinger, T., Waite, R., Hanson, C., & Ranganathan, J. (2019). *Creating a Sustainable Food Future*. Washington, DC: World Resources Institute.

Seinfeld, J., & David, L. (Creators) (1994). *Seinfeld* / The Pledge Drive [TV episode].

Seligman, M. E. P. (2011). *Flourish: A Visionary New Understanding of Happiness and Well-being*. New York: Simon & Schuster.

Seligman, M. E. P., Steen, T., Park, N., & Peterson, C. (2005). Positive psychology progress: Empirical validation of interventions. *American Psychologist*, *60*: 410–421. https://doi.org/10.1037/0003-066X.60.5.410

Sepúlveda-Loyola, W., Rodríguez-Sánchez, I., Pérez-Rodríguez, P., Ganz, F., Torralba, R., Oliveira, D. V., & Rodríguez-Mañas, L. (2020). Impact of social isolation due to COVID-19 on health in older people: Mental and physical effects and recommendations. *Journal of Nutrition, Health & Aging, 24*(9): 938–947. https://doi.org/10.1007/s12603-020-1469-2

Sforzo, G. A., Kaye, M. P., Todorova, I., Harenberg, S., Costello, K., Cobus-Kuo, L., Faber, A., Frates, E., & Moore, M. (2018). Compendium of the health and wellness coaching literature. *American Journal of Lifestyle Medicine, 12*(6): 436–447. https://doi.org/10.1177/1559827617708562

Sharma, A., Madaan, V., & Petty, F. D. (2006). Exercise for mental health. *Primary Care Companion to The Journal of Clinical Psychiatry, 8*(2): 106.

Sharma, M., & Rush, S. E. (2014). Mindfulness-based stress reduction as a stress management intervention for healthy individuals: A systematic review. *Journal of Evidence-Based Complementary & Alternative Medicine, 19*(4): 271–286. https://doi.org/10.1177/2156587214543143

Sheikh, M. (2020, November 11). 12 brand archetypes by Carl Jung (& how to use them). *Visme Blog*. https://visme.co/blog/brand-archetypes/.

Shepherd, G. M. (2012). *Neurogastronomy: How the Brain Creates Flavor and Why It Matters*. New York: Columbia University Press.

Shlisky, J. D., Hartman, T. J., Kris-Etherton, P. M., Rogers, C. J., Sharkey, N. A., & Nickols-Richardson, S. M. (2012). Partial sleep deprivation and energy balance in adults: An emerging issue for consideration by dietetics practitioners. *Journal of the Academy of Nutrition and Dietetics, 112*(11): 1785–1797. https://doi.org/10.1016/j.jand.2012.07.032

Shuster, A., Patlas, M., Pinthus, J. H., & Mourtzakis, M. (2012). The clinical importance of visceral adiposity: A critical review of methods for visceral adipose tissue analysis. *British Journal of Radiology, 85*(1009): 1–10. https://doi.org/10.1259/bjr/38447238

Silberman, A., Banthia, R., Estay, I. S., Kemp, C., Studley, J., Hareras, D., & Ornish, D. (2010). The effectiveness and efficacy of an intensive cardiac rehabilitation program in 24 sites. *American Journal of Health Promotion: AJHP, 24*(4): 260–266. https://doi.org/10.4278/ajhp.24.4.arb

Sims, D. (2015). Lack of employee engagement can be a costly disadvantage. https://bizjournals.com/nashville/blog/2015/10/lack-of-employee-engagement-can-be-a-costly.html (last accessed 29 October 2025).

Sinha, R., Gu, P., Hart, R., & Guarnaccia, J. B. (2019). Food craving, cortisol and ghrelin responses in modeling highly palatable snack intake in the laboratory. *Physiology & Behavior, 208*: 112563. https://doi.org/10.1016/j.physbeh.2019.112563

Skubisz, C. (2016). Naturally good: Front-of-package claims as message cues. *Appetite, 108*: 506–511. https://doi.org/10.1016/j.appet.2016.10.030

Sleiman, S. F., Henry, J., Al-Haddad, R., El Hayek, L., Abou Haidar, E., Stringer, T., Ulja, D., Karuppagounder, S. S., Holson, E. B., Ratan, R. R., Ninan, I., & Chao, M. V. (2016). Exercise promotes the expression of brain-derived neurotrophic factor (BDNF) through the action of the ketone body β-hydroxybutyrate. *eLife*, *5*: e15092. https://doi.org/10.7554/eLife.15092

Smith, G. D., & Ebrahim, S. (2003). "Mendelian randomization": Can genetic epidemiology contribute to understanding environmental determinants of disease? *International Journal of Epidemiology*, *32*(1): 1–22. https://doi.org/10.1093/ije/dyg070

Smith, R. P., Easson, C., Lyle, S. M., Kapoor, R., Donnelly, C. P., Davidson, E. J., Parikh, E., Lopez, J. V., & Tartar, J. L. (2019). Gut microbiome diversity is associated with sleep physiology in humans. *PLoS One*, *14*(10): e0222394. https://doi.org/10.1371/journal.pone.0222394

Spahn, J. M., Reeves, R. S., Keim, K. S., Laquatra, I., Kellogg, M., Jortberg, B., & Clark, N. A. (2010). State of the evidence regarding behavior change theories and strategies in nutrition counseling to facilitate health and food behavior change. *Journal of the American Dietetic Association*, *110*(6): 879–891. https://doi.org/10.1016/j.jada.2010.03.021

Speir, L. (2016, March 14). How hospital vending machines are slowly killing patients and staff: Nurse describes the farce of trying to heal people who are bingeing on junk in the waiting room. *Daily Mail Online*. http://dailymail.co.uk/health/article-3491347/Hospital-vending-machines-slowly-killing-patients-staff-Nurse-describes-farce-trying-heal-people-bingeing-junk-waiting-room.html (last accessed 29 October 2025).

Spence, C. (2017a). *Gastrophysics: The New Science of Eating*. London: Viking Penguin.

Spence, C. (2017b). Hospital food. *Flavour*, *6*: 3. https://doi.org/10.1186/s13411-017-0055-y http://rdcu.be/pRsy.

Spence, C. (2018). Background colour & its impact on food perception & behaviour. *Food Quality & Preference*, *68*: 156–166. https://doi.org/10.1016/j.foodqual.2018.02.012

Spence, C., & Keller, S. (2019). Medicine's melodies: On the costs and benefits of music, soundscapes, and noise in healthcare settings. *Music and Medicine*, *11*(4): 211–225. https://doi.org/10.47513/mmd.v11i4.699

Spence, C., Mancini, M., & Huisman, G. (2019). Digital commensality: On the pros and cons of eating and drinking with technology. *Frontiers in Psychology*, *10*: 2252. https://doi.org/10.3389/fpsyg.2019.02252

Spence, C., Navarra, J., & Youssef, J. (2019). Using ice-cream as an effective vehicle for energy/nutrient delivery in the elderly. *International Journal of Gastronomy & Food Science*, *16*: 100140. https://doi.org/10.1016/j.ijgfs.2019.100140

Spence, C., Okajima, K., Cheok, A. D., Petit, O., & Michel, C. (2016). Eating with our eyes: From visual hunger to digital satiation. *Brain & Cognition*, *110*: 53–63. http://dx.doi.org/10.1016/j.bandc.2015.08.006

Spence, C., & Piqueras-Fiszman, B. (2014). *The Perfect Meal: The Multisensory Science of Food and Dining*. Oxford: Wiley-Blackwell.

Spence, C., & Youssef, J. (2016, July 12). How to trick your brain into healthy eating. *The Guardian*. https://theguardian.com/lifeandstyle/2016/jul/12/how-to-trick-your-brain-into-healthy-eating (last accessed 29 October 2025).

Spence, C., & Youssef, J. (2021). Aging and the chemical senses: Implications for food behaviour amongst elderly consumers. *Foods*, *10*(1): 168. https://mdpi.com/2304-8158/10/1/168 (last accessed 29 October 2025).

Spencer, B., & White, J. (2015, September 2). Ban fast food giants from our hospitals, says NHS boss as he calls for crackdown on the amount of junk food on offer to patients. *Daily Mail Online*. http://dailymail.co.uk/health/article-3219032/Ban-fast-food-giants-hospitals-says-NHS-boss-calls-crackdown-junk-food-offer-patients.html (last accessed 29 October 2025).

Spencer, S. J., & Tilbrook, A. (2011). The glucocorticoid contribution to obesity. *Stress (Amsterdam, the Netherlands)*, *14*(3): 233–246. https://doi.org/10.3109/10253890.2010.534831

Spreckley, E., & Murphy, K. G. (2015). The L-cell in nutritional sensing and the regulation of appetite. *Frontiers in Nutrition*, 2: 23. https://doi.org/10.3389/fnut.2015.00023

Sprince, H., Parker, C. M., Smith, G. G., & Gonzales, L. J. (1975). Protective action of ascorbic acid and sulfur compounds against acetaldehyde toxicity: Implications in alcoholism and smoking. *Agents and Actions*, *5*(2): 164–173. https://doi.org/10.1007/BF02027359

Srivastava, J. K., Shankar, E., & Gupta, S. (2010). Chamomile: A herbal medicine of the past with a bright future. *Molecular Medicine Reports*, *3*(6): 895–901. https://doi.org/10.3892/mmr.2010.377

Stadlbauer, V., Horvath, A., Komarova, I., Schmerboeck, B., Feldbacher, N., Wurm, S., Klymiuk, I., Durdevic, M., Rainer, F., Blesl, A., Stryeck, S., Madl, T., Stiegler, P., & Leber, B. (2019). A single alcohol binge impacts on neutrophil function without changes in gut barrier function and gut microbiome composition in healthy volunteers. *PLOS One*, *14*: e0211703. https://doi.org/10.1371/journal.pone.0211703

Staff, M. (2017, January 11). Jon Kabat-Zinn: Defining mindfulness. *Mindful.* https://mindful.org/jon-kabat-zinn-defining-mindfulness/ (last accessed 29 October 2025).

Stefanikova, Z., Jurkovicova, J., Sevcikova, L., Sobotova, L., & Aghova, L. (2009). Association between tobacco smoke and nutritional behavior. *Epidemiology, 20*(6): S160. https://doi.org/10.1097/01.ede.0000362546.98667.d7

Stevens, J. C., Cain, W. S., Demarque, A., & Ruthruff, A. M. (1991). On the discrimination of missing ingredients: Aging and salt flavour. *Appetite, 16*(2): 129–140. https://doi.org/10.1016/0195-6663(91)90038-t

Stevenson, R. J., Francis, H. M., Attuquayefio, T., Gupta, D., Yeomans, M. R., Oaten, M. J., & Davidson, T. (2020). Hippocampal-dependent appetitive control is impaired by experimental exposure to a western-style diet. *Royal Society Open Science, 7*(2): 191338. https://doi.org/10.1098/rsos.191338

Stone, E. (2023, May 29). Navigating kashrut: Understanding the dietary laws in Judaism. *Judaicapedia.* https://judaicapedia.org/navigating-kashrut-understanding-the-dietary-laws-in-judaism/ (last accessed 29 October 2025).

Stone, H., & Sidel, J. L. (2004). *Sensory Evaluation Practices.* Redwood City, CA: Academic Press.

St-Onge, M.-P., McReynolds, A., Trivedi, Z. B., Roberts, A. L., Sy, M., & Hirsch, J. (2012). Sleep restriction leads to increased activation of brain regions sensitive to food stimuli. *American Journal of Clinical Nutrition, 95*(4): 818–824. https://doi.org/10.3945/ajcn.111.027383

St-Onge, M.-P., Mikic, A., & Pietrolungo, C. E. (2016). Effects of diet on sleep quality. *Advances in Nutrition, 7*(5): 938–949. https://doi.org/10.3945/an.116.012336

St-Onge, M.-P., Roberts, A. L., Chen, J., Kelleman, M., O'Keeffe, M., RoyChoudhury, A., & Jones, P. J. H. (2011). Short sleep duration increases energy intakes but does not change energy expenditure in normal-weight individuals. *American Journal of Clinical Nutrition, 94*(2): 410–416. https://doi.org/10.3945/ajcn.111.013904

Suni, E., & Rosen, D. (2009, April 17). Mastering sleep hygiene: Your path to quality sleep. *Sleep Foundation.* https://sleepfoundation.org/sleep-hygiene (last accessed 29 October 2025).

Suni, E., & Truong, K. (2023, May 18). 100+ sleep statistics. *Sleep Foundation.* https://sleepfoundation.org/how-sleep-works/sleep-facts-statistics (last accessed 29 October 2025).

Swinburn, B., Egger, G., & Raza, F. (1999). Dissecting obesogenic environments: The development and application of a framework for identifying and prioritizing environmental interventions for obesity. *Preventive Medicine, 29*(6 Pt 1): 563–570. https://doi.org/10.1006/pmed.1999.0585

Tacon, A. G., & Metian, M. (2008). Aquaculture feed and food safety. *Annals of the New York Academy of Sciences, 1140*(1): 50–59. https://doi.org/10.1196/annals.1454.003

Taheri, S., Lin, L., Austin, D., Young, T., & Mignot, E. (2004). Short sleep duration is associated with reduced leptin, elevated ghrelin, and increased body mass index. *PLoS Medicine, 1*(3): e62. https://doi.org/10.1371/journal.pmed.0010062

Teasdale, T. W., & Owen, D. R. (2005). A long-term rise and recent decline in intelligence test performance: The Flynn effect in reverse. *Personality and Individual Differences, 39*(4): 837–843. https://doi.org/10.1016/j.paid.2005.01.029

TED (Director) (2016, January 25). Robert Waldinger: What makes a good life? Lessons from the longest study on happiness / *TED* [video recording]. https://youtube.com/watch?v=8KkKuTCFvzI

TED (Director) (2023, January 10). The secret to a happy life—Lessons from 8 decades of research / Robert Waldinger / *TED* [video recording]. https://youtube.com/watch?v=IStsehNAOL8

Teixeira, P. J., Carraça, E. V., Marques, M. M., Rutter, H., Oppert, J.-M., De Bourdeaudhuij, I., Lakerveld, J., & Brug, J. (2015). Successful behavior change in obesity interventions in adults: A systematic review of self-regulation mediators. *BMC Medicine, 13*(1): 84. https://doi.org/10.1186/s12916-015-0323-6

Tempesta, D., Salfi, F., De Gennaro, L., & Ferrara, M. (2020). The impact of five nights of sleep restriction on emotional reactivity. *Journal of Sleep Research, 29*(50): e13022. https://doi.org/10.1111/jsr.13022

Thau, L., Gandhi, J., & Sharma, S. (2023). Physiology, cortisol. *StatPearls*. Treasure Island, FL: StatPearls. http://ncbi.nlm.nih.gov/books/NBK538239/

Thomas, D. T., Erdman, K. A., & Burke, L. M. (2016). Nutrition and athletic performance: American College of Sports Medicine joint position statement. *Medicine and Science in Sports and Exercise, 48*(3): 543–568. https://doi.org/10.1249/MSS.0000000000000852

Tidswell, E. (2023, October 25). Does Gen Z care about sustainability? Stats & facts in 2023. *Goodmakertales.com*. https://goodmakertales.com/does-gen-z-care-about-sustainability/#:~:text=When%20it%20comes%20to%20daily (last accessed 29 October 2025).

Tilman, D., & Clark, M. (2014). Global diets link environmental sustainability and human health. *Nature, 515*(7528): 518–522. https://doi.org/10.1038/nature13959

Toller, S. V. (1999). Assessing the impact of anosmia: Review of a questionnaire's findings. *Chemical senses, 24*(6): 705–712. https://doi.org/10.1093/chemse/24.6.705

Tomiya, M. T. O., Cabral, P. C., Arruda, I. K. G. D., & Diniz, A. S. (2017). Association between diet quality index, food and nutrient intake and metabolic parameters in adolescents from Recife, northeastern Brazil. *Nutrition Journal, 16*(1): 64.

Tomova, L., Wang, K. L., Thompson, T., Matthews, G. A., Takahashi, A., Tye, K. M., & Saxe, R. (2020). Acute social isolation evokes midbrain craving responses similar to hunger. *Nature Neuroscience, 23*(12): 1597–1605. https://doi.org/10.1038/s41593-020-00742-z

Torske, A., Bremer, B., Hölzel, B. K., Maczka, A., & Koch, K. (2024). Mindfulness meditation modulates stress-eating and its neural correlates. *Scientific Reports, 14*(1): 7294. https://doi.org/10.1038/s41598-024-57687-7

Tremblay, A., Wouters, E., Wenker, M., St-Pierre, S., Bouchard, C., & Després, J. P. (1995). Alcohol and a high-fat diet: A combination favoring overfeeding. *American Journal of Clinical Nutrition, 62*(3): 639–644. https://doi.org/10.1093/ajcn/62.3.639

Troisi, J. D., Gabriel, S., Derrick, J. L., & Geisler, A. (2015). Threatened belonging and preference for comfort food among the securely attached. *Appetite, 90*: 58–64. https://doi.org/10.1016/j.appet.2015.02.029

Tryon, M. S., Carter, C. S., DeCant, R., & Laugero, K. D. (2013). Chronic stress exposure may affect the brain's response to high calorie food cues and predispose to obesogenic eating habits. *Physiology & Behavior, 120*: 233–242. https://doi.org/10.1016/j.physbeh.2013.08.010

Tuorila, H., & Pangborn, R. M. (1988). Prediction of reported consumption of selected fat-containing foods. *Appetite, 11*(2): 81–95. https://doi.org/10.1016/s01956663(88)80008-4of

Turnwald, B. P., Bertoldo, J. D., Perry, M. A., Policastro, P., Timmons, M., Bosso, C., Connors, P., Valgenti, R. T., Pine, L., Challamel, G., Gardner, C. D., & Crum, A. J. (2019). Increasing vegetable intake by emphasizing tasty and enjoyable attributes: A randomized controlled multisite intervention for taste-focused labeling. *Psychological Science, 30*(11): 1603–1615. https://doi.org/10.1177/0956797619872191

Turnwald, B. P., Boles, D. Z., & Crum, A. J. (2017). Association between indulgent descriptions and vegetable consumption: Twisted carrots and dynamite beets. *JAMA Internal Medicine, 177*(8): 1216–1218. https://doi.org/10.1001/jamainternmed.2017.1637

Turnwald, B. P., & Crum, A. J. (2019). Smart food policy for healthy food labeling: Leading with taste, not healthiness, to shift consumption and enjoyment of healthy foods. *Preventive Medicine, 119*: 7–13. https://doi.org/10.1016/j.ypmed.2018.11.021

Ulrich-Lai, Y. M., Fulton, S., Wilson, M., Petrovich, G., & Rinaman, L. (2015). Stress exposure, food intake and emotional state. *Stress (Amsterdam, the Netherlands), 18*(4): 381–399. https://doi.org/10.3109/10253890.2015.1062981

Umar ibn Muḥammad Nafzāwī (15th century). *The Perfumed Garden. En.wikisource.org*. Retrieved August 1, 2024, from https://en.wikisource.org/wiki/The_Perfumed_Garden/Chapter_21

UMass Memorial Health (2024). MBSR 8-week online live. *UMass Memorial Health.* https://ummhealth.org/umass-memorial-medical-center/services-treatments/center-for-mindfulness/mindfulness-programs/mbsr-8-week-online-live (last accessed 29 October 2025).

Umberson, D., & Montez, J. K. (2010). Social relationships and health: A flashpoint for health policy. *Journal of Health and Social Behavior, 51*(Suppl.): S54–S66. https://doi.org/10.1177/0022146510383501

United Nations (2019). World population projected to reach 9.8 billion in 2050, and 11.2 billion in 2100. https://un.org/en/desa/world-population-projected-reach-98-billion-2050-and-112-billion-2100#:~:text=The%20current%20world%20population%20of,Nations%20report%20being%20-launched%20today (last accessed 27 August 2025).

United Nations (2022). Sustainable development goals report—United Nations Sustainable Development. https://un.org/sustainabledevelopment/progress-report/ (last accessed 27 August 2025).

University of Oxford (2017, March 16). Social eating connects communities. https://ox.ac.uk/news/2017-03-16-social-eating-connects-communities (last accessed 29 October 2025).

Urade, Y., & Hayaishi, O. (2011). Prostaglandin D2 and sleep/wake regulation. *Sleep Medicine Reviews, 15*(6): 411–418. https://doi.org/10.1016/j.smrv.2011.08.003

USDA (2020). *U.S. Department of Agriculture MyPlate* What Is MyPlate? https://myplate.gov/eat-healthy/what-is-myplate (last accessed 29 October 2025).

USDA (2023). Food waste FAQs. *Usda.gov*. https://usda.gov/foodwaste/faqs

USDA & USDHHS (2020). Dietary guidelines for Americans, *2020–2025. U.S. Department of Agriculture and U.S. Department of Health and Human Services.* https://dietaryguidelines.gov/sites/default/files/2021-03/Dietary_Guidelines_for_Americans-2020-2025.pdf

U.S. Department of Health and Human Services (2018). Physical activity guidelines for Americans. 2nd edition. https://health.gov/our-work/

nutrition-physical-activity/physical-activity-guidelines (last accessed 29 October 2025).

USDHHS (2024). Healthy people 2030. U.S. Department of Health and Human Services: Office of Disease Prevention and Health Promotion. Retrieved March 19, 2025 from https://odphp.health.gov/healthypeople/objectives-and-data/social-determinants-health

USDHHS (2025). The U.S. Surgeon General Advisory: Alcohol and cancer risk. *U.S. Department of Health and Human Services.* https://hhs.gov/sites/default/files/oash-alcohol-cancer-risk.pdf (last accessed 29 October 2025).

USFDA (2023). Spilling the beans: How much caffeine is too much? *U.S. Food and Drug Administration.* https://fda.gov/consumers/consumer-updates/spilling-beans-how-much-caffeine-too-much (last accessed 29 October 2025).

Utter, J., Larson, N., Berge, J. M., Eisenberg, M. E., Fulkerson, J. A., & Neumark-Sztainer, D. (2018). Family meals among parents: Associations with nutritional, social and emotional wellbeing. *Preventive Medicine, 113*: 7–12. https://doi.org/10.1016/j.ypmed.2018.05.006

Valdes, A. M., Walter, J., Segal, E., & Spector, T. D. (2018). Role of the gut microbiota in nutrition and health. *BMJ Clinical Research, 361*: k2179. https://doi.org/10.1136/bmj.k2179

Vale, M. J., Jelinek, M. V., Best, J. D., Dart, A. M., Grigg, L. E., Hare, D. L., Ho, B. P., Newman, R. W., McNeil, J. J., & COACH Study Group. (2003). Coaching patients on achieving cardiovascular health (COACH): A multicenter randomized trial in patients with coronary heart disease. *Archives of Internal Medicine, 163*(22): 2775–2783. https://doi.org/10.1001/archinte.163.22.2775

Valencia-Martín, J. L., Galán, I., & Rodríguez-Artalejo, F. (2011). The association between alcohol consumption patterns and adherence to food consumption guidelines. *Alcoholism, Clinical and Experimental Research, 35*(11): 2075–2081. https://doi.org/10.1111/j.1530-0277.2011.01559.x

Valenzuela, C. F. (1997). Alcohol and neurotransmitter interactions. *Alcohol Health and Research World, 21*(2): 144–148.

van den Broek, N., Larsen, J. K., Verhagen, M., Burk, W. J., & Vink, J. M. (2020). Is adolescents' food intake associated with exposure to the food intake of their mothers and best friends? *Nutrients, 12*(3): 786. https://doi.org/10.3390/nu12030786

Van der Gucht, K., Takano, K., Van Broeck, N., & Raes, F. (2015). A mindfulness-based intervention for economically disadvantaged people: Effects on symptoms of stress, anxiety, and depression and on cognitive reactivity and overgeneralization. *Mindfulness*, *6*(5): 1042–1052. https://doi.org/10.1007/s12671-014-0353-8

Vatansever-Ozen, S., Tiryaki-Sonmez, G., Bugdayci, G., & Ozen, G. (2011). The effects of exercise on food intake and hunger: Relationship with acylated ghrelin and leptin. *Journal of Sports Science & Medicine*, *10*(2): 283–291.

Vela, M. F., Kramer, J. R., Richardson, P. A., Dodge, R., & El-Serag, H. B. (2014). Poor sleep quality and obstructive sleep apnea in patients with GERD and Barrett's esophagus. *Neurogastroenterology and Motility: The Official Journal of the European Gastrointestinal Motility Society*, *26*(3): 346–352. https://doi.org/10.1111/nmo.12265

Vennemann, F. B., Ioannidou, S., Valsta, L. M., Dumas, C., Ocké, M. C., Mensink, G. B, Lindtner, O., Virtanen, S. M., Tlustos, C., D'Addezio, L., Mattison, I., Dubuisson, C., Siksna, I., & Héraud, F. (2015). Dietary intake and food sources of choline in European populations. *British Journal of Nutrition*, *114*(12): 2046–2055. https://doi.org/10.1017/s0007114515003700

Versace, F., Frank, D. W., Stevens, E. M., Deweese, M. M., Guindani, M., & Schembre, S. M. (2019). The reality of "food porn": Larger brain responses to food-related cues than to erotic images predict cue-induced eating. *Psychophysiology*, *56*(4): e13309. https://doi.org/10.1111/psyp.13309

Versluis, I., & Papies, E. K. (2016). The role of social norms in the portion size effect: Reducing normative relevance reduces the effect of portion size on consumption decisions. *Frontiers in Psychology*, *7*: 756. https://doi.org/10.3389/fpsyg.2016.00756

VIA Institute (2024). *VIA Character Strengths Survey & Character Reports*. https://viacharacter.org/.

Vicennati, V., Pasqui, F., Cavazza, C., Pagotto, U., & Pasquali, R. (2009). Stress-related development of obesity and cortisol in women. *Obesity (Silver Spring, MD)*, *17*(9): 1678–1683. https://doi.org/10.1038/oby.2009.76

Vinik, A. I. (2012). The conductor of the autonomic orchestra. *Frontiers in Endocrinology*, *3*: 71. https://doi.org/10.3389/fendo.2012.00071

Vlemincx, E., Van Diest, I., & Van den Bergh, O. (2016). A sigh of relief or a sigh to relieve: The psychological and physiological relief effect of deep breaths. *Physiology & Behavior*, *165*: 127–135. https://doi.org/10.1016/j.physbeh.2016.07.004

Voica, S. A., Kling, J., Frisén, A., & Piran, N. (2021). Disordered eating through the lens of positive psychology: The role of embodiment, self-esteem and identity coherence. *Body Image*, *39*: 103–113. https://doi.org/10.1016/j.bodyim.2021.06.006

Volkow, N. D., Fowler, J. S., & Wang, G. J. (2003). The addicted human brain: Insights from imaging studies. *Journal of Clinical Investigation*, *111*(10):

1444–1451. https://doi.org/10.1172/JCI18533. PMID: 12750391; PMCID: PMC155054

Volkow, N. D., Wang, G.-J., Tomasi, D., & Baler, R. D. (2013). The addictive dimensionality of obesity. *Biological Psychiatry*, *73*(9): 811–818. https://doi.org/10.1016/j.biopsych.2012.12.020

Voss, M. W., Nagamatsu, L. S., Liu-Ambrose, T., & Kramer, A. F. (2011). Exercise, brain, and cognition across the life span. *Journal of Applied Physiology*, *111*(5): 1505–1513. https://doi.org/10.1152/japplphysiol.00210.2011

Waldinger, R., & Schulz, M. (2023). The good life: Lessons from the world's longest scientific study of happiness. *Simon & Schuster*. https://simonandschuster.com/books/The-Good-Life/Robert-Waldinger/9781982166694.

Walker, R. J., Williams, J. S., & Egede, L. E. (2018). Pathways between food insecurity and glycaemic control in individuals with type 2 diabetes. *Public Health Nutrition*, *21*(17): 3237–3244. https://doi.org/10.1017/S1368980018001908. PMID: 30088467; PMCID: PMC6258341.

Wang, X., Ouyang, Y., Liu, J., Zhu, M., Zhao, G., Bao, W., & Hu, F. B. (2014). Fruit and vegetable consumption and mortality from all causes, cardiovascular disease, and cancer: Systematic review and dose-response meta-analysis of prospective cohort studies. *BMJ Clinical Research*, *349*: g4490. https://doi.org/10.1136/bmj.g4490

Wangchuk, S., Norbu, N., & Sherub, S. (2012). Impacts of cordyceps collection on livelihoods and alpine ecosystems in Bhutan as ascertained from questionnaire survey of cordyceps collectors. Royal Government of Bhutan. Jakar, Bhutan: UWICE.

Wansink, B., Payne, C. R., & North, J. (2007). Fine as North Dakota wine: Sensory expectations and the intake of companion foods. *Physiology & Behavior*, *90*(5): 712–716. https://doi.org/10.1016/j.physbeh.2006.12.010

Waters, A. (2010). *The Art of Simple Food: Notes, Lessons, and Recipes from a Delicious Revolution*. New York: Random House.

Watts, A. W., Rydell, S. A., Eisenberg, M. E., Laska, M. N., & Neumark-Sztainer, D. (2018). Yoga's potential for promoting healthy eating and physical activity behaviors among young adults: A mixed-methods study. *International Journal of Behavioral Nutrition and Physical Activity*, *15*(1): 42. https://doi.org/10.1186/s12966-018-0674-4

WebMD (2022). Beer: Is it good for you? *WebMD*. https://webmd.com/diet/beer-good-for-you.

WebMD (2024). The difference between animal protein and plant protein. *WebMDEditorialContributors*.https://webmd.com/diet/difference-between-animal-protein-plant-protein (last accessed 29 October 2025).

WebMD (n.d.). What is cortisol? *WebMD Contributors.* Retrieved July 18, 2024, from https://webmd.com/a-to-z-guides/what-is-cortisol

Webtribunal.net (2023). How many ads do we see a day? 17 insightful stats from 2023. https://webtribunal.net/blog/how-many-ads-do-we-see-a-day (last accessed 16 July 2024).

Weill Cornell Medicine (2015). Skinny fat. *Sandra and Edward Meyer Cancer Center.* https://meyercancer.weill.cornell.edu/news/2015-10-22/skinny-fat-breast-cancer-and-obesity (last accessed 29 October 2025).

West, E., & Krychman, M. (2015). Natural aphrodisiacs—A review of selected sexual enhancers. *Sexual Medicine Reviews, 3*(4): 279–288. https://doi.org/10.1002/smrj.62

West, S. G., McIntyre, M. D., Piotrowski, M. J., Poupin, N., Miller, D. L., Preston, A. G., Wagner, P., Groves, L. F., & Skulas-Ray, A. C. (2014). Effects of dark chocolate and cocoa consumption on endothelial function and arterial stiffness in overweight adults. *British Journal of Nutrition, 111*(4): 653–661. https://doi.org/10.1017/S0007114513002912

Whitaker, R. C., Phillips, S. M., & Orzol, S. M. (2006). Food insecurity and the risks of depression and anxiety in mothers and behavior problems in their preschool-aged children. *Pediatrics, 118*(3): e859–e868. https://doi.org/10.1542/peds.2006-0239

Whittemore, R., Melkus, G. D., Sullivan, A., & Grey, M. (2004). A nurse-coaching intervention for women with type 2 diabetes. *Diabetes Educator, 30*(5): 795–804. https://doi.org/10.1177/014572170403000515

Whitworth, L., Kimsey-House, H., Sandahl, P., & Sandahl, P. (2007). *Co-active Coaching: New Skills for Coaching People Toward Success in Work and Life.* Boston, MA: Davies-Black Pub.

Willett, W., Rockström, J., Loken, B., Springmann, M., Lang, T., Vermeulen, S., Garnett, T., et al. (2019). Food in the Anthropocene: The EAT-Lancet commission on healthy diets from sustainable food systems. *The Lancet, 393*(10170): 447–492.

Williams, A. (2015, March 15). Hospital patients and visitors accused of eating all the pies as boss of medical centre claims Greggs outlet is bakery firm's second-busiest shop. *Daily Mail Online.* http://dailymail.co.uk/news/article-2995944/Hospital-patients-visitors-accused-eating-pies-boss-medical-centre-claims-Greggs-outlet-bakery-firm-s-second-busiest-shop.html (last accessed 29 October 2025).

Williamson, A. M., & Feyer, A. M. (2000). Moderate sleep deprivation produces impairments in cognitive and motor performance equivalent to legally prescribed levels of alcohol intoxication. *Occupational and Environmental Medicine, 57*(10): 649–655. https://doi.org/10.1136/oem.57.10.649

Willis, J., & Todorov, A. (2006). First impressions. *Psychological Science, 17*(7): 592–598. https://doi.org/10.1111/j.1467-9280.2006.01750.x

Wilson, K. (2020). *How to Build a Healthy Brain: Reduce Stress, Anxiety and Depression and Future-proof Your Brain*. London: Yellow Kite.

Wise, F. M. (2010). Coronary heart disease—The benefits of exercise. *Australian Family Physician, 39*(3): 129–133.

Wolever, R. Q., & Dreusicke, M. H. (2016). Integrative health coaching: A behavior skills approach that improves HbA1c and pharmacy claims-derived medication adherence. *BMJ Open Diabetes Research & Care, 4*(1): e000201. https://doi.org/10.1136/bmjdrc-2016-000201

World Economic Forum (2023). 4 Ways to Reduce Food Waste in South-East Asia. *World Economic Forum*. https://www.weforum.org/stories/2023/07/food-waste-harvest-losses-southeast-asia (last accessed 14 January 2026).

World Health Organization (2007). Assessment of iodine deficiency disorders and monitoring their elimination: A guide for programme managers. 3rd edn. *World Health Organization*. https://who.int/publications/i/item/9789241595827 (last accessed 6 May 2025).

World Health Organization (2020). WHO reveals leading causes of death and disability worldwide: 2000–2019. https://who.int/news/item/09-12-2020-who-reveals-leading-causes-of-death-and-disability-worldwide-2000-2019 (last accessed 29 October 2025).

World Health Organization (2023). WHO updates guidelines on fats and carbohydrates. *World Health Organization*. https://who.int/news/item/17-07-2023-who-updates-guidelines-on-fats-and-carbohydrates (last accessed 29 October 2025).

World Health Organization (2024a). Physical activity. https://who.int/news-room/fact-sheets/detail/physical-activity (last accessed 29 October 2025).

World Health Organization (2024b). Tobacco. https://who.int/news-room/fact-sheets/detail/tobacco (last accessed 29 October 2025).

World Resources Institute (2019). Creating a sustainable food future: A menu of solutions to feed nearly 10 billion people by 2050. *Climate Change and Law Collection* [preprint]. https://doi.org/10.1163/9789004322714_cclc_2019-0020-134

WRAP (Waste and Resources Action Programme) (2008). *The Food We Waste*. Banbury, UK: Scientific and Education.

Xiong, R.-G., Li, J., Cheng, J., Zhou, D.-D., Wu, S.-X., Huang, S.-Y., Saimaiti, A., Yang, Z.-J., Gan, R.-Y., & Li, H.-B. (2023). The role of gut microbiota in anxiety, depression, and other mental disorders as well as the protective effects of dietary components. *Nutrients, 15*(14): 3258. https://doi.org/10.3390/nu15143258

Yamaguchi, S., & Ninomiya, K. (2000). Umami and food palatability. *Journal of Nutrition, 130*(4S): 921S–926S.

Yaribeygi, H., Panahi, Y., Sahraei, H., Johnston, T. P., & Sahebkar, A. (2017). The impact of stress on body function: A review. *EXCLI Journal, 16*: 1057–1072. https://doi.org/10.17179/excli2017-480

Yau, Y. H., & Potenza, M. N. (2013). Stress and eating behaviors. *Minerva Endocrinology, 38*(3): 255–267. PMID: 24126546; PMCID: PMC4214609.

Yeomans, M., Chambers, L., Blumenthal, H., & Blake, A. (2008). The role of expectancy in sensory and hedonic evaluation: The case of smoked salmon ice-cream. *Food Quality and Preference, 19*: 565–573. https://doi.org/10.1016/J.FOODQUAL.2008.02.009

Yoshikawa, A., Smith, M. L., Lee, S., Towne, S. D., & Ory, M. G. (2021). The role of improved social support for healthy eating in a lifestyle intervention: Texercise Select. *Public Health Nutrition, 24*(1), 146–156. https://doi.org/10.1017/S1368980020002700

YouGov survey results (2016). Crisp packaging. https://docs.cdn.yougov.com/jph9436cxb/InternalResults_161025_CrispPackagingwithGOR_W.pdf (last accessed 11 May 2023).

Young, D. R., Hivert, M.-F., Alhassan, S., Camhi, S. M., Ferguson, J. F., Katzmarzyk, P. T., Lewis, C. E., Owen, N., Perry, C. K., Siddique, J., Yong, C. M., & On behalf of the Physical Activity Committee of the Council on Lifestyle and Cardiometabolic Health; Council on Clinical Cardiology; Council on Epidemiology and Prevention; Council on Functional Genomics and Translational Biology; and Stroke Council. (2016). Sedentary behavior and cardiovascular morbidity and mortality: A science advisory from the American Heart Association. *Circulation, 134*(13): e262–e279. https://doi.org/10.1161/CIR.0000000000000440

Youssef, J., Mora, M., Maiz, E., & Spence, C. (2022). Sensory exploration of vegetables combined with a cookery class increases willingness to choose/eat plant-based food and drink. *International Journal of Gastronomy & Food Science, 28*: 100515. https://doi.org/10.1016/j.ijgfs.2022.100515

Zaalberg, A., Nijman, H., Bulten, E., Stroosma, L., & van der Staak, C. (2010). Effects of nutritional supplements on aggression, rule-breaking, and psychopathology among young adult prisoners. *Aggressive Behavior, 36*(2): 117–126. https://doi.org/10.1002/ab.20335

Zaccaro, A., Piarulli, A., Laurino, M., Garbella, E., Menicucci, D., Neri, B., & Gemignani, A. (2018). How breath-control can change your life: A systematic review on psycho-physiological correlates of slow breathing. *Frontiers in Human Neuroscience, 12*: 353. https://doi.org/10.3389/fnhum.2018.00353

Zahn, R., Moll, J., Paiva, M., Garrido, G., Krueger, F., Huey, E. D., & Grafman, J. (2009). The neural basis of human social values: Evidence from functional MRI. *Cerebral Cortex (New York)*, *19*(2): 276–283. https://doi.org/10.1093/cercor/bhn080

Zhang, Y., Zhang, X., & Lin, S. (2022). Irisin: A bridge between exercise and neurological diseases. *Heliyon*, *8*(12): e12352. https://doi.org/10.1016/j.heliyon.2022.e12352

Zhang, Z., Ye, Q., Law, R., & Li, Y. (2010). The impact of e-word-of-mouth on the online popularity of restaurants: A comparison of consumer reviews and editor reviews. *International Journal of Hospitality Management*, *29*(4): 694–700. https://doi.org/10.1016/j.ijhm.2010.02.002

Zou, R., El Marroun, H., Voortman, T., Hillegers, M., White, T., & Tiemeier, H. (2021). Maternal polyunsaturated fatty acids during pregnancy and offspring brain development in childhood. *American Journal of Clinical Nutrition*, *114*(1): 124–133. https://doi.org/10.1093/ajcn/nqab049

Index

Page numbers in *italics* refer to figures and page numbers in **bold** refer to tables.

Further praise for ***Culinary Psychology***

"This is one of the most eloquent and intellectually engaging works written on the deeper dimensions of culinary culture. When visionary minds converge, the result is a text that transcends traditional food writing and enters the realm of cultural philosophy. The book invites the reader to reconsider cuisine not simply as an art form, but as an intersection of geography, history, and human psychology. Through this lens, gastronomy becomes more than technique or creativity, it becomes a sustainable cultural expression shaped by place, people, and time. In an era where food systems, identity, and sustainability are central global conversations, this work stands as a revolutionary and timely contribution."

Natasha de Bourg, Culinary Strategist, Director, and Executive Producer, Classy Chef Productions Ltd.